2nd edition

Creative Leadership in Recreation

HOWARD G. DANFORD
Late of
Colorado State College

revised by
MAX SHIRLEY
University of Northern Colorado

ALLYN AND BACON, Inc.
Boston · London · Sydney

To the Memory of
HOWARD G. DANFORD,
teacher and friend,
whose dynamic and effective leadership
was an inspiration to so many and who
has left a lasting imprint on all who
labor to make life more meaningful.

. . . of a good leader
  who talks little
when his work is done,
  his aim fulfilled
They will say,
  "we did this ourselves."

       LAO-TZU

Library of Congress Catalog Card Number: 70-109596

Printed in the United States of America

ISBN: 0-205-02719-9

Seventh printing . . . November, 1975

Contents

nettes. Story dramatization. From charades to Shakespeare. Little
theatre and children's theatre. Arts and crafts. The values we seek.
Methods must harmonize with ends. The program in arts and crafts.

Preface

IN THIS REVISION, the goal has been to carry on Howard G. Danford's philosophy. His strong beliefs and advocation to high standards of ethics in his chosen profession were inspirational. It is my hope that his words will continue to affect the course of leadership in what he called "the coming era of recreation."

The other goal has been to have a book that is up-to-date and that renders a contribution to the field of recreation, particularly leadership. If there is any one thing upon which all professional people in the area of recreation agree, it is that leadership is by far the most important single factor in the successful operation of a program of recreation.

Two new chapters have been added: an introductory chapter which should be thought-provoking for students majoring in the field of recreation; and a chapter on leadership for the handicapped, one of the fastest growing areas in the profession. Also, a new section has been added on outdoor recreation, and all chapters have been updated.

This book proposes to consider the historical significance of leisure; the impact of leisure on modern society; the goals which leaders should seek through the recreation experience; the nature of human behavior; the nature of leadership and the competencies essential to its effective functioning; the selection and conduct of activities as a means of goal attainment; evaluation of leadership and of recreation; leadership for senior citizens and the handicapped; and the challenge of the future to the recreation leader. The unifying theme throughout the book is the concept that the leader is inescapably involved in the conduct of activities whose outcomes are multiple and that the quality of the outcomes will depend largely upon the quality of the leadership. In clearer terms, the creative leader of the future must be concerned with the achievement of goals other than simply fun and enjoyment, as important as they are. What these goals should be and how leadership functions to achieve them is the central thesis of this book.

Creative Leadership in Recreation was written to serve two major needs of the recreation profession: first, the need for a text for use by institutions of higher learning in the preparation of the creative leader in recreation; second, the need for a book which will assist the leaders presently employed to understand more fully the significance of their responsibilities and to discharge them in such a manner as to meet successfully the challenge which leisure makes to the human spirit.

I am indebted to many people who have helped make this revision possible. Special gratitude is expressed to my family, professional colleagues, and friends for their inspiration and encouragement. Appreciation is also expressed to many recreation educators and other professionals in the field of recreation.

Max Shirley
University of Northern Colorado

Chapter I

Introduction

IF ONE WERE to choose a single word to characterize contemporary life in the United States as we enter the decade of the 1970's, that word would be change. Every minute and every hour the world changes—for better or for worse.

CHANGE FOR BETTER

During the 1960's the pace and volume of these changes were so swift as to dazzle even the most sophisticated writers of science fiction. In this country, particularly in a generation of time, once formidable barriers have been broken on almost every frontier. We are in the generation of the electric toothbrush, the instant replay of world events, and the transplant of organs from one human to another. Through the Apollo space program men landed on the moon, proving that man and his machines could go higher, farther, faster, and stay there longer than ever had been demonstrated. Still man's search for new conquests moves on.

History records no other era when the tempo of change has been so rapid. The pace will continue and intensify. The 1960's are succeeded by the changing 1970's where a fast generation is enabled to move by sophisticated science, technology, and research rooted in the last decade. From this will come developments whose ultimate form can only be guessed at. But there is one certainty: the decade of the 1970's will produce profound changes in the American way of life.

CHANGE FOR WORSE

Change inevitably threatens vested interests, interrupts habits, creates distress, and finally results in the development of new social patterns. Social change is the forerunner of the appearance of social problems.

Social change generally sharpens conflicts of values. The bases for conflict exist in the facts of economic, political, and religious differences, in racial and ethnic variations, and in conflicts of interest which characterize complex societies. We have seen technology and science have a bright future, and yet if we look at our nation socially and are realistic concerning the future, there is room for some disillusionment or discouragement.

For the United States the 1960's were a time of internal crises. A close look at the country shows that never has so much well-being come to so many Americans as now. More and more, color television sets and swimming pools are becoming symbols of the "good life." In 1967 the Census Bureau reported a decline of nearly 25 percent since 1959 in the number of Americans living in poverty. Yet never have values seemed to be crumbling as they are today.

During the latter part of the 1960's we have had violence and defiance. During 1969 the Federal Bureau of Investigation reported that violent crime in the United States increased by 11 percent. While crime was increasing, poverty decreased and the nation was at a time of general prosperity.

Frustration and protest are the symbols of the nation as we enter the 1970's. The major barriers which confront this nation (and each citizen in his search for fulfillment) are seen in protest against the Vietnam War, famine and poverty, racial crises, illiteracy, reaction against crime and violence, and needed social reform.

Even with our internal strife we cannot afford to become a nation of despair. A society is to be judged more by what it does with its human resources than by what it does with its natural resources. The computer has placed man in a unique position, solving his work problems, yet at the same time de-individualizing him. Thus, we search for individuality and identity and we desire to change society. That the younger generation is disillusioned with the older one perhaps results in a "generation gap," where no one over thirty is to be trusted. The young people want to become involved, with a chance to shape the world in which they live. However, the present and future college generations are faced with the challenge of breaking the barriers of war, race, and poverty, and solving the complexities of a world which sometimes seems out of gear.

The recreation leader is an individual who functions at the very core of our social structure. So we challenge present and future recreation leaders to face up to change because change is the central fact of our age.

TYPES OF LEADERS

What kind of recreation leaders do we need in today's age of change?

The recreation leaders of today and the future have two obligations within the society in which they live and work. One is to preserve and maintain as a meaningful force those values held to be true from the past —love, truth, courage, friendship, honor, integrity, respect—which are timeless. On the other hand, the recreation leader has an obligation to be receptive to the world in which he must function. He must be able to speak the language of that world. He must be able to interpret truths to that world. This must be the overriding concern of all of us today—to be relevant in today's world, whether on a campus, on the job, or in the communities in which we live.

The recreation leader's role changes because recreation agencies will take on new responsibilities as their society changes and makes new demands, and as knowledge affects the goals of recreation. Clearly, to fulfill the leader's role today the student of recreation leadership will need to grow in certain basic areas of understanding.

BASIC AREAS OF UNDERSTANDING

Let us begin our study of leadership in recreation with a brief glance at five of the most important basic areas of understanding with which every student of recreation leadership should be thoroughly conversant. Each will be developed in greater detail later in the text.

1. *The Nature and Significance of Leisure.* The recreation leader understands the nature of modern leisure. He is able to comprehend leisure and its problems in the light of history and its role in the culture of

nations. He knows that leisure symbolizes freedom and opportunity; but he also knows that both freedom and opportunity require the making of choices which, in turn, places a high premium on education and leadership. He sees the relationship between work and leisure—that leisure is a complement, not the antithesis, of work; and that work is no longer a central life interest to large numbers of workers who now must find the real meaning of life in their leisure. He perceives that leisure can ennoble man or degrade him, and that the true test of its value is how it is used.

2. *The Goals of Recreation.* Vital to the leadership process in any area of life is the coöperative determination of goals, followed by the intelligent pursuit of these goals or values. Leadership means that people are to be led from where they are to where they wish to be. This implies action or movement, and movement implies direction, unless it is blind, purposeless movement, in which case there is no leadership.

To give direction, meaning, and purpose to a program is essential. Goals must be coöperatively determined by the leader and the group, be intellectually challenging, socially acceptable, arise out of the nature and needs of human beings in an urbanized, industrialized, and mechanized democracy, and be in harmony with the purposes of the organization administering the program of recreation. The superior leader, understanding all of this, becomes a philosopher as his ideals and his actions harmonize in a constant effort to achieve the higher values attainable through recreation.

3. *The Nature and Needs of Human Beings.* The recreation leader realizes that every conception of leadership is based necessarily upon certain assumptions about the nature of man. The leader works primarily with people and with activities. His success depends largely upon the extent to which he is effective in helping people achieve goals of importance to them and to the leader. This involves influencing the behavior of human beings. It can best be accomplished when the leader understands people, and possesses a deep insight into their nature and needs, their motivations and aspirations, their characteristics at various ages, and why they react as they do in relation to other people. He seeks constantly to further his knowledge of human relations, as a vital phase of leadership education, for the purpose of determining what works, what doesn't, and why.

4. *The Nature of Leadership.* The recreation leader understands that leadership is not something that occurs by chance, but it is an art which some day may become a science. He realizes that leadership involves changing the behavior of people and that this highly complicated process requires not only a knowledge of human beings, goals, recreation activities, and leisure, but also acquisition of definite and specific leadership skills.

5. *The Program of Activities.* The true purpose of leadership in recreation is to influence people in such a way as to effect progress toward

a realization of the values sought. The ends sought are inherent in human beings; the means by which these ends are reached are the activities comprising the program.

The superior leader differentiates clearly between ends and means. He has a comprehensive knowledge of recreation activities and their relative worth. He understands that activities are not of equal value—that many are worthless, cheap, inane, and trivial. He perceives the relationship between goals sought and the activities, or means, by which these goals are attained. He knows that values simply do not accrue from participation in activities in which such values are nonexistent.

The leader not only has a wide knowledge of recreation activities but he also possesses considerable personal skill in a few of these activities, leadership skill in a large number of them, and the ability to develop programs fitted to the nature, needs, and abilities of all the people.

Selected References

"America on the Brighter Side," *U.S. News & World Report,* September 2, 1968, p. 128.

Hoffer, Eric, "Leisure and the Masses," *Parks & Recreation,* 4, No. 3, March, 1969, p. 31.

Montgomery, William L., "Investing in Today's Youth," *Parks & Recreation,* 4, No. 1, January, 1969, p. 29.

The 1969 World Book Year Book (Chicago: Field Enterprises Educational Corporation, 1969).

Vannier, Maryhelen, *Methods and Materials in Recreation Leadership* (Belmont, Calif.: Wadsworth Publishing Company, Inc., 1966).

Chapter II

Leisure in American Life

THROUGHOUT THE AGES man has yearned for some freedom from the toil and drudgery required to earn a living. For most of his racial history leisure was the exclusive privilege of the wealthy few, a luxury which seemed always beyond his reach. Today, we Americans have more leisure than any people have ever had in the history of the world. For the first time, a nation has reached a point where almost all of its people are no longer preoccupied exclusively with securing food, clothing, and shelter.

Swift technological change has transformed our society so completely within the past century that an American living at the time of Abraham Lincoln would have felt more at home in the Rome of Julius Caesar than he would feel in Washington today. We live in an age of urbanization, mechanization, automation, computers, nuclear energy, space ships, rockets, man-made satellites, and jet-propelled transportation. Fantastic as these changes have been, there is every indication that the end is by no means in sight, that the world of tomorrow will not even remotely resemble the world of today, because we stand only at the threshold of the nuclear age with its unlimited possibilities for the enrichment of human life and its equally infinite potentialities for the complete extinction of human life.

A mountain brook begins as just a small trickle of water fed by the melting snows. As it moves toward the valley in the distance it grows by accretion through its many tributaries until eventually it becomes a raging torrent unrecognizable to anyone who observed it at its source. Leisure in America, one of the less tangible by-products, or outcomes, of our technological revolution, is similar to this mountain stream in its humble beginnings, its slow but steady growth, and its ultimate magnitude.

These figures tell a story unparalleled in human history. In 1850, of the total amount of energy used in producing goods and services in the United States, the muscles of men furnished 13 percent, machines 35 percent, and animals 52 percent. By 1950, machines provided 98 percent, men one percent, and animals one percent. In 1850, the average work week in industry and farming was seventy hours; in 1950 it had dropped to forty hours. Today an estimated six million persons work thirty-seven-and-a-half hours, thirty-five hours, or even less, with predictions for a 32-hour work week by 1975. Already, an electrical construction workers' union in New York City has a contract that is based on a twenty-five-hour work week. On the basis of a forty-hour work week, eight hours a day for sleep, and two hours for eating, the average industrial worker spends 2,080 hours a year on the job and has 3,030 hours off the job—and this assumes no vacation periods at all.[1]

Largely as a result of automation, the number of employees in manufacturing has decreased by 1,500,000 in the last six years although production has increased. In New York City alone, automatic elevators have displaced 40,000 operators. *Time* presents a picture of our increasingly automated world:[2]

In the highly automated chemical industry, the number of production jobs has fallen 3% since 1956 while output has soared 27%. Though steel capacity has increased 20% since 1955, the number of men needed to operate the industry's plants—even at full capacity—has dropped 17,000. Auto employment slid from a peak of 746,000 in boom 1955 to 614,000 in November. . . . Since the meat industry's 1956 employment peak, 28,000 workers have lost their jobs despite a production increase of 3%. Bakery jobs have been in a steady decline from 174,000 in 1954 to 163,000 last year. On the farm one man can grow enough to feed 24 people; back in 1949 he could feed only 15.

The Ford Motor Company opened an automated engine plant where an engine block could be made by forty-eight men in twenty minutes, whereas the same operation formerly required 400 men and forty minutes.

---

[1] Not all students of the problem agree on the amount of free time possessed by the average American worker. Sebastian de Grazia states that, "The great and touted gains in free time since the 1850's . . . are largely myth." He maintains that when the part-time worker is excluded from the calculations, the average full-time American worker puts in almost 48 hours a week. Furthermore, according to his statistics, he claims that the 25.2 hours of free time gained each week by the full-time worker since 1850 is reduced to approximately 8.5 hours by "moonlighting," going to and from work, "do-it-yourself" jobs, and household chores and shopping. The student is referred to: Sebastian de Grazia, *Of Time, Work, and Leisure* (New York: The Twentieth Century Fund, 1962), Ch. 3.

[2] "The Automation Jobless—Not Fired, Just Not Hired," *Time*, February 24, 1961, p. 69.

The shape of things to come is further indicated by Michael as he describes the fantastic products of man's creative genius in the realm of cybernation, a term which refers to both automation and computers:[3]

The U.S. Census Bureau was able to use fifty statisticians in 1960 to do the tabulations that required 4100 in 1950. . . . The R. H. Macy Company is trying out its first electronic sales girl. This machine is smart enough to dispense 36 different items in 10 separate styles and sizes. It accepts one—and five—dollar bills in addition to coins and returns the correct change plus rejecting counterfeit currency.

The almost superhuman qualities of some of these machines are described:[4]

Cybernated systems perform with a precision and rapidity unmatched in humans. They also perform in ways that would be impractical or impossible for humans to duplicate. They can be built to detect and correct errors in their own performance and to indicate to men which of their components are producing the error. They can make judgments on the basis of instructions programmed into them. They can remember and search their memories for appropriate data, which either has been programmed into them along with their instructions or has been acquired in the process of manipulating new data. Thus, they can learn on the basis of past experience with their environment. They can receive information in more codes and sensory modes than men can. They are beginning to perceive and to recognize.

The Ford company now has fifteen or twenty Unimates—the world's first automatic robot—which can be taught to perform 16,000 different functions. They can pour you a cup of coffee or lift a seventy-five-pound white-hot casting from a foundry.

What does all this mean to America? It means that we are involved in an economic and social revolution so vast in its implications that every aspect of our lives is affected today and will be increasingly affected tomorrow. Martin Greenberger asks, "What of the future? What can we expect as computers enter their third decade?"[5] He believes that on the basis of recent computer research, we can expect only a new wave of computer expansion with computer services and establishments beginning to spread throughout every sector of American life and reaching into houses, offices, classrooms, laboratories, factories, and businesses of all

[3] Donald N. Michael, *Cybernation: The Silent Conquest* (Santa Barbara, California: Center for the Study of Democratic Institutions, 1962), p. 15.

[4] *Ibid.*, p. 6.

[5] Martin Greenberger, "The Computers of Tomorrow," *Atlantic Monthly,* July, 1964, pp. 63–67.

kinds. To the recreation leader it means shorter working hours and a greater amount of free time for most, if not all, of the American people with the probable exception, for some time at least, of many managerial and technical workers, as well as members of the professions. The corollary of this is that the gift of free time will fall upon less capable or less able workers in all its abundance more as an affliction than as a blessing because they are very largely unprepared for it.

Leisure is a condition in which an individual is free from all obligations and thus is enabled to engage in activities without any compulsion whatsoever. Thus, the outstanding characteristics of leisure are freedom and the absence of necessity. A man of leisure is characterized by serenity and detachment. Being free of necessity, he participates in an activity solely for its own sake. The moment he plays golf to make a sale he is no longer at leisure because the state of necessity violates the concept of leisure. However, he may be completely absorbed and intensely engaged in what appears to be hard work, but he is doing so only for the satisfactions inherent in the activity itself.

Sebastian de Grazia indicates both the nature of true leisure and its relative absence in our work-oriented industrial society:[6]

> Perhaps you can judge the inner health of a land by the capacity of its people to do nothing—to lie abed musing, to amble about aimlessly, to sit having a coffee —because whoever can do nothing, letting his thoughts go where they may, must be at peace with himself. If he isn't, disturbing thoughts cut in and he will run to escape into alcohol or the flurry of activity called work.

Since leisure is uncommitted time when the individual is under no compulsion to do anything at all, but is free to do as he pleases, it naturally follows that he then reveals what he pleases to do. Leisure is largely a by-product of man's increasing control over nature, a gift of his creative genius to his fellow man. Like many similar products of man's creativity, leisure possesses tremendous possibilities for good and equal potentialities for evil. Just as nuclear power may enrich or destroy life, so may leisure lift the quality of human existence to new heights in America or lower it to depths of degradation never before attained.

There is no guarantee that leisure will prove to be a blessing to the American people; there is no guarantee it will prove to be a curse. If either

---

[6] de Grazia, *op. cit.*, p. 341. He does not, however, equate leisure with unproductiveness. He believes that free time is thought of as the opposite of work and, therefore, unproductive, but he believes that leisure and free time are two entirely different things. We shall continue to use the two terms interchangeably throughout this text as we do not believe that the American people are yet ready to accept any basic differences.

alternative were fixed and certain there would be no justification for a book designed to influence the outcome nor for our concern over the quality of leaders working in this area. The challenge lies in the uncertainty which exists. There is nothing inherently good or bad about leisure itself. Leisure is simply a key which unlocks the best and the worst in man. No one knows what the ultimate effect of leisure will be upon the individual and the nation—whether we are headed for a new age of Pericles or a Roman holiday. We do know, however, that leadership will prove to be the most important single factor in influencing the outcome. History is replete with examples of how leadership of a high quality has led nations to greatness and how poor or evil leadership has led them to destruction. How our people *use* their leisure will be the determining factor in its effect upon the individual and society. The intelligent use of leisure depends chiefly upon one's skills, interests, appreciations, understandings, and ideals. The role of the leader in helping our people develop these qualities and competencies is a vital one. Whether leisure in America becomes an asset or a liability depends, therefore, in large degree upon the quality of the leadership available for this increasing segment of our lives.

LEISURE IN HISTORICAL PERSPECTIVE

The student of history has one major advantage over the individual who knows no history. The happenings of today become more meaningful and significant when viewed against the backdrop of history than when seen only as current events, isolated from the previous experiences of mankind. By lengthening the historic perspective, the student of recreation gains the power to weigh and measure the facts, events, and proposals of his immediate society in terms of the totality of human experience. Thus, he is enabled to transcend the limitations of his present generation and draw upon the entire reservoir of human creativity which, in one sense, is the meaning of history. He learns that the centuries speak louder than the hours. Or, as Mumford puts it, "If we have not time to understand the past, we will not have the insight to control the future; for the past never leaves us and the future is already here."[7] Furthermore, no area of human endeavor deserves professional status, the respect of mankind in general, and of scholars in particular, unless the workers know thoroughly their own history.

---

[7] Lewis Mumford, *The Condition of Man* (New York: Harcourt, Brace and Co., 1944), p. 14.

Have other men in other times been confronted with what we term today the "problem" of leisure? If so, was it a problem to them? What did they do with their leisure? Was leisure in those days a good or a bad thing? What lessons can we learn from history that will help us profit from their experiences and avoid their mistakes? These are important questions, vital to our welfare. Let us turn now to see what lessons there may be for us from ancient Greece and Rome and from early America.

Leisure—The Basis of Grecian Culture

History provides a sound basis for belief in the constructive values of leisure for it reveals that all great cultures have been built upon a foundation of leisure.

Beginning almost 2,500 years ago, after centuries of preparation and sacrifice, Greece entered upon its Golden Age described by Shelley as "undoubtedly, whether considered in itself or with reference to the effect which it has produced upon the subsequent destinies of civilized man, the most memorable in the history of the world." During this period, Greece, and particularly Athens, reached pinnacles never before attained in sculpture, architecture, philosophy, literature, music, and drama. In the fifth century B. C., Athens burst into cultural glory to produce great philosophers like Socrates and Plato, playwrights like Sophocles and Aristophanes, sculptors like Phidias. The immortal temples of the Acropolis were all built within fifty years. This channeling of creative energy into cultural pursuits, which elevated Athens to one of history's loftiest peaks, was made possible largely through the work of slaves which freed the citizen to devote his time and energy to those activities deemed worthy of a freeman.

Leisure, at this period of Grecian history, meant opportunity—opportunity to use one's free time in a rewarding, nourishing, creative type of activity as innately satisfying to the individual as it was exalting to the state.

The Athenian looked down upon work as ignoble. Durant sums up his point of view:[8]

A freeman . . . must be free from economic tasks; he must get slaves or others to attend to his material concerns, even, if he can, to take care of his property and his fortune; only by such liberation can he find time for government, war, literature, and philosophy. Without a leisure class there can be, in the Greek view, no standards of taste, no encouragement of the arts, no civilization. No man who is in a hurry is quite civilized.

---

[8] Will Durant, The Life of Greece (New York: Simon and Schuster, 1939), p. 277.

For Aristotle leisure was far higher on the scale of values than work; in fact, it was the aim of all work and, along with theoretical wisdom and happiness, leisure represented the true purpose of human life.

A Roman Holiday

Rome provides the outstanding example in all history of the extent to which leisure misused can contribute to the degradation of a people. The most popular of leisure activities among the citizens of Rome about the time of Christ and for many years afterwards were those conducted in the circus, the stadium, and the amphitheater of which the most famous was the Colosseum. Never was a city so bountifully amused by plays, athletic contests, prize fights, horse races, chariot races, mortal combats of men with men or beasts, and naval battles on artificial lakes. So popular were the games that by A.D. 354 they were presented on 175 days in the year. Any freeman or woman could attend and apparently no admission was charged.

The most attractive entertainment of all was the bloodiest and the most brutal. Gladiators fought to the death and any who indicated a reluctance to die were prodded to bravery by red-hot irons. Mass battles were fought by thousands of men with desperate ferocity. Attendants passed among the fallen and probed them with sharp rods to see if they were feigning death. They killed any still living with blows on the head.

Durant describes the merciless and revolting spectacle:[9]

Condemned criminals, sometimes dressed in skins to resemble animals, were thrown to beasts made ravenous for the occasion . . . . The condemned man was sometimes required to play in no make-believe way some famous tragic role: he might represent Medea's rival, and be garbed in a handsome robe that would suddenly burst into flame and consume him: he might be burned to death on a pyre as Heracles; . . . he might play Mucius Scaevola and hold his hand over burning coals until it was shriveled up; he might be Icarus and fall from the sky into no merciful ocean but a crowd of wild beasts . . . Laureolus, a robber, was crucified in the arena for the amusement of the populace; but as he took too long in dying, a bear was brought in and was persuaded to eat him, piece by piece, as he hung upon the cross.

This was Roman recreation, or, at least, a highly popular aspect of it—bloody, cruel, inhuman, degenerate, revolting. As we contemplate the contrasts between the uses of leisure in Periclean Athens and Epi-

---

[9] Will Durant, *Caesar and Christ* (New York: Simon and Schuster, 1944), p. 385.

curean Rome, the words of William Hazlitt become especially meaningful: "Man is the only animal that laughs and weeps; for he is the only animal that is struck with the difference between what things are and what they ought to be." Their recreation reflected the qualities of their people and contributed to their further development. Each day's savagery called for greater horrors the next. Each member of the audience was less a human being when he left the Colosseum than when he entered.

When we look back across the centuries at Greece and at other great cultures of the past we realize that leisure, constructively used, was the foundation upon which their civilizations were erected. This is one of the vital lessons which history teaches the student of recreation—that leisure is the basis of culture and that the quality of a civilization is determined in large degree by how the people use their leisure. It is only when people cease to be occupied exclusively with the task of making a living that they are free to concern themselves with improving the quality of life. When a man is forced to devote almost all of his time and energy simply to the task of staying alive, it is futile to expect him to show any major interest in cultural activities either as a consumer or a contributor. The height to which the cultural stature of a nation rises generally will vary indirectly with the intensity of the struggle for existence engaged in by its citizens.

Russell points out that the leisure class[10]

contributed nearly the whole of what we call civilization. It cultivated the arts and discovered the sciences; it wrote the books, invented the philosophies, and refined social relations. . . . Without the leisure class, mankind would never have emerged from barbarism.

We can agree with Russell that leisure is the foundation upon which civilization is constructed, but disagree vigorously with the implication that the leisure of a few shall be supported upon the backs of the many. For democracy rejects any concept or proposal which aims to create a leisure elite at the expense of the masses.

Leisure in Early America

Leisure is a scarce commodity in primitive pioneer societies where the struggle for survival absorbs most of the time and energy of the people. The first settlers in America were confronted by a stubborn con-

---

[10] Bertrand Russell, "In Praise of Idleness and Other Essays." Reprinted in: Eric Larrabee and Rolf Meyersohn (eds.), *Mass Leisure* (Glencoe, Illinois: The Free Press, 1958), p. 103.

tinent which grudgingly yielded up a living only to those who directed all their energy to their work. Dulles paints the picture:[11]

The first settlers actually had very little time or opportunity to play. Harsh circumstances fastened upon them the necessity for continual work. In the strange and unfamiliar wilderness that was America, 'all things stared upon them with a weather-beaten face.' The forest crowded against their little settlements along tidewater, and they felt continually menaced by its lurking dangers. None knew when the eerie war-whoop of the Indians might break the oppressive silence. Starvation again and again thinned their ranks, and disease was a grim specter hovering over each household. Merely to keep alive in a land which to their inexperience was cruel and inhospitable demanded all their energy.

Two additional factors combined with economic necessity to arouse intense disapproval of leisure and recreation by the Puritans. The Church of England looked with favor upon many of the harmless diversions engaged in by the people in the early part of the seventeenth century. The Puritans, as a party of reform, made little effort to evaluate the worth of the various activities that the Church countenanced. They were religious dissenters; they were opposed to the Church; therefore, they were opposed to the "sinful pleasures" permitted by the Church. Their reaction is comparable to that of the individual who says, "I don't like him; I don't like anything about him; I don't even like the way he combs his hair." It may not be a sensible reaction, but it is a very human reaction.

Furthermore, the Puritans, a middle-class group, resented the wealthy classes partially because of the large amount of leisure they enjoyed. They, too, wanted leisure, but they couldn't have it; therefore, it was evil and no one should have it. Thus, their intolerance was tridimensional in origin, stemming from economic necessity, spiritual reform, and economic envy.

The ruling powers in the colonies, both north and south, Puritan and Anglican, passed numerous laws prohibiting idleness and all amusements and requiring everyone to work. Bowling was outlawed at Jamestown and an indifferent worker could be "condemned to the galley for three years." The General Court of the Massachusetts Bay Colony stipulated that "no person, householder or other, shall spend his time idly or unprofitably, under paine of such punishment as the Courte shall thinke meet to inflict." The Virginia Assembly in 1619 decreed that any idle person should be condemned to compulsory work. Massachusetts and Connecticut outlawed dice, cards, quoits, bowls, ninepins, and shuffleboard. Dancing and the theatre also were prohibited.[12]

---

[11] Foster Rhea Dulles, *A History of Recreation: America Learns to Play* (New York: Appleton-Century-Crofts, Inc., 1965), p. 4.
[12] *Ibid.*, pp. 4–6.

The enactment of laws prohibiting certain activities is a fairly reliable indication that these activities were being engaged in by some of the people. It is reasonable to believe that most of America's early settlers would have welcomed leisure and reaction had it not been for the situation in which they found themselves. Had they chosen, or been permitted to choose, the easy life New England might well have been doomed. Unfortunately, ideas often persist long after the environmental conditions which produced the ideas have disappeared. Puritanism has much to its credit, but it must bear most of the blame for fastening upon its descendants a concept of the innate sanctity of work and a guilt complex in relation to leisure and recreation. The Puritanic tradition which denies the need for, and importance of, recreation has been the seedbed from which an enormous crop of evils has sprung and which still plagues us today.

LEISURE IN MODERN SOCIETY

To the Greeks in the days of Pericles, leisure was an opportunity for creative expression through cultural activities; in early America, leisure was despised and prohibited by law. What does it mean in the lives of people today? To find where you are going you must know where you are as well as where you have been.

Labor and Leisure

Leisure can be fully understood only as we see it in relation to work. Nothing in this world stands completely isolated and alone; and nothing can be fully understood except as it is seen in its major relationships. The true meaning of a boat can be understood only in relation to water; an airplane in relation to air; a fork in relation to food; and light in relation to darkness. One of the marks of the intelligent man is his ability to see relationships. Let us examine leisure in its relationship to work.

The leisure of the ancients was made possible by human slavery while mechanical slaves have been largely responsible for releasing us from a life of toil. This highly mechanized industrial society has been productive of much that is good in American life. Living standards for the average man, at least from the standpoint of material welfare, are the highest in the history of the world. Man is no longer a beast of burden bowed down beneath the weight of unremitting toil and forced to endure a hard and painful life in which leisure is but a hopeless yearning. And yet, seldom is any major alteration in the lives of people wholly good. Before the industrial revolution much of work challenged the whole of man and, in many instances, provided a large measure of creative satisfaction. The shoemaker, upon completing a pair of shoes, surveyed his handiwork with deep pride and joy because he had shaped and fashioned them with his own hands and mind.

Now the worker in a shoe factory may operate a machine which punches out the eyelets, and all day long he performs this one simple operation—monotonous, boresome, repetitive, and noncreative. Only a small fraction of his total powers are employed by his work. There is little exercise for the body, no challenge to the mind, no appeal to the emotions, and yet man is all of these. Thus, the new technology has condemned industrial man to lead a fractionalized life while on the job, calling into play only a part of his total self, and denying him the personal satisfaction, pride, happiness, and sense of purpose and meaningfulness which used to characterize much of his work.

Since work, for a large proportion of our population, fails to provide opportunities for balanced growth and development it is evident that leisure must assume a more important role than mere cessation from toil. Leisure must serve a rehabilitative or therapeutic function. It must provide opportunities for the worker to repair the damage done by the machine; to achieve organic balance and regain the wholeness of personality destroyed by his work. Thus, through his leisure man may compensate for the deprivations suffered while on the job, provided he engages in activities that challenge his total powers, exercise the entire body, stimulate the intellect, and satisfy his creative impulses.

Once work was a focal point of man's life and the chief function of leisure was to refresh his spirit and renew his energy so that he might labor more effectively. A number of studies reveal that work is no longer a central life interest, at least for industrial workers. Dubin reports on his research among industrial workers:[13]

Our research shows that for almost three out of four industrial workers studied, work and the workplace *are not* central life interests. . . .

---

[13] Robert Dubin, "Industrial Workers' Worlds." Reprinted in: Eric Larrabee and Rolf Meyersohn (eds.), *Mass Leisure* (Glencoe, Illinois: The Free Press, 1958), pp. 215, 219, 225.

Factory work may now very well be viewed by industrial workers as a means to an end—a way of acquiring income for life in the community. . . .

In particular, work is not a central life interest for industrial workers when we study the informal group experiences and the general social experiences that have some affective value for them. Industrial man seems to perceive his life history as having its center outside of work for his intimate human relationships and for his feelings of enjoyment, happiness and worth.

Any discussion of work and play should point out the impossibility of drawing a sharp line between the two because what is play to one may be work to another. The sedentary worker may take a five-mile hike as part of his recreation, but the postman is not likely to do so. The motive is the important factor in differentiating between recreation and work. Where the element of necessity exists the activity is work.

Four stages in the development of leisure .in relation to work have evolved in this country over the past three centuries, or are still in the process of evolving:

1. Leisure is rejected completely as an evil thing and prohibited by law.
2. Leisure exists for the sole purpose of renewing man's powers to the end that he might work more effectively.
3. Leisure exists to compensate man for the deprivations suffered while on the job. It is not the antithesis of work, but a complement of work. In this concept, work is still of primary importance while leisure occupies a secondary role, although a more important one than in the two previous stages.
4. Leisure is the goal, the end, the purpose of work. Work is a means of acquiring the necessary income so that one may be free to achieve in his leisure the happiness, enjoy the intimate human relationships, experience the satisfactions of creative achievement, and discover the deeper meanings of life no longer to be found in his work. In short, leisure replaces work as the central life interest of mankind. In work man makes a living; in leisure he makes a life. Leisure has risen above the level of *recreation* to the level of *creation*.

A direct relationship often exists between the nature of a man's work and the nature of his leisure activities. The individual who is exposed to constant boredom and monotony while on the job needs to experience in his leisure some adventure, thrills, and excitement if he is to be a healthy and happy person. Heron's studies of the effects of exposure for prolonged periods of time to a rigidly monotonous environment reveal that such exposure "has definitely deleterious effects. The individual's thinking is impaired; he shows childish emotional responses; his visual perception becomes disturbed; he suffers from hallucinations; his brain-wave pattern changes."[14] Heron concludes that, "In this age of semi-automation when . . . many industrial workers have little to do but keep a constant watch on instruments, the problem of human behavior in monotonous situations is becoming acute."[15]

Unfortunately, large numbers of our people seem to be chasing a will-o-the-wisp in their frantic efforts to escape from the drabness of their work. They seek relief from the emptiness of their lives through such forms of excitation as gambling, alcohol, narcotics, scenes of violence or passion enjoyed on the television or motion picture screen, or in some other equally unsatisfactory struggle with the tediousness of time. But the escape from "the great emptiness" is but a brief delusion since it has been achieved by a type of excitation which, like a drug, must be taken in ever greater quantities in order to get the same effects. Thus, leisure too, becomes a void and as boresome as one's work.

The reason for this is that leisure to be enjoyable presupposes some absorbing interest inherently satisfying to the basic need of man. For example, self-expression through a cultural activity, such as painting, gives to leisure a satisfying content which frequently it lacks. But just as a man cannot enjoy a book unless he has developed skills, interests, and appreciations in reading, so must he have been educated for the cultural use of leisure in other respects. He, frequently, is unfit for leisure because the schools may have neglected this aspect of his education and because his work provides no opportunities for practice in the art of creative self-expression. The worker is not an artisan as was his grandfather; he is a cog in a vast industrial machine. Since neither his work nor his education prepares him for creative self-expression, his leisure takes mainly a receptive instead of an expressive form. Considered from this standpoint we are probably less fit for leisure than any previous generation. This fact, together with our failure to recognize the obligations as well as the pleasures of leisure, renders leisure potentially more dangerous to our society today than at any previous time in our history.

On the Bright Side

Proof of the misuse of leisure by Americans exists on every hand but the picture is by no means an entirely dark one. As Kaplan puts it, "Yet there is considerable evidence that aesthetic interests have never been

---

[14] Woodburn Heron, "The Pathology of Boredom," *Scientific American*, January 1957, p. 56.
[15] *Ibid.*, p. 52.

pursued more genuinely in the history of this country or with greater variety and independence."[16] He presents proof of the cultural explosion:[17]

Quantitative evidence on the present state of the arts is abundant: expenditures in 1957 of 500 million dollars for concert tickets, 80 million dollars for classical records, 166 million dollars for hi-fi equipment and tapes, and 40 million dollars for published concert music and teaching pieces. . . . In 1934 recordings of Beethoven's Ninth sold less than 500 copies; in 1953 and 1954 Toscanini's recording of this work was purchased by almost 150,000 persons.

The ten symphony orchestras of 1900 had increased to 1,385 in 1965. There are now over 700 opera groups in the country. A sampling made by the American Music Conference in 1967 indicated that over 20 million Americans play the piano, 11 million, the guitar, 800,000, the accordian, and about half a million, the ukulele.

Music is not the only creative area in which the cultural revolution seems to be taking place. We have more than 5,000 community theater groups; an estimated two million persons paint regularly in their leisure time, and the audience or clientele of art exhibitions runs into the many millions.[18]

Also, there is evidence of a remarkable growth in active, wholesome recreational pursuits. The most surprising development in the leisure economy has been the growth of the swimming pool business. In 1950 there were only 3,600 residential pools in the whole country. The Tile Council of America, Inc. estimates there are now about a million privately owned pools, or one for approximately every 200 people in the United States.

There were around 6,784,000 outboards in use in 1966 and over $500 million worth of them were sold in 1966. The annual Sports Participation Survey of the Athletic Institute revealed that during 1965 some 33 million anglers and hunters, in 700 million recreation days (any part of a day in which hunting and fishing occurred), traveled 31 billion passenger miles and spent over $4 billion in pursuit of fishing and hunting.

About 20 million hunters spend $1 billion each year. Bowling has become a $1 billion yearly business. At least 8,525,000 golfers spend $750 million a year for golf expenses. Approximately 22,500,000 Americans take part in softball, 20,000,000 in shooting sports, 8,000,000 in target archery, 5,000,000 in skiing, 57,000,000 in bicycling, and 39,300,000 in boating.

---

[16] Max Kaplan, *Leisure in America* (New York: John Wiley and Sons, Inc., 1960), p. 301.

[17] *Ibid.,* pp. 206–207.

[18] *Ibid.*

Over 50 million people visited our national parks in 1955, 72 million in 1960, and approximately 133 million in 1966.[19]

A Time for Choices

Leisure is a time for choices, a measure of alternatives. The numerous decisions which the individual must make in his leisure was indicated by Jacks when he defined leisure as "that part of a man's life where the struggle between white angels and black for the possession of his soul goes on with the greatest intensity."[20] There is much truth in the statement, "What a person is depends upon what he does when he has nothing to do." For when people are free to choose what they shall do they reveal their deeper selves. What a man does when he is on the job he may do from necessity, but what he does in his leisure he does by choice. Therefore, the decisive factor in determining the worth of leisure becomes inevitably the nature of the choices which people make. Upon the nature of these choices rests in large degree the welfare of both the individual and society.

It has begun to dawn upon the American public consciousness that leisure is not an unmixed blessing and that many of our hopes and expectations for leisure appear to be falling far short of even a reasonable degree of fulfillment. One universal temptation of leisure is the temptation of the easy choice. The immediate and obvious instance of this is the unwillingness of millions to choose the active, vigorous life over the sedentary and inactive which requires a minimum of effort, both mental and physical. It is easier to watch an athletic contest than to play in one so we are a nation of spectators at athletic contests. Why exert oneself learning to play golf when one can watch the experts perform on the television screen? And why spend years attempting to master a musical instrument when by the mere turn of a dial one can listen to far better music than he can ever hope to produce himself? Leisure, instead of being a stimulant for the channeling of the creative energies of the American people into cultural pursuits, as was true with the Periclean Greeks, has too frequently deteriorated into a sedative, an inducement to enervation and an encouragement to inertia.

The student of leisure who reflects seriously upon this aspect of human life and society is impressed very deeply by the quality of freedom

---

[19] Donald E. Hawkins (ed.), *Recreation and Park Yearbook—1966* (Washington, D.C.: National Recreation and Park Association, 1966), p. 17.

[20] L. P. Jacks, *The Education of the Whole Man* (New York: Harper and Brothers, 1931), p. 58.

which characterizes leisure and all the implications inherent in this fact. Leisure is uncommitted time, a time for choices, a new dimension of freedom. When a man is free to determine for himself his own course of action it becomes immediately apparent that the possibilities are limitless—for good or for evil. Shall this freedom be for millions simply the freedom to stagnate, to endure the tediousness of time which means nothing more than a vast emptiness in their lives? Is it to be an opportunity for the enrichment of life through participation in creative activities which exalt and ennoble man, challenging the best that is in him? Or shall it be freedom to descend the toboggan slide leading to dissipation and degradation? Shall this new leisure be the means by which man experiences an awakening sense of civic responsibility and an increasing involvement in community life or shall it further his withdrawal into the shell of his own personal, petty, and selfish interests? Is it to be the freedom to suffer the bitterness of rejection by our fellow men or to enjoy the self-respect and happiness accruing from acceptance as one of the group? Could our leisure become more leisurely, bringing into our lives greater serenity to the end that we might rest, relax, reflect, and "possess our souls" before we die? Might not this precious gift of leisure become a time for greatness, as it was for the Periclean Greeks, rather than an invitation to vice and moral decadence?

This freedom of choice which lies so uniquely at the heart of the leisure problem imposes upon the individual a heavy obligation to insist not upon the right to do what he chooses, but rather to accept the responsibility of choosing to do what is right.

The Threat of Leisure

Leisure can be either an asset or a liability depending upon the manner in which it is used. Many of the vices that disfigure and poison our civilization have their origin in the efforts of human beings to escape the dullness and the drabness of lives devoid of creative activity. We spend billions of dollars each year on national defense, and rightly so, but it is well to remember that no great civilization of the past was ever destroyed from without until it had first destroyed itself within. Our democracy has proved it can stand the test of war. Whether it can stand the test of leisure and survive is quite another matter. Alger presents the threat when he says: "A civilization that creates a leisure which it cannot rationally use may well be in greater danger of destruction than one that has no leisure at all."[21]

---

[21] George W. Alger, "Leisure—for What?", *The Atlantic Monthly,* 135, April 1925, p. 492.

The task with which we are confronted is the same that other civilizations have faced and failed to solve. For while leisure, constructively used, was the foundation upon which Grecian culture was erected, a few hundred years later its misuse was a factor in the downfall of Greece. No other civilization in the history of the world has been able to "withstand the combination of time and money in the hands of its masses." However, the conditions which threaten us are not insolvable; we still have the power to control our own destiny. Alger presents the challenge:[22]

The great problem before us today is to create a civilization that does not degenerate under leisure. This can be done only by setting in operation forces making for a culture that recognizes, as no civilization since the fall of Rome has been required to do, that leisure is and must be a means and not an end; that its true value is measured by what we do with it— by whether it lifts us or lowers us in the great world of intangibles, the world not of material but of spiritual values.

LEISURE CHALLENGES THE SCHOOLS

Intelligent human beings are free to learn from the tragedies of the past and how to avoid repeating them. If we accept the concept that man has, at least in part, the power to direct his destiny and if we believe in education as a vital means of influencing this direction, the importance of the school as an instrument for converting leisure into an asset of tremendous significance becomes immediately apparent. Leisure is a time when choices must be made. Selection of one course of action over another is dependent primarily upon a sense of values, appreciations, understandings, interests, and skills, all of which, basically, fall within the province of education.

Let us state the problem in somewhat different words. People do in their leisure, if opportunities are available, what they like to do and they like to do that which gives them enjoyment, happiness, and satisfaction. In general, people like to do what they do well and dislike to do what they do poorly. A high degree of skill in an activity is the best single guarantee of interest in, liking for, and desire to participate in that activity. Not many people, for example, are clamoring for an opportunity to demonstrate their total ineptness on the tennis courts and golf courses of this nation.

---

[22] *Ibid.*

The School Educates for Leisure

It follows, therefore, that education for leisure is the major, unique and continuing responsibility of the school in relation to recreation. In a nation where leisure constitutes more than half of the waking hours of its citizens there can be no possible justification for the failure of the schools to prepare young people for the creative use of their leisure time. Here is one of education's finest opportunities to demonstrate its effectiveness as a vital force in man's efforts to reach his goal of the "good life."

If the school is to be successful in the development of leisure skills, interests, and appreciations their acquisition must not be left to chance but must be planned for and sought as intelligently and deliberately as are other goals which the school seeks. Thus, it is clear that a major task of the school is helping students acquire life-long interests, appreciations, and skills in art, music, dramatics, outdoor education, crafts, dance, sports and games, and in many other desirable activities, including hobbies. How this can best be done is education's problem but its solution will be facilitated if the educators will remember that people in their leisure, if given an opportunity, generally prefer to participate in those activities which are satisfying and enjoyable; that the *manner* in which teachers present their subjects determines in large measure the degree of interest and enjoyment of the students; that people are not likely to enjoy as adults activities they disliked when they were young; that people usually enjoy that which they do well; and for this reason, teachers should do their utmost to help students reach the highest possible level of performance, as skill is a basic factor in the making of wise choices among leisure activities. Mediocrity should never be tolerated when excellence is possible.

Education for leisure is not something extra to be tacked on to education nor does it involve telling people what they should do in their free time. It consists primarily of awakening and stimulating their creative faculties and providing opportunities for creative expression so that whenever leisure is available they will chose for themselves those activities that are eminently satisfying to the nature of man.

Additional suggestions designed to assist the school in carrying out more effectively its role as leisure educator include:[23]

A special committee should be established by the school to explore each area of the curriculum to determine its possible contributions to leisure education.

---

[23] Howard G. Danford (ed.), *School Recreation—National Conference Report* (Washington, D.C.: American Association for Health, Physical Education, and Recreation, 1960), p. 8.

Literature, for example, should be taught with a view to making it more meaningful and enjoyable to students while in school, and increasingly more satisfying as long as they live.

Science should be taught in a way to bring out the excitement, curiosity, and adventure resident in the exploration field trips. A life-long recreation interest in ornithology or botany may result.

It is also the school's responsibility to provide opportunities wherein the various recreation activities taught can be practiced, interests deepened, and skills perfected. These opportunities might include establishment of clubs around some of the common interests, intramural participation, and provision of school and community facilities for further enjoyment of these interests.

The schools should strive to utilize as many direct experiences as possible in recreation education. For example, teachers should take their students on more field trips, as well as bring more life into the classroom by inviting guest demonstrators and lecturers.

The school's responsibilities in the area of recreation may, and frequently do, go far beyond leisure education to include direct operation of the program of public recreation. Or the school may pool its personnel, finances, and facilities with another governmental agency for the joint operation of a community recreation program. No matter what plan of administration is in effect, school buildings and grounds should be made available for recreation when needed. They belong to the people and should be used by the people. The extensive use of school facilities for community recreation pays high dividends both to the people who use them and to the school. As the school widens its services to the community, it increases the number of its friends who now identify it as a center of community life, happiness, and enriched living for all the people. Its prestige rises, its influence grows, and its support develops. School officials who have the vision to see the school as a great social institution, directly involved in the maintenance of an active, virile community life, will welcome the opportunity to open its doors to the people seeking recreation.

THE RELATIONSHIP OF
RECREATION TO EDUCATION

Unfortunately, partially because of our Puritan background, recreation has not yet been accepted universally as an area of life comparable in importance with education. The recreative arts still occupy the role of the poor relation. Some share of responsibility for this situation rests upon the recreation people for their failure to define terms and relationships; establish, clarify, and agree upon values of a highly significant nature; interpret these higher values to the public; substitute vital experiences with cultural values for the many trivial and meaningless activities which so frequently characterize their programs today; attract into the field a higher quality of personnel; and measure the effectiveness of their work in terms of progress made in realizing the values previously agreed upon.

The Meaning of Recreation

Recreation is any socially desirable leisure activity in which an individual participates voluntarily and from which he derives immediate and continuing satisfaction. Manifestly, recreation must help meet certain basic human needs otherwise it will not be satisfying, and it must contribute to the socialization of the individual else it will not be socially desirable.

Since human beings differ, that which is recreation to one may not be recreation to another. Assuming that an activity meets all other standards, the decisive factor is that of motivation. If the individual engages in an activity for the sheer fun of doing so, it is recreation; if he does so because of an outer compulsion, such as the need for money, the activity is work. Leisure, the time when recreation takes place, becomes far more meaningful and significant when it is earned through work; and work, without leisure as one of its rewards, is endless drudgery. Thus, labor and leisure, work and recreation, are not antagonistic but complementary in nature. The good life consists neither of all one nor all the other, but of both.

Unity Through Excellence

The relationship of recreation and education is an extremely close one. Many of the activities taught by the school as an integral part of education are exactly the same activities as those comprising the program of recreation. There are no essential differences between literature and volleyball taught in school and the same interests enjoyed during one's leisure. The extent to which youth and adults participate voluntarily during their leisure in activities taught by the school is one direct measure of the effectiveness of teaching.

Teachers generally use a more formal approach to subject matter and are more concerned with educational outcomes, while recreation leaders are more interested in the enjoyment of the activity. Students may be compelled by law to go to school; no such compulsion exists in the recreation situation. The absence of any element of compulsion magnifies the importance of a high quality of leadership in recreation.

Recreation leaders are realizing more and more that fun, although very important, is not, by itself, enough, and are conducting activities in such a way as to achieve other values related to human welfare and the enrichment of life without sacrificing the value of enjoyment. Recreation, so conducted, *is* education. Among the characteristics of recreation which enhance its educational possibilities are these:[24]

(1) it is freely chosen—therefore the individual is in a state of readiness for the activity with no artificial motivation necessary; (2) it is enjoyable, interesting, and purposeful, else the individual would not participate; and (3) since many of the recreation situations are highly emotionalized they possess great potentialities for learning.

When teachers present their school subjects in such a manner as to stimulate greatly the interests and heighten the enjoyment of their students, then education may become recreation. The higher the quality of education and the higher the quality of recreation the more closely do they merge and become indistinguishable.

Recreation and education should be seen in synthesis rather than in separation. Certainly, both can profit greatly by this union. Recreation needs to free itself from the inane, useless, trivial, and cheap; to lift its sights and seek values of vital significance to the individual and society; and to select activities within which these values reside and conduct them in such a manner as to realize the values sought. In short, recreation needs to become far more educational than it is at present. On the other hand, education can be greatly improved by the addition of some of the interest, joy, and zestfulness that characterize recreation. Many educators need to free themselves from the fallacious notion that man can be divided into a mind and a body; that the mind is superior and the body inferior; and that education is a vitally important process involving the mind and emphasizing intellectual development, while recreation is a relatively insignificant operation centering around the body, amusement, fun, and frivolity.

Recreation and education should be an indivisible unity. On their highest levels they are indistinguishable. The Greeks understood this because their word for leisure is *skole*, the English "school." They saw the relationship of education and recreation centuries ago. Our recent

---

[24] Howard G. Danford, *Recreation in the American Community* (New York: Harper and Brothers, 1953), p. 119.

discovery of the educational possibilities of recreation and the importance of vitalizing education through recreation constitutes a milestone of profound significance in the development of these areas of human activity.

Selected References

Alger, George W., *Education for Leisure* (Washington, D.C.: American Association for Health, Physical Education, and Recreation, 1957).

Danford, Howard G., ed., *School Recreation—National Conference Report* (Washington, D.C.: American Association for Health, Physical Education, and Recreation, 1960.

De Grazia, Sebastian, *Of Time, Work, and Leisure* (New York: The Twentieth Century Fund, 1962).

Douglass, Paul F., ed., "Recreation in the Age of Automation," *The Annals of the American Academy of Political and Social Science,* 313, September 1957. Entire issue is devoted to recreation.

Dulles, Foster Rhea, *A History of Recreation: America Learns to Play* (New York: Appleton-Century-Crofts, Inc., 1965).

Durant, Will, *The Life of Greece* (New York: Simon and Schuster, 1939).

Hawkins, Donald E., ed., *Recreation and Park Yearbook—1966* (Washington, D.C.: National Recreation and Park Association, 1966).

Jacks, Lawrence Pearsall, *Education Through Recreation* (New York: Harper and Brothers, 1932).

Kaplan, Max, *Leisure in America* (New York: John Wiley and Sons, Inc., 1960).

Larrabee, Eric and Meyersohn, Rolf, ed., *Mass Leisure* (Glencoe, Illinois: The Free Press, 1958).

Mead, Margaret, "The Patterns of Leisure in Contemporary American Culture," *Annals of the American Academy of Political and Social Science,* 313, September 1957.

Muggeridge, Malcolm, "The Real Opiate of the Masses," *New York Times Magazine,* November 23, 1959.

Neumeyer, M. H. and Neumeyer, Esther, *Leisure and Recreation* (3rd ed.), (New York: The Ronald Press Company, 1958).

Pieper, Josef, *Leisure: The Basis of Culture,* Trans. by Alexander Dru, (New York: Pantheon Books, 1952).

Chapter III

Understanding Human Behavior

LEADERSHIP CAN FUNCTION effectively only as it operates upon the solid rock of understanding with respect to the nature of human beings and why they behave as they do. The key to constructive guidance of human behavior is an insight into the forces, drives, or needs that feed the springs of human action and provide the motivating influences that energize and direct human beings. A more adequate understanding of people and their behavior is the most vital of all the bases for the solution of problems confronting the recreation leaders of our time.

Two distinct limitations must be recognized at this point: (1) there is no general agreement among behaviorial scientists with regard to many aspects of human behavior. In fact, one is impressed and somewhat appalled by the diversity and complexity of their viewpoints; and (2) it is outside the limitations of this book to present a comprehensive account of the various theories of human behavior or a detailed analysis of the physiological, sociological, and psychological characteristics of the various age groups. Hence, this chapter will present only a brief overview of some of the most important facts and beliefs shedding light upon human beings and human behavior—facts which appear to possess special significance for the recreation leader.

Our approach to the problem of human behavior is frankly a perceptual one with emphasis upon the human being as an organic unity motivated by the need for personal adequacy as perceived by himself.

THE CHALLENGE TO LEADERSHIP

To the playgrounds and community centers of this nation come children and adults with many kinds of problems and varied forms of behavior. Leaders must work with children who fight and children who are afraid to fight; children who are team players and children who are selfish individualists; children who are honest and truthful and children who steal and lie; children who constantly seek the limelight and those who are withdrawn; children who welcome suggestions and those who resent suggestions; children who are liked and accepted and children who are disliked and rejected; adults who possess a sense of dignity and worth and adults who have no confidence in themselves; and adults who lose their heads when beaten in a softball game and others to whom defeat is a matter of relative unimportance.

The first step in dealing effectively with any problem is understanding the nature of the problem. Whether these children and adults will be treated by the leader in ways conducive to the attainment of goals significant both to themselves and to the society of which they are a part will be determined in large degree by the leader's insight into such problems of human nature. Understanding human nature, he is better able to manage it and is not trapped by his lack of knowledge into trial and error experiments often with disastrous results. It is only as we understand why people behave as they do, what the forces are which drive them on, that we are able to influence their behavior more effectively. Stated simply, a leader is a person who influences the behavior of another and the extent of his influence is measured in large degree by the breadth and depth of his understanding of human nature.

THE UNITY OF MAN

No fact of human nature possesses greater significance to recreation leadership than the principle of organic unity, the wholeness of man. This means that there is no such thing as mind or body existing as separate and unrelated segments of man. He is not a mind *and* a body, but a totality, an integrated unitary whole in which mind and body are one—interdependent, inseparable, indivisible. The very word "individual," in its original meaning, indicates an indivisible, unitary being.

Aristotle believed in this unified concept of man and his point of view is supported by modern scientists. However, throughout recorded history, others have argued that man existed as separate parts, primarily body and mind, or soul, and, although housed together, these parts were neither closely nor harmoniously related. Wherever this "atomistic" view of man prevailed the effect upon recreation generally was disastrous. For example, the doctrine of asceticism which existed in certain parts of the world during the early Middle Ages was an offshoot of dualism, the theory that man was divided into body and soul. The ascetics believed that body was evil while soul was good; that the two were continually at war with each other; and that mortification of the flesh, resulting in purification of the soul, was the surest road to eternal salvation. Thus, among many of the ascetics, a keen rivalry arose for the austerity championship. Starvation, sleeplessness, solitude, poverty, filth, disease, celibacy, and many other forms of humiliation and self-denial characterized their lives. Anything which contributed to the joy and happiness of the individual was bitterly condemned and rigorously avoided. There was no place for recreation in the life of any individual who held such a concept of the nature of man.

A more modern and less extreme expression of belief in man's divisibility exists in the prevalent and pernicious concept that education is concerned with things intellectual while recreation is involved almost exclusively with such physical or relatively nonintellectual activities as games, sports, crafts, music, and drama in which amusement and fun, but no higher values, may be the outcomes. Since education is supposed to deal with the intellect and recreation with the nonintellectual aspects of man's nature, such as the body and the emotions, a hierarchy has developed over the years with education ranked at the top of the order and recreation far down the list.

A heavy burden of responsibility for the relatively low status of recreation in comparison with education must be borne by those persons in recreation who discount the contributions recreation should make to the total development of the individual and to those values related to democratic citizenship, and confine their efforts primarily to fun and entertainment. They, too, fail to understand the unified nature of man, for this concept of the inseparable wholeness of the individual means that the whole person reacts and interacts to, affects and is affected by, the total environment. The whole child comes to the playground and the community center; body, mind, spirit, and emotions are involved in every recreation experience. He is affected by every aspect of the recreation situation—by the leader, his playmates, the equipment, supplies, and facilities, the weather, noise, and a myriad of other factors. He responds to every situation, not as a body, nor as an intellect, nor as a bundle of emotions, but as a whole person. Since he reacts as a whole to every situation, he will be affected morally, socially, mentally, and physically by everything he does. Therefore, the recreation leader must be concerned with total, rather than with partial, outcomes.

THE MEANING OF MAN'S UNITY
TO RECREATION LEADERSHIP

The implications of the unified nature of man to recreation leadership are numerous and precise. What are some of the most important of these meanings?

1. Man exists as an integrated, whole person. He reacts as a whole to the total situation. That which affects one part of man affects the whole man. When recreation leaders accept this concept of organismic unity it follows that they must be concerned with total outcomes—with emotional responses, human relationships, social, moral, and ethical impacts, intellectual outcomes, and physiological values. Whether they desire it or not, the recreation people are inescapably involved in the conduct of activities whose outcomes go far beyond fun, enjoyment, and relaxation.

   A boy playing softball on a playground team is having fun, but since the "whole person" is involved many other things are also happening to him. He is active, therefore physiological outcomes, either good or bad, are certain to result, and skills, either properly or improperly executed, are engaged in. His intellectual operations may involve the learning of rules and the making of intelligent decisions during play. These intellectual operations interlock with the development of social behavior as he responds to his teammates, his opponents, the officials, spectators, and to his coach, or leader. The emotions may be aroused in many of these responses. Moral and ethical choices may have to be made.[1]

   Thus, the youth reacts with all of himself to the softball experience and the recreation leader must be directly concerned with all of the outcomes. If he shuts his eyes to moral and ethical values he may develop a skillful player who is also a bully, a liar, a cheat, and a thief. If he ignores social behavior he may contribute to the development of non-coöperative, selfish individualists whose sole concern is themselves. If physiological results seem unimportant a few serious injuries may invoke the wrath of parents upon him. When we accept

---

[1] See pages 226–228 for a discussion of moral values in softball.

the concept of the unified nature of man, it is imperative that we accept its corollary—that outcomes of the recreation experience are multiple and their nature will depend largely upon the quality of the experience. It follows, therefore, that professional leadership in recreation will plan and conduct programs in such a manner as to achieve those values that heretofore have been considered as being associated with recreation, but not among its central purposes.

2. The true worth of recreation can best be judged in terms of its total effect upon the whole individual, not merely upon a few parts of him.

3. The economic life of man, in many instances, has become so highly specialized that he is unable to function as a whole person. He lives a fractionalized existence while on the job. Hence, leaders should provide opportunities for the whole man to participate in activities demanding the exercise of all his talents.

4. Classifying recreation activities as physical or mental is unscientific and a denial of the unified nature of man.

5. Since the whole person reacts to the whole situation, the recreation leader should give careful consideration to every aspect of the recreation experience—sanitation, ventilation, equipment, supplies, facilities, lighting, noise, congestion, all factors that might produce feelings of insecurity or embarrassment, factors that promote individual growth toward competency and adequacy, his own leadership practices, and many other elements.

WHY PEOPLE DO WHAT THEY DO

We cannot understand human behavior unless we know what is important to people and what they are trying to achieve when they behave or misbehave. In our efforts to observe the behavior of people as a basis for deepening our understanding, we may either assume the point of view of an outsider and observe the behavior of others or we may make our observations from the point of view of the behaver himself. This attempt to understand human behavior in terms of how things seem to the individual is known as the "perceptual" approach and is the point of view expressed in this chapter.

As You See Yourself

Every man is the center of his own universe; not the man we see, but the self as he sees himself. How a man sees himself will determine largely what he thinks and how he behaves. For example, if you look upon yourself as being handsome and popular with the girls, your thoughts and your behavior at a party are likely to be quite different from what they would be if you perceived yourself as an ugly, backward, self-conscious, and socially inept wallflower.

A person's ideas about himself are derived from many sources. Combs and Snygg point out:[2]

. . . The self is the product of the individual's experience. Each of us discovers who he is and what he is from events that have occurred in his lifetime, but most particularly from the ways he has been treated by those close to him in the course of his growing up.

The self is not simply a physical entity, a body, but is the entire personality, "that unique being known as John Jones or Sally Smith." In the lifelong construction of one's concepts of self, no part of this edifice is so important as the foundation laid in early life when the child first discovers from his family whether he is liked or disliked, accepted or unaccepted. The evolvement of the self is described by Combs and Snygg:[3]

Each of us has literally thousands of more or less discrete perceptions of himself in all kinds of situations. Among them are such perceptions of his physical self as being blue-eyed or brown-eyed, tall or short, fat or thin, blond or brunette. One will also have concepts of himself in social or judgmental terms when he sees himself as being afraid or unafraid, acceptable or unacceptable, liked or unliked, able or unable. The number of self perceptions a person may possess will be almost unlimited, but for each person they are unique to himself. They are his experience of himself. All perceptions of the self a person has at a particular instant we call the phenomenal self, or the perceived self. It is the phenomenal self which each human being is forever seeking to maintain.

Believing and Behaving

The boy who perceives himself to be the toughest teenager in the community will act quite differently on the playground from one whose self-image involves a perfect gentleman. Thus, the behavior of a person is determined largely by the concepts he possesses of himself. These perceptions need not be based upon facts as seen by others. It is sufficient if the individual believes they are facts. A dramatic illustration of this truth was

---

[2] Arthur W. Combs and Donald Snygg, *Individual Behavior* (rev. ed.) (New York: Harper and Brothers, 1959), p. 157.

[3] *Ibid.,* p. 44.

revealed by Lecky[4] in his study of children who were poor spellers. He found that regardless of the difficulty of the words, they made about the same number of errors per page. He concluded that since they viewed themselves as poor spellers they were spelling in terms of their concepts. They learned to spell with far greater success as methods were used to help them change their concepts of themselves as spellers.

There are, of course, limitations to the height an individual may rise propelled by belief in himself, but undoubtedly many millions of people in this world could lift their standards of productivity and happiness immeasurably simply by elevating their concepts of themselves. The man who knows he can't speak in public, the boy who is certain he'll never be a good hitter in softball, the girl whose life is embittered by a deep feeling of her own unattractiveness, and the woman who all her life has wanted to drive an automobile, but is positive she would be a failure—all are prisoners of their own self-perceptions and will remain so until they change the concepts they hold about themselves. How a person acts in any given situation depends upon how he perceives himself and the situation in which he is involved. The degree to which we are successful in understanding human behavior will vary directly with our ability to understand the nature of people's perceptions.

The Search for Personal Adequacy

Man, like all other parts of the universe, seeks constantly to maintain his organization. The organization he strives to maintain is the self as he perceives his self; not just the physical self, for if this were the case he would never engage in dangerous activities, but the total self of which he is aware. A boy who perceives himself as a courageous individual might accept a dare involving the risk of his life in order to maintain this particular concept. Simple maintenance of one's present self, however, is not enough because just as a person seeks to put in the bank enough money to care for unforeseen emergencies that may arise in the future, so, too, does he strive to enhance, or build up, the self against the crises of tomorrow. In either case, whether he seeks simply to maintain himself as he is or to build himself up still further in his own eyes and, he hopes, in the eyes of others, there is but one basic need he is attempting to satisfy—the need for adequacy or self-realization.

This constant striving to maintain and enhance the self, this insatiable quest for personal adequacy, this all-powerful drive aimed at the intensi-

---

[4] P. Lecky, *Self-Consistency: A Theory of Personality* (New York: Island Press, 1945).

fication of our perceptions of individual worth and value is the universal clue to an understanding of human behavior. Everything a person does becomes meaningful when viewed as an attempt to maintain or expand his concepts of self-esteem and adequacy. Looking through this window into the mind and heart of man we can understand why Bill spends hundreds of hours practicing for the city golf tournament; why Mary accepts the difficult task of editing the youth center newspaper; why Jim writes magazine articles for which he receives no monetary compensation; why Jack is highly irritated when the results of a softball game he pitched and won failed to get into the newspaper; and why Bob is miserable when he failed to get on a junior baseball team. We can even understand why Dick wears such loud neckties; why Mrs. Jackson gives so many parties; why Mr. Brown practically bankrupts himself to buy a Cadillac; why Gene is the loudmouth roughneck of the playground; why Mr. Stevens erects a forty-foot television aerial when one ten feet high would be just as effective;[5] and why Nancy prefers being a member of the high school student governing body to being in the senior dramatic club.[6]

All people seek the same goal—satisfaction of the basic need for adequacy—but the ways by which they express this need may be as numerous and varied as the individuals themselves.

One or Many Needs?

Students of human behavior do not agree on the number of basic human needs. Some list as many as forty; Combs and Snygg suggest but one. In Chapter Four of this book a discussion of goals centers upon how recreation should contribute to the satisfaction of certain basic needs. Among these are the need for activity, mental health, recognition, acceptance, and adventure or zest in life. There is really no conflict here with the point of view that but one basic need exists. The individual seeking activity, mental health, recognition, acceptance and relief from boredom is, in reality, striving for personal adequacy. For our purposes, we may look upon the needs presented in Chapter Four as sub-needs, goals, or milestones along the road which leads to personal adequacy or enhancement of the self.

---

[5] Vance Packard, *The Status Seekers* (New York: David McKay Company, Inc., 1959), p. 70. See Packard for an extremely comprehensive list of ways by which Americans seek status and prestige.

[6] C. Wayne Gordon, *The Social System of the High School* (Glencoe, Illinois: The Free Press, 1957), p. 50. Gordon's study showed that high school students joined school organizations for prestige reasons and that, among girls, the high school governing body ranked first in prestige.

SOME IMPLICATIONS FOR LEADERSHIP

Your conception of the nature of human beings will determine the leadership methods and techniques you will use in working with them. If you believe, for example, that man is the victim of his environment and that his behavior is determined by environmental forces acting upon him, then you will seek to develop skill in the manipulation of the proper forces at the proper times. You will utilize coercion, force, power, and a type of motivation consisting of more or less subtle forms of reward or punishment for what you consider to be proper or improper behavior.

If you believe in the perceptual view of behavior, rather than the environmental, you will conduct yourself as a leader in quite a different manner. For this view of behavior emphasizes that man is not completely at the mercy of his environment, but, at least in part, controls his own destiny. How a person thinks and behaves are determined largely by how he sees himself and his environment. How he sees himself and the world in which he lives is a personal matter, arising within himself, and is not directly open to manipulation by you as a leader. You cannot *make* people perceive nor can you *force* them to change their concepts.

Thus, we see that intelligent and purposive leadership must be conceived and executed in the light of one's understanding of human behavior, and that leadership with a perceptual point of view will function quite differently from leadership based upon any other concept of human nature. We are concerned here with identifying a few of the most important implications of the perceptual view to recreation leadership. A more complete development of these implications will be found in Chapter Four.

1. How people behave depends upon how they perceive themselves and their environment. Perception is a highly personal, an internal, process not open to direct manipulation from the outside. Therefore, the challenge to leadership is to help provide experiences through which the individual may enjoy success in his search for adequacy or self-esteem. This growth approach rejects coercion, manipulation, and force as leadership techniques and emphasizes instead the quality of the recreation experience supplemented by persuasion, understanding, effective communication, and mutual recognition of interests in the discovery of goals and their attainment.

2. If we would influence human behavior we must find out how a person views himself and his environment, since how he thinks and behaves

are determined largely by the concepts he holds about himself and his abilities. Therefore, the leader must become sufficiently close to a child to discover what the child thinks of himself. If he views himself as characterized by incompetence, rejection, failure, and inadequacy he will act this way. The leader must help this child rebuild a feeling of competence by guiding him into activities in which he can experience success, assist him in the development of skills, emphasize the principle of progression in the conduct of activities so that he may experience success early in the activity, and provide him with numerous opportunities to associate with, and be accepted by, the socially desirable individuals and groups with which he wishes to be identified. The leader who places a high premium upon human dignity and the worth of the individual will know what to do with the child who feels unliked, unaccepted, and unable.

3. Every human being seeks his own enhancement. If an individual is closely identified with others, feels a sense of oneness with them, he will advance the interests of the group as a means of advancing his own. The isolated, the rejected, "lone wolf" type of person is dangerous to society because he recognizes no interests but his own. The leader will be constantly on the alert to discover these inadequate people and help them become liked and accepted by the socially desirable individuals and groups which they admire. This is an important step toward their being accepted by and acceptable to society at large.

4. Every individual is motivated by the quest for self-enhancement, but the manner in which this drive is expressed varies widely. Therefore, leaders must offer broad and diversified programs in which everyone can find an opportunity to excel and thus gain status and self-esteem. Furthermore, leaders must relate what they want people to do to their quest for self-enhancement. For example, if a leader wishes to interest a child in crafts he must lead this child to see that participation in crafts will result in heightened status, prestige, and self-esteem. If he is unable to show this connection between the craft program and the child's personal interests, it is quite likely that this particular child will remain completely indifferent to crafts as a leisure activity.

5. Competition as a factor in recreation has many values. However, where most of the opportunities for success depend upon competitive achievement, an equal number of opportunities exist for the losers to experience failure, threat, and insecurity. Therefore, leaders will plan and conduct programs in which numerous opportunities are offered individuals for success and self-enhancement measured by standards appropriate to the age and experience of the individuals rather than by their ability to beat one another. Thus, emphasis will be upon creativity, spontaneity, individual excellence, a maximum of challenge and a minimum of threat.

AN ANATOMY OF MOTIVATION

We all know some people who seem to possess an inner fire, some hidden source of energy, that drives them on to heights that others, with greater talent, never reach. The difference between them may be that those who get to the top are strongly motivated while the others lack this energizing force. Manifestly, the leader who can tap this reservoir of human energy will be far more effective in his efforts to influence people than will be the leader who knows very little or nothing about motivation.

All of us are motivated by a continuous search for the enhancement of ourselves as we see ourselves. When it appears that an individual's behavior is unmotivated it is only because we do not understand his goals. Thus, a boy's unwillingness to join the drama club may cause the leader to think he is unmotivated and has no desire to improve himself culturally. The boy, however, may see no relationship between membership in the drama club and his quest for greater self-esteem until one day he sees a picture of the club members in the local newspaper. When this happens, he may *perceive* the matter differently and seek admission into the club. The problem of changing his behavior is not one of motivation but of helping him to perceive differently.

The task of a leader, therefore, who seeks to influence the behavior of others is basically a problem of perception. People will behave differently when they see themselves and the world in which they live differently. When a boy sees a drama club as a means to self-enhancement his behavior is not the same as when he perceives no such connection. A major task of the leader is to help people change the way they see themselves and the world about them.

"A Long Way from Understanding"

A student who attempts to find out all he can about motivation in recreation by reading the published research studies on this problem should save his time and energy because such studies are almost non-existent. He will find it necessary to turn to studies of motivation in general or of motivation in the area of education and then apply the findings to recreation. But even here not much has been done. Fox points out that ". . . it is astonishing that so little research on motivation in school learning has been conducted during the past decade."[7]

Gardner presents some problems and raises some questions which, in light of our present knowledge of motivation, are unanswerable:[8]

We are a long, long way from understanding the complexities of individual motivation. We understand very imperfectly, for example, the inner pressures to excel which are present in some children and absent in others. We don't really know why, from earliest years, some individuals seem indomitable, while others are tossed about like the bird in a badminton game. Differences in energy and other physiological traits are partially responsible. Even more important may be the role of early experiences—relations with brothers and sisters, early successes and failures. We know, for example, that high standards may be a means of challenging and stimulating the child or, depending on the circumstances, a means of frightening and intimidating him.

Speaking of adults, he asks:[9]

Why do some individuals come to defeat early and live out their lives in resignation while others seem capable of endless renewal, rising from defeat, learning and growing, constantly discovering new resources of energy and spirit.

We must conclude from the above that human nature is extremely complex and there is much that we don't know about it. There are, however, some things we do know about motivation and others that we think we know. It is well to be aware of our limitations and seek to extend our knowledge in this area, but because much remains unknown we are not excused from using intelligently that which is known.

Light on the Path

The individual participates in recreation because he wants to—for the fun, joy, happiness, and other values that accrue from taking part. Children are compelled by law to go to school and to engage in studies that are not inherently interesting to many of them. Hence, the motivational task of the teacher is an imperative one. Fortunately for the recreation leader, however, the compulsion or drive motivating people to attend a playground or community center arises not within legislative bodies

---

[7] Raymond B. Fox, "The Dearth of Recent Research on Motivation," *The Clearing House*, December 1960, pp. 239–243.

[8] John W. Gardner, *Excellence* (New York: Harper and Brothers, 1961), p. 104.

[9] *Ibid.*

but within human beings. Nevertheless, influencing young people and adults to take part in activities that are new to them, to behave in socially desirable ways, and to seek values worthy of human beings in a democratic society are all goals which can best be achieved by leaders who understand, and are skilled in, the art of motivation.

Students of motivation have debated for many years the relative effectiveness of intrinsic and extrinsic incentives. Research of the last ten years has shed very little light upon this problem. About the only safe conclusion we can draw from these recent studies of incentives is that human beings react differently; some are highly motivated by intrinsic incentives, some by extrinsic incentives, and some are not motivated by either. We believe, although experimental evidence is lacking, that intrinsic incentives are better than extrinsic. This means, until research proves otherwise, that the leader must use a variety of incentives.

All human behavior is directed toward satisfying the need for self-enhancement. It follows from this assumption that an individual will change his established ways of behaving for one of two reasons; to satisfy this need more adequately or to avoid a decrease in the satisfaction of this need. If an individual sees in an activity the promise of benefits in harmony with his efforts at self-enhancement, he is far more likely to engage in this activity than if the promise did not exist. Motivation thus becomes a process of helping the individual to perceive self-enhancement as an outcome of participation in a particular activity.

Behavioral scientists agree that human beings generally do tend to choose activities with pleasant consequences and to avoid those with unpleasant ones. Among the "pleasant consequences" which the leader should utilize as a means of motivation are praise, peer approval, reward, and success. Leaders should insure that individuals experience success frequently and regularly throughout all phases of participation, but particularly in the earlier, and generally more difficult, stages. Since the intensity of a drive varies with a person's nearness to his goal, leaders should assist in the selection of reasonable sub-goals, especially for children whose perspective is relatively short.

Several theories of learning agree that reward facilitates learning more effectively than does punishment; that learning motivated by success is preferable to learning motivated by failure; too intense motivation, especially fear, pain, and anxiety may prove relatively ineffective because of accompanying distracting emotional states; and intrinsic motivation is preferable to extrinsic motivation.[10]

---

[10] *Learning and the Teacher*. Washington, D.C.: Association for Supervision and Curriculum Development, 1959, pp. 161–162.

Extrinsic incentives are those which lie outside the activity itself. We give Bill a ribbon if he wins the hundred yard dash in the city track meet, but the relationship between the ribbon and the dash is strictly an artificial one. Shall we use ribbons, medals, certificates, trophies, plaques, and other kinds of rewards to entice boys and girls into recreation activities? What effect does the use of such lures have upon them? If Bill runs the hundred yard dash just to win a ribbon is he learning that there are real values inherent in the running which far overshadow in importance the cheap ribbon for which he ran? And is it not a function of good leadership to help children and youth to discriminate between real and superficial values?

Some rewards can be quite vicious in their effects upon children, as the following true story indicates. In a midwestern city where the author was director of recreation for a number of years, a playground director was so desirous of winning his interplayground softball games that he promised an ice cream cone to each boy who should hit a home run in any of these games. Things went well for a while with the miniature Babe Ruths collecting their prizes at the conclusion of each game. However, after a few days, spurred on by their love for ice cream, the boys got together and decided to demand an ice cream cone for all three-baggers. The director, who could resist everything but pressure, acceded to their demands. The boys again conspired and came out with the conviction that doubles also were worthy of a payoff. The director again bowed to the inevitable. But even this was not enough for the mercenary athletes who presented further demands that any kind of a hit be rewarded. The director, sensing by this time that motivation was not as simple a matter as he had thought, but feeling he was in too deep now to withdraw, again agreed to pay off, buoyed up by the belief that he had hit rock bottom and things could get no worse. It was at this point he made his second mistake, because his little bandits, appetites for ice cream as completely uninhibited as their morals were perverted, issued an ultimatum that they would play no more unless they received an ice cream cone in advance of each game. This attitude of the softball players permeated the entire playground and, when the directors attempted to influence children to participate in crafts, dance, music, drama and other activities, they were met with the stock question, "What's in it for me?" The problem eventually was solved by a city-wide policy stipulating that no awards of any kind could be issued with the exception of certificates from the central office, but the effects upon the children involved were not so easily removed.

All extrinsic motivation is not necessarily bad, but we should covet for every child the high-level motivation which arises from within the individual and which seems to sustain itself. The leader may have to rely at times on extrinsic incentives, but one measure of good leadership is the degree to which individuals are influenced to reject these superficial rewards in favor of those more permanent satisfactions arising out of an understanding of how participation in an activity can contribute to the fulfillment of that basic and universal need—the need for enhancement of the perceived self.

IN KEEPING WITH ONE'S ABILITIES

In the process of growing up, all human beings pass through a series of growth and developmental levels. Within each of these stages the individual will differ in his interests, abilities, needs, capacities, potentialities, and characteristics. These stages do not constitute watertight compartments nor are all persons within each stage at exactly the same point in their development. Perhaps we need to change our way of thinking, placing less emphasis on the rigid categories of childhood, adolescence, maturity, middle-age and old age, and thinking instead of the continuing stream of life, each age flowing normally and properly into the next. There is no average person. Individuals differ in rate and ultimate level of development. This well-known principle of individual differences possesses many implications for recreation leadership. It emphasizes the importance of taking into consideration deviations from the norm. On the other hand, the leader who understands the numerous factors and forces which characterize human beings and influence their behavior at varying stages in their lives is able to provide them with satisfying experiences appropriate to their own developmental level. Questions regarding the timeliness of activities, the readiness of a child for any given experience, the nature of his needs, capacities, and potentialities, and whether it is economical, for example, to expend time and energy, in teaching a nine-year-old boy to play baseball or to wait until he is more mature, must all be answered in terms of growth and development.

Whatever our goals may be in recreation at any growth level we should attempt to achieve them through experiences and measures which harmonize with the individual's abilities and potentialities at that level. Jersild states:[11]

---

[11] Arthur T. Jersild, *Child Development and the Curriculum*. New York: Bureau of Publications, Teachers College, Columbia University, 1946, pp. 9–10.

Whether our aim is to prepare a child for a life of crime or of saintliness, a life of cutthroat competition or friendly coöperation, a life in a horse-and-buggy era or in a machine age, our efforts will best be repaid if what we offer him at any period in the growth span is adapted to his capabilities at that stage.

Students should understand that much is known about growth and development and numerous books have been written on this subject.

Only a minute portion of the available knowledge can be included in the remainder of this chapter. An attempt has been made to select that which appears to possess greatest significance for the recreation leader.

The Middle Years of Childhood—Ages 6-12

An age range of six years is a very long time in the lives of children. A child of six differs in many ways from one of twelve, yet these middle years constitute a period featured by a number of distinctive characteristics. It is with these general characteristics of this age group that we are primarily concerned.

HOW THEY LOOK.   This is a period of slow physical growth between two spurts. Eye-hand coördination is improving, but still is not of high quality. Boys begin to show an increasing superiority over girls in muscular strength and in sustained energy output. The attention span lengthens. Intellectually, they look upon life as a great adventure and seek information and new experiences with avid curiosity. They are imaginative and love rhythmical sounds and movements; sex differences begin to appear in the latter stages; hero worship is strong as is the desire for recognition; and leadership abilities begin to appear. The three most striking characteristics of this age group, however, are: (1) the struggle for independence from adults through the medium of the peer group; (2) the expression of sheer vitality through continual participation in vigorous movement and the relationship of motor ability to the drive for self-esteem; and (3) increasing sex differentiations.

Gordon describes this first characteristic:[12]

. . . the needs for increasing self-direction and attaining selfhood may be seen in the struggle for independence from adults. The child of school age is working on the developmental task of gaining more independence from the family group. Since he still has security needs and lacks the strength to really "go it alone,"

---

[12] Ira J. Gordon, *The Teacher as a Guidance Worker* (New York: Harper and Brothers, 1956), p. 129.

his peer group serves as a source of power to him, a new security base from which to wage the war of the apron-string and psychological umbilical cord. It is ironic, perhaps, that in his fight for selfhood and against the demands of the adult he creates a group with rigid conformity demands and, to some degree harsher standards than he is resisting; but at least the peer group is his creation, and the demands are being made as part of the price one pays to "fight the good fight."

The fight, however, is not solely to get away from something; it is of equal, or even greater, importance that he get *into* something—the gang. He passionately wants in. If he is rejected and in desperation seeks reunion with adults, not only is he labeled "teacher's pet" or "mamma's boy," but as an outcast from the group is denied many vital experiences basic to his development. The peer group constitutes a subculture all its own and the child who belongs actually lives in two different societies. His organized group has its own body of customs, traditions, games, knowledge, beliefs, values, loyalties, rules, and rituals transmitted from generation to generation, demanding in nature and powerful in effect.

At no other period in life is the need for vigorous movement so compelling nor its satisfaction so passionately pursued. For sheer vitality this age group stands alone. Motor skills serve as a high road to status and a badge of admission into the peer group. If a youngster is lacking in most of the skills which are involved in the play of his age group, he is, at best, tolerated grudgingly and labeled "butterfingers" or barred completely from many of its activities.

Among the younger children in this age group, play is largely informal. As they grow older, large muscle activities of a team nature become popular because of the gang urge. Competition is emphasized. One can fight for personal glory and the team at the same time.

Sex differences begin to appear at the middle of this period. Boys go through a period when they want nothing to do with girls. Boys like rough games such as football, wrestling and boxing; also marbles, guns, kites, fishing, bicycles, tools, and machinery. Girls prefer dolls, rope jumping, jackstones, hopscotch, dressing up, playing house, dancing, and sewing. Boys associate with boys and girls with girls. Girls are more emotional than boys except where aggression is concerned. Boys have more scholastic and behavior problems than girls. Boys care little for dancing, but with girls it is almost an obsession.

WHAT IT MEANS.   Among the activities leaders should provide for younger children in this age group are all kinds of simple crafts, puppetry, rhythmic movements to music, singing and rhythm band; group games that include everyone but do not demand special skills, such as Tag, Squirrel in Trees, Brownies and Fairies, Hide and Seek, London Bridge, and relays, collecting, and nature activities. Activities in which the child may express himself as an individual are vital as a means of preserving, expressing, and further developing those unique aspects of personality which the group, by its insistence on conformity, tends to destroy.

The desire for vigorous activity is so powerful that the leader needs to guard against too much of it by proper scheduling. An occasional quiet hour or the intermingling of less active games with the more vigorous will provide desirable relaxation.

While most of the games of this age are competitive, among the younger children this competitive element should not be too intense. Their games should be informal, happy-go-lucky, joyous, and loosely organized. They should be under no pressures to win. When these pressures become so great that when the child makes a mistake he cannot have fun, the game has lost its recreative aspects and its values have become suspect. "Nature makes no jumps" and children do not become fiercely competitive all at once about the age of nine.

One of the most important responsibilities of the leader who is concerned with the emotional well-being of children is to help every child gain acceptance into a group of his choice.

Many opportunities should be given children to practice and grow in personal independence. These should include officiating, functioning as a leader, planning activities, working on committees, and issuing supplies. Care should be taken not to alienate a child from his group by artificially investing him with adult powers. Encourage creativity, originality, and individuality rather than submissive conformity. This means, among other things, that some activities will be of an unusual nature and will appeal to but a few children. The criterion of numbers is not wholly valid in program building.

Provide a wide variety of activities so that many children may experience success and gain self-esteem. The number of "underdogs" will vary directly with the narrowness of the program. Emphasize sportsmanship, proper skill development and, if necessary, give special attention to the less skillful youngsters. The good leader is also a good teacher. Both team and individual sports should be included in the program for older children. Encourage noncompetitive activities such as hiking, bicycling, skiing, swimming, social recreation, and square dancing. Beating someone is not the supreme objective of life.

Adolescence—Early Teens to Early Twenties

Adolescence is a period of continuing change in youth extending from about the age of eleven for girls and thirteen for boys to maturity in the early twenties. Neither the beginning nor the ending of adolescence is as clear-cut as we have indicated since there is considerable individual variation. The two-year lag between boys and girls poses some definite problems for recreation leaders.

HOW THEY LOOK.   In early adolescence growth is rapid and marked by poor coördination. The growth spurt is most noticeable in the increase in height. The height and weight of girls may equal or even exceed that of boys. In later adolescence boys become relatively bigger, heavier, and stronger. Girls are at a disadvantage in some motor activities because of the wider pelvis and other anatomical differences. The younger adolescent seemingly possesses unlimited energy plus a hunger for skill in physical activities and the status which accompanies it. Growth toward and attainment of sexual maturity is the dominant feature of physical development during adolescence.

Stone and Church describe what they call "a spectacular developmental mismatching of boys and girls" in the early adolescent years:[13]

The average junior high school is populated by young ladies and male children. This makes little difference to the boys who are still woman haters, but entails some hardships for the girls, who are ready for masculine companionship. Their male contemporaries are uninterested and uninteresting . . . a school dance is likely to be characterized by the young ladies towering over and dragging around grudging and grubby escorts who would rather be playing baseball . . . . It is possible that this developmental disparity in the junior high school years is responsible for the fact that girls thereafter seek boy friends who are older than they.

Youth, at this time, reach the peak of their abilities in most physical activities. Speed, strength, coördination, and the ability to acquire new skills are at their maximum. Somewhere about fifteen or sixteen years of age boys begin to catch up to the girls in maturity and they have more interests in common. However, the boys still prefer team sports while there is a tendency on the part of the girls to prefer such individual or dual activities as tennis, archery, badminton, golf, swimming, and dancing. Unfortunately, during the latter period of adolescence, when physical powers are highest, a decline in participation in vigorous activities sets in and a rise in sedentary pursuits takes place.

The adolescent who differs from the norm, or what he thinks is the norm, in height, size, rate of growth, and state of maturity frequently

---

[13] L. Joseph Stone and Joseph Church, *Childhood and Adolescence* (New York: Random House, 1957), p. 286.

becomes emotionally disturbed over the differences. He is more concerned, however, about his social than his physical well-being. Acceptance by, and identification with, the group is the very breath of life to him. Havighurst states:[14]

The most potent single influence during the adolescent years is the power of group approval. The youth becomes a slave to the conventions of his age group. He must wear only the clothes that are worn by others, follow the same hair style, and use the same slang. Yet this conformity seems limited to the externals of life. In their inner life adolescent boys and girls are still individuals, and sometimes individualistic to an extreme.

The older adolescent begins to show a preference for smaller and more select groups. Social growth is toward fewer and deeper interests, more dignified adult behavior, and more formal social activities.

Adolescents are troubled about many questions, but especially those involving relationship of the sexes. Moral development takes place. Many teen-agers are bored with continually doing things that seem to possess no vital significance either to themselves or to society in general. They resent the extended apprenticeship to maturity which presently they must serve.

A powerful drive for independence, for more freedom from adult supervision, for self-determination characterizes the adolescent. His struggle to escape from adult protection is not wholly what it appears to be since he still wants the assurance that when the going gets rough some adult in the background will be there to help.

WHAT IT MEANS. A broad program will be provided consisting of sports and games, arts and crafts, music, dramatics, dance, social recreation, community service, hobbies, clubs, reading, and other socially desirable leisure activities in which youth express a desire to take part. Both small and large group activities involving both sexes, or but one, will prove popular. Small group activities at the early teen level generally are confined to members of one sex and are primarily active. Examples are organized teams in baseball, football, softball, and volleyball for boys. Older adolescent boys still prefer group games, but girls evidence a tendency toward such individual or dual activities as tennis, archery, horseback riding, badminton, table tennis, ice skating, golf, swimming, and dancing. At the upper level of this age group boys begin to express greater interest in these activities. The well-planned program will reflect these changing inter-

---

[14] Robert J. Havighurst, *Human Development and Education* (New York: Longmans, Green and Company 1953), p. 112.

ests. Joint participation by older boys and girls in the more vigorous athletic activities, such as volleyball, will emphasize social values rather than competition and victory.

The leader will do his utmost to raise the level of skill of all youth since motor skill at this age, as throughout most of life, contributes to poise, self-confidence, a sense of adequacy and self-esteem, and is a key which often unlocks the door to social acceptance by the peer group. Three errors should be avoided by the leader: (1) the tendency to concentrate one's efforts on the few "stars" and neglect the far larger number of unskilled youth, a condition considerably aggravated by current practice in many public schools; (2) failure to encourage the older adolescent to concentrate on no more than two sports and to seek excellence in both, rather than try to master several and succeed in none; and (3) perpetuation of a tendency toward stifling conformity in sports participation characterized by narrow, limited, poverty-stricken programs consisting only of a few of the most popular sports. Why should we try to make football, baseball, or basketball players out of all American boys? The truly superior leader will encourage individuality and personal distinctiveness in youth by guiding them into some leisure activities in which the "herd" does not take part.

The dominant need in adolescent youth, as in all human beings, is the need for self-enhancement. In their quest for this goal they travel along two main highways: (1) that which leads to an ever-greater degree of independence from their parents; and (2) that which leads to acceptance and approval by the peer group. In a sense, they are not separate highways since the greater the involvement with the peer group, the more independent one becomes of his parents. If our children are to grow into mature, self-reliant, and responsible adults who can think and act for themselves, we must give them experiences in which they can bear responsibilities, be self-reliant, think for themselves, and even make mistakes, provided the consequences are not too severe. When it is necessary to oppose an adolescent's unwise idea, the leader will do so in such a way as not to damage his extremely sensitive ego.

Youth should be given an opportunity to share in planning and operating their programs. Many recreation programs for adolescent youth have failed because they were denied any part in their inception and management; many have failed because these young people were burdened with responsibilities beyond their capacities. Those who would burden youth with responsibilities for which they are unfitted and those who would deny youth experiences leading to growth in self-direction are equally guilty of sinning against young people and the democratic process.

The most successful youth programs are those planned and conducted by youth and adults working together in an atmosphere characterized by friendliness, mutual respect, and the recognition of common interests.

Adolescence in America, partially for economic reasons, is a prolongation of childhood status and a denial of adult status. Youth possess unlimited energy and a tremendous desire to use it in constructive activities meaningful to themselves and of significance to the community. They want to prove their worth and one outstanding way to do this is through some important form of community service. Hartley and Goldenson reveal an insight into this aspect of the nature of the adolescent:[15]

They resent being treated as children and are aching to show that they aren't immature. Most of them have reservoirs of energy that are waiting to be channeled and organized, and even those who appear inert and apathetic rarely lack the energy—it is only blocked by conflicts, self-consciousness, or feelings of inadequacy. It can be released, and their difficulties relieved at the same time, if they discovered new opportunities to work constructively with others. Moreover, many teen-agers are bored with endless hours spent in "just sitting around gabbing," to use their phrase for it. They are ready to "do something"—and it's up to us to show them the possibilities that exist practically at their doorstep.

Among the possibilities of community service which may enlist the energies and enthusiasms of adolescent youth are city beautification projects, such as tree planting, presenting concerts, and other types of recreation programs in homes for the aged, veteran's hospitals, and similar institutions; providing volunteer recreation leadership for crippled children and other handicapped persons, and assisting in Community Chest campaigns. Most American youth are fully aware of their *rights* in a democracy; it is not so certain they are as completely aware of their *responsibilities*. Thus, the leader contributes to the development of democratic citizenship by teaching youth that among the responsibilities of the good citizen is the rendering of some form of service to the community from which he receives so much.

Gardner puts the problem succinctly!

To be needed is one of the richest forms of moral and spiritual nourishment. And not to be needed is one of the most severe forms of psychic deprivation. There is danger in a conviction on the part of young people that they are not needed by their own community.[16]

---

[15] Ruth E. Hartley and Robert M. Goldenson, *The Complete Book of Children's Play* (New York: Thomas Y. Crowell Company, 1957), p. 272.

[16] Gardner, *op. cit.*, p. 152–153.

Adulthood—The Early and Middle Years

The young and middle-aged adults are the forgotten people in recreation. Less is known about their characteristics and less effort is expended by recreation departments in the development and operation of programs geared to their needs, abilities, and interests than is true with any other age group discussed in this book. Their need for recreation, however, is just as great as that of any other group.

HOW THEY LOOK.   Development does not end with the termination of adolescence. Routine, inevitable changes occur with age which affect the individual's use of leisure. For example, beginning rather early, physical vigor and stamina decline, neuromuscular skills fade, reaction times become slower, recuperative powers are reduced, sensory acuity is diminished, and the battle against overweight is launched. The Census Bureau reported that 27.7 was the median age of the nation's population as of July 1, 1968, whereas it stood at 30.3 years in 1952.

Early adulthood is a period of storm and stress in which the task of finding a marriage partner and then learning how to adjust to one's spouse so that life may be a happy one for both, is of primary importance. Shifts in family roles and responsibilities take place rapidly as the individual starts in an occupation, selects a mate, begins a family, rears children, manages a home, accepts a civic responsibility, and looks for new and congenial friends with whom he can associate socially for many years.

Among the most important characteristics of the mature adult which possess relevance for the recreation leader, Stone and Church list the following: His emotions are more stable and his accumulated experiences broaden his understandings and deepen his sensitivities. Vigorous interests make him more interesting. He is at peace with himself because he knows and accepts his weaknesses and limitations. He has developed the capacity to entertain himself and he requires a certain amount of solitude. He is deeply committed to democratic values and he will judge people by the standards he applies to himself. He has grown in human relationships, needs and seeks close human attachments, and is willing to pay the price which these close personal involvements cost in emotional wear and tear. Although not a reformer, he is deeply concerned with social problems and their alleviation. He is conscious of his own mortality and has acquired the ability to face the certain expectation of death with composure. The authors sum up their concept of the mature adult:

. . . the adult with a capacity for true maturity is one who has grown out of childhood without losing childhood's best traits. He has retained the basic emotional strengths of infancy, the stubborn authority of toddlerhood, the capacity for wonder and pleasure and playfulness of the pre-school years, the capacity for affiliation and intellectual curiosity of the school years, and the idealism and passion of adolescence. He has incorporated these into a new pattern of development dominated by adult stability, wisdom, knowledge, sensitivity to other people, responsibility, strength, and purposiveness.[17]

WHAT IT MEANS. Young adults continue to enjoy many of the activities in which they engaged as adolescents. The extent of their participation generally depends upon the opportunities provided by the community and the degree of skill developed in these activities. Three major trends in their use of leisure put in an early appearance: (1) increased participation in such activities as golf, bowling, sailing, water skiing, and photography which many adolescents cannot afford; (2) gradual transition from the more vigorous to the less vigorous sports—basketball gives way to volleyball, tennis to golf, and baseball to bowling; and (3) both small and large group activities increasingly involve both sexes in social programs with more and more sedentary pursuits, such as cards, checkers, and chess.

Among the social activities planned and conducted jointly by the members and leaders of the highly successful Young Adult Club of Madison, Wisconsin are the following: social, folk, and square dances, dance instruction, singing, special holiday parties, talent shows, picnics and wiener roasts, scavenger hunts, a chess club, and a mandolin and guitar club. Such a program not only enriches the lives of these young adults by helping to meet the basic human need for recreation, but it provides numerous opportunities for them to associate in varied and wholesome social situations thus leading to a better understanding between the sexes. While the stated purposes of a recreation department seldom include the promotion of successful marriages, nevertheless, this is one of the desirable by-products of an effective program of recreation for young adults.

Few outstanding differences exist between a program of recreation for young and middle-age adults. As one grows older and assumes greater family, occupational, and civic responsibilities he may find it necessary to reduce the amount of time previously devoted to recreation beyond the home. Leaders will provide more activities in which the entire family can take part, or in which fathers and sons and mothers and daughters will be interested. Popular activities will include picnics, wiener and marshmallow roasts, family nights, arts and crafts for all ages, group singing, and family participation in such activities as swimming, volley-

---

[17] Stone and Church, *op. cit.,* p. 345.

ball, bowling, shuffleboard, table tennis, badminton, archery, horseshoes, hunting, fishing, and camping.

Good leadership, recognizing the declining vigor of the middle-age adult, will modify the rules in certain sports and establish age classifications. In volleyball, for example, leagues for men over thirty-five years of age might be organized with the net lowered from eight feet to seven feet, six inches. Adults at all age levels will be encouraged to share in planning and operating their recreation programs.

How much emphasis should we place upon group activities for the older adult? Certainly not as much as for the younger adult, for as an individual advances in years the scope of his social contacts narrows in accordance with his desire for fewer but closer friends. Yet, there should be a limit to this withdrawal tendency. Perhaps the best answer to this question is given by Donahue:[18]

A great philosopher has taught us that human social life is comparable to a group of porcupines sleeping on the ground on a wintry night. Should they roll together to gain warmth, they are apt to injure one another with their prickly spines. Should they then roll apart to avoid pain, their sacrifice of proximity renders them isolated and exposed to the chill night. We may conclude that porcupine comfort and contentment are to be found in their discovery of the perfect distance.

We may define perfect distance as a state of separation that achieves warmth without intrusion and independence without isolation.

The Older Adult—Over 65

In 1966 there were more than 18 million people in the United States who were sixty-five years of age or older. It is estimated that this age group will number approximately twenty-five million by the early 1970's.[19] This increase both in number and proportion of the aging constitutes a serious problem with several vital ramifications among which are health and medical care, housing, employment security, retirement, institutional care, citizenship participation, and recreation. It is not our purpose to discuss these problems nor even to explore all the characteristics of the aging. Rather, a brief presentation will be made of those distinctive qualities with which the recreation leader should be familiar as they have a bearing upon either the nature of the recreation program or the manner of its presentation.

18 Wilma Donahue and others (eds.), *Free Time—Challenge to Later Maturity* (Ann Arbor: The University of Michigan Press, 1958), p. 78.

19 Bureau of the Census in U.S. Department of Commerce, *The U.S. Book of Facts, Statistics & Information for 1968* (New York: Essandess, 1967), p. 10.

HOW THEY LOOK. There are approximately one hundred aged females for every eighty males in the United States and the disproportion is expected to become greater. More than 95 percent of persons living beyond retirement age are suffering from some type of chronic disease.[20] The gradual decline in the physical capacities of the individual which began in early adulthood is now accelerated and includes a decrease in strength; an increase in reaction time; body temperature adjusts more slowly and incompletely to cold or heat; cardiac output is decreased; general visual acuity decreases; hearing loss, especially for men, proceeds rapidly; repair of body tissues after injury is slowed; and shortness of breath develops.

The accidental death rate rises sharply among the aged. During a recent year 19,500 persons died from falls within the home. Of this total, approximately 15,000 were sixty-five years or over. Persons over sixty-five spend two and one-half times more time in hospitals than those under sixty-five.

The aged comprise a major proportion of the patients in our mental hospitals. Kleemeier points out that in a recent year "25 percent of all United States mental-hospital patients were over sixty-five years of age, although only 8.1 percent of the total population was over this age."[21] Suicide statistics reveal that the suicide rate rises throughout life, reaching its highest point at the oldest age levels.

Donahue states that the mental powers of an individual do not decline as rapidly as do the purely biological functions.

It is possible, however, for mental function to be maintained at maximum performance or even to be increased for many years. Cerebral capacity begins to weaken only in later years and then relatively slowly. At the age of seventy, a person is still as capable as at fifty. At eighty, the intellect is the equivalent of that of the twenties.[22]

The social and psychological effects of aging equal and often exceed in importance the physical results. We live in a work-oriented society. This means that our people place a higher value upon work than is the case in many other nations. Work is valued for its own sake. It is an end in itself, not simply a means to an end. A man's life revolves largely about

[20] James E. Birren (ed.), *Handbook of Aging and the Individual* (Chicago: The University of Chicago Press, 1959), p. 305.

[21] Robert W. Kleemeier, "The Mental Health of the Aging," in *Aging in Western Societies*, Ernest W. Burgess (ed.) (Chicago: The University of Chicago Press, 1960), p. 263.

[22] Wilma Donahue, "The Human Machine at Middle Age," in *Aging in Today's Society*, Clark Tibbitts and Wilma Donahue (eds.) (Englewood Cliffs, New Jersey: Prentice-Hall Inc., 1960), p. 112.

his work; most of his friends are people with whom he works. Work is an anchor that stabilizes his life and prevents him from drifting aimlessly. Work in our society gives purpose, direction, significance, and meaning to life. It is even a mark of status and prestige; a man is known and respected partially because of the nature of his work. When we think of Bill Jackson we think of Bill Jackson, the plumber; or Jack Graham, the teacher; or Frank Haskin, the golf professional.[23]

Take away all of this, deny a man an opportunity to work, which is what happens when retirement is forced upon him, and you may create a void in his existence so wide and deep as to constitute a personal tragedy that may embitter all the rest of his life. Add to this the loss of a spouse, relatives, or friends; the decline of physical vigor and attractiveness; the lessening of mental efficiency; the threat to his financial and emotional security; the release from both family and civic obligations; and the increase of leisure with its attendant loneliness, boredom, and time for introspection. The cumulative psychological impact may be disastrous, generating a sense of uselessness and rejection and emphasizing the apparent meaninglessness of existence, both of which undermine his self-respect and smash hard at his ego.

We should not assume that the retirement years of all older persons are empty and unhappy. Many look forward to the transition from labor to leisure with feelings of happiness and contentment. Life at this time is rich and meaningful to them. These are the people who are free from handicapping anxiety, who remain active, and who began cultivating their leisure interests in childhood, youth, and adulthood. Unfortunately, they appear to be in the minority as a number of studies have obtained judgments from older adults as to the happiest period of their lives; most commonly so designated was young adulthood, ages 25–45, with youth next, and then childhood. A study by Landis revealed that only about 5 percent so rated the years 45–60 and 60 and over. Most of those who said they were happiest in old age were either divorced or widowed and had been unhappy in marriage.[24] This does not imply that old age is generally a period of unhappiness, but it does imply that certain factors in the lives of aged people are operating to reduce the relative degree of happiness.

Other characteristics of the aged include a tendency to be conservative, resentful of change, somewhat dogmatic, extremely sensitive to criticism, desirous of recognition, "set" in their ways, and easily offended.

[23] Exceptions to this general observation with respect to the importance of work in the lives of people exist chiefly in industry where frequently work is no longer a central life interest. See pages 15-18 for a discussion of this point of view. However, even when a man does not like his work, it may be better than no work at all.

[24] Judson P. Landis, "What Is the Happiest Period in Life?" *School and Society*, June 1942, pp. 643–645.

WHAT IT MEANS. The significance of these characteristics falls into three categories: (1) the purposes which a recreation program for the aged should seek; (2) types of activities desirable; and (3) effective methods which should be utilized.

Medical science has been a major factor responsible for increasing the span of life in this country. According to the 1966 *Vital Statistics Report* of the U.S. Department of Health, Education, and Welfare, the life expectancy in the United States male is 66.9 and in the female is 73.7. But a life which has length without depth is simply existence. If life for the aged is to be two-dimensional, if it is to have depth as well as length, if it is to possess meaning, significance, and vitality, social science must match the efforts of medical science and help enrich the lives of this increasing segment of our population. One of the ways this can be done is through a program of recreation, wherein the latent talents of these people will be channeled into constructive leisure activities which challenge their abilities, restore their sense of individual worth, build new friendships, and create a new happiness that endures throughout the twilight of their lives.

No one ever outgrows the need for physical activity. Activity is a characteristic of the living organism at all ages and the failure of older people to remain active, provided overexertion and strain are avoided, in the long run results in deterioration. The aging enjoy dancing, shuffleboard, picnics, boat rides, pool, gardening, camping, group games, and horseshoes.

In addition to the physical activities, programs for the aging frequently include card parties, potluck suppers, group singing of the old songs and musical programs with members of the group presenting instrumental solos or duets, stunts and talent programs, simple dramatics, all kinds of parties, especially those celebrating birthdays, golden wedding anniversaries, and other special occasions in the lives of club members, movies, armchair travels, and hobbies. Without special encouragement and assistance from the leader the older person seldom will participate in creative activities. Nor is he primarily interested in activities of an adult education nature since ambition and expectations for the future generally motivate participation in such activities. Many of the aged have little of either remaining.

Highly skilled leadership is basic to the successful operation of a program of recreation for the aged. A leader may be successful with youth and unsuccessful with this group. Specialized knowledge, skills, and techniques are essential. A leader must understand these old people and be patient with them. They want to follow a routine; they resent change as it gives them a sense of insecurity. Their feelings are easily hurt and they carry a grudge for some time. The leader must not try to dominate them nor, on the other hand, permit the more aggressive members to do so. The limitations of the aged must at all times be considered with respect to program, facilities, and finances. Some activities should be conducted which enable the aged to retain contact with younger people. Complete segregation is undesirable.

Recreation programs for the aging, under good leadership make an extremely significant contribution to the enrichment of their lives. But, as important as they are, we should not make the mistake of believing that they solve the total problem of the aged in this nation. Recreation cannot, at the present time, in a work-oriented society, provide a role sufficiently meaningful that it will serve as a work substitute and do psychologically for the aged what work did for them in their period of maturity. The attitudes of our people toward work and status roles have developed over a period of too many years for them to change overnight. The task of the recreation leader is to work with the aged in developing the best possible program of recreation. A further function of the leader, as a citizen and a social engineer, is to join with other members of society in creating a point of view that attaches social significance to any position occupied by old people. The present statusless role of the aged in the United States is a creation of the minds of men and it can be changed by the minds of men.

Selected References

Birren, James E., ed., *Handbook of Aging and the Individual* (Chicago: The University of Chicago Press, 1959).

Bortz, Edward, *Creative Aging* (New York: Macmillan, 1963).

Burgess, Ernest W., ed., *Aging in Western Societies* (Chicago: The University of Chicago Press, 1960).

Combs, Arthur W. and Snygg, Donald, *Individual Behavior* (rev. ed.) (New York: Harper and Brothers, 1959).

Crow, Lester D and Crow, Alice, *Human Development and Learning* (New York: American Book Company, 1956).

Donahue, Wilma and others (ed.), *Free Time—Challenge to Later Maturity* (Ann Arbor: The University of Michigan Press, 1958).

Friedman, Eugene A. and Havighurst, Robert J., *The Meaning of Work and Retirement* (Chicago: The University of Chicago Press, 1954).

Gordon, C. Wayne, *The Social System of the High School* (Glencoe, Illinois: The Free Press, 1957).

Hartley, Ruth E. and Goldenson, Robert M., *The Complete Book of Children's Play* (New York: Thomas Y. Crowell Company, 1957).

Havighurst, Robert J., *Human Development and Education* (New York: Longmans, Green and Company, 1953).

Ireland, Ralph R., "The Significance of Recreational Maturation in the Educational Process: The Six 'Ages of Play'," *The Journal of Educational Sociology.* XXXII, No. 7, 1959, 356.

Stone, L. Joseph and Church, Joseph, *Childhood and Adolescence* (New York: Random House, 1957).

Tibbitts, Clark and Donahue, Wilma, *Aging in Today's Society* (Englewood Cliffs, New Jersey: Prentice-Hall, Inc., 1960).

Williams, Jesse Feiring and Kitzinger, Angela, *Health for the College Student* (New York: Harper and Row, 1967).

Chapter IV

Goals for Recreation

TWO MEN START OUT on separate journeys. One knows precisely where he wants to go and how to get there. Since he has a perfectly clear conviction of what he should do, he acts upon it without hesitation; he is sure of himself; he has decided what direction to take. The second traveler has only a vague notion of his destination. He knows he must go somewhere so he keeps moving, but his movements are hesitant, uncertain, vacillating, indecisive. The behavior of the first traveler is intelligent because it is directed toward a specific, clear-cut, and worthwhile goal; the behavior of the second is unintelligent because it lacks purpose and direction.

No leader can be truly effective in his work unless he knows where he wants to go. Leadership implies *movement*—influencing and persuading people to take some kind of *action*—to go from where they are to where they want to be. But in what direction shall we lead them? We can lead them around in a circle, creating an impression of vigorous action, and end up exactly where we started. We can lead them into activities that degrade man or we can lead them into leisure experiences that uplift and exalt the human spirit. For recreation is never simply recreation. It is either good or bad recreation, and whether it is good or bad depends upon what it does to the human beings who take part in it. This means, of course, that if leadership is not blind it must know where it is going, or where it wants to go. We must understand quite clearly what our goals are and how to achieve them, otherwise, like the second traveler, we too, will get nowhere simply because we don't know where we want to go. The worth of a leader will be no greater than the values that he seeks. Almost 2,500 years ago Socrates emphasized the importance of a clear understanding of goals or values when he warned, "If a man does not know to what port he is sailing, no wind is favorable." No matter what else a worker in recreation may be, he is no leader unless he knows the goals toward which his efforts and those of the group are directed and is skilled in the means by which he seeks to achieve them. For the object of every group is to realize its goals and the main function of a leader is to help it do so.

A PROFESSION HAS
COMMON IDEALS AND COMMON GOALS

Many years ago John Collier, a great friend and critic of recreation, charged the recreation leaders in this country with "conducting pigmy programs, seeking pigmy results, amid giant opportunities." Collier's criticism is still valid because, as a profession, we have no clear conception or conviction as to what our goals should be and, as a result, our work lacks direction, purpose, and significance. Many of our leaders have what might be called a professional inferiority complex due primarily to our failure to reflect seriously upon the future of our civilization, the values by which men in a democracy should live, and the contribution recreation should make to a realization of these values. History teaches us that no society can survive unless it has values in which the majority of its members believe deeply, and that threats to that society originating from the outside are less dangerous than the slow, subtle, corrosive wearing away of faith in the ideals which first contributed to its greatness.

Leaders Must Seek Higher Values

The truly great leader, therefore, is not simply a technician highly skilled as an organizer, teacher, and director of leisure activities. He must care deeply about life and destiny. He must gain a deeper insight into the possibilities of recreation as a contributor to those higher values which enrich the lives of human beings in a democratic nation. One source of satisfaction to the professional man is the conviction that the values he seeks in his work are not trivial but are vital, purposeful, and highly significant, both to himself and to society. Dostoevsky tells us what happens to men engaged in unimportant work:[1]

---
[1] Fyodor Dostoevsky, *The House of the Dead* (London: William Heinemann, Ltd., 1915), p. 19.

The idea has occurred to me that if one wanted to crush, to annihilate a man utterly, to inflict on him the most terrible of punishments so that the most ferocious murderer would shudder at it and dread it beforehand, one need only give him work of an absolutely, completely, useless and irrational character.

The members of a profession everywhere have common ideals and common goals which furnish a force that unites them, binds them together, and provides a rallying point for the profession. The more vital these values are, the greater becomes their power to inspire and to unite those who seek them, for when men carry the same ideal in their minds nothing can divide them. Unity of purpose, however, should never be confused with unanimity of opinion.

A fundamental question that must be answered before any consideration can be given to the identification of specific goals is, "Should recreation have any values outside itself?" Is recreation an end in itself? When I play golf, may I not play simply because I enjoy playing, or must I also be concerned with the possible health values of the game? Why can't I read a book just for the fun of reading it? Or must I be a kind of academic hypochondriac eternally concerned with my cultural improvement? Is it possible that simple enjoyment is a sufficient goal for the individual, but insufficient for a recreation department, a social institution, expending tax funds and faced with the responsibility of justifying its expenditures?

The answer to this question has three facets:

1. Activities are means, not ends. The professional leader never confuses means with ends. In a democracy, the individual personality is supreme. Institutions exist to serve man. Man is not the servant of institutions. All activities, equipment, supplies, and facilities have one outstanding purpose only—to enrich the lives of people by contributing to their fulfillment as individuals and as effectively functioning members of a democratic society. Thus, we see that an activity has no value in itself. It has value only as it contributes something of worth to a human being, as man, in a democracy is the measure of all things. To say that recreation is an end in itself is a denial of the democratic tenet which affirms the supremacy of man over things.
2. In Chapter Three we learned that a child is a whole person who reacts as a totality to the total environment. Body, mind, spirit, and emotions are involved in every recreation experience. Since he reacts as a whole to every situation, he will be affected morally, socially, mentally, and physically by everything he does. Recently, the author was teaching an eleven-year-old boy to play golf. His most difficult task was not teaching him how to hold a club nor to hit the ball; it was persuading him to tell the truth about his score. Therefore, the recreation leader must be concerned with total, rather than with partial, outcomes.

3. The goals of the individual and those of the department or leader frequently differ. A boy may enter a track meet solely to win a ribbon and status, but the leader may seek fitness and fair play as well. Probably no volleyball player ever entered a game to strengthen his moral fiber, but the good leader teaches him to call the foul if he touches the net. There need be no conflict between the fun or enjoyment goal of the participant and other values sought by the leader. As a matter of fact, everyone has more fun when each respects the rights of all the others.

A housewife, when making orange juice, attempts to squeeze from an orange all the juice that's in it. She would be considered wasteful if she did not. The leader who is willing to settle for the fun value only, when other vital goals also are attainable without doing violence to the fun objective, is like the wasteful housewife who accepts a 50 percent return on her investment when 100 percent is possible.

Inherent in the recreation experience are many values. Some are quite obvious, such as the fun value; others might be called "hidden" values since to so many people they are almost obscure. One of the marks of a superior leader is his ability to discover for himself all the outstanding values an activity has to offer. Certainly, the ability to discover the higher values is a mark of intelligence. Of all the characteristics which distinguish the great from the mediocre leader, none equals this in importance: the great leader is aware of the higher values that reside in each activity and is highly skilled in their attainment. The ordinary leader sees only the obvious and achieves only the tangible.

ALL HUMAN BEINGS SEEK GOALS

People do what they do in order to satisfy the need for self-enhancement, self-esteem, or personal adequacy. This is why they join groups. The group appears to promise the individual a better opportunity for happiness, personal fulfillment, and enhancement of the self than would be available to him outside the group. For example, a boy joins a baseball team because it enables him to have fun, satisfy the need for recognition, and the need for acceptance.[2] The activities of the team are motivated by the needs of its members in such a way that they are directed toward

---

[2] In Chapter Three constant reference is made to the one basic need for personal adequacy or self-enhancement. When we refer to such needs as the need for acceptance, recognition, and others, we are not being inconsistent as, in actuality, recognition and acceptance are basic to, and part of, self-enhancement.

goals. One of these goals might be the development of a sufficiently high degree of individual and team skill so that some victories could be won, thus resulting in a measure of recognition for the players.

In an effort to reach this goal of victory, the players may participate in numerous practice sessions and subject themselves to an arduous training program. They will remain members of this team or group just so long as their membership continues to be rewarding or satisfying to them. This is tantamount to saying that the degree of satisfaction derived from the team depends upon the extent to which the team enables them to achieve their goals. This explains why so many teams disband after losing a high proportion of their games.

Since the individual joins a group because it apparently promises to aid him in achieving a significant goal, and since the holding power of the group is measured by its goal-achieving ability, we see that goals are of vital importance to the organization and functioning of all groups.

Research Turns The Spotlight on Goals

The man who knows precisely what he wants has a major advantage over the individual whose doubts about his goals result in actions that are uncertain, hesitant, and irresolute. This is equally true with groups. The morale of a group and the personal satisfaction of its members are usually high in proportion to the clarity of its goals and its effectiveness in reaching them.

A number of studies have turned the spotlight on goals, revealing facts basic to effective leadership in recreation. These facts should be understood by all who desire to attain competency in this area of work. The most important are as follows:

1. The more clearly a group member understands the group goal, the greater is his feeling of group belongingness. Also, the greater is his willingness to accept influence from his group.
2. The members of a group will more readily accept and strive to achieve those goals they have decided upon themselves, or, at least, have had a share in selecting, than those in whose determination they have had no part.
3. The attainment of a group goal must be within the power of the group. The members will not exert themselves in an attempt to achieve a goal they deem beyond their reach.
4. Acceptance into a group depends more upon the extent to which the individual under consideration shares the ideals or goals of the group than upon personal glamour.
5. Goals determine programs. Not only is the goal the primary element

in determining the nature of the program to be developed, but it also influences in large degree the kind of group which will be involved in it.

6. Different sets of goals may exist and the good leader must bring about some degree of harmony among these often conflicting purposes or values as the attainment of program objectives is unlikely when leader and group goals are at cross-purposes. Among these different sets of goals may be those of the group and its individual members, the goals of the leader, and the goals of the recreation department.

7. The primary function of a leader is to assist the group in reaching its goals. Therefore, leadership can be judged good or bad mainly in terms of its effectiveness in meeting this particular responsibility.

8. The leader must have his own goals, otherwise his work will lack purpose and direction. He cannot be expected to exercise a type of leadership that goes beyond the level of the values or ideals in which he believes. A river can rise no higher than its source.

A knowledge of values provides a group with common goals which is an important factor in developing professional solidarity; it provides a basis for interpreting the recreation department to the public and for evaluating both program and personnel; and it serves as a guide for selection of program, supplies, facilities, and leaders. Lacking a knowledge of goals, recreation personnel will wander in the dark doing a myriad of things simply because they have always done them, or because others are doing them, or because someone in authority tells them to do them— none of which is a very good reason for doing anything.

GOALS ARE DETERMINED BY THE PEOPLE INVOLVED

Under democratic leadership the selection of goals should be a responsibility of the group in coöperation with the leader. Many studies have revealed the ineffectiveness of leaders who ignored the wishes of the group and attempted to impose their own personal set of goals upon the members. Hemphill's[3] study of 500 leaders, 365 of whom were successful and 135 unsuccessful, showed that two of the six factors basic to success were: (1) the leader set group goals with the members; and (2) he helped them reach the group goals.

---

[3] John K. Hemphill, *Situational Factors in Leadership* (Columbus, Ohio: Ohio State University, 1949).

Some important questions must be raised at this point for the problem of goal selection is not as simple as it may appear. Can youth be trusted to choose goals worthy of pursuit by a department of recreation supported by tax funds? Shall complete freedom be granted immature youth in goal selection or are there some limits to a child's freedom, even in a democracy? Has a leader a right, or even a responsibility, to attempt to guide both youth and adults into the acceptance of goals which are not strictly of their own choosing? Should a leader seek latent goals—goals which to him are clear, valid, and worthy of attainment—but of which the group is not aware, or but dimly aware?

Answers to these vital questions depend upon an understanding of certain basic facts. First, every experience a child has adds something to the sum total of his character, either to his strengths or to his weaknesses. There are no neutral experiences; they build up or they tear down. The quality of the experience is the decisive factor. Unless we can assume this to be true there is no particular reason for a recreation department; one activity would be as good or bad as another and the outcomes of participation would be the same. The existence of a recreation department is based on the assumption that it does make a socially significant difference whether, for example, youth engage in crude and vulgar dances or in rhythmic expressions of beauty and refinement. When a community decides that the leadership and the opportunity for such an activity shall be provided by the recreation department rather than by a cheap night club, it does so in the conviction that the outcomes of the experience will be on a substantially higher level. Therefore, recreation leaders, representing a social institution in a democratic nation, are faced with an imperative responsibility to seek values that will preserve and strengthen the way of life in which the nation believes. There need be no neglect of the fun value or other worthwhile goals deemed important by the group, but there is no justification for a leader to achieve only one or two goals when others of equal or greater importance may at the same time be readily attained. One of the marks of a superior leader is the ability to lead others to rise higher in their discovery, pursuit, and achievement of goals.

There are definite limits to the freedom of youth in a democracy. No one should be free to choose goals nor engage in activities which jeopardize unduly the safety of themselves and others, or which result in the destruction of property. The leader, as a representative of adult society, must impose limitations prohibiting illegal, immoral, and unethical behavior no matter how far removed from the desires of the group such prohibitions may be. Within these necessary limitations, however, the area of freedom should be broad and the leadership democratic.

GOALS FOR AMERICAN RECREATION
ARE TO BE DISCOVERED IN
THE DEMOCRATIC IDEAL

If the goals suggested by one person are to be accepted and acted upon by another, the second person should understand and agree with the steps by which the first arrived at these goals. Otherwise, he is a slave, in the words of Plato who defined a slave as one who executes the purposes of another.

We live in a democracy. Democracy is both a political and a social philosophy. It constitutes a kind of package deal of values which our forefathers believed in so deeply that they fought and died for them. Within the past half century we have engaged in two world wars and conflicts in Korea and Vietnam in which hundreds of thousands of young Americans lost their lives and many billions of dollars were expended. All of this vast expenditure of blood and wealth seemed worthwhile only as it was related to the preservation of democracy and the values associated with it.

Whatever course of action we pursue, whatever activities we conduct, the purpose should be significant; an insignificant purpose is not worth the time and energy required to realize it and discredits both the department and the leaders who seek it. The truly significant purposes which we as leaders, employed by a social institution in a democratic nation, should seek are those which arise out of the urgent needs of our people and our democratic society. The great and fundamental purposes for which we should strive and which give meaning, significance, and vitality to all our efforts are those which relate to the development of the individual within a framework of social and moral purpose.

These are not superficial values, shallow and transient. In every period of history and under every kind of social organization, there persists, essential and indispensable, a set of values by which the proper role of each individual is determined. The perpetuation of a particular society, such as democracy, depends in large degree upon the ability of that society to develop in its citizens those qualities that are in harmony with its prevailing doctrines and that result in the kind of behavior essential to citizens in a virile democracy. For democracy cannot work except as its citizens possess the qualities needed to make it work.

But is it the responsibility of recreation leaders to seek social, moral, and ethical values leading to the development of democratic citizenship?

Isn't this the job of education? It should be apparent that no single social force can discharge this vital responsibility and that no single social force can wash its hands of the matter and remain aloof. Even if we could persuade ourselves that such values are no concern of recreation leadership, honesty would force us to admit that moral values, for example, taught in school could easily be vitiated on the playgrounds if no one cares whether or not they exist. The conscience of the recreation leaders of this nation will not permit them to forget the words of Arnold Bennett: "Thus...ideals die; not in the conventional pageantry of honored death, but sorrily, ignobly, while one's head is turned . . . ."

Let the sponsors of recreation have deep convictions about the tremendous importance of fun, and joy, and happiness as outcomes of recreation. They are vital aspects of the good life; there is no need to be ashamed of them, nor to apologize for them. But let them beware of a program that seeks no other values, unless they are satisfied with playing a relatively unimportant and trivial role in the drama of community and national life. There is no reason why a boy cannot have fun playing on a softball team and at the same time grow in the qualities that mark the good citizen in a democracy. The goals of personal fulfillment and democratic human relationships must become our deepest concern, our professional preoccupation, our passionate obsession.

By dedicating ourselves to the highest goals of our society our own lives take on a meaning and significance which they hitherto have lacked. There is exhilaration in intense effort expended for a great cause and one of the outcomes of this effort is true happiness which, as John Mason Brown puts it, "comes from squandering ourselves for a purpose." There is no higher purpose to which the recreation leaders of this nation can dedicate themselves than the preservation and strengthening of democracy as the best way of life known to man.

Many of the values, therefore, which we consider important in this country have their origin in the democratic faith which, in turn, derives many of its concepts from Christian ethics. Perhaps the most basic of all the tenets of democracy and of Christianity is belief in the sacredness of human personality, in the inherent worth of the individual, in the dignity and value of human life. Since belief in the supreme importance of the individual is the foundation upon which the edifice of democracy is built, it follows naturally that we should begin our search for goals by asking this question: How can recreation enrich the lives of human beings?

This emphasis on the welfare of the individual and his personal development as a goal of all democratic institutions is indicated by the President's Commission on National Goals:

The paramount goal of the United States was set long ago. It is to guard the rights of the individual, to ensure his development, and to enlarge his opportunity. It is set forth in the Declaration of Independence drafted by Thomas Jefferson and adopted by the Continental Congress on July 4, 1776. . . .

. . . The status of the individual must remain our primary concern. All our institutions—political, social, and economic—must further enhance the dignity of the citizen, promote the maximum development of his capabilities, stimulate their responsible exercise, and widen the range and effectiveness of opportunity for individual choice.[4]

RECREATION HELPS SATISFY BASIC HUMAN NEEDS

The welfare and happiness of people depend in large measure upon the degree to which basic human needs are satisfied. Man's behavior is motivated by his needs. He does what he does in an attempt to satisfy these needs. He eats to satisfy the biological *need* for food; he sleeps because he *needs* sleep. Other needs, psychological in nature, and powerful in effect, drive him on to various forms of behavior. The extent to which these needs are met is, in a very large sense, a measure of his happiness and personal fulfillment; the extent to which they are unmet is a measure of human frustration, maladjustment, unhappiness, and, in many instances, illness or death.

Among the needs of the individual to which recreation can make a major contribution are the following:

Recreation Helps Satisfy the Need for
Activity and Counteracts the Effect of Soft
and Easy Living

One of the basic needs of human beings is the need for movement or activity. When man is sufficiently active to meet his biological needs the outcomes include enough strength, coördination, endurance, and vitality to meet the requirements of daily living, as well as any emergencies that may arise. Fitness also implies that the individual will have sufficient

---

[4] U. S. President's Commission on National Goals, *Goals for Americans* (Englewood Cliffs, N. J.: Prentice-Hall, Inc., 1960), pp. 1, 3.

strength and energy for off-the-job responsibilities, for recreation, and for productive participation in home and community affairs.

While we need to know far more than is known at present regarding the relationship between exercise and health, a number of studies indicate that exercise does make a positive contribution to health in the following ways:[5]

1. Regular exercise can play an important part in the prevention of overweight and thereby help prevent deaths from degenerative disease associated with obesity.
2. A high level of physical activity throughout life appears to slow the development of coronary heart disease, at least partially by decreasing the cholesterol level.
3. Regular exercise helps preserve good muscle tone and other physical characteristics of youth, retards the onset of the marks of aging, and probably contributes to a longer life.
4. The fit individual is able to meet emergencies more effectively and thus avoid disability and even death.

Muscles grow and develop and remain strong chiefly as a result of exercise; they weaken, become soft, and atrophic when unused. Organic power was no problem for primeval man. He had to be active or he died. Confronted constantly by savage beasts and savage men his survival depended upon his ability to fight or flee and the vigorous activity involved in both contributed to his organic development.

Biologically man has changed very little over the past fifty thousand years but his environment has undergone a complete transformation. Urbanization and technological developments have materially reduced opportunities for vigorous movement. The inventive genius of mankind has dedicated itself to making life easier for all of us. Our automobiles are good examples of the trend toward greater ease, more comfort, and softer living. We now have power brakes, power steering, power windows, and power seats. No exercise any more when we go places! If it happens to be to the grocery store the electric eye opens the door for us, a cart carries our packages to the counter, and a boy puts them in the car. Elevators carry us upstairs; electric carts transport us about the golf course; machines do our work for us—even think for us; we take our athletics sitting down in front of the television screen; we sit at the movies, in front of the radio, and at the bridge table. We are fast becoming a nation of sitters with biological deterioration the inevitable result.

[5] Adapted from Fred V. Hein and Allan J. Ryan, "The Contributions of Physical Activity to Physical Health," *The Research Quarterly of the American Association for Health, Physical Education, and Recreation,* May 1960, p. 279.

A life of ease and softness threatens both the individual and the nation. No nation can be strong if its individual citizens are weak. The late President Kennedy described the situation and sounded the alarm:[6]

But the harsh fact of the matter is that there is also an increasingly large number of young Americans who are neglecting their bodies—whose physical fitness is not what it should be—who are getting soft. And such softness on the part of individual citizens can help to strip and destroy the vitality of a nation.

For the physical vigor of our citizens is one of America's most precious resources. If we waste and neglect this resource, if we allow it to dwindle and grow soft then we will destroy much of our ability to meet the great and vital challenges which confront our people. We will be unable to realize our full potential as a nation.

Throughout our history we have been challenged to armed conflict by nations which sought to destroy our independence or threatened our freedom. The young men of America have risen to those occasions, giving themselves freely to the rigors and hardships of warfare. But the stamina and strength which the defense of liberty requires are not the product of a few weeks' basic training or a month's conditioning. These only come from bodies which have been conditioned by a lifetime of participation in sports and interest in physical activity. Our struggles against aggressors throughout our history have been won on the playgrounds and corner lots and fields of America.

Thus, in a very real and immediate sense, our growing softness, our increasing lack of physical fitness, is a menace to our security.

The choice lies with the individual. He can choose the inactive, sedentary life or he can choose the life of action. If he chooses the former, he violates a fundamental law of nature, the law of use. This law decrees that that which is used grows, develops, and becomes strong; and that which is unused becomes soft and deteriorates. When man violates a law of nature he is compelled to pay a penalty, which in this case may be organically tragic for the individual and potentially disastrous to the nation.

History may not repeat itself in our case, but it has repeated itself so many times that no one who is familiar with the lessons which it teaches can regard the situation with anything other than acute apprehension. We have more wealth and more leisure than any nation has ever had in the history of the world. Let the historian, Durant, sound the warning:[7]

It is almost a law of history that the same wealth that generates a civilization announces its decay. For wealth produces ease as well as art; it softens a people to the ways of luxury and peace, and invites invasion from stronger arms and hungrier mouths. . . .

---

[6] John F. Kennedy, "The Soft American," *Sports Illustrated*, December 26, 1960, p. 16.

[7] Will Durant, *Our Oriental Heritage* (New York: Simon and Schuster, 1954), pp. 222, 259.

. . . A nation is born stoic and dies epicurean . . . If victory comes, if war is forgotten in security and peace, then wealth grows; the life of the body gives way, in the dominant classes, to the life of the senses and the mind; toil and suffering are replaced by pleasure and ease; science weakens faith even while thought and comfort weaken virility and fortitude. At last men begin to doubt the gods; they mourn the tragedy of knowledge and seek refuge in every passing delight. Achilles is at the beginning, Epicurus at the end.

Recreation Contributes to Mental Health

We live in what has been called the "Age of Anxiety." The details of life in this "Age" differ but its central theme for a large portion of the population is the same: rush, deadlines, pressure, decisions, responsibility, fears, threats to the ego, frustrations, maladjustments, uncertainty, anxiety, and tension. Its outcomes all too frequently are unhappiness, no peace of mind, stomach ulcers and other psychosomatic disorders, delinquency and crime, alcoholism, drug addiction, mental illness, and suicide. Tension also appears to be a factor in many deaths from heart and circulatory diseases, the leading cause of death in this country.

In a desperate search for relief man turns this way and that. Hundreds of thousands have turned to drugs—tranquilizers to quiet our nerves, a pill to soothe our stomachs, another to lower our blood pressure, drugs to put us to sleep at night, and others to pep us up in the morning. As the tempo of life increases, so does the demand for drugs. The American public now is consuming more than three billion barbiturates annually; more than 50,000,000 prescriptions for tranquilizers are written each year. A bottle of sleeping pills on the dresser has become almost a symbol of our disordered society.

Almost half of all hospital beds in the United States are filled with mental patients. Approximately 5,000,000 persons are alcoholics. Suicide annually claims more than 21,000 victims. Over one million die each year from heart and circulatory diseases. Ulcer sufferers number more than 2,000,000. Tension is a factor in a large proportion of these cases. It is estimated that more than half of all patients who go to a general practicing physician for treatment have no discoverable organic cause for the symptoms of which they complain. Their trouble is psychosomatic or emotional in origin.

Surely there must be a better way of releasing one's tensions than through drink, drugs, and death. Can recreation provide socially acceptable escape valves so that man in his leisure can find relief from the suffocating weight of things and demands which threaten both his sanity and his life? This question can best be answered after a brief inquiry into the causes and nature of tension.

Implanted in man by his Creator is a mechanism, sometimes called the "fight or flight" mechanism, whose purpose is similar to that of the passing gear in a modern automobile, namely, to enable him to meet emergency situations more effectively. Triggered chiefly by the emotional states of fear, anger, and worry the organism is prepared for action as the following physiological changes take place: (1) the heart beats faster; (2) blood pressure rises; (3) respiration is speeded up; (4) blood is driven away from the digestive organs and sent in greater quantities to the muscles, lungs, and brain; (5) the adrenal gland is stimulated; and (6) muscle tension rises.

In the case of primitive man, following the preparatory stage, either fighting or fleeing ensued. In either situation, after the vigorous activity was over the organism returned to normal, the tension disappeared, and relaxation resulted. Modern man, however, has no such relief. Restrictions imposed by civilization forbid fighting; nor can he run from his fears or his worries. So he bottles up his emotions, represses his aggressive drives, and carries his tensions with him constantly.

Unfortunately, emotions simply cannot be bottled up over a long period of time without damage to the organism. One of the most important discoveries of Freud was that when emotions cannot be expressed and relieved through normal voluntary activities they may become the cause of chronic mental and physical disorders. Man has become too civilized for his own good.

Strecker and Appel call attention to increasing evidence that these bottled up emotions[8]

may, as it were, become concentrated in individual organs of the body with the result that coronary heart disease, high blood pressure, asthma, peptic ulcer, colitis, arthritis are prone to develop. More frequently nonspecific physical symptoms of fatigue, tenseness, lack of strength, indigestion, insomnia occur on this basis . . . If, for one reason or another, this emotional energy is not used in some activity, it will not just evaporate and disappear. It is a law of physics that energy does not just disappear; it continues to accumulate, to increase in charge until it may even reach explosive proportions which demand discharge.

Primitive man had no need for drugs with which to escape from his tensions; he escaped by fighting and running. Modern man must discover socially acceptable substitutes for these primitive escape valves and

[8] Edward A. Strecker and Kenneth E. Appel, *Discovering Ourselves* (2nd ed.) (New York: The MacMillan Company, 1944), pp. 128–129.

engage in them. Menninger emphasizes the vital role of recreation in the maintenance of mental health:[9]

Psychologically, recreation is one of the best outlets for pent-up emotions, particularly hostile feelings. This is most obvious in competitive games in which there is running, hitting, throwing. It applies equally, however, to sedentary games like chess, bridge, poker.

As psychiatrists we heartily endorse and strongly recommend that every individual develop a hobby or an organized program of play for himself. There is much less interest in hobbies and recreational activities among psychiatric patients prior to their illness than among well-adjusted persons. Hobbies do not necessarily prevent a mental illness, but their cultivation seems to tend to the development of a more stable personality by providing even a momentary diversion from stress.

Many recreation activities are, in a very real sense, sublimated fights or, in other words, satisfactory social outlets through which tensions are released and aggressive drives expended. Thus, man may achieve a compromise between certain forces within himself and opposing demands of a civilized society. Recreation is not by any means an antidote for all the *dis-eases* of our troubled world, but the hope which it offers to those who are willing to make the effort to help themselves is based both upon the age-old experiences of man and the findings of modern science.

Recreation Adds to the Joy of Living

Life becomes richer, happier, and more meaningful when certain basic human needs are satisfactorily met. Among these is the psychological need to experience a sense of creative achievement, to acquire status or recognition, to be somebody; the need for acceptance, to belong, to be a part of something bigger than one's self; the need for variety or change in life, some zest, adventure, challenge, some relief from monotony and boredom; and the need to feel that at least some of life's activities have significance, purpose, and meaning.

Recreation lacks meaning unless it adds to the joy of living, to the sum total of human happiness. Happiness is important in a world of so much unhappiness. Fun is a part of the good life; life without it would not be worth living. Unless people have fun they will not participate in our activities. Fun, therefore, is a perfectly legitimate goal of recreation.

For those who have the knowledge and skill to use it, leisure provides

---

[9] William C. Menninger, *Psychiatry in a Troubled World* (The MacMillan Company, 1948), p. 359.

the opportunities to experience the satisfactions which make life worth living. They have learned the joys of skillful participation in sports and games; the deep satisfactions of creative achievement in the arts and crafts; the delights of personal fulfillment attained through the rich lore of the libraries; the growing revelation of the wonders of nature acquired through experiences in the out-of-doors; the feeling of self-respect and social approval accompanying membership in one or more of recreation's many clubs and other groups; the awakening sense of civic responsibility arising out of participation in community life; and, finally, the consciousness that life, after all, does have depth, vitality, and meaning.

RECREATION CONTRIBUTES TO DEMOCRATIC CITIZENSHIP

A recreation department in America is a social institution in a demo-cratic nation. Therefore, leaders are under obligation to seek social, moral, and ethical values that will preserve and strengthen democracy. A further reason why growth in democratic human relationships should be sought by recreation leadership lies in the very real danger that exclusive emphasis upon values related primarily to development of the individual may result in the production of a nation of selfish, ruthless, non-coöperative, egotistical individualists. Strength is a desirable quality, but the strong man may use his strength to injure those who are weaker than he unless his strength has been developed in relation to a standard of conduct, a code of behavior, based upon moral and ethical principles. Democracy provides such a code which serves to guide men in their relationships with other men. We have a responsibility, shared by the home, school, and other social institutions, to do everything in our power to help develop in chil-dren and youth those unique qualities or characteristics which distinguish the good citizen in a democracy. The degree to which democracy functions effectively varies directly with the extent to which its citizens possess the qualities necessary to make it function effectively—and its citizens are not born with these qualities.

The leader, therefore, must find his goals on two levels—the level of the individual and the level of society, because[10]

when the general interest is over-accented, freedom declines and may disappear; first controls, then paternalism supervene. On the other hand, if individual

[10]U. S. President's Commission on National Goals, *op. cit.,* p. 48.

interest utterly neglects social needs, anarchy is the end result. The consequence of either extreme is loss of liberty.

The Democratic Citizen Has a High Regard
for the Welfare of All Human Beings

High among the unique characteristics of the democratic citizen is respect for human personality, belief in the inherent worth of the individual, in the dignity and value of human life. Stated more simply, the democratic citizen believes that the most important thing in the world is another human being; that buildings, grounds, supplies, equipment, institutions, and government exist to serve men rather than that men exist to serve governments and institutions.

The recreation leader, therefore, will judge the worth of all activities he conducts in terms of their effects upon the individual human beings who participate in them. The test of every activity will be: What does it do to people? Does it help meet basic human needs or does it harm people, make them selfish, callous, and indifferent to others? What kinds of social attitudes does it foster? Does it advance the cause of democracy by helping to develop the qualities of the good citizen? These are the only valid tests by which to judge the worth of activities in recreation.

The leader must be constantly alert for opportunities to cultivate in youth this most basic of all qualities of the democratic citizen—respect for human beings. The following account of an actual happening in a recreation situation illustrates how as simple an activity as a relay may make a vital contribution to development of this quality.

A leader was preparing to conduct a relay and as the children took their positions one boy, about eleven years of age, stood out among the others because he was so crippled by spastic paralysis that he could hardly walk, let alone run. He moved with a slow, shambling, awkward gait which would have been ludicrous had it not been for his misshapen and twisted body. It seemed a cruel and thoughtless error to expose this crippled boy to the ridicule of his playmates because, manifestly, he could not possibly compete on an equal basis with the others.

David was the third runner on his team. The race began and the first runners charged down around the goals and back to touch the outstretched hands of the second. Finally, it was David's turn and he started off with that lurching, awkward, half-stagger no faster than a slow walk. Immediately his three opponents, with no word from the leader, slowed their progress from what had been a fast run to match exactly the slow pace set by David. Thus, all three maintained their relative positions while David was "running" and, along with all the other children, shouted encouragement to David who finally crossed the finish line with a look of exaltation on his face and a great cheer ringing in his ears. The race then continued at full speed.

Following the relay the leader was asked what had happened. She said that plans for it had been made the day before when David was not present. The children wanted the relay but a question about David was raised. They decided that if he were kept out of the relay his feelings would be hurt; if he were allowed to take part and everyone ran as fast as he could, his feelings also would be hurt. This was their solution. These children demonstrated by their conduct in the relay that "belief in the inherent worth of the individual" and "respect for human personality" were not simply meaningless, high-sounding phrases but that they had become a vital part of their lives, a guide to their behavior toward others. This is one example of how a good leader should conduct activities, whenever possible, in such a manner as to enrich and ennoble the lives of the children taking part. Again, the decisive factor was the quality of the experience, something with which recreation personnel need to be increasingly concerned.

The Democratic Citizen Coöperates for the Common Good

Our economic system is characterized by a high degree of specialization. A corollary of specialization is interdependence. Whenever the workers in any one industry go on strike all of us are affected. We do not believe in a police state. Democracy is predicated upon the theory that people, with a few exceptions, will work together coöperatively in a common effort to achieve common goals without the necessity of legal compulsion. This theory is sound only when the citizens learn the art of coöperation in their youth and prefer it to conflict as a way of life. Recreation can make an important contribution to the development of this quality by guiding youth to work together as members of teams and share in the use of equipment and supplies; by sacrificing one's personal interests in a game, such as softball, in order to advance the welfare of the team; and by leading youth to see that if coöperation is essential to success in a game and to the enjoyment of other activities in recreation, it is equally important in life outside the play world.

The Democratic Citizen Obeys the Law

A fatal weakness in many democracies of the past was their failure to unite liberty with order. When the citizens of a democracy refuse, in large numbers, to obey the laws of their own making their type of government is in grave danger.

The extent to which delinquency and crime exist in this nation, as well as the general disrespect for law which appears to characterize large numbers of Americans, constitute a major threat to our democracy. The rules of games which govern the child's play world are comparable to the laws of organized society. Recreation leaders have a splendid opportunity to develop in youth respect for these rules, to lead them to see that the purpose of rules is to protect the rights of all and to guarantee that everyone will be given an equal share of the good things in a game. They must also lead youth to see that if obedience to game rules is essential to enjoyment of the game and protection of the players so, too, is obedience to law necessary to the good life in the community at large.

The Democratic Citizen Seeks Excellence in Preference to Mediocrity

One of the most difficult problems with which democracy has been confronted throughout history is how to reconcile the apparent conflict between the individual and the group. Where emphasis on the individual is cultivated to the neglect of the general welfare, the ruthless rise to positions of power and the law of the jungle prevails. This is what eventually happened in ancient Athens; rampant individualism was a more powerful factor in the loss of Athenian liberty than was Philip of Macedon.

The reverse of individualism is the tendency to emphasize the importance of the group, to belittle the individual, to arrive at all decisions through committee action, to demand that the individual conform to group thought, and to believe that all men are equal in their abilities and their talents. Since the group dominates the individual, and since the majority of all normal groups is composed of average individuals, group thought, group action, and group standards must of necessity be mediocre or average in quality. Mediocrity never gives birth to excellence.

Our nation is faced with the same problem with which other democracies have been confronted in the past—how to encourage the development of individual talent and to utilize it in constructive efforts for the benefit of mankind. Can we lead youth to understand that all men are equal before the law and should have an equal opportunity to develop their innate capacities to their highest potentialities, but that men are not equal in the nature and extent of these capacities? Can we teach them that while democracy emphasizes the importance of the "common man," the good citizen selects the "uncommon man" to be his representative because he prefers exc llence to mediocrity? We cannot afford mediocrity in office because it represents a deterioration in society. Aristophanes, in his brilliant satire, "The Frogs," described such a deterioration in ancient Athens:

> The men that stood for office,
>   Noted for acknowledged worth,
> And for manly deeds of honor,
>   And for honorable birth;
> Trained in exercise and art,
>   In sacred dances and in song.
> All are ousted and supplanted
>   By a base ignoble throng.

Commager, the eminent historian, raises this vital question:[11]

How can you explain the outburst of genius in the Athens of Pericles and Sophocles, the Florence of Michelangelo and Raphael, the England of Hakluyt and Shakespeare, the Copenhagen of Hans Andersen and Kierkegaard and Thorvaldsen, the Vienna of Haydn and Mozart and Beethoven? Also, that out of America emerged in a single generation Washington, Franklin, Jefferson, Hamilton, John Adams, James Wilson, John Jay, James Madison, John Marshall, and a score of others.

The explanation, he believes, is that excellence is contagious. He might have added that mediocrity also is contagious. In a society where everybody is interested in music, where musicians have attained excellence of the highest order and are admired above all men, where pictures and articles praising them appear constantly in the press, and statues glorifying their memories adorn the public parks, every boy will want to be an outstanding musician. In the words of Plato, "What is honored in a country is cultivated there."

Recreation leaders must teach the language of excellence to youth, cultivating a taste for the beautiful in crafts, in art, in music, and in dance. The sports participant will be taught never to be satisfied with mediocrity when excellence is possible. The challenge to excellence will include the concept that there is some kind of excellence within the reach of everyone. One aspect of good leadership will be a constant endeavor to stretch every youngster in terms of his own capacities. Youth will be taught that excellence comes only to those who are willing to pay the price of excellence; that excellence is a product of many, many hours of hard work, of struggle, of striving for perfection; of careful, intensive preparation, of attention to minute detail; that there is no royal road to excellence, and those who seek

---

[11] Henry Steele Commager, "Urgent Query: Why Do We Lack Statesmen?," *The New York Times Magazine,* January 17, 1960, p. 21.

a short cut to it will end up with mediocrity or worse; and that excellence is a product of self-sacrifice and unselfishness.

The part played by the leader in the stimulation and cultivation of excellence cannot be overemphasized. In general, it may be said that the leader will get whatever standard of performance he expects or demands. To quote Gardner:[12]

We are beginning to understand that the various kinds of talents that flower in any society are the kinds that are valued in the society. . . .
More and more we are coming to see that high performance, particularly where children are concerned, takes place in a framework of expectation. If it is expected it will often occur. If there are no expectations, there will be little high performance.

The Life of the Democratic Citizen Is Regulated by a Code of Behavior Based on Moral and Ethical Values

The student of history who seeks the causes of the decay of any civilization invariably finds that they are multiple in nature. There is no single cause. But he also will discover that certain factors appear and reappear so consistently that they might almost be referred to as chronic causes of the downfall of civilizations and of nations. High among these persistent and destructive influences is a deterioration in the moral fiber of the people. Durant sums up the corruptness of the Greeks in the fifth century B. C. by saying, "The Greek might admit that honesty is the best policy, but he tries everything else first." He further points out that their lack of moral restraint and corrupt individualism were major factors in their downfall.[13]

Again, Durant emphasizes the moral factor in appraising the reasons for the fall of Rome:[14]

Moral decay contributed to the dissolution. The virile character that had been formed by arduous simplicities and a supporting faith relaxed in the sunshine of wealth and the freedom of unbelief; men had now, in the middle and upper classes, the means to yield to temptation, and only expediency to restrain them.

---

[12] John W. Gardner, *Excellence* (New York: Harper and Brothers, 1961), p. 101.

[13] Will Durant, *The Life of Greece* (New York: Simon and Schuster, 1939), pp. 294, 670–71.

[14] Will Durant, *Caesar and Christ* (New York: Simon and Schuster, 1944), p. 667.

In our own nation, within recent years, certain ominous signs have appeared which seem to indicate that the moral and ethical behavior of large numbers of our people either is on the downgrade or that we are becoming increasingly aware that it never was as high as we once had thought it was.

Evidence exists on every hand. Policemen in many cities throughout the nation have coöperated with criminal elements or actually have robbed the people they had sworn to protect. College athletes have accepted bribes from gamblers. A climate of fraud has descended at times upon television, radio, various government agencies, big business, and many other aspects of American life. Gibney deplores the disintegration of moral standards:[15]

Never in our history has the practice of fraud been so dignified by constant use and acceptance. Last year, by conservative estimate some five billion dollars . . . changed hands under innumerable desks, counters, or expensive restaurant tables in kickbacks, pay-offs, or bribes. The country's employers lost more than half a billion to embezzling employees, from pilfering shop workers to absconding assistant secretary-treasurers . . . . A half billion went down the drain in home-repair frauds alone.

We Americans have a tendency to say whenever anything goes wrong, "There ought to be a law." However, much of the evil in the world cannot be controlled by law. Law can't prevent a man from betraying a friend nor a woman from spreading malicious gossip about another. Is it too much to expect simple truth and honesty from people without passing laws to compel them to be truthful and honest? What is needed is not more laws but a standard of behavior that will help guide men to act as they should act, with the compulsion originating from within themselves rather than from enactments of legislative bodies. Where can we find such a standard of conduct? Lord Moulton, Member of Parliament and learned English judge, proposed such a standard some years ago.

All human conduct, said Lord Moulton, can be classified into three major categories which he calls "Domains." One is the Domain of Positive Law. In this great area of human action the behavior of an individual is prescribed by law. For example, he is not free to drive his car as he chooses. He must obey the speed laws, possess a driver's license and, perhaps, an inspection sticker.

The next area of human behavior is the Domain of Freedom of Choice. Here a man may do as he pleases. He is under no compulsion; he is free to make choices. He may wear a hat or go bare-headed, visit

---

[15] Frank Gibney, *The Operators* (New York: Harper and Brothers, 1960), p. 6.

the community center or the tavern, order apple or cherry pie, and go to bed at ten o'clock or at eleven.

Lying between these two areas is a third the importance of which is greater than either of the others. Lord Moulton calls it the Domain of Obedience to the Unenforceable. He explains it by saying that when it first became clear to the passengers and crew that the Titanic was doomed, the cry went up, "Women and children to the lifeboats first!" With but few exceptions the men stood back, even though knowing they faced almost certain death, and helped guide the women and children into the lifeboats. There was no law compelling them to do so. They acted as they did in response to a moral code, a code of honor, a personal standard of conduct arising out of an inward compulsion to behave like decent, honorable gentlemen. This is the kind of behavior needed so desperately in America today, for the true greatness of a nation, says Moulton, is measured by the length and breadth of this area of human conduct in which men obey the Unenforceable. When the great majority of a nation's citizens conduct themselves as decent, honorable, upright, law-abiding human beings, not because of laws and the fear of punishment, but because of a self-discipline based on moral and ethical values, one may rest assured that this nation is headed toward greatness.

The implications of the foregoing to the recreation leaders of the nation are quite definite and precise. Two illustrations will clarify both our opportunities and responsibilities: (1) A boy is playing center field in a closely contested game of softball. The batter hits a line drive to him which he cannot reach standing up. He dives for the ball, rolls over, and comes up with it in one hand. The umpire can't tell whether the ball was caught or trapped so he calls the boy in and asks him. The boy looks the umpire in the eye and says he trapped the ball. (2) The final game is being played to decide the city-wide volleyball championship. The score is tied at 13 all. A boy goes high in the air, hits the ball into the opposing court and the referee signals a point for his team. However, the boy who hit the ball throws up his hand and tells the referee that the tip of one finger had touched the net. The point is canceled and his team later loses the game and the championship.

In both instances the boys obeyed the Unenforceable. They faced a moral problem and they made a moral choice among three competing courses of action. They could have lied and no one but they would have known; they could have told the truth; or they could have said, "You're the official, you call it," and been evasive. They proved to be self-disciplined young men acting in accordance with a standard of conduct based on moral and ethical values. There are numerous situations, constantly occurring in our recreation activities, especially in the program of sports and games, which test the moral fiber of the boys and girls participating in them. They also test the quality of the leaders who should utilize these opportunities to give youth some understanding of what democracy means in terms of human relationships and what is meant by Obedience to the Unenforceable.

Make no mistake about it. These social, moral, and ethical values are vital to our way of life. Democracy, a monument of the spirit, will not stand untended as will our monuments of concrete and steel. It must be nourished in each generation by the abiding faith and dedication of devoted men and women. The world has never been and never will be safe for democracy for "every good and excellent thing . . . stands moment by moment on the razor edge of danger and must be fought for." Let us never make the mistake of assuming that the ability to chin one's self a half dozen times is more important to society than personal integrity; or that skill in hitting a golf ball is more vital than simple honesty in counting the score. Morality and ethics have become old fashioned words in many parts of our land and have been replaced by a cheap cynicism that justifies almost any act as long as it is instrumental in achieving the end desired. One of the great and continuing challenges to the recreation leaders of America is to conduct their activities in such a manner as to contribute to the development of self-disciplined, ethical citizens who respect the dignity and integrity of others.

We have discussed the goals which intelligent and dedicated leaders should strive to achieve through the recreation experience. Some may be appalled by the magnitude of the task and may shrink from a responsibility so complicated and so vast. There can be no return, however, to the early days of the play movement in this nation when the goals of recreation were simply to keep the children off the streets, out of trouble, and out of the hearing of adults. The higher the human intellect rises in the discovery of aims for recreation the greater becomes the contribution of its leaders to the enrichment of human life. In the early days there were valid excuses for conducting "pigmy programs, seeking pigmy results, amid giant opportunities," but that time is past. The emphasis in the future must be placed upon the discovery of these giant opportunities; the selection of activities in which these higher values reside; the exercise of leadership practices effective in achieving the values; and, above all, the preparation of broadly educated leaders, sensitive to the needs of human beings and of a democratic society, and who combine the competencies of the leader, the teacher, and the social engineer. This is the kind of leader who understands that humans are never finished; they are always in a state of change. They can sink to utter degradation or rise to moral heights. Whatever happens is not a matter of chance, but is the result of human volition. The ultimate goal of the leader is to give himself to this struggle of mankind toward the improvement of human life.

Selected References

Alger, George W., "Leisure—For What?", *The Atlantic Monthly* 135, April 1925, p. 483.

The Commission on Goals for American Recreation, *Goals for American Recreation* (Washington, D.C.: American Association for Health, Physical Education and Recreation, 1964).

Danford, Howard G., *Recreation in the American Community* (New York: Harper and Brothers, 1953).

Educational Policies Commission, *Moral and Spiritual Values in the Public Schools* (Washington, D.C.: National Education Association, 1951).

Huizinga, Johan, *Homo Ludens—A Study of the Play Element in Culture* (Boston: The Beacon Press, 1950).

Larrabee, Eric and Meyersohn, Rolf, *Mass Leisure* (Glencoe, Illinois: The Free Press, 1958).

————, "Leisure Could Mean a Better Civilization," *Life,* December 28, 1959, p. 62.

Nash, Jay B., *Philosophy of Recreation and Leisure* (St. Louis: C. V. Mosby Company, 1953).

Robbins, Florence Greenhoe, *The Sociology of Play, Recreation, and Leisure Time* (Dubuque, Iowa: Wm. C. Brown Co., 1955).

Romney, G. Ott, *Off the Job Living* (New York: A. S. Barnes Company, 1945).

Slavson, S. R., *Recreation and the Total Personality* (New York: Association Press, 1946).

Tibbitts, Clark and Donahue, Wilma (eds.), *Aging in Today's Society.* Edman, Irwin, "On American Leisure," Soule, George, "The New Instar," Englewood Cliffs, N.J.: Prentice-Hall, Inc., 1960), p. 208, p. 22.

U.S. President's Commission on National Goals, *Goals for Americans* (Englewood Cliffs, N.J.: Prentice-Hall, Inc., 1960).

Chapter V

The Nature of Leadership

SOMEWHERE, AGES BACK in man's primeval past, he made the remarkable discovery that game could be killed and enemies defeated far more successfully when he joined with others in a coöperative effort than when he hunted or fought alone. This was the beginning of leadership among men because whenever men have worked together for some common purpose a leader has emerged. Leadership does not come into being automatically or by accident.

THE IMPORTANCE OF LEADERSHIP

The higher or more complex the society, the more important leadership becomes as a means of solving the problems which require for their solution the deep insights and sound judgments of the leader working coöperatively with the group. It may be said, therefore, that man's chief interest and concern about leadership originate from his desire to master his environment through group effort. Thus, leadership is to be found in all kinds of groups from the simplest to the most complex. There is the leader of the hunting pack, the leader of a children's play group, the captain of a football team, the chairman of a committee, president of a school board, head of a family, leader of a political party, president of a corporation, champion of a school of philosophy, dictator of a nation, and prophet of a religion. The list is endless, for leadership emerges wherever men come together in groups to achieve common goals.

Leadership is by far the most important single factor in the successful operation of a program of recreation. Without good leadership no recreation department can succeed regardless of the many other assets it may possess. Therefore, every possible effort should be made to understand the nature of good leadership, to determine what works, what doesn't, and why. This, in essence, is the basic purpose of this chapter.

What is Leadership?

To practice the art of leadership effectively, the potential leader needs to have a clear idea of what leadership is. Much remains to be discovered about leadership since it involves human beings and their relationships with one another. Human beings are complicated organisms and research in the area of human relations is only a few decades old as contrasted with several centuries of progress in the physical sciences. Nevertheless, more than 500 recent studies, carried out primarily in about twenty-four leadership research centers within the past three decades in the United States, now provide us with more basic information regarding the nature of leadership than had been collected during the entire previous century.

Leadership is a process of stimulating and aiding groups to determine, or to accept, common goals and to carry out effectively the measures leading to the attainment of these goals. In other words, leadership is what a person does to help a group decide upon common goals and then achieve them. Three factors, or conditions, must be present before leadership can exist: (1) a group of two or more persons; (2) goals or common tasks to be pursued; and (3) at least some of the group members must have different responsibilities—where all have the same duties no leader exists.

Leadership in recreation is concerned with all aspects of the situation which help make it possible to achieve the objectives important to the department and to the group. Leadership is planning ways and means of moving toward these objectives. Leadership is securing the facilities, equipment, and supplies needed if the group is to function effectively in its pursuit of the goals. Leadership is teaching the basic skills, social and moral behaviors, and group strategies essential to success. Leadership is the assignment of specific responsibilities to each member of the group. Leadership includes providing information which the group needs for intelligent action. Leadership helps establish a friendly atmosphere within which the members can work coöperatively without fear, anxiety, or insecurity. Leadership assists each individual to achieve a measure of success, inspires him to seek excellence in everything he does, and influences him to accept the common good as his highest aim. These are the most important things a superior leader does.

THEORIES OF LEADERSHIP

Leadership, as described in the two preceding paragraphs, places emphasis on leader behavior, on performance, on what the leader does in relation to the group, and the problem to be solved, rather than upon possession of a combination of alleged leadership traits or qualities. This is one of the most revolutionary of all the newer discoveries in leadership research. Prior to the evolvement of this particular theory of leadership, which will be described later, two other theories were popular and still are accepted today, either wholly or in part, by many people. Students of leadership in recreation need to understand these theories if they are to have any broad comprehension of the many and varied aspects of leadership. For just as a receding glacier leaves remnants of itself which affect the land forever, so, too, does each theory leave its marks upon the minds of men and upon each succeeding theory.

The Trait Theory

This also is known as the "Great Man" theory for it originally was based on the assumption that leaders are born, not made, and they were born members of the aristocracy. Only men of a distinctive stamp, marked for leadership from birth by virtue of their possession of unusual traits, could possibly rise to positions of eminence. If you wanted to learn about leadership, you simply studied these leaders, determined what traits they possessed, and there you had the key to an understanding of leadership.

At first it was assumed these "leadership" traits were handed down from one person to another chiefly through heredity. Later on, according to Gordon,[1]

. . . the modified theory held that leadership was a function of traits and characteristics that were *acquired* chiefly through experience, education, and special training. . . . A person by virtue of possessing the traits of leadership would somehow acquire the role of leader. Furthermore, a person so endowed, it was believed, would emerge as a leader in many, if not most, group situations.

If the trait theory is valid, all leaders should possess approximately the same traits. A number of research studies, however, have exploded

---

[1] Thomas Gordon, *Group-Centered Leadership* (Boston: Houghton Mifflin Company, 1955), p. 47.

this theory by proving that very few traits are common to all leaders. Ross and Hendry report on a study by Bird in 1940 which found seventy-nine traits mentioned in twenty different studies, only five percent of which were common to four or more investigations. The authors conclude, "The most discerning examination of the relation between these personality traits and leadership demonstrates a complete failure to find any consistent pattern of traits which will characterize leaders."[2]

Stogdill further undermined the trait theory when he examined 124 studies on the relationship of personal factors to leadership and was unable to find any consistent pattern of traits characterizing all leaders. He summarized:[3]

A person does not become a leader by virtue of the possession of some combination of traits, but the pattern of personal characteristics of the leader must bear some relevant relationship to the characteristics, activities, and goals of the followers. Thus, leadership must be conceived in terms of the interactions of variables which are in constant flux and change.

In short, the attempt to distinguish leaders from nonleaders on the basis of traits has not proved successful.

Leadership as a Function of the Group

As dissatisfaction with the trait explanation of leadership grew, leading thinkers in this field began to look upon leadership solely in its relationship to the group. Leadership is viewed as the performance of such acts as helping the group to establish goals, assisting it to achieve the goals, creating a friendly climate within which the interactions among members will be improved, providing the group with the facilities, equipment, and supplies necessary for the attainment of its goals, and building a feeling of group unity and solidarity.

Leadership, according to this theory, centers not in one person alone, but resides in the group. All members of the group perform many different functions depending on the needs of the group and the abilities of the members. All members are potential leaders and do exhibit leadership behavior to some degree.

---

[2] Murray G. Ross and Charles E. Hendry, *New Understandings of Leadership* (New York: Association Press, 1957, pp. 18–19).

[3] Ralph M. Stogdill, "Personal Factors Associated with Leadership: A Survey of the Literature," *Journal of Pychology,* January, 1948, p. 64.

Leadership as a Function of the Situation

Doubts with respect to the validity of the "group" theory of leadership arose when careful observers noted that an individual might be a leader in one group but not in another. The captain of a baseball team, for example, might be an inspiring leader on the ball diamond and a total failure as leader of a discussion group in the classroom. Or the captain of a football team might exhibit superior leadership abilities when asked to lead a group in demonstrating the punt formation, but lose all his confidence when charged with the task of leading the same group in solving the problem of writing a letter of application for a teaching position.

It began to appear that the qualities or traits possessed by potential leaders must be related to the situation, the problem to be solved, or the goals to be pursued. The leader must be superior to the members of the group in some respect that is of importance in goal attainment—stronger, if the task demands strength; more intelligent, if intellectual ability is required; more articulate, if verbal persuasion is called for; more skillful, if skill is significant. This is what Stogdill meant when he said that the "personal characteristics of the leader must bear some relevant relationship to the characteristics, activities, and goals of the followers."

IMPLICATIONS OF THE SITUATIONAL THEORY OF LEADERSHIP TO RECREATION

This latest theory of leadership includes a number of important implications for recreation. The most important are:

1. No longer should we compile lengthy lists of traits which all recreation leaders presumably should have and then attempt to find or develop leaders who possess them. Rather, we should study the various situations, groups, and problems with which the leader will be involved and determine what he should know, the skills he should acquire, and other competencies needed if he is to be successful in establishing mutual goals and carrying out the measures essential to attainment of these goals.

   This does not mean complete unconcern for the qualities of leaders. We certainly desire leaders who possess high moral and ethical qualities and who exemplify in their conduct other qualities of the good citizen in a democracy. But these are specific qualities which are necessitated by the nature of the goals and of the situation in which the individual is to function as a leader. In other words, these qualities are relevant to the situation just as superior intelligence is relevant to helping a group achieve its goals in the realm of higher mathematics, but not particularly related to the problems involved in leading a group of six-year-olds in "Drop the Handkerchief."

2. Leaders are made, not born. Leadership is not something mysterious and magical, but is a pattern of competencies consisting primarily of knowledge, skills, insights, and attitudes that people can learn and develop. After we have determined the specific knowledge, skills, insights, and attitudes which persons need if they are to be successful leaders in the varied situations existing in the field of recreation we then must provide an education that will prepare them for as many of these situations as possible. A broad range of experiences, both as an observer and as a leader, should be an essential part of this preparation.

3. Since the competencies required in a leader are determined in large degree by the demands of the situation in which he is expected to function as a leader, the recreation administrator should study the situation carefully before assigning a leader to a specific task. He should ask himself this question: "Do the qualifications of this leader prepare him to meet the demands of this particular situation better than any other leader in our department?" At least as equal an emphasis should be placed upon appraisal of the situation as upon appraisal of the leader. An individual might prove to be an excellent leader of a teen-age club and a total failure as leader of a club for the aged.

The nature of leadership and the traits of leaders will differ from group to group and from situation to situation. Although no recreation department will find it possible to provide a different leader for each different group, every effort should be made to match specific abilities with those situations in which these abilities may bear the most fruit.

4. Groups generally choose leaders that are superior in certain characteristics or skills relevant to the situation in which the group finds itself. For example, the leader may be more skillful, a better speaker, more intelligent, stronger, or be a better organizer. Although groups operating within the recreation department generally cannot be given an opportunity to choose their leaders, the effectiveness of the assigned leaders will be enhanced if they do possess one or more superior traits of value in helping the group reach its goals. For this reason, students preparing for recreation leadership responsibilities should be encouraged to seek excellence in as many areas as possible.

5. A leader is effective only as the members of the group respond to him and he to them. One test of a leader is the extent to which he can get people to follow him. The leader is as dependent upon the non-leaders as they are upon him. Thus, leadership is a two-way process, a product of the interaction of human beings and not solely a matter of status or position. A person does not become a leader simply because

he is employed as a leader and designated as one by the recreation department. He becomes a leader only when he behaves as a leader and is accepted by the group as a leader. This means that the leader must be able to get along with others. He must be a warm, friendly, coöperative person because no one can be a successful leader without followers, and he will have followers only if the people like and respect him.

6. Leadership must not be looked upon as a factor in isolation from other factors. Leadership can be understood only in relationship to the group, to the individual members of the group, to the situation, the problems, goals, and needs of the group, and to the interactions of the members with the leader and with one another. Any attempt to understand leadership other than in these relationships is certain to fail.

DEMOCRATIC AND AUTOCRATIC LEADERSHIP

Social institutions in a democratic nation should contribute to democratic values. Democratic ends cannot be attained by autocratic methods. The one study which has contributed most to an understanding of the differences in the techniques and outcomes of democratic and autocratic leadership is the study by Lewin, Lippitt, and White at the University of Iowa.[4]

In 1938, these psychologists undertook to explore the nature of leadership by organizing two sets of experimental groups of boys, one of which was dominated by a dictatorial leader and the other by a democratic leader. A third group evolved accidentally when one of the "democratic" leaders created an atmosphere quite different from that achieved by the other "democratic" leaders. This third type of leadership was termed "laissez-faire." Leadership techniques and results differed materially in each group.

Autocratic Leadership

In this group the leader determined policy, established goals, decided what was to be done and how, assigned tasks to individuals, allocated

---

[4] Ralph K. White and Ronald Lippitt, *Autocracy and Democracy* (New York: Harper and Brothers, 1960).

work companions to each member, and, in general, dominated the group.

The boys reacted either aggressively or submissively under autocratic leadership and exhibited more dependence and less individuality. The boys were quarrelsome and when the leader left the room, tended to stop work almost entirely. The impulse to aggression resulted in the search for and persecution of scapegoats, apparently as a means of ego satisfaction denied by the nature of the leadership. Most of the scapegoat behavior was directed not against the leader but against other members of the group. More destruction of property and more demands for attention occurred in this group. More work was done, but the boys showed less originality and creative thinking in their work than was shown under democratic leadership.

Democratic Leadership

Matters of policy were determined by the group in coöperation with the leader. Throughout the program, group members were encouraged to participate in decisions and to choose their own work companions. The leaders created an informal and friendly climate by displaying no concern about their status and dignity. They took off their coats, worked with the boys, indicated that they were enjoying the work, and evidenced a "sensitive awareness of and respect for the status needs of the boys." Stimulating self-direction, characterized primarily by encouraging the boys to offer suggestions and then following them up, was emphasized by the democratic leaders. Both the leader and the group participated in establishing goals and in determining what steps should be taken to achieve them. While freedom was an important factor in the situation, leadership was a very active thing involving both careful planning and skillful action.

The findings demonstrated conclusively that democratic leadership produces measurably different results than does autocratic or *laissez-faire* leadership. Among these results were less aggressive behavior, less dependence upon the leader, greater originality, more friendliness, more group-mindedness, more readiness to share group property, and more genuine interest in the work. Both work and play goals were achieved and the members continued to work even when the leader was absent. This phase of the experiment proved that, "of all the generalizations growing out of the experimental study of groups, one of the most broadly and firmly established is that the members of a group tend to be more satisfied if they have at least some feeling of participation in its decisions."[5]

---

[5] *Ibid.*, p. 260.

Laissez-faire *Leadership*

Virtually no control was exercised over the group, each member being permitted to shift for himself to a great extent.

The members expressed considerable discontent with the situation during meetings. The work done was poorer in quality and reduced in quantity. Much time was wasted in arguments and in purely personal discussions. Group activity was less efficient and less satisfying. There was a lack of clear goals. The boys stated a definite preference for their democratic leaders.

This study emphasized, as does no other leadership study, that just any kind of a recreation program, conducted without regard to method, will not yield worthwhile results. The achievement of democratic outcomes calls for a particular kind of recreation, conducted by a particular kind of leader, in a particular kind of way.

TYPES OF LEADERSHIP

Four major types of leadership exist in American recreation at the present time activity and group leadership, administrative leadership, civic or community leadership, and educational leadership.

Activity and Group Leadership

This type of leader works directly with people as they participate in recreation activities. He may be a playground or community center leader or he may be director of a symphony orchestra. In any case, he has been given official leadership status, involving formal authority, is the head of his group or groups, and is skilled in activities and their conduct. He also understands people and is effective in working with them.

Administrative Leadership

This leader's role is primarily an executive one involving organizing and administering. His major task is to provide the best possible conditions for the effective functioning of the activity or group leaders. Just as the most important responsibility of a superintendent of schools is to provide those conditions within which superior teaching can take place, so, also, should the administrative leader in recreation understand that the purpose of administration is to facilitate attainment of the values deemed important by the department of recreation. He must be capable of understanding the culture within which he exists, know how cultural concepts influence people in recreation, and be effective in helping society achieve a higher cultural level in its uses of leisure.

Civic or Community Leadership

These are lay leaders who may serve as members of boards, commissions, councils, committees, or other citizen groups which can provide effective support to the local recreation department. Their most valuable function is helping to bring together into a harmonious working relationship the professional leaders in recreation, on the one hand, and the social forces of the local community, on the other. They also can make a vital contribution by interpreting the work of the professional leaders to the community.

Educational Leadership

This person is typified by the recreation educator in the colleges and universities among whose chief responsibilities is the professional education of recreation personnel. Preferably, he should have had many years of successful practical experience both as an activity leader and as an administrative leader in recreation, but he also should be a frontier thinker in his field. He should be an educator in the very best sense of the word. He should be a scholar, broadly educated, a cultured individual who can understand and appreciate the relationships existing among areas of knowledge and the implications of this knowledge and these relationships to human beings as they face increasingly the problem of leisure in an industrialized, urbanized, and mechanized democracy. He must understand leisure and its uses as a factor of historical significance in the rise and fall of civilizations. Not only is he charged with the responsibility of transmitting a highly specialized body of knowledge to his students, but he should add to this body of knowledge through his personal writings and research and those of his students. By the very nature of his responsibility, he will, at all times, be in some degree of conflict with many other leaders in the field and with the culture in which he teaches. Teaching of the highest quality involves an element of discontent with things as they are, since this kind of teaching constantly seeks improvement and improvement calls for change. Many people do not want to change and they resent individuals who do.

The more closely we study these four types of leadership, the more apparent it becomes that they overlap. Attempts to separate them completely, to convert them into water-tight compartments, are as futile as they are arbitrary. One of our difficulties is that more than one type of leadership frequently devolves upon one person. The administrative leader, for example, must also exercise an educational function with his staff, work harmoniously with community groups, and, in the smaller departments, he may even conduct activities.

This four-type classification of leadership does throw light on the fact that leadership in recreation is complicated, varied, and diverse. Although major emphasis in this book will be placed on the activity or group leader, students should understand that much of what is written will apply to all leaders since their common elements far outnumber their dissimilarities.

PRINCIPLES OF LEADERSHIP

Principles are fundamental beliefs based on fact. They serve as guides to action or to better understanding. Unfortunately, in many instances leaders have depended not upon principles for the formation of judgments but upon such aids as tradition, current practice, best guess, and authority, each of which may prove to be unsound.

What is the origin of these principles? Where do they come from? Are they infallible and eternal? Does the art of leadership consist simply of memorizing a list of basic principles and then putting them into practice? Do basic principles of leadership change as the situation changes or are they universal in their application? These are important questions and they must be answered if the student is to have a clear understanding of the role which principles should play in recreation leadership.

From the experiences of man, his nature, and the nature of the society in which he lives are derived the principles by which the leader is guided. Lacking principles as guides to action, he is dependent upon rules, methods, current practice, authority, and tradition, none of which may be valid in any given situation. While principles should not be revered as eternal truths since they rest on a factual foundation which will change in the light of progress made in the behavioral sciences, nevertheless, they are the best guides we know of and professionally minded leaders prefer to place their reliance upon principles as a basis for determination of procedure.

The art of leadership, however, does not consist solely of memorizing a list of principles and then applying them in a mechanical fashion to the appropriate situations. Leadership is not that simple. Leadership involves working with human beings, and human nature is a highly unpredictable element. A knowledge of principles will prove to be extremely helpful to the leader, but successful leadership is a complicated phenomenon. Just as no two people are identical, so are no two situations, groups, or problems exactly alike. Therefore, the leader may expect to find a great variety of problems which do not lend themselves to any rigid, inflexible, standard-ized solutions. Leadership must be elastic, flexible, and sensitive to the distinctive factors and conditions characterizing each situation confront-ing it. A knowledge of principles is indispensable to good leadership, but it must be supplemented by sound judgment and common sense. In summary, despite the importance of principles, they do not offer a ready-made solution to leadership problems.

A limited number of principles are presented and discussed briefly at this point. Only those which appear to possess greatest significance for recreation leaders are set forth here.

1. *Leadership must be based upon a sound philosophy of recreation.* A leader without a sound philosophy of recreation is like a navigator with-out a compass. Philosophy is concerned with purposes, values, goals, and leadership is important only as it makes possible the attainment of these goals. Unless a leader clearly understands the values he should seek through recreation, and unless these values be worthy ones, his work is without meaning and without direction. Things are done, but there is no good reason for doing them. It is not enough merely to encourage peo-ple to take part in activities without regard to what happens to them while they are participating. We must be concerned with the quality of the experience and its effect upon the behavior of those who experience it. Leadership is but a means to an end, and the end is the realization of the goals which all concerned deem important.

2. *Leadership is dedicated to the principle of involvement.* The heart of the democratic ideal is belief in the worth and dignity of the individual. If you truly believe in the supreme importance of the indi-vidual, then it naturally follows that you will respect people for what they are and give them an opportunity to share in the coöperative formulation and accomplishment of plans and decisions which affect them. The leader who professes belief in the worth of people but denies them a chance to demonstrate their worth is giving nothing but lip-service to democracy.

The democratic leader believes that "everybody is smarter than any-body" and he attempts to mobilize all the abilities inherent in the group. Faith in human intelligence is closely allied to belief in the worth of the individual. Democracy rejects any concept of leadership which centers in one individual's, or a small group of individuals', exclusive power to make decisions for the group, because history shows that in this direction lies dictatorship. Instead, democracy believes in the universality of leader-ship—that leadership is not the exclusive prerogative of the few, but may be expected to flower in all men to the extent that each individual is encouraged to make his contribution to the common cause in such a manner that no one person dominates the group. One of the major func-tions of democratic leadership, therefore, is the fostering of leadership in others to such a degree that the leader finds himself working with a group, all of whose members are leaders within varying limits. Thus, democratic leadership, through its efforts to create strong, responsible, self-reliant individuals capable of both thinking and acting for themselves, seeks to make itself increasingly unnecessary. Conversely, autocratic lead-ership strives to make itself increasingly indispensable.

Another powerful argument in favor of the principle of involvement lies in the fact that people more fully understand, appreciate, and support those ideas and decisions in whose formulation they have participated. This democratic concept calls for widening the area of common concern so that all persons involved may feel themselves to be partners in a com-mon enterprise. If a teen-age dance is to be conducted, its leader will meet with youth representatives to plan with respect to such items as time, place, music, decorations, admission price, supervision, dress, refreshments, and rules of behavior. The group is much more likely to attend the dance and help enforce the regulations agreed upon because they look upon it as *their* dance and *their* rules, than if the leader had made all the decisions. In short, the leader plans *with* people rather than *for* people.

3. *Effective leadership depends in large measure upon the leader's insight into the nature of man and his behavior.* Every conception of lead-ership is necessarily based upon certain assumptions about the nature of man and his behavior. This point of view is presented in detail in Chapter 3 and needs no elaboration here.

4. *Leadership functions in harmony with the principle of individual differences.* Four major implications of this principle to recreation leader-ship warrant consideration: (1) since each human being is different from all other human beings, this very uniqueness lies at the heart of our belief in the preciousness of human life; (2) the uniqueness of each individual means that mass methods of working with people must be rejected in favor of the individual approach; (3) special assistance should be given

by the leader to the unskilled, the unable, and the unaccepted, but the talented individual also should be encouraged and assisted to reach his highest possible level of excellence; and (4) an extremely broad and diversified program must be provided so that everyone may find something of interest and value in which he can participate with some degree of success and satisfaction.

5. *Leadership is shaped and fashioned both by the group and by the situation.* Leadership of a senior citizen's group will be different from leadership of a teen-age club. The leader of an adult discussion group will behave differently from the leader exercising an instructor's role in teaching fifteen-year-old boys how to play volleyball. The degree of democracy practiced by a leader conducting a meeting of a playground council comprised of adults will be considerably more pronounced than that practiced by a leader faced by the problem of getting forty six-year-old children out of a burning building. The variables in each of the above instances are the nature of the group and the character of the situation.

One of the ways by which the group affects the leadership is through its degree of maturity. The less mature a group is, the stronger must be the leadership. As the group grows in maximum effectiveness, as its members develop greater self-reliance, responsibility, and self-discipline, a less dominant style of leadership is indicated.

Every situation stipulates certain modes of leadership behavior. As an illustration of how the situation affects leadership, let us consider two quite different situations. In the first situation the leader is confronted with the problem of how to organize and operate an adult softball program for a city of 50,000 population. He calls a meeting of the managers of all teams desirous of entering league competition and discusses the various problems with them. He seeks their advice and counsel. Through friendly and coöperative efforts a softball constitution is adopted providing for a high degree of self-direction under expert but unobtrusive guidance from the recreation department. In this situation the leader operates quite democratically.

Now, let's see how a completely different situation requires an entirely different style of leadership. A volleyball team for teen-age boys is being organized in a community center. All boys eligible for the team are given an equal opportunity to try out for it, and equal amount of time for practice, an equal chance at the volleyballs, and an equal share of the coaching efforts. They may even share equally in arriving at such decisions as days and hours of practice, number of games to be played, who shall be the opponents, methods of transportation to and from games, how expenses shall be met, and whether refreshments shall be served after the home games.

They do not decide democratically how the hands should be held while making the chest pass nor how the skills involved in executing the serve should be performed. They do not participate in selection of the team. These duties are the teacher's, and the essential functions of the teacher in the coaching of a team are to develop both individual and team skills and strategies. The recreation leader is both a leader and a teacher. Whenever possible he uses democratic procedures, but in matters demanding a high degree of technical "know-how" he instructs and directs the group. In his role as teacher the leader cannot function as democratically as he can in other roles. He should understand, nevertheless, that even the teacher can be so autocratic as to elicit feelings of hostility, apathy, and withdrawal thus nullifying in large degree his teaching efforts, no matter how superior they may be from the strictly technical standpoint.

6. *Compatibility must exist between means and ends.* One of the basic elements in the moral teachings of Mahatma Gandhi dealt with this problem of ends and means, "that means are always as important as the ends; that it is not good enough to have a good end in view, but the means you adopt to reach that end are at least as important. If you adopt wrong means, evil means, to attain a good end, the evil means do not lead you to that good end at all."[6] Furthermore, the adoption of bad means to reach good ends results in the transmutation of the good ends into bad ones. War cannot end wars, autocratic methods cannot produce democratic citizens, and force cannot cultivate friendship. What we do, not what we desire, shapes and fashions our personalities.

The superior recreation leader recognizes this inviolable connection between ends and means. He understands that a recreation department is a social institution in a democratic nation. As such, its personnel have a responsibility to contribute to the preservation and improvement of democracy. Democratic ends cannot be achieved by autocratic methods. The means or methods must harmonize with the values sought. When we practice autocratic leadership we are creating the kinds of leaders who would subvert democracy. Even if it be true that democratic leadership at times may be less efficient than autocratic leadership, nevertheless, it nourishes values that are vital to the way of life in which we so deeply believe.

An additional and vital reason exists why we should emphasize democratic methods in recreation. As the leader of the free nations America is attempting to convey to the peoples of the world an image of democracy as the best way of life known to man. The measure of our faith in

---

[6] Jawaharlal Nehru, *Visit to America* (New York: John Day Company, 1950), pp. 181–182.

democracy is most likely to be judged by the extent to which our leaders practice democracy in all their relationships with others. Our recreation leaders bear an equal share of responsibility with other leaders to demonstrate their conviction that a system which grants to free men the right to arrive at their own decisions is superior to a system which imposes upon the many decisions made by the few.

7. *Leadership establishes an organizational structure for effective operation.* An unorganized group is simply a mass of people and sometimes a mob. Therefore, leadership determines the roles to be played by each member of the group, assists in the determination of the goals or values to be sought, the means by which these goals shall be achieved, and facilitates the work of the various members as they carry out their different assignments.

8. *The effectiveness of leadership is measured by the degree to which it attains its goals.*

This principle implies that good leadership must have a clear understanding of its goals and be skillful in their attainment. These goals must be accepted by the members and they should exist at both the level of the individual and the level of society. Our goals must relate both to individual development (personal fulfillment) and to the development of competency in human relations (society). The leader knows that a drive increases in intensity as it nears its goal. Remote goals may lack the power to motivate people. Therefore, reasonable and attainable intermediate goals are agreed upon which lead step-by-step to the major goals. Leadership in recreation must be particularly scrupulous in its methods since evil means will not lead to good ends. The means are of equal importance to the ends.

9. *Leadership seeks a compromise between the extremes of individualism and equalitarianism.* Two hazards jeopardizing the lives of sailors in ancient times were Scylla, a dangerous rock on the Italian side of the Strait of Messina, and Charybdis, a whirlpool on the Sicilian side. Thus, "between Scylla and Charybdis" came to mean between two evils or dangers, either one of which could be safely avoided only by risking the other. Extreme individualism and equalitarianism are the Scylla and Charybdis of the modern leader. Let us see what each means and why both should be avoided.

Lying at the heart of the democratic ideal is belief in the worth and dignity of the individual. We believe that in a democracy the individual should be free to develop his innate abilities to the utmost. High on the scale of values sought through recreation are those which relate to self-realization or individual fulfillment. We believe in free enterprise which means we believe in individual performance on a competitive basis.

But too much of anything is not good for people. Just how far should the individual be permitted or encouraged to go? The cult of the individual, when carried to an extreme, results in the law of the jungle where each individual seeks to advance his own personal, selfish interests with no concern whatsoever for anyone but himself. The most aggressive and ruthless move into positions of power and those less able to compete suffer bitterly.

Thus, we see that leadership should encourage individual performance and display of talent, but there are limits beyond which it should not go.

The leader must work with the group, help establish its goals, persuade its members to accept the department's goals, and guide them in the measures which lead to goal attainment. The leader also helps to create a friendly, permissive, coöperative climate within which the members are encouraged in creative self-expression and to work together for the common welfare. Up to this point, it is difficult to find fault with the group concept. Yet, the pendulum can swing too far here just as it frequently does in the realm of super-individualism.

When the concept of the equality of man is so misconstrued as to mean that all men are equal in their abilities, talents, and contributions, the evils spawned by such a misconception frequently include the following: since everyone is equal, all have a right to share equally in decision-making, so everything of importance must be decided by the group, the committee, the council or the organization; the group demands conformity to group thought and action which means all display of initiative, talent, originality, creativity, independence, and high intelligence is vigorously discouraged because it threatens the self-esteem of the less able members who are in the majority; the individual is judged not on the basis of his ability to perform but on his willingness to conform; the incentive to excel, to achieve excellence, to explore new frontiers withers as the individual is smothered by the group; the dry rot of mediocrity sets in; the individual is protected from judgments made on the basis of performance as he hides within the anonymous mass; and the leader plagued by doubts about his ability to handle the job, escapes the burden of personal responsibility by, theoretically at least, abdicating his position of leadership and allowing the group to make the decisions which are rightfully his to make.

The problem confronting leadership at this point is twofold: (1) to encourage the individual to be an individual, to seek excellence in preference to mediocrity, to resist with all his power any tendencies of the group to crush out of him his uniqueness or to demand of him total loyalty; but, at the same time, to employ his talents in constructive efforts for the benefit of mankind, to understand that no man can live wholly outside the group, and that the good life consists in part of joining with others in a common effort to improve the lot of all; and (2) to practice what he teaches others, to be a leader in actuality as well as in name, to recognize that a leader cannot function in isolation from the group, but to refuse to place complete reliance upon the group with its standard of mediocrity, and to accept the responsibilities which develop upon the leader.

One of the marks of the truly great leader is his ability to achieve the values related to the highest possible development of the individual within a framework of social and moral purpose, or, in short, to navigate a course between the Scylla of rampant individualism and the Charybdis of deadening equalitarianism.

10. *Leadership accepts responsibilities and risks.* This principle is closely related to the preceding principle. Superior leadership involves innovating, pioneering, exploring, investigating, and initiating. No particular leadership ability is required to persuade people to move in a direction they already have taken. Most of the progress made by mankind throughout the ages has been initiated by a few superior individuals—the great leaders of history.

Leadership of this kind involves great personal risk; it is hazardous. It is dangerous to be different in a conformist society. The nonconformist is no longer regarded as a heretic and punished by death as he was a few hundred years ago, but his life is not exactly a bed of roses simply because the penalties imposed by society are more subtle than they used to be.

There is no merit in being different just for the sake of being different, but the individual who lacks the courage to be different when he believes that is the right thing to do is no leader in the deeper meaning of the term.

11. *Leadership operates in harmony with the principle of multiple chances.* This principle is based on the assumption that every normal human being is potentially capable of excellence at some level and in some activity; and that leadership will persevere until each individual discovers those opportunities best suited to his particular talents. The leader, functioning as coach of a boys' softball team, will not give up on a boy because he fails as a first baseman, but will give him a chance to make good at all other positions. If he fails completely as a softball player, the capable leader, carefully analyzing the boy's abilities, will encourage him to participate in other activities in which the probability of success appears greater.

12. *Leadership seeks to expand the interests of people.* Among the responsibilities of a leader is the building of a program of recreation activities sufficiently attractive to people that they will participate in

large numbers. One way of doing this is to find out from people what they are interested in and would like to take part in. This is known as the *expressed desires* approach to program construction. There are two grave weaknesses in this approach: (1) the recreation interests and desires of people are limited by their experiences; and (2) it ignores the fact that one of the major functions of leadership is to expand the recreation horizons of people by introducing them to new interests and helping them develop understandings, appreciations, and skills in new activities that will make life happier, more meaningful, and more significant.

People cannot be expected to express a desire for an activity about which they know little or nothing and in which they have no skill. Folk dancing to one who has never experienced it, represents no compelling urge. The child who has never heard of aerial tennis will manifest no great interest in it nor any urgent desire to play it. People are not born with their leisure interests, but develop them as opportunities are presented and encouragement is given to learn new activities and acquire new skills. That which is of no interest when unknown frequently becomes an absorbing hobby when known.

Leaders who are content to limit their programs to activities in which children and adults already possess an interest are taking the path of least resistance leading to narrow, limited, sterile programs unworthy of themselves and unfair to their communities.

13. *Extreme discrepancies between the intelligence of potential leaders and their followers militate against the exercise of leadership.* A number of studies support the assumption that successful leaders are more intelligent than those they lead. However, the leader must not be too superior or the followers will reject him. Stogdill reports on an important study:

Hollingsworth found that "among children with a mean IQ of 100, the IQ of the leader is likely to fall between 115 and 130 IQ. That is, the leader is likely to be more intelligent, but not too much more intelligent than the average of the group led." Observation further showed that a child of 160 IQ has very little chance of being a popular leader in a group of children of average intelligence but may become a leader in a group of children with a mean IQ of 130. One of the difficulties in this connection seems to be concerned with communication. The average child cannot comprehend a large part of the vocabulary employed by a child of unusually superior intelligence to express exact meanings in relation to his more mature and complicated interests. Differences in interests, goals, and activity patterns also act as barriers to joint participation, which is a necessary condition for group leadership.[7]

Additional reasons why the highly intelligent individual may fail as a leader are:

---

[7] Stogdill, *op. cit.*, pp. 44–45.

1. He may not understand, appreciate, or exhibit sensitivity to the problems which concern the group.
2. The members of the group may resent his superiority because of the threat to their own egos. He gives them an inferiority complex.
3. He may leave the group because it is no longer rewarding to him.

A number of other studies support Hollingsworth's findings. Apparently, in a democracy, the group prefers to be led by the average man even though his leadership may be inferior to that which the more intelligent leader could provide. This, no doubt, throws light on what may have appeared to be questionable leadership choices within our own social, political, and professional groups over the years. It seems doubtful if geniuses would make good recreation leaders. Recreation administrators should consider the intelligence of their leaders when making assignments and attempt to match the most intelligent leaders with the most intelligent groups. Highly intelligent leaders who find themselves working with relatively unintelligent groups would do well not to make any unnecessary display of their superior intellectual talents.

14. *Leadership anticipates difficulties before they arise and acts to prevent them.* The successful leader, when planning any event, looks ahead, visualizes possibilities, anticipates, foresees, and predicts largely on the basis of past experience, his knowledge of human nature, and his ability to estimate degrees of probability. In terms of his anticipation he takes whatever action is necessary to prevent or mitigate the foreseen difficulty.

A few examples will illustrate the principle. A playground leader, thinking through problems involved in the issuance and care of supplies, foresees that some children will be forgetful while others will be dishonest. Hence, he is certain that an effective system of checking these supplies in and out must be established to prevent the loss of many valuable items. He does not wait until some equipment is lost and then take preventive measures; he anticipates this difficulty in advance of its occurrence and acts to prevent it. Another leader plans to take a group of young children on a trip from the playground to the zoo. He looks ahead and visualizes the possibility that some parents might wish to pick up their children at the playground while he has them at the zoo. So he sends a permission form home the day before the trip for the parents to sign.

A street dance to be held at night is planned by the playground leaders. Strings of light bulbs will be used to light the area. The leaders know that light bulbs have a tendency to burn out so they check all of them the day before the dance and provide a number of replacements in case some burn out during the dance. The woman leader realizes that a common type of accident among teen-age girl softball players is sprained or broken fingers caused by pointing the fingers directly toward the ball when attempting to catch it. She anticipates that such accidents may occur to her girls and instructs them carefully in advance of play how they should hold their hands while catching a ball.

15. *Leadership attempts to realize as large a return as possible on all facilities, activities, and services.* A group of boys is playing volleyball in a community center. One boy goes high in the air to spike the ball, but as he starts his jump his left hand brushes lightly the lower part of the net. The leader sees the foul, but the referee does not. The leader stops play, calls the boys around him, and tells them how the players on all the great volleyball teams in this country throw up a hand and call this kind of foul on themselves since no referee can possibly see it. He points out that volleyball is a game played by gentlemen who have developed an extremely high standard of ethical conduct, and that even in the national tournament this kind of moral behavior prevails. Under another leader who shuts his eyes to happenings of this nature a considerable amount of fun, exercise, and skill development may result from play; under this leader, in addition to fun, exercise, and skill, growth in moral behavior is taking place. One is satisfied with a 50 percent return on the investment by the recreation department; the other seeks 100 percent. This is the primary meaning of the principle in relation to activities.

With respect to facilities, the principle emphasizes the importance of utilizing school buildings for recreation purposes in the late afternoons, at night, and on Saturdays. It points to the desirability of lighting outdoor play areas so they may be used over a longer period of time. It raises this question in the minds of all leaders: How can I render more effective service so that the people of this community may receive the greatest possible return from their recreation investment?

16. *Leadership is based on continuous evaluation.* Evaluation is a process of determining the extent to which leadership has accomplished what it set out to accomplish. Evaluation begins with a statement of the goals to be sought and ends with an appraisal of the degree to which these goals have been realized. Evaluation is both a continuous and a coöperative process involving participation by all persons affected by the leadership. Without evaluation there is no way of determining whether leadership is good, poor, or mediocre; with evaluation, both strengths and weaknesses are discovered which is the first step toward the improvement of leadership.

The community which supports the recreation department has a proper concern that the program pays adequate dividends on its investment. The morale of the leaders will be much higher if they know that they are achieving results. Effective evaluation provides the solution to both problems.

THE LEADER AS A PROFESSIONAL MAN[8]

The leader has responsibilities not only to his followers, his department, and his community, but also to his profession. No occupation becomes a profession simply because those who engage in it call it a profession. An area of work achieves professional status only when it possesses certain specific characteristics just as a building becomes a house, not a barn, nor a gymnasium, nor an auditorium, only when it possesses certain unique features. Among the characteristics of a profession is the display of professional behavior, attitudes, and workmanship by its practitioners. In the final analysis, the public judges a profession by what it knows about the members of this profession. Just as no code of honor will work unless there are honorable men to make it work, so there can be no profession unless there are members who exhibit the characteristics of professional men.

The professional leader is motivated primarily by ideals of service rather than by money. He is in recreation because he loves it and he would not be in any other type of work even if he could be. He believes that people, not activities or facilities, are the most important thing in the world and that the basic purpose of recreation is to enrich the lives of people. He judges the worth of an activity and everything he does in terms of its effect on people. If it hurts people the activity is bad; if it enriches the lives of people it is good. Since people are the most important thing in the world, the professional man respects all human beings and is interested in their welfare. In all his relationships with people, he treats them as he would like to be treated. He is friendly and he likes people.

He is an educated man who has undergone a prolonged period of preparation for his work. Not only is he educated with respect to what should be done in recreation and how to do it; he also knows why. He knows the values which should be sought through recreation in a democracy, and he is deeply committed to democratic ideals and values. He seeks constantly to improve himself professionally. He knows that education is a continuous process which is never ended, so he reads constantly and attends professional meetings in an attempt to keep abreast of new discoveries in the sciences which underlie his field of work. He knows that no man is well educated in his particular field unless he is conversant

---

[8] This section with minor alterations first appeared as follows: Howard G. Danford, "The Marks of a Professional Man in Recreation," *Journal of Health, Physical Education, and Recreation,* November, 1960, p. 31.

with the fields that are closely related to his own. Therefore, he seeks to understand and appreciate the work of his professional colleagues in education, health education, physical education, sociology, psychology, and others. Not only does the professional man attempt to master a body of knowledge, he also seeks to contribute what he can to this body of knowledge through research, writing articles or books, and in any other way he can.

He voluntarily joins his professional societies or associations, pays his dues, attends meetings, and contributes both time and energy to furthering the work of his profession and elevating its standards. When he accepts membership on a professional committee he contributes to the work of this committee to the best of his ability.

He conducts himself at all times in such a manner as to enhance the prestige and dignity of his profession. He knows that people judge a profession by the individuals who are in it and that undignified conduct on his part will hurt his profession in the eyes of the public. His professional life and conduct are regulated by a code of behavior based on moral and ethical principles. He spreads no malicious gossip about his professional colleagues nor does he engage in the practice of attacking persons in related areas of work.

The professional man seeks to exclude from the profession those who are not qualified to enter it. He is interested in the exercise by the state, or by the profession itself, or by both, of some form of control over who may enter into the most responsible recreation positions. He wants no quacks, frauds, or unfit individuals in the profession.

He is a team player, not a prima donna. He prefers coöperation as a way of life. He works with all agencies and individuals in the community on matters of common concern. He recognizes that many groups or agencies in a community have a stake in recreation and that he holds no divine charter from above granting him an exclusive monopoly on public recreation. He is not characterized by professional jealousy nor by an all-absorbing desire for credit. He is motivated primarily by the ideal of public service and he understands that credit for what he does is much more likely to come as a by-product of good work than when it is sought directly.

He insists on high standards of excellence in his work; he is not satisfied with mediocrity but is constantly working to upgrade his professional performance. A professional person is curious, welcomes new ideas, experiments, creates, originates, and is never quite satisfied with things as they are. He is motivated by a spark of discontent with what has been and what is now. He seeks perfection although he never quite achieves it, for when a person believes he has achieved perfection he no longer possesses this important quality of the professional man. He does not ridicule new ideas but welcomes them, studies them, and, if they are good, adopts them whenever possible.

And finally, the professional man in recreation enjoys life. He has fun; he is no stuffed shirt, no kill-joy. For how can he lead others in joyous living if he doesn't live joyously himself? But he does not forget that the public will respect his profession and accord to it the dignity and status it should have only when its members conduct themselves in such a manner as to merit respect.

A CALL TO GREATNESS

Transcending in importance all other needs in recreation today is the imperative need of superior leadership. The contributions of a recreation department to the life of a community will rise no higher than the quality of its leaders. Potentially, leisure, as in ancient Greece, is an opportunity for greatness; time in which to live life at its fullest; time to fashion a new Golden Age as our people channel their creative energies into cultural pursuits that ennoble both the individual and the nation; time to join with others in community activities that elevate the tenor of human relationships and strengthen our democratic society.

If our people are to meet successfully the challenge which leisure makes to the human spirit, the individual who plans and directs these leisure programs must be something more than a play leader, an athlete, or a part-time employee whose primary interest is in some area other than recreation. He must understand leisure and its problems in the light of history and its role in American culture. He must have a sense of the mission of recreation in a democratic society. He must be far more concerned with the achievement of social, moral, and ethical values than with methods and techniques, except as they lead to these ends.

Since he will lead others in cultural activities, he must be a cultured individual himself. It will be a part of his task to instruct people in skills, understandings, and appreciations, therefore, he must be an educator. He can be effective in his leadership role only as he understands human behavior, and for this reason he must become a psychologist. His responsibilities will include understanding and influencing the social forces which affect society as well as working coöperatively with other agencies and groups in the community, so he must assume the role of a sociologist. He is a philosopher, because the values in which he so deeply believes guide his every action.

There are not many leaders of this high quality in the field of recreation today, but the number is growing constantly. No profession ever came into being fully grown. Each had its lowly beginnings and gradually over the years achieved mature professional status by paying a price in terms of standards elevated through intensive study, hard work, and self-discipline. Above all, competent personnel render a distinctive and extremely valuable social function in the community. Leadership in recreation is climbing the ladder of professional status in America. It has come a long way since the inception of the recreation movement. As the quality of leadership improves, society will recognize the increasing social significance of its work, thus enabling it to complete with even greater facility the long climb ahead.

Selected References

Bass, Bernard M., *Leadership, Psychology, and Organizational Behavior* (New York: Harper and Brothers, 1960).

Cartwright, Dorwin and Zander, Alvin, *Group Dynamics* (White Plains, N.Y.: Row, Peterson and Company, 1953).

Corbin, A. Dan, *Recreation Leadership* (2nd ed.) (Englewood Cliffs, N.J.: Prentice-Hall, Inc., 1959).

Gardner, John W., *Excellence* (New York: Harper and Brothers, 1961).

Gordon, Thomas, *Group-Centered Leadership* (Boston: Houghton Mifflin Company, 1955).

Jennings, Eugene E., *An Anatomy of Leadership* (New York: Harper and Brothers, 1960).

Kraus, Richard, *Recreation Today: Program Planning and Leadership* (New York: Appleton-Century-Crofts, 1966).

Liveright, A. A., *Strategies of Leadership* (New York: Harper and Brothers, 1959).

Robinson, F. Willard, "Moral Aspects of Educational Leadership," *The Clearing House,* 34, No. 7, 1960, p. 387.

Ross, Murray G. and Hendry, Charles E., *New Understandings of Leadership* (New York: Association Press, 1957).

Stogdill, Ralph M., "Personal Factors Associated with Leadership: A Survey of the Literature," *The Journal of Psychology,* 25, 1948, p. 35.

Vannier, Maryhelen, *Methods and Materials in Recreation Leadership* (Belmont, Calif.: Wadsworth Publishing Company, Inc., 1966).

White, Ralph K. and Lippitt, Ronald, *Autocracy and Democracy* (New York: Harper and Brothers, 1960).

Wriston, Henry M., "The Individual in a Conformist Society," *Overview, I,* No. 12, 1969, p. 48.

Chapter VI

The Road to Values

A LEADER IS TEACHING a group of children to play a simple game of tag. The children play for the fun of it, but the leader seeks two additional values or goals: (1) the biological objective of fitness promoted through vigorous running; and (2) strengthening the moral fiber of the children by teaching them to tell the truth when they are tagged. Fun, fitness, and morality are the ends; the game of tag is the means. The superior leader never confuses ends and means, but he recognizes their inviolable connection.

A number of questions arise at this point. Why was tag chosen? Was it chosen by the leader, by the children, or by both? Should the values a leader seeks determine the program, or are other factors involved also? What are these factors? Could the goals of fun, fitness, and morality have been realized just as effectively through other activities as through tag? Are all activities equal in value? If not, how can you tell which activities harbor which values? When certain specific values reside in an activity do they automatically accrue to those who participate in the activity? Are there any guides that will aid a leader in developing programs of high quality for his community?

These questions and their answers lie at the heart of the leadership problem as it relates to the development of programs of recreation in American communities today. The leader must gain a deeper insight into the possibilities of recreation as a contributor to those higher values which enrich the lives of human beings in a democratic nation. The primary purpose of this chapter is to shed light upon establishing important values in regard to the above questions.

THE PROGRAM AS THE MEANS

The program of a recreation department is more than just a list of recreation activities in which people engage. Rather, it consists of all the organized leisure experiences provided by the department through which its leaders seek to achieve the goals deemed worthwhile by the department. The program, therefore, is to be conceived as including, in addition to the customary recreation pursuits, all of the coöperative activities which both youth and adults share with leaders while planning and operating their own recreation. Thus, included within the meaning of the term "program" will be such experiences as serving on the playground safety patrol, the community center council, or the executive committee of the youth recreation association; acting as a volunteer official for playground softball games; issuing supplies; serving as a member of the softball commission; and contributing one's time and energies to the many forms of civic activity through which the patrons of a recreation department may render service to their community.

Activities are means. They should be selected and conducted by leaders for the specific purpose of achieving certain values in which the department, the community, and the participants believe. This implies that leadership should be clear in the identification of its goals, careful in its selection of activities through which these goals are to be reached, and effective in the methods by which the activities are conducted.

THE INEQUALITY OF ACTIVITIES

If every leisure activity had equal value, the problem of program planning would be a relatively simple one. The leader could reach blindly into a grabbag of interests or activities and, regardless of what he came up with, the results still would add up to a desirable program. But activities are no more equal in value than men are equal in wealth or intelligence. The tendency to activity is a fundamental characteristic of human beings, but the expression of this characteristic takes various forms. The individual may find outlets for his drive to action that run the gamut of human possibilities from those pursuits which are illegal or antisocial in nature to those which result in physical, mental, or moral deterioration; then on up the scale of values to a wide variety of activities which, although perhaps not harmful, nevertheless, are trivial and useless; and, finally, at the top of the ladder are those activities of highest quality and value which contribute both to the individual and society and are measurable in terms of the extent to which they help meet basic human needs and further the development of democratic human relationships.

A complicating factor here is the extent to which an activity may be of high value to one individual and of lesser value or even harmful to another. A vigorous game of basketball may be very worthwhile for a healthy teen-ager and quite dangerous to a man of forty-five who is out of condition. Touch football for boys possesses considerably more value than it does for girls. A play may be high on the scale of values for a mature adult group, but unfit for immature adolescents. Thus, we see that any attempt to classify activities in terms of values must involve consideration of individual differences in human beings.

A most important task of the leader is to work with others in selecting the good and rejecting the bad. He will have no difficulty eliminating illegal activities from the program because the law tells him what is bad. How is he to judge, however, the relative merits of the literally thousands of available leisure activities among which a discriminating choice must be made? Where can he discover guidelines by which he can find his way out of this dark jungle of thousands of activities good, bad, and useless to the broad uplands of intelligent selection? Before attempting to answer this question, let us see what mistakes in program planning many leaders have made in the past so that we may learn from their errors.

UNSOUND APPROACHES TO PROGRAM PLANNING

The leader may look to the past for answers to his questions. What shall be the program on our playground? Let's find out what the program has been for the past several years and do the same things. No effort is made to appraise the worth of an activity in terms of values sought. What has been is right. This is known as the *traditional* approach to program building. Its major weaknesses reside in its blind devotion to the past, its failure to utilize in the continual improvement of the recreation program the growing fund of knowledge from the behavioral sciences, and its disregard of the basic obligation of all social institutions to change as the needs of the time and place change.

If the leader visits other playgrounds to find out what their programs are and decides to follow their lead, he is utilizing the *current practice* approach. Do what the others do! Two grave weaknesses invalidate this approach: (1) what others are doing may be wrong; and (2) even if what they are doing is right for their communities, it may not be right for his.

A third approach to program construction involves finding out what the people want to do and then letting them do it. Pass out a checklist of many possible activities, ask the people to check those in which they are interested, and build your program around these activities. Surely this makes sense. Give the people what they want! This is the *expressed desires* approach to the development of a program. Reasonable though it appears (and it does have value), it cannot be accepted as a thoroughly sound technique of program building because: (1) the recreation interests and desires of people are limited by their experiences; and (2) one of the most important functions of leadership is to lead the people from where they are into new interests and new activities which enrich life beyond anything they have ever known before.

A fourth approach to program construction is the *authoritarian* approach. When the superintendent of recreation and his assistants or supervisors make all decisions with respect to activities and send out this uniform program to their leaders in somewhat the same manner as the Lord handed down the Ten Commandments to Moses, the authoritarian technique is being employed. Or, when the leader denies to his followers any opportunity to share in program building, the same criticism applies. If the recreation personnel possessed the wisdom of the Lord no criticism of this technique would be admissible. Since they do not, its weaknesses are found in its faulty assumptions that: (1) all wisdom resides in the recreation staff, and (2) that uniformity is a desirable characteristic of recreation programs.

It should be pointed out that none of these approaches is wholly valueless. If an activity has proved to be successful in the past it may still have value for the present; that which is operating effectively in a neighboring city has proved its workability; unless people are interested in the activities you offer they will not come to your playgrounds or community centers, thus denying you an opportunity to lead them into new interests; and program decisions made by members of the recreation staff are based upon years of experience, observation, and education. Nevertheless, after granting these approaches their full measure of possible strength, their weaknesses are so numerous and grave as to cause their rejection as a major form of guidance by professionally-minded leaders.

If these approaches are not wholly reliable, where do we find our guides? We should be satisfied with nothing less than excellence in program because: (1) it is the major reason why people come to our centers; (2) important values cannot accrue from poor programs; and (3) great harm may be done both to the community and to the cause of recreation by ill-advised activities. A further reason exists why students of recreation should be greatly concerned over the quality of the leisure experience provided by recreation departments. Despite the outstanding achievements by a number of individual cities, and signs of broad public interest in the improvement of programs in many others, it must be admitted that much of public recreation is extraordinarily poor. Many of the activities are exceedingly inane. Many of the dramatic, musical, arts and crafts, dance, and sports activities are poorly chosen, unrelated to values, improperly conducted, and inadequately evaluated. Musselman reports representatives of Utah saying, "We offer children a tremendous flurry of very dead stuff."[1] And yet, there is no reason why we should be satisfied with mediocrity in program. Leaders cannot go too far beyond the interests and experiences of the people with whom they work, but the superior leader will reject the cheap and common and seek to cultivate the tastes of his followers for excellence in all that they do.

FORCES AND INFLUENCES
AFFECTING THE PROGRAM

Recreation programs are shaped and fashioned by a variety of forces and influences and no leader can function effectively in his role as program planner unless he is aware of these forces and operates in harmony with them. Some of the most important are presented briefly.

Increase in Leisure

As the people of a community gain more leisure, programs of recreation must be expanded to meet their needs. In 1850 the average work week for farmers and laborers was approximately seventy hours. By 1950 it had dropped to forty hours and the prediction for 1975 is thirty-two hours. At the conclusion of a twelve-hour day the average individual had neither the time nor energy for much recreation. An eight-hour day supplemented by two complete days of leisure each weekend provides both time and energy for extensive participation in recreation. The recreation program must reflect this continual growth of leisure. There seems little

---

[1] Virginia Musselman, "Ten Challenges to Program," *Recreation*, December 1960, p. 468.

doubt that while the quality of our programs may reasonably be expected to improve, the primary difference between the program of today and that of tomorrow will be a matter of quantity and greater variety.

The Growth of Cities

Within the past century the United States has been transformed from a predominantly rural people to a nation of city dwellers. In 1860, only one out of five persons was included in our urban population; in 1960, this figure had increased to 69.9 percent. From 1950 to 1960, the total population increase for the nation was 18.4 percent, but the urban population increase was 26.4 percent as contrasted with a rural population increase of only 8.3 percent. In 1960, the urban population which constituted nearly 70 percent of the total population was concentrated on slightly more than one percent of the land area of the country.[2]

In its implications to program planning in recreation, this concentration of our people in cities equals or exceeds in importance any single force or influence existing on the American scene and, for this reason, must be examined at some length.

The city, like most creations of man, is neither all good nor all bad. Its advantages, many and varied, need not be recounted here. Many of its evils, however, have become so malignant and so chronic as to threaten the foundations of our democratic society. Its leaders understand these evils and the part which recreation can, and should, play in counteracting them; they will then be enabled to shape their programs accordingly.

Down through the ages the spotlight of history has been focused upon the rise of various cities to greatness, revealing the brilliance of their cultural contributions to civilization, and then depicting the tragedy of their deterioration, decay, and disappearance from the center of the world's stage. Among the best known instances are Babylon, Athens, Rome, Memphis, Carthage, Syracuse, and Timbuctoo. Patrick Geddes, more than a generation ago, traced the rise and fall of cities through six stages. The first stage is the rise of the village community. The second, which he called "Polis" is characterized by "civic unity and common vision of life symbolized in Temple or Cathedral." In the third stage, signs of weakness put in an appearance. The tendency toward individualism threatens to disrupt old social bonds.

---

[2] *United States Census of Population, 1960, Number of Inhabitants* (Washington: U. S. Department of Commerce, Bureau of the Census, 1961), p. xiv. These figures relate only to conterminous areas of the United States.

Then comes the fourth stage in the life of cities which marks the beginning of the decline. Among its characteristics are a concentration upon bigness and power, standardization, weakening of the moral sense, bureaucratism, failure of direct action, lack of a common life and participation in activities directed at a common goal, and diversion of energy from the making of a life to the making of a living. The fourth merges into the fifth stage which is marked by widespread moral apathy, disappearance of a sense of civic responsibility, and a tendency on the part of each group and each individual to ignore completely the common good and to take for itself whatever it can get away with. The sixth, and final, stage pictures the death scene of the city.

Looming high among the inherent weaknesses of the city is a breakdown in community life. There is nothing complicated or mystifying about what constitutes a good community. In a good community people do things together. There are numerous opportunities for associations. Associations are the life of a community. Without them life is barren and drab.

The people are friendly in the good community. They enjoy a common social life. A generation ago everyone in the community, regardless of age or economic status, went to the ice cream socials, church suppers, spelling bees, picnics, band concerts, and harvest festivals. Entire families took part, and the banker rubbed shoulders with the blacksmith, the teacher with the farmer, and the laborer with the executive. Today, in our cities, community life, in many instances, has almost completely vanished. One of man's major tragedies is his lack of involvement and concern in matters that affect the community at large.

People in cities suffer from social isolation. They are physically near but socially distant. The life blood of a community and of human society is widespread participation in a meaningful, purposive group life characterized by an emotional quality compounded of friendliness, social responsibility, mutual confidence, and a feeling of oneness.

It is imperative, therefore, that every effort be made by the recreation leader, joined with others equally concerned with the welfare of the nation and with the improvement of living, to do everything in his power to put together again our disintegrated communities. If the essence of community life is associating in constructive activities of common concern, then programs must include these activities through which the bonds of friendship and of mutual understanding may be strengthened. Many of the walls which set people apart and create friction and ill-will, such as differences of race, religion, economic and social status, and education can be broken down through community singing, dancing, clubs, arts and crafts, drama, social recreation, and other activities which emphasize coöperation, friendliness, and a sense of oneness. Every effort, also, must be made to compensate for the lack of open spaces for vigorous participation in activities yielding biological results. The program must reflect this need by an emphasis upon vigorous activities that can be carried on in community centers, playgrounds, gymnasiums, and even in backyards and the home.

Thus, leaders may catch a vision of themselves as social engineers making a most significant contribution to the revitalization of community life in the urban areas of the nation.

Changes in Population

Since programs are planned for people, any major change in population is certain to influence a well-planned recreation program. Changes, other than urbanization, include total growth in population; changes in the number of persons in, and the proportion of, certain age groups to the total population; mobility; and population shifts.

If the rate of increase in total population which prevailed during the past decade continues throughout the 1960's, recreation leaders in 1970 must plan programs for approximately 33 million more people. In the spring of 1968 the U.S. Census Bureau recognized officially that the United States is a nation of 200 million individuals. Furthermore, there is every indication that increased emphasis must be placed upon meeting the needs of older persons who are comprising an ever-greater proportion of the population. In 1966 there were more than 18 million people in the United States who were sixty-five years of age or older. It is estimated that this age group will number approximately 25 million by the early 1970's. Women will increasingly outnumber men at older age levels. In 1960 there were one hundred aged females for every eighty-three males aged sixty-five years and over.

Not only will the number and proportion of the aged increasingly affect recreation programs, but the growing trend toward retirement for men at sixty-five has important implications. Tibbitts and Donahue report that in 1850 only 5 percent of men sixty-five and over had retired from work; this figure increased to 35 percent in 1900; to 55 percent in 1950; and the authors predict it will reach 70 percent in 1975.[3]

Population shifts both in mass and in terms of individuals affect recreation programs. A general population shift westward has been taking

---

[3] Clark Tibbitts and Wilma Donahue, eds., *Aging in Today's Society* (Englewood Cliffs, N.J.: Prentice-Hall, Inc., 1960), p. 16.

place ever since we became a nation. The center of population, during the past century, has shifted from south-central Ohio to south-central Illinois, a distance of approximately 350 miles. Then, too, Americans are a mobile people, moving frequently within cities, from city to city, and from state to state. In March, 1958, nearly three million people had moved from one of the main geographical areas of the United States to another within the preceding twelve months.[4] The newcomer in a community frequently feels and is treated as an "outsider" with damaging psychological effects both to children and adults. Leaders should plan programs designed to introduce these newcomers to others in the community and create in them a feeling of acceptance and belonging. An increase in services to suburban areas will no doubt take place in the future as greater numbers move out from congested city areas and as the legislation needed to make these services possible is enacted.

Environmental Factors

Programs must be planned for specific situations. These situations may differ in many respects. The differences determine in large degree both the scope and nature of the program. For example, a winter recreation program for a city in the Colorado Rockies will include skiing and ice skating, but these activities will not be offered in a southern Florida community.

Among the environmental factors of greatest significance to leaders planning programs are the following:

1. *Natural Resources.* The extent of a community's natural resources is a measure of its wealth. Poverty-stricken communities cannot afford extensive programs of recreation and their residents generally do not have the time, the interests, or the desire to participate.
2. *Climate.* Both the quantity and the quality of recreation programs are influenced by climate. In many southern communities outdoor playground programs are conducted on a year-round basis while in the north these give way to ice skating, skiing, ice boating, ice hockey, and numerous indoor activities within community centers. Anyone who has ever visited a playground in the south during July or August is well aware of the effect of heat upon program. In the middle of the afternoon checkers in the shade is far more likely to be observed than a fast game of basketball.

[4] Interdepartmental Committee on Children and Youth, *Children in a Changing World* (Washington, D.C.: White House Conference on Children and Youth, 1960), p. 7.

3. *Geography.* In Florida, a state with many thousands of lakes, recreation will include boating, sailing, canoeing, water skiing, swimming, and fishing. Less emphasis will be placed upon these activities in Nevada. A large and enthusiastic mountain climbing club is active on the University of Colorado campus, but none exists at the University of Florida. Mountains, lakes, oceans, rivers, forests, plains— all influence the recreation program.

4. *Population Distribution.* One aspect of this factor, urbanization, already has been discussed at some length. A recreation program in a sparsely settled region will be different from one in a metropolitan area. There will be less of it in the first place. It is probable that enough chess players reside within six blocks of one another in Milwaukee to form an active chess club. In certain desert or mountainous regions of our nation attempts to organize a similar club would be ludicrous.

5. *Facilities.* Facilities are an influence of vital importance. Programs cannot be conducted in a vacuum. If you have a swimming pool, you can operate a swimming program. Tennis courts, gymnasiums, bowling alleys, handball, volleyball, and horseshoe courts, playgrounds, ball diamonds, auditoriums, shops, dance floors, archery ranges, and hockey rinks are all forces which shape the recreation program. Even in the operation of as simple an activity as an hour-long program of social recreation for twenty teen-age boys and girls, the leader must select those activities that can best be conducted with the available facilities. If, for example, chairs are bolted to the floor and cannot be moved, this one fact alone will determine the choice of many activities.

War and the Threat of War

Throughout human history war has been a powerful force in shaping the destiny of mankind. An outstanding example is the degree to which war influenced every aspect of life in ancient Sparta. All education was aimed solely at producing an effective warrior. The national ideal revolved about courage, endurance, martial skills, and the willingness to die for the nation. This concentrated, almost fanatical, devotion by the entire nation to a single goal was induced by the situation in which the Spartans found themselves—a relatively small nation surrounded by enemies who constantly threatened its survival. Unfortunately, where the challenge of survival has taken precedence over all other values, as was true in Sparta, the cultural life of a nation is smothered by its efforts simply to keep alive.

For the first time in the history of the world man now possesses the power to destroy human life completely. From now on we Americans must live in a world in which the threat of total extinction hangs over us like the sword of Damocles, perilous, grim, unremitting. The need of recreation to bring a measure of relaxation in a tension-ridden world certainly will increase. The imperative need for fitness which has characterized every nation threatened by war will bring about a more careful selection of activities designed to produce improvements in both physical and mental health. It is quite probable also that recreation programs will place greater emphasis upon survival activities in the out-of-doors. But of even greater importance than any of these emphases is the challenge to intensify the devotion of our people to democracy, to expand the potential fulfillment of the individual, to strengthen his moral fiber, and to elevate the quality of human relationships. It is only when men have learned to live together that the threat of war will vanish from the earth. There is no higher goal to which the recreation leaders of America can dedicate themselves.

Advances in Science and Technology

Industrialization, mechanization, and automation must be considered vital forces affecting recreation in America. Science expressed in terms of the industrial arts, or technology, has elevated our material standard of living far beyond that of any other nation. It is chiefly responsible for the leisure we possess. The machine has been the great liberator, freeing us from a life of drudgery, and giving to us a multitude of *things* many of which complicate our lives and possess the power both to enrich and to impoverish us. The automobile, as an illustration, may be used to take us on fishing trips, to the mountains for skiing, to the golf course, to the community center, and on trips to our magnificent national parks. On the other hand, it is an instrument of death which annually slaughters between 40 and 50 thousand Americans and it has contributed materially to the softening of our people.

Television sets in 65 million American homes have brought the entire world into our living rooms, broadening our interests, deepening our appreciations, often stimulating reading, travel, and the development of hobbies, opening cultural doors hitherto closed, and creating an exciting sense of participation in the affairs of the world. Television, however, absorbs 2.6 billion man-hours per week compared with a total of 1.9 billion man-hours per week devoted to all productive economic activities in our country. The average person watches television over twenty hours a week.[5] Many of the programs are poor in quality, emphasizing crime, sex,

[5] Max Kaplan, *Leisure in America* (New York: John Wiley and Sons, Inc., 1960), p. 222.

and violence; they blunt sensibilities, drain away energies, present distorted and perverted views of life, intensify boredom, exert a pernicious influence on children, and further contribute to the softness of the nation.

Improving Economic Conditions

Not only has family income been rising steadily during recent years—in 1967 the median family income nationwide stood at a healthy $8,000—but family spending patterns show higher levels of living according to a White House Conference report:[6]

In 1901 the average city family had to spend about 80 percent of its income on food, housing, and clothing, and had only 20 percent left for all other items. Even with the increased cost of living, the average city family in the last decade has been able to pay for its food, housing, and clothing with less than 60 percent of its income, leaving more than 40 percent for other things.

The incomes of people affect the recreation program in a number of ways. The great increase in the number of golfers within the past quarter of a century is attributable in large part to the fact that more people can afford to play golf today. The same is true of increased participation in horseback riding, both snow and water skiing, motor boating, photography, skin diving, travel, and many other activities.

Higher personal incomes generally mean a larger budget for the recreation department and also permit it to offer more activities for which a fee may be charged, such as golf and adult education classes. On the other hand, in a wealthy community, participation in public recreation programs often is reduced as people build their own residential swimming pools, join private golf clubs, develop their own backyard playgrounds, and go on lengthy vacations.

The Impact of Education

The extent to which the schools educate, or fail to educate, students for leisure through the development of skills, interests, and appreciations is a major influence on the recreation program. Let us cite just one illustration. If, in a certain community, the city supervisor of physical education persuades all of the men on his junior and senior high school staffs to emphasize the teaching of volleyball on a high level, organizes interschool

---

[6] Interdepartmental Committee on Children and Youth, op. cit., p. 15.

competition, issues varsity letters as for any other sport on the interscholastic program, publicizes the games in the newspapers and over television and radio, and enhances the prestige of the players in every possible manner, the recreation leaders, within a few years, can develop a broad program of volleyball for men and boys. They cannot do it without the support of the schools since leisure choices, skills, and attitudes are dependent very largely upon education.

Specialization and Interdependence

We live in the most highly specialized and interdependent society the world has ever known. The leader needs to understand how these two facts are interrelated and what they mean to the development of a recreation program.

In the days of George Washington the average man could do many things well. He might be a combination farmer, blacksmith, carpenter, weaver, statesman, author, amateur veterinarian, butcher, and cook. As a result, he was not dependent to any great degree upon anyone else. Today the situation is changed entirely. In medicine, for example, the general practitioner has been largely displaced by the specialist who may be a pediatrician, urologist, internist, gynecologist, cardiologist, dermatologist, endocrinologist, or any one of several other specialties.

Today a man is a teacher, a salesman, a lawyer, a steelworker, an elevator operator, a merchant, a farmer, a railroad engineer, or a bus driver. The more specialized he becomes the less he has in common with other men and the more dependent he is upon others.

Our society has become so complex and our people so dependent upon one another that small groups of workers in key industries can injure millions of their countrymen simply by not working. If the steelworkers go on strike today, you and I are affected tomorrow. The behavior of an individual is no longer simply his own concern. It concerns all of us. Everytime we drive our car we place our lives in the hands of other drivers. Our welfare and our safety rest not solely upon ourselves, but equally upon the good judgment, skill, coöperation, and understanding of others. There are no unimportant people in our interdependent society.

Common interests, common concerns, and common experiences are essential to weld together a society threatened by disintegration arising out of specialization. Another danger exists in the fact that the greater the degree of specialization the less will man have an opportunity to exercise all his talents while on the job.

Three emphases are indicated for the program of recreation: (1)

activities involving teamwork, coöperation, and sharing should be stressed and leaders should make every effort to strengthen the qualities essential to success, among which concern for the welfare of others and coöperation rank high; (2) activities should be conducted which attract people from all walks of life, cutting across lines of specialization and class stratification, creating warm social climates, and emphasizing friendliness and goodwill; and (3) leadership should encourage individuals to participate as informed and responsible citizens in helping to solve the social, economic, and political problems of their community, state, and nation.

Alienation of Youth from the General Culture

In the early days of our nation a boy became a man with all of the responsibilities and the respect accorded to such a role, at a much earlier age than is the case today. Forced now by society to remain children over a longer period of time with no vital role to play, youth in many instances have rebelled and created a subculture in conflict with adult culture. Goodman raises a pertinent question:[7]

During childhood, they played games with fierce intensity, giving themselves as a sacrifice to the game, for play was the chief business of growth, finding-and-making themselves in the world. Now when they are too old merely to play, to what shall they give themselves with fierce intensity?

Sorenson suggests a partial answer by discontented youth: "Juvenile delinquency is, in part, a protest, subconscious and inarticulate, against a society which gives to the rising generation no role which absorbs its energies and focuses its aims."[8]

A recreation department, as a social institution, has a direct obligation to help induct youth into the adult society and leaders should plan activities with this end in view. It is not an easy task to provide opportunities for youth to take some important part in a society that does not need them. Whatever is done must have real significance and purpose for youth are quick to sense pretense and superficiality. Some years ago, in Madison, Wisconsin, the park department acquired additional park acreage and requested assistance in planting a number of trees. The Youth Council mobilized the youth of the city who carried out the project with great enthusiasm. The boys did most of the heavy labor while the girls

---

[7] Paul Goodman, "Youth in the Organized Society," *Commentary,* February 1960, p. 104.

[8] Roy Sorenson, "Directions for the Future," *Recreation,* November 1960, p. 441.

provided food for the famished workers. In addition to many similar
activities of a community service nature, which Albert Schweitzer calls
"adventures in self-sacrifice," youth should be encouraged to share responsibilities with recreation leaders in planning and conducting their own
programs of recreation.

Changes in Family Life

More than 25 million women are employed today of whom 60 percent
are married. Four out of every ten have children of school age. Since
the wife seldom works at the same place as her husband and the children
are excluded from the work phase of their parents' lives, the family
solidarity must come from common activities engaged in during leisure.
Frequently the modern home has become a hotel, a point of departure
from which members of the family disperse to their separate groups and
activities, returning only to sleep. Commercialized recreation has increased
at the expense of former family functions in this area. Recreation departments often contribute to the separating of families by conducting activities on strictly an age basis. If family nights are held, the family may
arrive and depart as a unit, but participation is by age groups or the
parents are entertained by the children.

The desirability of family recreation, within limits, rests primarily
upon these facts: (1) it contributes to family solidarity; (2) provides vital
experiences in the lives of children which profoundly affect their developing sense of adequacy; (3) establishes desirable attitudes toward recreation
as a part of the good life; (4) enables parents to achieve a greater depth
of understanding of their children and a more significant level of comradeship with them.

Leaders should provide many activities that will help to bring
members of the family closer together. Some of the most effective means
are family night programs in which the entire family plays together,
father-and-son and mother-and-daughter projects, games, picnics, hobbies,
fishing, boating, horseback riding, and hiking. Family memberships in golf
clubs and similar organizations should be encouraged.

Advisory services should be provided for parents interested in developing backyard playgrounds, and mimeographed or printed plans should
be made available giving detailed information on the construction of
facilities for such activities as shuffleboard, horseshoes, badminton, croquet
golf, loop and paddle tennis, box hockey, outdoor fireplaces, and homemade
games. Many recreation departments have conducted social recreation

courses for parents, emphasizing activities that can be played in the home by the family.

All good things, however, can be overdone, including family recreation. "Togetherness," like perfection, palls on an individual if he gets too much of it. Appreciation for one another can be developed by permitting each member of the family a certain measure of privacy and freedom. Parents who try to assume the role of "pal" with their children, according to Stone and Church, are making a serious mistake. ". . . there is no sight more pathetic than a father or mother trying to be a 'pal' to son or daughter (not that there is any lack of things they can enjoy doing together). But there are plenty of peers around to serve as pals, and the child needs his parents as parents—which means as adults and not as pseudo-children."[9]

Increasing Emphasis on Health and Fitness

Many factors have focused the attention of the American people upon the need for health and fitness to a greater degree than ever before in our history. These factors include: (1) an increased awareness of the softening effects of sedentary living upon the health and vitality of the nation; (2) a growing concern over the magnitude of the mental health problem; (3) implications of the extraordinarily high proportion of men rejected under Selective Service Act examinations; (4) the threat of war and its corollary, the need for fitness; (5) an expanding body of evidence derived from clinical observations and experimental studies pointing to definite health values in exercise and other forms of recreation; and (6) widespread dissemination of information by leaders on the national scene warning the people of the need for recreation and urging appropriate action.

All the ills which plague Americans cannot be solved through recreation, but many of them can be alleviated by a more intelligent use of leisure. Leaders should welcome this emphasis and utilize it as a stimulus to greater participation in vigorous activities contributing to fitness. In the transformation of the American people from a nation of spectators at athletic contests to a nation of participants in the vigorous life, recreation leaders must play a dominant role.

---

[9] L. Joseph Stone and Joseph Church, *Childhood and Adolescence* (New York: Random House, 1957), p. 223.

Forces Generated by New Insights from Research

As research in the behavioral sciences provides us with deeper insights into the nature of human beings, programs are being modified in light of these new understandings. Gordon's study of adolescent social behavior in the high school is an example of this type of research. This study revealed that the dominant motivation impelling adolescent youth to join student organizations was a desire for status. Therefore, they sought admission into the organization or organizations which ranked highest in the prestige hierarchy of the school's social system.[10]

All the implications of this excellent study cannot be explored here, but it does point to the absolute necessity for leaders to invest some of their activities for youth with status value otherwise they may discover a complete lack of interest.

A number of recent studies indicate that the class position of an individual in society is a definite factor in his choice of leisure activities. Reissman reports that the upper-class people "read more books and magazines, attend church more frequently, belong to more organizations, and more often hold office in those organizations"[11] than do people in lower-class positions regardless of whether position be measured by occupation, income, or education.

A study by White adds to the evidence that the uses of leisure are conditioned by social class. He states:[12]

The upper middle class selects libraries, home diversions, and lecture-study groups more often than other classes, whereas the two lowest classes use parks and playgrounds, community chest agencies, church, museums, and commercial entertainment relatively more often.

He concludes, "It is clear that the tendency to choose leisure activities on the grounds of membership in a particular social class begins in adolescence and becomes more pronounced in maturity."[13]

The superior leader will keep abreast of the most important research in recreation and use the findings for the continual improvement of his program.

[10] C. Wayne Gordon, *The Social System of the High School*. Glencoe, Ill.: The Free Press, 1957, p. 131.

[11] Leonard Reissman, "Class, Leisure, and Social Participation," *American Sociological Review*, February 1954, p. 83.

[12] R. Clyde White, "Social Class Differences in the Uses of Leisure," *The American Journal of Sociology*, September 1955, p. 145.

[13] *Ibid.*, p. 150.

We have discussed the major forces and influences which affect the recreation programs in this nation. A thorough knowledge of these forces is essential if the leader is to construct and operate an effective program for any situation. Still further assistance must be provided the leader, however, if he is to answer intelligently some of the questions raised on the first page of this chapter and other questions of equal importance. Who should select the activities for the program? What should be the nature of the activities? How shall their worth be judged? These and many other problems can best be solved by leaders using as their guides to thought and action a few fundamental, guiding principles of program planning.

PRINCIPLES OF PROGRAM PLANNING

Twelve basic principles which appear to possess greatest value for leaders planning programs are now presented. They are based upon facts derived from the nature of human beings, the nature of the society in which we live, and from the experiences of leaders who have faced and solved similar problems.

1. *The program should consist of many and varied activities related to the needs, interests, and abilities of all the people.* This principle is based primarily upon the fact that human beings differ in many respects. A good program must be broad in scope if it is to provide a wide range of choice for all the people regardless of age, sex, race, or any other differences. In accordance with this principle, those programs are weighed in the balance and found wanting in which the following conditions exist: adequate opportunities for boys but not for girls; numerous sports for the athlete, but nothing for the lover of music or drama; softball and basketball leagues for young men and boys, but no horseshoes or volleyball for the older man; competition in excess, but no social recreation; activities for the highly skilled while the "dubs" and the handicapped are ignored; much for the white people and little for the Negro; a wide range of choices for the individual while the family is forgotten; and emphasis upon a program for children with the young adult disregarded.

If all other things are equal, that program is best which offers to all the people in a community equal opportunity to make the most satisfying use possible of their leisure.

2. *The program should consist of activities in which reside the values sought by leadership.* If we may assume that a recreation department, as a social institution in a democratic society, is truly concerned with the future of our civilization and the values by which men live, it follows naturally that activities should be selected which, when properly conducted, will enable us to achieve the values deemed important by the department and the society in which it exists. Leisure, according to this concept, is not merely for diversion or amusement, but is an opportunity to participate in activities which contribute to self-fulfillment within a framework of social, moral, and ethical purpose.

Musselman presents the challenge in stirring words:[14]

Behind the skills we can teach, beyond the programs we can provide, *must* come a deliberate strong emphasis on the basic values of life. Let no one say this is not the business of recreation or that it should nòt be its major objective. If we place more emphasis on strength, fleetness of foot, quickness of eye and of wit than we place on respect for human dignity, appreciation of goodness and beauty, and responsibility for the rights and privileges of all, then we are slated for oblivion, and we do not deserve the title of youth-serving or character-building agency.

After we have agreed upon the goals to be sought, we then must select the activities in which these values reside. There is no point in digging for gold where no gold exists. If we seek to strengthen the quality of coöperation, activities should be selected in which participants must work together as members of a team. If moral values are the goal, we would not choose calisthenics as the means since honesty and truthfulness are not demanded for successful participation. If we desire to teach obedience to law as a quality of the good citizen in a democracy, an activity such as basketball would be conducted and the importance of obedience to the rules would be emphasized, followed by efforts to bring about a transfer of this quality to life beyond the game. A dance may be the means of developing in youth certain social graces in relation to the opposite sex, but we would not seek these values in horseshoe pitching. Creative expression and love of beauty may be realized through arts and crafts, but do not exist in a game such as Drop the Handkerchief. Specific values exist in specific activities and leaders worthy of the name will prove capable of discovering the relationship between ends and means.

3. *The worth of an activity should be assessed in terms of its effects upon human beings.* The ultimate test of any activity is what happens to

---

[14] Musselman, *op. cit.*, p. 486.

the individual as he takes part in it. In other words, what does it do to people? Does it help meet basic human needs, nourish the personality, humanize, deepen and refine it, intensify the individual's concern for the welfare of others, foster desirable social attitudes, stimulate a desire for excellence, and strengthen the moral fiber? Does it enrich life? Or does it place restrictions upon the human spirit, thwart it, limit its capacity for coöperation and human association, and cultivate the selfish, callous, and ruthless aspects of our nature?

These are the major questions that must be answered when selecting activities for a recreation program. Place boxing under the spotlight of these questions, answer them honestly, and then decide whether any activity belongs in a program dedicated to the welfare of the individual when the success of a participant is measured by his ability to injure his opponent.

Let us turn the spotlight of this principle on one other activity frequently found in recreation programs. In Beater Goes Round, players stand in a circle facing in, with hands behind them. One player runs along outside the circle with a knotted towel or rolled up newspaper in his hand. As stealthily as possible he places the towel in the hands of a player in the circle who immediately begins striking the player to his right and continues to do so all the way around the circle unless the player being struck is a faster runner than the "Beater." When a large, fast, and strong player beats a small, slow, weak, and sensitive youngster several times in the course of this "game," with the action accompanied by taunts, ridicule, and sadistic shouts from the onlookers, the effects on all concerned are not likely to be good in terms of the welfare of the individual or of society. The activity leads back to the direction of tribal patterns and is reminiscent of the practice of savage American Indians forcing white captives to run the gantlet as a prelude to death by torture.

All activities of this nature have one element in common—the attempt to evoke laughs and derive pleasure through ridiculing and embarrassing human beings. The victim frequently is a shy, withdrawn, extremely sensitive child whose inferiority feelings are accentuated and whose sense of inadequacy is further enhanced. Damage also is done to the personalities of the other children as they assume the role of bully and aggressor, developing sadistic tendencies rather than an attitude of sensitivity and sympathy for the weak and unfortunate. In a democracy which believes in the dignity of man and the sacredness of human personality, such activities have no place in a program of public recreation.

4. *The program should not only reflect the culture in which it exists but seek to improve it.* The leader must operate within a culture which

is so completely and so inextricably a part of his experience as to over-shadow almost all else in determining the nature of the recreation program. Activities highly popular and socially approved in one community are taboo in another. Community mores and traditions may limit or enrich the program.

What is culture? It is an accumulation and refinement of the experiences of billions of human beings who have preceded us. It is a pattern of beliefs, attitudes, customs, traditions, and ways of behaving which man learns, accepts, and practices. We are born into these social ways, must accept them, and can affect them only to the slightest degree. To ignore them or to attempt to construct a program in direct conflict with the culture is to court both personal and professional disaster. It is important to note that the culture varies from country to country, from generation to generation, from community to community, and from group to group within a community. Thus, a single code of behavior does not regulate the conduct of people. Rather, they conform to the standards established by the various subcultures with which they are affiliated.

The culture and the subcultures condition the recreation program. Dancing is emphasized in many communities while in some others it is considered evil and is forbidden. Basketball is king in Indiana and football in Texas. The enthusiasm of truck drivers for bird-watching clubs is likely to be somewhat less than phenomenal. Leaders who possess an intimate understanding of the values in which people believe can select activities that the community will accept and support. For example, initiating a community center program for youth with bridge and cribbage tournaments in a conservative neighborhood of strong religious beliefs may be offensive to the people and bring about violent opposition to the recreation department. On the other hand, enthusiastic support may be won by a program emphasizing basketball, dramatics, and folk dancing.

It is our responsibility as leaders to develop programs acceptable to the culture, but we have an equal responsibility to enrich the culture. It also is our duty to oppose vigorously those groups in the community that would offer programs harmful to youth or destructive of the values in which we believe. As leaders we should work constantly to improve the quality of leisure experience, viewing the culture not as an inflexible entity incapable of being changed, but as a challenge to excellence.

There will be many times when we shall be discouraged by our inability to improve that which should be improved. When those times come our spirits may be lifted and our energies renewed by recalling the wise words of Jefferson, counseling the newly created University of Virginia:

We cannot always do what is absolutely best. Those with whom we act, entertaining different views, have the power and the right of carrying them into practice. Truth advances and error recedes step-by-step only; and to do to our fellow men the most good in our power we must lead where we can, follow where we cannot, and still go with them, watching always the favorable moment for helping them to another step.

5. *The program should enlarge the interests of people and lead on to more satisfying and rewarding experiences.* An effective program must provide activities in which people are interested; otherwise they will not participate. Therefore, the expressed desires of people must be used as one criterion for the selection of a program, but they should serve only as a starting point and never as a basis for a complete program. The interests and desires of people are limited by their experiences and leaders must seek to widen horizons rather than perpetuate limitations. Walter Lippman points out, "The essence of statesmanship consists in giving people not what they want but what they will learn to want." The same might be said of recreation leadership.

Some years ago we were faced with the problem of opening a number of community centers in Madison, Wisconsin. In an effort to build a program that would attract a large number of people 4,000 checklists of thirty-two different activities were distributed by the parent-teacher associations. Among these activities was shuffleboard, in which almost no one expressed any interest because there were no shuffleboard courts in the city and the game was relatively unknown. However, ignoring the lack of interest, we painted several courts on the terrazzo floors of our basement playrooms and placed shuffleboard on the program. In one center a cribbage league involving approximately seventy-five adults met once a week in a room where shuffleboard courts had been painted. League play began at 7:30, but the center opened at 7:00. During this thirty minutes the leader casually pushed shuffleboard discs along the courts which attracted the attention of some cribbage players who had arrived early. Apparently without premeditation and only as a time-killing measure, the leader soon had a number of beginning shuffleboard players in action. Next week these, and others, came even earlier to play this new game and within a few weeks so great was the interest that a shuffleboard league was organized for play on a different night.

We had similar experiences with photography, dramatics, square dancing, archery and many other activities. Adults, especially, are skeptical and apathetic towards the unfamiliar and the leader must use intelligence, good judgment, and ingenuity in his efforts to lead them into the enrichment and adventure of wider recreation experience. Influencing people to discard their blind-alley interests which lead nowhere except to boredom and emptiness in favor of creative and cultural activities with their promise of satisfying and rewarding experiences is one of the highest forms of leadership.

6. *The program should provide activities in which interest persists over many years.* All activities need not be of such a nature that they can be engaged in for many years, but programs should include far more of this kind of activity than they do now.

We have created in America a hierarchy of sports which has no place in a democratic nation. The schools and colleges are the greatest offenders in this respect, but our recreation departments also are guilty of contributing to the creation of this hierarchy. Sports in this nation are arranged with the successive levels determined not by the total values residing in each sport for the participants, but by the prestige or status each accords to the players, with the amount of prestige measured largely by the number of spectators who attend the games. The money paid by the spectators is a major factor in maintaining the hierarchy. The volume of publicity enveloping a sport contributes to its status value, adds to the number of spectators, which, in turn, increases the revenue for further promotion of the sport, thus attracting more spectators which adds to its status value—*ad infinitum.*

At the top of this hierarchy in most communities is football, followed by basketball, baseball, and track and field. Since all human beings, and especially adolescent youth, seek status or self-enhancement, the boys turn out in large numbers for these sports. Down at the bottom of our sports' totem pole are such activities as tennis, golf, swimming, and gymnastics—relatively unimportant according to prevailing concepts, but since they are varsity sports and letters can be won, they are accorded a small measure of recognition, a few boys try out for the teams, and a handful of spectators show up for the matches.

The fullest measure of contempt and lack of interest is reserved for those sports "unworthy" of inclusion on the interscholastic or intercollegiate programs. These include volleyball, badminton, archery, table tennis, horseshoes, shuffleboard, and handball. Seldom, in any high school or college in America, can an official volleyball or horseshoe court be found, nor anyone who can teach these sports as they should be taught. The boy who prefers volleyball to basketball or archery to football frequently is looked upon as a peculiar individual, not quite normal in certain important respects.

Four serious indictments of this condition of affairs appear: (1) the boy who participates in nothing but one of the "big four" sports has only an impoverished experience; (2) the skills, interests, and appreciations he has developed seldom continue beyond school days except as he assumes the role of professional or spectator; (3) many thousands of boys are discouraged from developing skills and interests in individual or dual sports which they could enjoy throughout life; and (4) vast numbers of spectators are created out of the "dubs" incapable of stardom in the "only sports that really count."

This situation has been described at some length because recreation leaders must cope with it even though they may have had no share in its creation. It is not an easy problem to solve because it involves the culture of our people, but we should do all in our power to counteract its pernicious effects.

First, we should emphasize as strongly as possible that there are no major and minor sports. All sports are major to the people who are interested in them. Since in a democracy the most important thing in the world is a human being, it follows naturally that an activity is important or unimportant only in terms of its significance to a human being. Second, we should cease measuring importance in terms of numbers of participants or numbers of spectators. If only a dozen people are interested in archery, must we wait until a hundred are interested before we add archery to the program? Third, we should do all in our power to give praise and recognition to excellence in every sport so that some status value may accrue to the horseshoe pitchers and the croquet champions. Fourth, we should insist on excellence in facilities, equipment, supplies, and leadership for every sport. One of the reasons why horseshoes has almost died out on the playgrounds of this nation is our failure to provide official courts and horseshoes and to teach boys how to throw an "open" shoe. We insist on excellence for football, basketball, baseball, and track, but are willing to accept mediocrity and worse in many of our other activities. And, finally, we should add more and more activities to our programs which people can enjoy throughout most of their lives. In the area of sports, this means more emphasis on such individual and dual sports as archery, aerial tennis, badminton, bowling, croquet, fly casting, handball, horseshoes, paddle tennis, roller skating, ice skating, skiing, tennis, golf, swimming, and shuffleboard.

We have interpreted this principle in terms of sports only, but it applies to other aspects of the program as well. For example, we should place more emphasis on the creative and cultural activities, on hobbies, and on activities in the great outdoors—camping, hiking, fishing, hunting, canoeing, boating, sailing. Everytime we develop in youth skills and interests in these types of activities we not only are making an important contribution to their present life, but we are making an investment in a rich and meaningful leisure throughout most of their remaining years.

7. *The program should emphasize meaningful relationships among activities.* In Chapter 3 we learned that man is an organic unit, a whole person in whom all the parts function harmoniously in relationship to all other parts. When he throws a baseball the arms, legs, mind, muscles, bones, and all other parts must work together. If they fail to do so, he cannot throw effectively. When the various parts of a human being fail to work together, we say the individual is in a disintegrated condition. When they work together as they should, we say he is an integrated person.

Leaders can contribute to the integration of an individual by conducting programs which reflect the principle of integration. This means that whenever possible programs should consist of activities in which meaningful relationships exist. Youth should be made aware of these relationships because each activity becomes more meaningful as it is seen in relation to other activities than if seen in isolation. For example, the building of chariots in a playground craft club may command some interest as an isolated activity, but how much more meaningful it becomes if the boys see it in relation to racing in miniature Olympic Games, stories of the ancient Greeks told by the leader, a play about the Greeks, singing some Grecian songs, making Grecian costumes, and taking the Olympic oath.

Music, pageantry, costuming, clowning, stunts, crafts, drama, dance can all be interesting by themselves, but combined in a circus with each activity related to all the other activities and presented before several thousand specators, they take on added interest and significance as they become parts of an integrated whole.

A good example of integration can be found in party programs built around a central theme such as Halloween, St. Patrick's Day, Thanksgiving, and Christmas. Each activity becomes more meaningful as it is seen in relationship to the integrating theme.

One further example. Let us assume that a playground schedule calls for storytelling at 9:30, crafts at 10:00, and a checker tournament at 11:00. The superior leader ties these three activities together into a meaningful relationship by telling children about the history of checkers, teaching them to make their checkers and checker boards, and then conducting the tournament with the children using their own checkers and boards. The storytelling, crafts, and tournament comprise an integrated program because the three parts are related. The traditional playground program jumps about from one activity to another with no effort made to establish meaningful relationships.

As leaders become better prepared for their work; as they learn more about the unified nature of man; and as they understand more fully how integrated programs make a greater contribution to the integration of human beings than do uncoördinated programs, we may expect that in the future they will demonstrate an even greater ability in discovering the expanding relationships among activities in recreation.

8. *Program planning and operation is a coöperative undertaking and involves both leader and participant.* This is the principle of involvement discussed on page 94. Applied to program planning, it means that all participants, or their representatives, shall be invited to contribute to the planning of their own activities provided they have a constructive interest in the quality of the program.

Three major reasons exist why leaders should invite participants to share responsibility for program planning: (1) democratic values are best achieved through democratic methods; (2) group judgment on matters of this nature, arrived at through the free exchange of ideas and the mutual harmonizing of different individuals, is likely to be sounder than the judgment of any one person no matter how wise that one person may be; and (3) people will participate in and support to a far greater degree those programs they have had a share in planning than those someone else has planned for them.

The leader who has faith in group judgment and democratic procedures does not believe that wisdom automatically emerges from an uninformed group. Ignorance compounded many times still adds up to ignorance. Nor do the advocates of democratic leadership propose that well-educated and experienced leaders abdicate their positions and permit immature youth to make decisions on matters about which they know little or nothing. Superior leaders, however, constantly seek to develop leadership in others, to widen the area of common concern so that all may feel themselves to be partners in a common enterprise, and to regulate the amount of responsibility carried in terms of one's abilities.

Leaders also will encourage participants to take an active part in operating various phases of the program. For example, adult athletic leagues are best administered when the players or managers elect representatives to a governing body generally known as a commission. Youth may be invited or elected to serve on playground, community center, or youth councils; on program committees, safety patrols, and clubs for athletic officials; or they may render effective service at a dance as a member of the decorations committee, the welcoming committee, or the refreshments committee. One mark of superior leadership is the extent to which it brings about a high degree of involvement on the part of many people in the conduct of their own affairs.

Numerous opportunities exist for the involvement of adults in various aspects of the recreation program. They may serve on the recreation commission, the advisory recreation council, and on many playground and community center councils or committees. Their services are extremely valuable as officers or committee members of a number of sports clubs or associations, such as the tennis, golf, bowling, horseshoe, swimming, and shuffleboard associations. The theatre guild and music association alone provide opportunities for more than a hundred men and women volunteer workers. Leading citizens may be invited to serve as judges in all kinds of events—pet shows, hobby shows, lantern parades, drama tournaments, music festivals, and backyard playground contests. Or they may present awards, crown queens, and preside at meetings.

The more extensive and intensive the degree of involvement on the part of people in the planning and management of their own recreation the more fully do they appreciate it, support it, and accept it as their own. It becomes *their* program. They have a stake in it. It becomes a vital part of their lives, something to treasure, to expand, to interpret, and, if need be, to fight for.

9. *The program should be sufficiently flexible to permit adaptation to varying situations.* Among the forces and influences which affect the nature of recreation programs are numerous variables which differ to so great an extent from region to region, city to city, and even from neighborhood to neighborhood within a city that any attempt to develop a rigid, inflexible program is certain to fail. A single, uniform program prepared by the central office staff and distributed to all leaders throughout the city is inadvisable unless leaders are permitted to make whatever adaptations are necessary to fit the program to the unique situation in which they are working.

10. *Grouping is a significant factor in programming and its implications should be examined carefully.* Is it better to group individuals on a narrow age basis for participation in recreation or should we conduct activities in which various age groups intermingle? Does the answer to this question depend upon the nature of the groups and the activities? Does it really matter how we do it, provided the plan places no restrictions on participation?

All activities do not lend themselves to participation by varied age groups. Tackle football is no game for middle-aged men or elementary school boys. Both youth and adults, however, can enjoy together music, crafts, drama, many hobbies, and sports and games, such as volleyball, swimming, gymnastics, bowling, tennis, golf, shuffleboard, table tennis, skiing, ice skating, and horseshoe pitching.

There are certain real values to be derived from a mixture of age groups participating in a common activity which are not realizable on a segregated age basis. For example, the first year the author taught school all eight grades were under his instruction. The youngest student was six; the oldest seventeen. Each grade listened to each of the other grades recite and by a kind of academic osmosis each individual soaked up some learning just by being exposed to all the others. Furthermore, the younger children "looked up to" the more capable older students, selected them as their "models," imitated them, and were helped by them both in the classroom and on the playground. Thus, the less skilled and able children were inspired to greater heights of individual performance by the older and more capable youth. This stimulus to growth and development emerges only where a wide age range exists. Segregation by age tends to establish mediocrity as the norm, confirm immaturity, and remove the power of this particular society to evoke high performance from its members.

A similar experience while observing members of the Madison, Wisconsin, Turners, a social and gymnastic organization, confirmed these conclusions. Entire families ranging from three-year-old toddlers to aged grandparents spent several hours each week in the gymnasium working strenuously on various phases of gymnastics. The older and highly skilled performers inspired and taught the younger and less skilled who made remarkable progress surrounded, as they were, by numerous examples of excellence. Excellence is contagious just as mediocrity is contagious and frequently the basic cause of highly skilled performance is simply the power of the group to evoke it.

Dodson points out that we have segregated on an age basis so strictly "that the only meaningful reference group a person has today is his peers." Furthermore, this practice "tends to sever the thread of historical continuity between the generations." A child should learn to participate in many leisure activities with his uncles, aunts, grandfathers, and grandmothers.[15]

This contact with the generations is shortened and in many instances severed. Family, in the large sense, is weakened. Hence, the controls are those of the peers, rather than of family tradition.

Dynamic programming faces no more serious issue than this of grouping in its many ramifications. Sensitivity to the trends, and intelligence in dealing with them may be one of the major tasks facing those whose job in the years ahead is that of assisting America to use this growing amount of leisure to achieve more fulfilled lives.

11. *Program development should be positive in direction but gradual in pace.* Begin with a few activities, experience success with what you are doing, and expand gradually, all the while constructing your program on a

---

[15] Dan W. Dodson, "The Dynamics of Programming," *Recreation,* November 1961, p. 485.

solid foundation of values. The program should be properly interpreted and expertly administered. Rapid overexpansion followed by embarrassing retrenchment may damage or retard development of your program for many years.

A basketball league might be the single seed from which could grow a broad community center program within a period of two or three years, whereas an attempt to begin with a full-grown program could prove disastrous. The leader must avoid the twin evils of excessive speed and gross inertia.

12. *Continuous evaluation is an important factor in program improvement.* If the road to values lies through program, the only valid test of the effectiveness of a program is the degree to which it leads to the values previously agreed upon. Thus, a program can really be justified only by the extent to which the established goals have been achieved. Since program justification, change, and expansion should all be based upon facts derived from evaluation, we reasonably should expect that considerable progress has been made over the years in the development of evaluative devices in recreation. Unfortunately this is not the case. Enrollment or attendance figures are reported, but head counting is bookkeeping, not evaluation. To know that 50,000 people attended your community centers during the month of January is interesting and important, but it tells nothing about what happened to these people while they were in the centers—and this is extremely important provided you believe that recreation should serve some worthy purposes.

The measurement of the extent to which recreation achieves certain vital purposes is one of the most needed, but one of the least popular, areas of research. Almost no studies, designed to find out what happens to people when they engage in recreation, have been made. There seems little doubt that a great deal can and should be done to appraise the value of the leisure-time offerings of recreation departments. If American recreation prizes results in terms of individual development and of social, moral, and ethical growth, its leaders must find and utilize the means of determining whether or not these results are actually being achieved.

A LIST OF ACTIVITIES

The following compilation of recreation activities provides an insight into the scope, nature, and diversity of the materials which departments may draw upon for the construction of their programs. Students should be aware of the limitations to be found in any list of this nature: (1) the things men do in their leisure are so numerous and diverse that any list is certain to be incomplete; (2) the classification system followed here is only one of several that might have been used; (3) many activities could have been categorized under more than one heading; and (4) no attempt is made to indicate the particular age group for which an activity is most appropriate.

Despite these limitations the list of activities should be helpful to leaders as they attempt to provide the best possible programs for their communities.

Games and Sports

Group games for younger children

Birds fly	Forest lookout	Rabbit chase
Brownies and fairies	Fox and geese	Redlight
Bull in the ring	Frog in the sea	Relays
Cat and rat	Hare and hounds	Slap jack
Circle chase	Hide and seek	Spider and flies
Circle stride ball	Hill dill	Squirrel in trees
Club snatch	Last man	Tag games
Corner spry	Numbers change	Three deep
Crows and cranes	Poison	
Dodgeball	Prisoner's base	

Individual and dual sports and games

Aerial tennis	Glider soaring	Rifle shooting
Archery	Golf	Roller skating
Badminton	Handball	Roque
Bicycling	Hand tennis	Sailing
Billiards	Hopscotch	Shuffleboard
Boating	Horseback riding	Skiing
Bobsledding	Horseshoes	Skin and scuba diving
Bowling	Ice boating	Squash
Box hockey	Ice skating	Swimming
Canoeing	Jacks	Table tennis
Coasting	Kite flying	Tennis
Croquet	Loop tennis	Tetherball
Croquet golf	Marbles	Tobogganing
Curling	Model airplane flying	Top spinning
Dart baseball	Motor boating	Track and field
Diving	Paddle tennis	Trap shooting
Fencing	Pistol shooting	Wrestling
Fly casting	Quoits	Yachting

Gymnastics and stunts

Apparatus play
Back bend
Backward roll
Baton twirling
Cartwheel
Forward roll
Hand balance

Handstand
Hand wrestling
Handspring
Head stand
Indian wrestling
Jump stick
Lariat throwing

Pyramid building
Rooster fight
Rope jumping
Snap up
Trampoline
Tumbling

Team sports or athletics

Baseball
Basketball
Captain ball
End ball
Fieldball
Field hockey
Football

Hit pin baseball
Ice hockey
Kickball
Lacrosse
Newcomb
Polo
Soccer

Soccer baseball
Softball
Speed ball
Touch football
Tug of war
Volleyball
Water polo

Arts and Crafts

Art metal craft
Basketry
Beadwork
Block printing
Candle making
Cardboard construction
Card weaving
Carving—soap, wood, bone
Cellophane craft
Ceramics
Cookery
Copper foil
Cork work
Drawing
Dyeing
Etching
Finger painting
Furniture refinishing

Gimp craft
Hooking
Jewelry making
Knitting
Leafprints
Leathercraft
Making posters, bulletins, scrapbooks, toys, and recreation games and supplies
Metalcraft
Millinery
Modeling—wood, clay, sand
Mosaic crafts
Needlework
Painting
Papercraft
Photography

Plaster casting and carving
Plastic crafts
Pottery
Printing
Puppets
Quilting
Reed and raffia
Sculpture
Sewing
Shell craft
Sketching
Snow sculpture
Stagecraft
Tincraft
Weaving
Woodcraft

Dance

Ballet
Clog
Creative rhythms for children

Folk
Modern
Social

Square
Tap

Drama

Charades	Impersonations	Plays
Children's theatre	Marionettes	Puppetry
Circuses	Minstrel shows	Shadow-plays
Community theatre	Monodrama	Skits
Creative drama	Musical dramas	Story dramatization
Dramatic stunts	Pageants	Storytelling
Dramatizations	Pantomime	Traveling theatre
Festivals	Peep shows	Water pageants

The Language Arts

Book clubs	Foreign language clubs	Stage, radio, and
Business and social	Forums	television writing
letter writing	Lectures	Storytelling
Creative writing	Public speaking	Television and radio
Debates	Reading	speaking
Discussion clubs	Spelling bees	

Music

Vocal

A cappella choir	Choruses	Quartets
Action songs	Group singing	

Instrumental

Accordion	Mandolin and guitar	String quartets
Bands	groups	Symphony orchestras
Bugle corps	Ocarina choirs	Ukulele orchestras
Harmonica bands	Rhythm bands	

Nature and Outing Activities

Astronomy	Flower shows	Oyster roasts
Bird watching and	Gardening	Pet shows
feeding	Hiking	Picnicking
Camping	Hunting	Trailing games
Caring for pets	Indianlore	Travel
Cave exploration	Mountain climbing	Tree identification
Clambakes	Nature clubs	trips
Fishing	Nature museum	Zoos

Collections

Arrowheads	Fossils	Sea shells
Butterflies	Minerals	Water life
Driftwood		

Field trips to art galleries

Museums	Parks	Zoos

Community Service Activities

City beautification.

Membership on clean-up squad, playground or youth council, leaders' club, officials' club, safety patrol, and supplies committee.

Participation in community projects, such as tree planting, forestry control, and hospital aides.

Service on athletic council or commission, playground and community center council, park, school, or recreation board.

Volunteer leadership on playground or community center, as scoutmaster, as coach of a junior athletic team, or with programs for shut-ins.

Judging contests, making costumes, and transporting the handicapped and the aged to playgrounds or community centers.

Serving in community chest campaigns.

Social Activities

Amateur nights	Hay rides	Scavenger hunts
Banquets	Marshmallow and	Social dancing
Barbecues	wiener roasts	Square dancing
Barn dances	Parties	Social games
Basket suppers	Birthday	Table games
Bonfire and skit night	Block	Treasure hunts
Candy pulls	Costume	Teas and coffee hours
Card games	Hard times	Visiting
Family nights	Holiday	

PROGRAM ORGANIZATION

From these preceding lists of activities and many others which are available, the leader must assume major responsibility for constructing programs for various groups and situations. The activities in their present form are bulky and unwieldy. How shall they be arranged for efficient use? Generally, departments are guided in their program organization by two major factors:

1. TIME. For the effective operation of a playground program, it is essential to schedule on a seasonal, weekly, and daily basis. The seasonal schedule is simply a compilation of all major activities planned for the summer. It is then broken down into weeks, days, and hours. Examples of a combined daily-weekly schedule for a playground and for a community center are given below:

Cincinnati Recreation Commission

SUGGESTED DAILY-WEEKLY PROGRAM FOR SUMMER PLAYGROUNDS

Time	Children under 8	Children 9–11	Children 12 and over
9:30–10:00	Flag raising. Getting out equipment, inspecting apparatus and grounds; distributing game supplies; posting announcements or organizing groups for morning play.		
10:00–11:00	Apparatus play Sandbox play	Low organized games	Group and team games Practice for contests and tournaments
11:00–12:00	Group and singing games Active games Storytelling	Crafts and stunts Quiet games Folk and square dancing Singing	Folk and square dancing Crafts
12:00–1:00	Free play	Free play	Free play
1:00–2:00	Storytelling and story acting Apparatus play	Group games and relays Apparatus play Dramatics	Group games and relays Individual games and athletic stunts
2:00–3:00	Sandbox play Free play activities Quiet games	Quiet games Free play activities Preparation for future events	Organization of team games Practice for league games Preparation for special or feature events

Cincinnati Recreation Commission
SUGGESTED DAILY-WEEKLY PROGRAM FOR SUMMER PLAYGROUNDS

Time	Children under 8	Children 9–11	Children 12 and over
3:00–4:00	Crafts Dramatics Apparatus play Singing games Taking part in special events	Contests, tournaments or special features Crafts Singing for fun	Special features Contests Tournaments League games Crafts Singing for fun
4:00–5:30	Sandbox play Quiet games Singing for fun	Storytelling Dramatics Quiet games Meeting of clubs	Dramatics Quiet games Preparation for community events
5:30–6:00	Collecting game materials and playground supplies; checkup on playground.		
6:00–8:30	Playground used by young people or adults for team games and for informal play. Twilight leagues for young people and adults; informal, individual and team games; special neighborhood programs and demonstrations.		

Cincinnati Recreation Commission
NORTH FAIRMOUNT COMMUNITY CENTER PROGRAM

Day	Time	Grade	Activities	Time	Grade	Activities
Mon.	3:30–4:00	1–8	Free play	6:30–8:00	5–8	Dance instruction
	4:00–5:00	1–4	Circle and relay games	6:30–8:00	5–8	Billiards and table games
	4:00–5:00	6–8	Billiards and table games	8:00–9:00	7–12	Teen Council
	5:00–6:00	1–4	Quiet games	9:00–10:00	7–12	Dramatics, ping pong
	5:00–6:00	6–8	Billiards and table games	9:00–10:00	7–12	Billiards and table games
Tues.	3:30–4:00	1–8	Free play	6:30–8:00	5–12	Singing
	4:00–5:00	1–4	Crafts	6:30–8:00	5–12	Billiards, table games
	4:00–5:00	5–8	Quiet games	8:00–9:00	7–12	Dancing, tumbling
	5:00–6:00	1–4	Low organization games	8:00–9:00	7–12	Billiards
	5:00–6:00	5–8	Crafts	9:00–10:00	7–12	Crafts
				9:00–10:00	7–12	Table games, billiards
Wed.	3:30–4:00	1–8	Free play	6:30–8:00	5–12	Social games
	4:00–5:00	1–4	Tumbling	6:30–8:00	5–12	Table games
	4:00–5:00	5–8	Billiards and table games	8:00–10:30	5–12	Teen-age dance
	5:00–6:00	1–4	Dramatics			
	5:00–6:00	5–8	Singing			
Thur.	3:30–4:00	1–8	Free play	6:30–8:00	5–12	Tumbling, dancing
	4:00–5:00	1–4	Ping pong, fist ball	6:30–8:00	5–12	Billiards, table games
	4:00–5:00	5–8	Billiards and crafts	8:00–9:00	7–12	Tumbling, dancing
	5:00–6:00	1–4	Low organization games	8:00–9:00	7–12	Billiards, mental games
	5:00–6:00	5–8	Crafts	9:00–10:30	7–12	Volleyball, ping pong
				9:00–10:30	7–12	Billiards

Cincinnati Recreation Commission
NORTH FAIRMOUNT COMMUNITY CENTER PROGRAM

Day	Time	Grade	Activities	Time	Grade	Activities
Fri.	3:30–4:00	1–8	Free play	5:00–6:00	1–4	Relays
	4:00–5:00	1–4	Rhythm Band	5:00–6:00	5–8	Tumbling
	4:00–5:00	5–8	Circle Games	6:30–10:00	7–8	Pre-Teen Dance

WEEKLY PROGRAM OF THE U.S. GRANT SOCIAL CENTER
Milwaukee, Wisconsin

CHILDREN'S PROGRAM—*Grades 3–8, 3:30–5:15*

Time	Day	Activity
3:30	Tuesday, Thursday, Friday	Boys' basketball, Table games
3:30	Tuesday	Junior Athletic Club Cooking crafts—3rd, 4th grades
4:30	Tuesday	Cooking crafts—5th, 6th grades
3:30	Tuesday, Thursday, Friday	Girls' Clubs, Boys' Clubs
3:30	Tuesday, Thursday	Active games
6:00	Tuesday, Thursday	Girls' volleyball
3:30	Thursday	Beginners' tumbling—boys Stamp Collectors' Club Art class
4:30	Thursday	Advanced tumbling—boys
4:30	Thursday	Tumbling for girls
3:30	Friday	Wrestling Junior Optimist Club for 10–12-year-old boys Camera Club Folk and square dance

TEEN'S PROGRAM

Tuesdays and Thursdays, 7:30–9:30 p.m., and
Saturday afternoons, 1:00–4:30

Conditioning (weight-lifting)	Junior high dances	Girls' Club Room
Billiards	Senior high dances	Senior High Club—Tuesday
Boys' clubs	Co-Rec clubs	Volleyball Club—Thursday
Table tennis	Girls' volleyball league	Junior High Club—Thursday
Girls' clubs	Hi Fi Room	
Boys' basketball leagues	Game Room	
Service club	Co-Recreation Room	
Newspaper staff	Table games	
	Juke box	

In addition to the above schedule and program, basketball league play for seventh and eighth grade youth is conducted on Saturday mornings from 9:15–11:45.

ADULT PROGRAM

A limited adult program is conducted at this center on Tuesday and Friday evenings, 7:30–9:30, as follows:

Day	*Activity*
Tuesday	Serving
	Crafts
Friday	Cake decorating
	Millinery

Special events, such as Mother and Daughter Parties and Father and Son Athletic Banquets, are scheduled throughout the season. Also, Golden Age Clubs meet on Tuesdays, Thursdays, and Fridays from 12:30–3:30.

2. DEGREE OF ORGANIZATION REQUIRED. Careful, detailed planning, long in advance of their presentation, is necessary if some activities are to be successful. Also, the leader must give to these activities constant supervision while they are in operation. On the other hand, many activities require a minimum of advanced planning, very little instruction, and almost no supervision as they seem to function under their own power as self-directed activities.

Many departments refer to the more highly organized and supervised activities as their *core* program, since they represent a central body of materials, often required of all centers, definitely scheduled, and the hub around which other phases of the total program revolve. Frequently, the core program will include the following activities:

Arts and crafts
Athletics—both intra- and
    interplayground games
Dance
Drama
Group games and relays

Individual and dual sports
Music
Nature and outing activities
Social activities
Storytelling

Leaders must understand that the scheduling of activities on a specific time basis, as indicated above in the playground schedule, does not mean the same thing to the participants as it does to the leader. To the leader it means that he follows a fairly definite and specific daily time schedule, thus providing a reasonable degree of planned order and coherence to the program. Participants know in advance when activities are scheduled, but there is no compulsion on their part to follow this schedule. Twenty children may be taking part in the crafts program at the hour scheduled, but a hundred or more may be scattered over the playground playing paddle tennis, croquet, checkers, swinging, sliding, or engaging in many other kinds of activities of a self-directed nature. This is no indictment of the leader. One characteristic of a well-organized playground is the number and variety of activities going on at one time. The leader should be concerned, however, if he is unable to interest many children in the scheduled activities. Either the program or the leadership, or both, may be at fault. Nevertheless, the provision of numerous opportunities for free, loosely organized, self-directed play, wholly voluntary and completely unregimented, also is a mark of good leadership. The following brief list indicates the kinds of activities in which children and youth will participate with a minimum of motivation and supervision provided they have been taught properly and a fair degree of skill has been developed:

Aerial tennis	Hand tennis	Sand play
Apparatus play	Hopscotch	Shuffleboard
Basketball goal shooting	Horeshoes	Table games—checkers,
Box hockey	Jacks	chess, dominoes
Croquet	Loop tennis	Table tennis
Croquet golf	Marbles	Tennis
Handball	Paddle tennis	Tetherball

Another type of activity from the standpoint of degree of organization required is the *special event*. A special event is what the name implies, an event that is unusual, out of the ordinary; it occurs generally only once during the season, necessitates detailed planning, represents a high point of interest, often attracts people as participants and spectators who are not regular patrons, and possesses public relations value beyond that of the routine type of activity since it serves as a show window for the department. Among events of this nature are:

Amateur night	Easter egg hunt	Pageant
Arts and crafts exhibit	Family night	Pet show
Band concert	Fishing rodeo	Picnic
Block party	Hobby show	Traveling theatre
Circus	Lantern parade	Treasure hunt
Festival	Motion pictures	Wiener and marshmallow
Doll show	On-wheels parade	roast

Special events may be limited to a single center or a number of centers may come together. In Madison, we divided the city into two sections for the lantern parade both to reduce the distance which the children must travel and the number of participants for greater ease of handling. All playgrounds combined their efforts for the annual circus. Pet shows were conducted as individual playground events.

CREATIVE IDEAS IN PROGRAMMING[16]

Many new, unusual, and excellent program ideas are being put into practice by recreation departments throughout the country. Summarized in this section are a few activities possessing exceptional merit and indicating that creativity is a highly desirable attribute of recreation leadership.

Albuquerque, New Mexico

SPANISH CULTURE NIGHT: The music coördinator in the Albuquerque Public Schools Recreation Department divides the sixty-two elementary schools into four groups. She selects a centrally located school in each group and meets with all of the fourth, fifth, and sixth grade teachers in that group. At these meetings she instructs the teachers in traditional Mexican, New Mexican, and Spanish dances. From the four groups of schools twenty teachers are selected who would like to have their classes perform during Spanish Culture Night. The children dance in native costumes made by themselves. Each year several thousand people attend this colorful and cultural program which is held in a high school gymnasium.

Atlanta, Georgia

TULIP FESTIVAL: The Atlanta Parks and Recreation Department presents annually, in coöperation with the Atlanta Tulip Study Club, a Tulip Festival involving approximately 600 dancers completely costumed by the Department, even to the extent of wooden shoes. Dutch dances are performed along the walks of Hurt Park. Other program features include numbers by the Atlanta Recreation Chorus and adult dance groups.

The central theme of the occasion is the coronation of the festival queen. The queen and her court, heralded by trumpeters, march to the throne in full evening attire. Then the program is presented in their honor. The setting for the event is a park in which thousands of tulips from Holland are in full bloom. The Burgomaster generally is the mayor of Atlanta. Large crowds attend this event which not only is splendid recreation, but also superior public relations.

---

[16] All the material for this section was provided by superintendents of recreation in the cities listed.

Cincinnati, Ohio

BOYS' RECREATION CLUB: The Fulton Recreation Club, established exclusively for boys sixteen through nineteen years of age, was opened late in 1960. The building was equipped with all kinds of sports, games, and recreation equipment, including pool tables and automatic bowling games. A complete set of automobile tools was purchased along with a manual on automobile repair and an area behind the building was lighted where the boys might tinker on autos. An outside lighted basketball court was installed.

Activities included basketball, volleyball, weight-lifting, trampoline, numerous table games, cards, punching bag, table tennis, television, radio, books, record player, and study facilities.

The new venture was an immediate success. After only two months of operation, 280 boys had joined the club and attendance had reached 3,445. Hours of operation were Mondays through Fridays from 3 to 10 p.m., 10 a.m. to 3 p.m. on Saturdays; and on Sunday from 1 to 6 p.m. A judge of the county juvenile court was consulted in setting up this project and gave it his unqualified approval.

Jefferson County, Kentucky

ROCKING CHAIR FISHING DERBY: Senior citizens, sixty years or older, who like to fish are invited to an all-day picnic. Generally, they bring their own rocking chair and fishing equipment, but the Department will furnish all equipment, if necessary. Awards are given to both men and women who catch the largest fish and the most fish.

CLOWN CONVENTION: This event was established to meet the numerous requests for clown entertainment. Each summer playground furnishes as many clowns as possible for the convention and an original clown skit. The convention meets at the end of the playground season with each group putting on its skit in an auditorium. Following the program a parade is conducted through downtown Louisville. The clown dressed in the most unusual costume is declared "clown of clowns," and becomes president of the convention for the coming year.

Long Beach, California

HOBBY SHOW: The first city-wide Hobby Show was organized by the Long Beach Recreation Department in 1934 and was viewed by 2,000 persons over a two-day period. Seventeen annual shows have been held since 1934 with the 1961 show attracting 58,800 visitors and extending over a period of four days.

Recent shows have been so extensive as to necessitate use of the entire Long Beach Municipal Auditorium with its approximately 34,000 square feet.

The Long Beach Hobby Clubs Council, consisting of forty-five club representatives, assists the Department with the show by serving as guards, relief for paid personnel, and helps with the purchase of various supply and equipment items. The Council also provides funds for publicizing the show, including the purchase of 50,000 matchbook covers in coöperation with the Long Beach Match Cover Club.

Approximately 135 booth locations are made available. In 1961, sixty-nine clubs exhibited, representing a membership of from six to 3,000 persons; eighty-nine individual exhibitors displayed. Among the various groups participating in a recent Hobby Show were the following:

A. A. U. Judo (put on many demonstrations)	Shell Clubs
Amateur Fencers Club	Aquarium Club
American Reloaders (old rifles)	Bow Club
Associated Radio Amateurs	Quick Draw Gun Club
Radio Control Planes Club	Match Cover Club
Fuchsia Society	Wood Carvers Club
Garden Club	Art Clubs
Cactus Club	Sketch Clubs
Begonia Club	Crafts Clubs
Amateur Orchid Growers	Magic Club
Coin Clubs	Puppetry Clubs
Stamp Clubs	Square Dance Clubs
Telescope Club	Folk Dance Clubs
Reptile Club	Round Dance Clubs
Kart Club	Camera Clubs
Car Club	Button Club
Boat Clubs	Public Library

The manager of the Hobby Show lists five factors as basic to success of the show:

1. Pre-planning—Detailed planning begins three months in advance of the show with the floor plan laid out two months before the event. At this time, it is available to the exhibitors.
2. Rules—Rules covering operation of the show are strictly and impartially enforced.
3. Keeping the show non-commercial—No commercial activity of any kind is permitted during the show. No advertising is permitted, nor can

exhibitors take orders or sell anything during the show. The general public likes to be able to visit the displays without being irritated by persistent salesmen.

4. Good public relations with exhibitors—Department representatives visit the exhibitors daily in an effort to maintain friendly relationships as well as take care of any of their display needs.

5. After-show thank you's—These are directed not only to exhibitors but to all groups and individuals coöperating in the show.

A unique aspect of the show is that it is a "working" show, rather than simply a display. Exhibitors actually work on their hobbies whenever possible in an earnest effort to "sell" their hobbies to the viewers.

SATURDAY SPORTS PROGRAM FOR JUNIOR HIGH SCHOOL BOYS: This is an outstanding example of how a municipal recreation department and a public school system can coöperate to offer a broad program of athletic activities for boys on Saturday. It is designed to meet the needs of the more highly skilled boys for wholesome recreation through vigorous competitive athletic games and contests. Publicity is kept to a minimum and participation on a purely spectator basis is discouraged.

The year's program consists of six-man flag football in the fall, basketball and gymnastics during the winter months, and track and field and baseball in the spring. The fourteen junior high schools are divided into two seven-team leagues with all contests scheduled on Saturday mornings. A round-robin schedule is operated in flag football, basketball, and baseball with a playoff between the league winners. In track and field and gymnastics, each team participates in two practice meets followed by a league meet. Those who qualify in their league meet participate in an all-city meet.

Grade level is the basis of team and individual participant classification. Teams are coached by the regular physical education teachers of each school a maximum of five hours a week. For this service the teachers are paid by the school district as play directors while on Saturday they are paid for four hours by the Municipal Recreation Department.

Direct responsibility for administration of this excellent program rests with the Recreation Department, but the establishment of broad policies and regulations is carried out jointly by the Department and the schools.

Selected References

Butler, George D., *Introduction to Community Recreation* (4th ed.), (New York: McGraw-Hill Book Company, Inc., 1967).

Chapman, Frederick M., *Recreation Activities for the Handicapped* (New York: The Ronald Press Company, 1960).

Corbin, H. Dan., *Recreation Leadership* (2nd ed.) (Englewood Cliffs, N.J.: Prentice-Hall, Inc., 1959).

Danford, Howard G., *Recreation in the American Community* (New York: Harper and Brothers, 1953).

Danford, Howard G. (ed.), *School Recreation—National Conference Report* (Washington, D.C.: American Association for Health, Physical Education, and Recreation, 1960).

Dodson, Dan W., "The Dynamics of Programming," *Recreation*, LIV, No. 9, 1961, 455.

Hartley, Ruth E. and Goldenson, Robert M., *The Complete Book of Children's Play* (New York: Thomas Y. Crowell Company, 1957).

Kaplan, Max, *Leisure in America* (New York: John Wiley and Sons, Inc., 1960).

Krug, Edward A., *Curriculum Planning* (rev. ed.) (New York: Harper and Brothers, 1957).

Larrabee, Eric and Meyersohn, Rolf (eds.), *Mass Leisure* (Glencoe, Illinois: The Free Press, 1958).

Leisure and the Schools (Washington, D.C.: American Association for Health, Physical Education, and Recreation, 1961).

Mulac, Margaret E., *Leisure—Time for Living and Retirement* (New York: Harper and Brothers, 1961).

Musselman, Virginia, "Ten Challenges to Program," *Recreation*, LIII, No. 10, 1960, 467.

The Nation and Its Older People—Report of the White House Conference on Aging (Washington, D.C.: U.S. Department of Health, Education, and Welfare, 1961).

The Recreation Program (rev. ed.) (Chicago: The Athletic Institute, 1963).

Sorenson, Roy, "Directions for the Future," *Recreation*, LIII, No. 9, 1960, 412.

Traxler, Arthur E. (ed.), *Curriculum Planning to Meet Tomorrow's Needs* (Washington, D.C.: American Council on Education, 1960).

Vannier, Maryhelen, *Methods and Materials in Recreation Leadership* (Belmont, Calif.: Wadsworth Publishing Company, Inc., 1966).

Wylie, James A., "A Survey of 504 Families to Determine the Relationships Between Certain Factors and the Nature of the Family Recreation Program," *The Research Quarterly*, 24, No. 2, 1953, 223.

Chapter VII

Social Recreation

SOCIAL RECREATION IS one of the most delightful forms of recreation with its emphasis on friendliness, sociability, fun, happiness, and such social graces as courtesy, kindliness, and fair play. Through this medium in which the competitive element is de-emphasized and congenial human relationships constitute a major goal, superior leadership may contribute to the achievement of social unity, a quality greatly needed in the typical American community today. It is difficult to dislike a person with whom one sings, dances, and plays games.

The program of social recreation presented in this chapter consists of the following types of activities: social mixers, party games, relays, dramatic fun, brain teasers, and pencil and paper games. Music, especially group singing, and dancing are important aspects of social recreation. They also are major areas of the general program of recreation and, for this reason, are given more thorough consideration in Chapter 9. All activities have been selected with considerable care. There are many activities in social recreation that are trite, unpopular, and ridiculous. The authors have taught or participated in all of the activities included in this chapter and know from personal experience that, properly presented to an appropriate age group, they will be popular as well as effective media for the attainment of important values. The list of activities is not large, nor is it intended to be. Many excellent games are not included, but can be found in the numerous books on social recreation. The purpose of this chapter is not to present a complete program of social recreation, but rather to indicate how leadership seeks to attain certain goals through this particular medium.

PLANNING THE PROGRAM

Careful, detailed, painstaking planning is the foundation upon which a successful program of social recreation is based. It is now, for the first time in this book, that students must put to practical use their knowledge of the basic principles of leadership and of program planning discussed in the two preceding chapters. A principle unused is valueless.

Let us assume that you have accepted an invitation to conduct a program of social recreation. What planning should be done in advance of the event? The principle of anticipation requires you to look ahead and attempt to anticipate all difficulties that may arise so that you may prevent them; it calls for you to secure certain information and to act in terms of this information.

What the Leader Should Know

Among the most important things the leader should know as a basis for advance planning are: (1) age of the participants; (2) sex; (3) number in the group and how well the members know one another; (4) their educational, social, cultural, and recreational skill levels; (5) their physical condition; (6) the facilities available—size, shape, general condition; (7) equipment and supplies available; (8) type, length, and time of party desired; (9) funds available for prizes and decorations; (10) extent and nature of assistance you may depend on from the group; (11) nature of the sponsoring organization, and name, telephone number, and address of the organization's representative with whom you are to work. With this information the leader can proceed in an intelligent manner to plan a program that will meet the needs and abilities of a specific group in a specific situation.

What the Leader Should Do

The principle of involvement points the way toward one important function the leader should perform in the course of his advance planning. He should involve a number of people in the planning and carrying out of their own party. This may be done largely through the establishment of committees.

1. Secure the appointment of committees. Among the most important party committees are program, publicity, decorations, facilities and supplies, finance, refreshments, welcoming, and clean-up. All social recreation programs do not require the elaborate preparations implied in these committee recommendations, but whenever possible the members should participate actively in the planning and conduct of their program.

2. Develop a balanced program consisting of a variety of activities selected from social mixers, party games, relays, dramatic fun, brain teasers, music, dance, and pencil and paper games.

3. Have available more activities than you expect to use so there will never be an occasion when you lack material.

4. Arrange the program so that more than one activity may be conducted while the group is in a certain formation thus reducing the number of times you must move the group about. If you end a grand march in columns of eight, two or more relays or line games should follow, rather than a circle game followed by a single game. Or, when you finish Circle 4 Mixer you are in perfect position for Squirrel in Trees, but not for a relay.

5. Plan a program that is no longer than one hour and fifteen minutes, or at the most, an hour and a half.

6. Build the program around a central theme whenever possible. Such a theme provides the party with a unifying idea which ties everything together into meaningful relationships. Among the various types of popular parties with an easily identifiable theme are:

April Fools' Frolic	Golden Age	Paddy (Irish)
Birthday	Halloween	Potluck
Christmas	Hard times	Progressive
Circus	Hawaiian	Rodeo
Country	Hobo	Sadie Hawkins
Diploma Doings	Italian	Sailor
Easter	Lincoln's Birthday	Shower
Father's Day	Mother's Day	St. Valentine's Day
Fiesta	New Year's Eve	Thanksgiving
Fourth of July	Oriental	United States
Gay Nineties		

7. Arrange your activities in approximately the following order:
   a. Something for the early comers
   b. One or two social mixers
   c. A simple relay or relays
   d. A party game—perhaps two
   e. An easy folk or square dance
   f. A party game while seated
   g. A brain teaser or a pencil and paper game, or both

    h. Some dramatic fun

    i. Group singing.

This order may vary somewhat with the age of the group, length of time available, and certain other factors. Any suggested schedule of this nature should be looked upon as being completely flexible. If refreshments are planned they should be served about three-fourths of the way through the program and followed by relatively inactive party games, dramatic fun, and group singing.

8. In accordance with the principle of anticipation take no chances that everything will be all right just because someone else was assigned certain responsibilities. Arrive at the scene of the party early enough to check on equipment, supplies, room or gymnasium, decorations, and similar items. Are there ample song sheets for all? Is the room temperature comfortable? Are chairs available and located properly? Does the record player work or is the piano where you want it? These, and many similar questions, will be raised by the leader who is unwilling to leave such important matters to chance.

STRATEGIES OF LEADERSHIP

Vital to the success of any program of social recreation is the degree of social intelligence displayed by the leader as he works with human beings in activities involving group participation. The suggestions listed below are designed to assist the leader in achieving a level of performance sufficiently high to enable him to attain the goals of good interpersonal relations which social recreation seeks.

1. Be enthusiastic and show it; smile, have fun, and keep a laugh in your voice. People will take their cues from you.
2. Never embarrass anyone. This implies that activities should be easy; skillful performance is relatively unimportant; minor mistakes are overlooked; and games are avoided in which some have fun at the expense of others. Be patient, helpful, sympathetic, and kind. Relax, be human, and let your sense of humor show. It has been aptly said that a good social recreation leader "is limber, loving, and a little bit loony."
3. Know your activities and be skilled in their presentation. Confidence is based on knowledge and skill. In general, these steps should be followed in introducing a new game:
    a. Place the group in formation
    b. Name the game
    c. Explain it briefly; avoid long, drawn-out explanations

       d. Demonstrate it, if necessary
       e. Ask for questions
       f. Start immediately
       g. Observe play carefully and make whatever changes are necessary to improve it
       h. Encourage players or teams verbally
       i. Stop play before interest begins to lag and introduce a new activity.

4. Adapt the activity to the ability level of the group. For example, a game or relay may involve running if youth are taking part, but should be changed to walking if women in high-heeled shoes are playing. Also, be prepared to adjust to conditions and situations you were unable to foresee, such as a variation in the number of participants anticipated or a lack of game supplies.

5. Use a whistle sparingly, if at all. It is best to use it only as a signal for the group to become quiet so instructions may be given. When it is used for more than one purpose the group frequently is confused, since it can't tell for which purpose it is blown.

6. Stand where you can be seen and speak so you can be heard. Act in a confident manner. Any evidence of a lack of confidence on your part will quickly be sensed by the group and will constitute a major handicap. Never try to outtalk an inattentive group. Secure attention by a short, sharp blast on your whistle, raising your hand, or just standing quietly.

7. Never choose up sides because of the embarrassment to those chosen last. Use some impersonal method of dividing into teams.

8. If awards are presented they should be inexpensive.

9. Use words that people understand and supplement verbal instructions with gestures when desirable. For example, when you instruct a group to move in a counterclockwise direction indicate what you mean by a sweeping movement of the arm. Also, raise your voice at the end of a sentence when you wish to stimulate action; in starting a contest or relay say, "Ready—go!"

10. Dress appropriately for the occasion. What is appropriate depends upon such factors as the nature of the event, its location, the group, and even the day. When in doubt you would do well to lean toward conservatism.

SOCIAL MIXERS

The purpose of the social mixer, as the term implies, is to create a situation in which people must intermingle and meet numerous other people, many of whom they may never have met before. Americans are not particularly a cold, reserved, dignified people whose social inhibitions cause them to withdraw into a shell when they come into contact with strangers, but they frequently give this impression. Thus, the mixer is often called an "ice breaker" because it is designed to thaw out the icy exterior behind which so many people hide, and reveal the real, friendly, sociable human being behind it.

The values sought are fun, sociability, friendliness, and the extension and improvement of interpersonal relationships in a group situation.

Fun Around the Clock—Fourth Grade and Up

Distribute to all a copy of the material shown below. They also will need pencils. Explain the activity in this manner:

"Folks, in just a moment I shall call out a certain hour. For example, if I call 7:00 o'clock, you should immediately try to locate someone in the room who was born the same month as you. Introduce yourself and write his or her name on the proper line. I shall give you a very short time to do this, so work fast. Then I shall call another hour. In about five minutes I shall stop the game and we'll see who has collected the largest number of names. Here we go—6:00 o'clock!"

LEADERSHIP SUGGESTIONS.   Have available a number of extra pencils for those who may have none. Use assistants to pass out the sheets so as to avoid a delay which may endanger the success of your program. Allow not more than thirty seconds between your calls of hours. During the game don't stand aloof from the group; show an interest in the activity by mingling, exhorting, and laughing with the players. At the end of the game call the players together and ask, "How many have five or more names? Will you raise your hands? How many have seven or more?" In this way the winner is determined. Raise the winner's hand in exaggerated fashion, praise him, and if a prize is to be given, award a candy kiss or some equally inexpensive item.

	First Name	Last Name
1:00 A stranger to you	_____	_____
2:00 Same color of hair as yours	_____	_____
3:00 Same color eyes as yours	_____	_____

4:00 Same size shoes as yours   _____ _____

5:00 Opposite sex (exchange names)   _____ _____

6:00 Same height   _____ _____

7:00 Born same month   _____ _____

8:00 Same number of brothers or sisters   _____ _____

9:00 Same color dress or tie   _____ _____

10:00 First initial same as yours   _____ _____

11:00 Dislike same things   _____ _____

12:00 Same hobby   _____ _____

Barter—Fourth Grade and Up

Give everyone ten beans and a numbered slip of paper. Explain the activity as follows: "Now, I'm sure all of you would like to know just how good a salesman you are without it costing you anything. Here's your chance to find out. When I say 'go' you will approach another player and either try to sell your number for as many beans as possible or buy his number for as few beans as possible. Then you go from player to player trying to 'hook' each one for as much as you can at the same time trying to protect yourself against the slick, high-pressure salesmen in this group. If you can't do business immediately with a person, don't waste time on him. Go get yourself another victim. In about five minutes I shall blow a whistle and all bartering must stop then. Oh, by the way, one number has been chosen as a lucky number. Both the holder of the lucky number and the salesman who has the most beans will be given magnificent prizes. Ready—go!"

LEADERSHIP SUGGESTIONS.   Prepare the beans and numbers in advance by placing them in small envelopes about 3 × 4 inches. Stop the game at the end of five minutes; call out the time remaining at three and four minutes. At the end of the game call everyone together and ask all to raise their hands who have twenty or more beans, then twenty-five, thirty, and up until the winner has been determined. Also, ask, "How many have no beans at all?" As in the previous game, mingle with the players, laughing and joking with them.

Odd or Even—Fourth Grade and Up

This game is similar to Barter in many respects. Distribute ten beans, but no numbers. Explain the game somewhat as follows: "Years ago, folks, a man often was known by his ability as a horse trader. In this game we're not trading horses, but we are trading beans. Let's find out who the best bean trader is in this group. All of you have ten beans. Hide some of these beans in one hand, go up to someone, put your closed hand out, and ask him, 'Odd or even?' If he guesses 'even' and you do have an even number of beans in your hand you must give him these beans. However, if he guesses incorrectly he must give you the number of beans you have in your hand. Any questions? Ready—go!"

Circle Four Mixer—Third Grade and Up

All are in a circle facing counterclockwise. A good pianist playing a lively march will add zest to the activity. The leader describes the game in this manner: "When the music starts everyone will march around the circle in the direction you are now facing, keeping time to the music. When the music stops everyone must try to get into a small circle of just four people with hands joined. If more than four are in your circle you must squeeze them out. Those who do not get into a circle of four shall come into the center of the large circle and I'll tell you what to do before we play the game a second time. Ready—march!"

After the grand scramble to get into a small circle is over and the rejectees have come to the center of the circle the leader proceeds with the explanation: "Now this time we do exactly the same thing only you cannot make your small circle with the same four people that you did before. At least one person must be different. These lost souls in the center here will try to get into a small circle again when the music stops. Let's hope they're more successful this time."

LEADERSHIP SUGGESTIONS: Five or six minutes will be long enough for this game. Be sure that the pianist plays a rather fast and snappy march and that she stop at irregular intervals, none of which exceeds fifteen seconds. If piano music is not available use a record player, clap, or count, but some kind of music is best. Don't ridicule those who fail to get into a small circle; laugh and joke with them. After playing for a while with four in a circle, change to five, but be sure that the total number playing is not divisible by either four or five. It may be necessary to caution boys against being too rough with the girls when they "battle" for a place in the small group.

Famous Persons—Youth and Adults

Clip from magazines or newspapers pictures of famous or well-known persons and put on each a number beginning with one. Pin a picture on the back of each player and give each a score sheet as shown below. Describe the game as follows: "On the back of each of you is a picture of a well-known or famous person. When the signal is given you are to see how many of these famous people you can identify. When you do recognize one, write the name on your score sheet opposite the number identical with the number on the picture. Also write on the same line the name of the person on whose back the picture is pinned. Do not reveal to anyone the name of a famous person recognized."

LEADERSHIP SUGGESTIONS.   Some magazine pictures will be quite dark and numbers will not show up on them. When this occurs, cut out small one-inch squares from white paper, put the number on these, and staple them onto the picture. It is best to pin the pictures on the backs of people as they enter the room where the party is being held, thus avoiding a delay in the program later on. Caution all at this time not to reveal the names of any persons recognized. At the end of the game, call the group together and determine the winner by calling off the names of both real and famous persons from a master list compiled by an assistant during the pinning procedure.

Score Sheet for Famous Persons

	Name of real person	*Name of famous person*
1.		
2.		
3.		
4.		
5.		
6.		
7.		
8.		
9.		
10.		
11.		
12.		
13.		
14.		

15. _____
16. _____
17. _____
18. _____
19. _____
20. _____
21. _____
22. _____
23. _____
24. _____
25. _____

Split Proverbs—Senior High and Adults

Select a number of the longest proverbs you know and write each on a slip of paper. Cut each slip into three pieces and give each guest one piece. Then describe the game: "Each one of you has a slip of paper on which is written one-third of a well-known proverb. The purpose of this game is to put the parts of each proverb together. So, in just a moment when the signal to begin is given, you are to start proverb hunting by locating the other two people who have the missing parts of your proverb. When you have found them, all three of you should come to the front of the room, report to me, and stand with your third of the proverb in front of you so that, reading from left to right, the proverb is complete. Now, let's see who will be the first ones up here."

Here are some proverbs that may be used:

A fool and his money are soon parted.
Never look a gift horse in the mouth.
A rolling stone gathers no moss.
Birds of a feather flock together.
A bird in the hand is worth two in the bush.
It takes two to make a quarrel.
Who steals my purse steals trash.
Keep your eyes wide open before marriage, half shut afterwards.
There's many a slip twixt the cup and the lip.
Early to bed and early to rise makes a man healthy, wealthy, and wise.
Discretion is the better part of valor.
You may lead a horse to water, but you can't make him drink.
It's a long lane that has no turning.
He who lies down with dogs gets up with fleas.

What's sauce for the goose is sauce for the gander.
You cannot have your cake and eat it too.
Laugh and the world laughs with you; weep and you weep alone.
It's an ill wind that blows nobody good.
People in glass houses shouldn't throw stones.
In the kingdom of the blind, the one-eyed are kings.
He who pays the piper calls the tune.
The pen is mightier than the sword.
Necessity is the mother of invention.
Too many cooks spoil the broth.
Marry in haste and repent at leisure.
An apple a day keeps the doctor away.
It takes a thief to catch a thief.
Half a loaf is better than no bread.

LEADERSHIP SUGGESTIONS. Many books recommend cutting the proverbs only in half, but our experience with this game indicates that it is much too easy to find your partner when this is done. The game is over almost before it begins. Leaders should avoid the twin errors of making a game too easy or too difficult. After all, or nearly all, have lined up in proper position, announce the winners and have each group read its proverb.

Name Bingo—Youth and Adults

Give each person a sheet of paper and ask that he draw four horizontal and four vertical lines in such a manner that the paper is divided into nine boxes. Two of the vertical lines must be at the ends of the horizontal lines. The leader then describes the game: "Each of you has a sheet of paper with nine boxes. In just a moment go around the room and get the names of nine people, writing a different name in each box. When you have finished I shall call out the names of various people here. Whenever I call a name that appears in one of your boxes you should cross it off with your pencil. The first person to cross off three names in a row horizontally, vertically, or diagonally should call out 'Name Bingo.' He will be the winner."

LEADERSHIP SUGGESTIONS. The number of boxes should vary with the size of the group. It is recommended that nine boxes be used if the group has less than thirty members; if thirty to fifty, then use sixteen boxes; and if over fifty, have the players draw twenty-five boxes. If a check on the accuracy and honesty of the winner is desired have an assistant write the names as you call them and check his list against the winner's list. Have some extra pencils on hand.

PARTY GAMES

Jungle Din—All Ages

Before anyone has arrived for the party, hide throughout the room a fairly large number of candy kisses or peanuts in the shell. Divide the group into teams, preferably with about six to ten players on a team. Assign a captain to each team. Explain the game as follows: "We're going to have a lot of fun with this game, but before we can begin it is necessary that each team go into a huddle and choose some animal or fowl it would like to represent. Be sure to select one whose call, cry, or bark is easily imitated: for example, sheep with their baa—baa; or a turkey with its gobble-gobble-gobble. Do this now, and then I'll explain the game. Are you ready? Listen carefully. Hidden around the room in all kinds of hiding places are many candy kisses. When I give the signal all of you will start hunting. When you find a candy kiss you are to give the call of your animal or fowl. You must not pick up the candy kiss. Only your leader can pick it up; your job is to call your leader, stand guard over the treasure until your leader arrives, and then go find another. When I blow the whistle to end the game come back into your lines where you are now and your captain will count the candy kisses your team has found. The winning team will be the one with the most kisses. One final point—if a member of the dog team finds a candy kiss and barks over it no one from any other team may claim it. The first one to find it, gets it. I'm sure you'll all be fair about this. Let's go!"

LEADERSHIP SUGGESTIONS.   Peanuts are cheaper, but if you don't want shells on the floor it's better to use candy. Be sure to hide at least as many pieces of candy as there are players—more if possible. Regardless of the number of players, divide into at least four teams; if there are fifty players use six teams. Don't choose up teams as this will embarrass those chosen last. An easy way to group party members for this type of activity is simply to count off by whatever number you wish on a team and have all the one's, two's, three's and on up get together. Or, you can give them a number on a slip of paper as they arrive. Still a third method is to end a grand march in files of four or eight and use these groupings as your teams. After the teams have selected their animals, ask the captains to call out the name of the animal so there will be no duplications. Emphasize the importance of fair play in that the good sport will not pick up a candy kiss if he is not a leader and he will not try to claim a treasure found by another.

During the game the leader should exhort one and all to let everyone know they have found a kiss by the vigorousness of their yelling.

The game is well named Jungle Din, with emphasize on the second word.

Hunters, Guns, and Rabbits—Fourth Grade and Up

This is one of the very best social recreation games for all groups above the third grade. The author has taught it hundreds of times and it has never failed to capture the enthusiasm of the players.

Divide the players into an even number of teams. Players on a team stand side by side and face the members of the opposing team from a distance of eight to ten feet. If six teams are playing, they will line up in these positions:

1	2	3	4	5	6
X	X	X	X	X	X
X	X	X	X	X	X
X	X	X	X	X	X
X	X	X	X	X	X
X	X	X	X	X	X
X	X	X	X	X	X
X	X	X	X	X	X
X	X	X	X	X	X
8′		8′		8′	

Teams one and two play against one another as do three and four, and five and six.

GAME DESCRIPTION. "The purpose of this game is to score points by outwitting your opponents. In just a moment your team will go into a football huddle and decide whether you will be hunters, guns, or rabbits. Don't let the other team know what you are going to be. When you have made up your minds, come back into your present position. Now, listen carefully. If you think the other team is going to be guns, you should be hunters because hunters can shoot guns. If you have a hunch they are going to be rabbits, then you should be guns because guns shoot rabbits. If you believe they will be hunters, you should be rabbits because hunters cannot catch rabbits. Go into your huddles now, make your choice, come back into line, and I'll tell you what we'll do next.

"All right, we're ready to go. When I give the signal, if you are guns, you will point an imaginary gun at your opponents. If you are hunters, you will simply stand with your hands on your hips. If you are rabbits, put your thumbs on your temples, hands open, palms out, and flap your hands back and forth like the ears of a rabbit as you jump up and down. Ready—go!"

Bedlam breaks out especially when opposing teams both point guns at one another or do the rabbit hop at the same time, thus constituting a tie game.

LEADERSHIP SUGGESTIONS. If a blackboard is available write these reminders so all can see:

Hunters beat guns
Guns beat rabbits
Rabbits beat hunters

Announce that the team first scoring three points is the winner. Speed in the huddle generally is achieved by stating that the players at the ends of the lines nearest you will serve as captains. In calling out "Ready—go," drag out the "Ready," thus heightening the suspense and adding to the fun. Point out the winning teams after each game and comment on the ties.

Ping Pong Football—Third Grade and Young Adults

Divide into an even number of teams with six to ten players on a team. For each two teams an official, a table tennis table, and ball are necessary. Two teams to a table are arranged in such a manner that the players of one team are standing along one side and one end while the other team protects the other side and end of the table.

GAME DESCRIPTION. "You are about to take part in the football game of the century. Just before your official places the ball in the center of the table you will crouch or kneel down so that your chin is on a level with the table. When the ball is placed on the table you will blow with all your might attempting to blow the ball off the table on your opponent's side or end. Any time you do this your team scores a point. Also, if the ball touches the chin, face, or any other part of a player's body or clothing a point is scored against his team. The winner is the team that first scores five points. Let's see who are the biggest blowers here, but be careful you don't swallow the ball."

LEADERSHIP SUGGESTIONS. Use assistants as officials and instruct them to call all fouls whenever the ball touches a player. If each team has but five or six players and the ping pong table comes apart in the middle, use only half a table as the entire table may be too large an area for this number to protect. Teach players that the good sportsman calls his own foul when the ball touches him; praise those who do. Let the winners at each table play for the championship while the losers play one another.

Streets and Alleys—Fourth Grade and Up

Players are arranged in several parallel lines of equal numbers, hands joined, and facing the leader. The lines are about three feet apart. In this position the spaces between the lines are known as streets.

	X		X		X		X
	X		X		X		X
O Leader	X	Street	X	Street	X	Street	X
	X		X		X		X
	X		X		X		X

When the leader calls out "alleys," the players make a quarter-turn to the right and join hands with others in line thus forming four alleys. Two additional players are in the game; one chases the other in a game of tag.

GAME DESCRIPTION. "As you stand facing me now you have formed three streets between your lines. When I call out 'alleys,' all of you should turn one-quarter turn to the right and join hands thus forming four alleys. John is trying to catch Mary by chasing her through the streets and alleys. At no time may either one break through the lines; they must go around the ends. If John catches Mary, then Mary must chase John. Ready—go!"

LEADERSHIP SUGGESTIONS. Call out "streets" and "alleys" often as these quick changes add to the fun and complicate the chase. Have the two runners trade places frequently with two players in line so that many may have the pleasure of running. Stress the importance of acknowledging immediately the fact that you are tagged. Suggest that adults walk fast rather than run.

Ha Ha—Twelve Years and Up

Divide into groups of six to ten seated in small circles. Assign one person to be the judge in each group.

GAME DESCRIPTION. "Everyone likes to think that he can control his emotions. This game will give you a chance to find out just how good you are at self-control. The purpose of the game is not to laugh or even to have the slightest flicker of a smile on your face at any time. If you laugh or smile you are out of the game and must move your chair back out of the circle. The winner is the player in each group who resists the longest the temptation to laugh or smile. The game begins when one player says, 'ha.' The player to his left says, 'ha, ha.' The third player may try to force a laugh with a sing-song, 'ha, ha, ha, ha, ha, ha, ha!' The judge waves out of the game anyone who laughs or smiles. All right, let's see who the champion sourpuss of each group is."

LEADERSHIP SUGGESTIONS. Locate the various groups far enough apart so that they will not interfere with one another. Demonstrate the game with a centrally located group. Give examples of almost sure-fire laugh provokers such as a short, sharp ha; high, falsetto ha's; deep, bass, slowly spaced ha's; and a combination of all of these. The individual who can long resist the almost overpowering urge to laugh is rare indeed.

This Is My Nose—Twelve Years and Up

Keep the groups in the same small circles as in the "Ha Ha" game although it will be best if they enlarge them slightly. One person in each group is "It" and stands in the center of the circle.

GAME DESCRIPTION. "It" moves slowly around the circle, suddenly stops in front of a seated player, grasps some part of his body, such as his elbow, with one hand and says, 'This is my nose.' He then immediately counts to ten. The seated player in front of whom 'It' stops must grasp his nose and say, 'This is my elbow,' before 'It' reaches ten or he becomes 'It' and the former 'It' takes his seat."

LEADERSHIP SUGGESTIONS. This game is not as easily learned as are some of the games previously explained in this chapter. The leader should explain the game carefully and demonstrate slowly with a centrally located group. Emphasizing the importance of "It" concealing until the last possible moment the place where he plans to stop and start his count. It will help to tell the seated players they must always grasp their noses while "It" never does.

Ghosts—Twelve Years and Up

Retain the same small-group formation as in the two previous games.

Designate one player in each group to be timekeeper. This is an old game, but an excellent one. Not only is it thoroughly enjoyable but it is also educational in that it broadens one's vocabulary and helps one learn to spell.

GAME DESCRIPTION. "The purpose of this game is to avoid adding the last letter thus completing the spelling of a word. Two-letter words do not count and proper nouns are not allowed. Let's all watch this group play for a moment. Mary will start a word with the first letter; John, to her left, must add a letter as does each person when it comes his turn. Now, if Mary begins with 't,' John adds 'r'; Bill tries 'a'; and Alice submits 'j'; Jack, whose turn it is, may doubt if Alice knows of any word beginning with the letters 'traj' so he challenges Alice. If Alice cannot name such a word she becomes a third of a ghost. On the other hand, if she says she was spelling trajectory, then Jack becomes a third of a ghost. In either case, the player to Jack's left begins a new word. You are allowed thirty seconds in which to add a letter or challenge. After you miss three times you are a full ghost and out of the game. Then you must try to get the remaining players to talk with you and if any do, they become ghosts and are out of the game. The winner is the only non-ghost left in the game. Please understand that if Alice had added 'm,' thus spelling tram, and some player called out that this was a word, Alice would have become a third of a ghost even if she protested that the word she had in mind was tramp."

LEADERSHIP SUGGESTIONS. Instruct the timekeeper to notify the player involved when he has five seconds remaining. Point out that fairness prohibits helping other players in any manner. Establish the rule that no word may be spelled more than once in any one game.

RELAYS

Relays are one of the most inexpertly conducted types of activities in the entire program of recreation, not because of any difficulties inherent in their nature, but because leaders neglect to observe a few simple techniques basic to their successful conduct. The most important of these include:

1. The starting and finishing lines should be clearly defined.
2. Emphasize that each runner must stay *back of* the starting line until

his hand has been touched by the preceding runner—provided it is this type of relay.

3. In most relays, teams should consist of not more than eight or ten players. When larger numbers are involved on each team there is too much waiting for one's turn and the time required to conduct the relay is too long. There is no particular fun standing around for a long period of time when these delays could be eliminated simply by having more teams with fewer players per team.

4. If some teams have one less player than the others, instruct the captain to have one player run twice.

5. If the relay involves running or walking to a goal and returning, establish a type of goal around which the player runs. A chair, an Indian club, a volleyball standard, or even a book on the floor may be used. Running to a line on the floor and returning is unsatisfactory because of the constant temptation to cheat by not quite reaching the line plus the difficulty of judging whether the runners actually did reach it. Never run to a wall because of the hazard involved.

6. When the last runner of a team crosses the finish line the entire team should sit down, thus clearly identifying the order of finish. If adults are playing this may be changed to leaning over and placing their hands on their knees. Also, it is usually better to substitute walking for running when adults are involved.

7. Penalize children and youth for infractions of the rules by stopping them at the point of infraction and sending them back to start over again or by deducting points from their team's total. Relays possess considerable potential value for strengthening the moral fiber of youth provided they are conducted properly. Conversely, if the leader ignores cheating the youngsters learn that anything goes as long as you can get away with it. It is no justification for a leader to ignore cheating in a relay on the grounds that this is a party in which fun and sociability are the sole goals and the feelings of children may be hurt if penalties are administered for unfair conduct. The manner in which the penalty is administered—with a smile and perhaps a humorous comment— need not be hypercritical, but you are responsible for the quality of the experiences which these children have under your leadership and must remember that every experience leaves its mark, either for good or evil, upon their developing personalities.

If adults cheat in social relays the leader might say, "Now, folks, I noticed that some of us apparently misunderstood the rule which requires you to go around the Indian club rather than cut across in front of it. I'm sorry I failed to make this clear. Now, let's try it again." Do not identify the offender under any circumstances. If he's a confirmed cheater, it is too late for you to reform him. Check him off as a lost soul and forget about him.

Shock Relay—Fifteen Years and Up

Divide the group into teams with eight to sixteen members each, standing side by side and holding hands. The teams are in parallel columns about six feet apart.

DESCRIPTION. "When I say 'go' in just a moment each of you leaders who are at this end of the lines, will squeeze the hand of the person next to you; he will squeeze the hand of the third person, who, in turn, will squeeze the hand of the fourth. The shock is thus transmitted along your team to the last player who then immediately squeezes the hand of the player who just squeezed his. The shock is then sent back up the line to your leader who, upon receiving it, immediately raises his hand. The team which first transmits the shock down and back is the winner. There are two important things to remember: (1) this is an opportunity you have been looking forward to for a long time—to squeeze your boy or girl friend's hand; and (2) no hand squeezing until your hand has first been squeezed."

LEADERSHIP SUGGESTIONS. It is essential that the teams have an equal number of players. If they do not, use the extra players as judges, or, if only one team lacks a player, you should play with it. Announce the winners each time.

Chair Relay—Twelve Years and Up

Teams consisting of not more than eight players line up in single file back of a common starting line. Directly in front of each team and thirty feet away is a folding chair, folded up and lying on the floor.

DESCRIPTION. "When the signal to run is given, the first player on each team will run to the chair in front of him, open it, sit on it, lift his feet and click his heels together once, get up and fold the chair, leaving it on the floor as it is now, run back, and touch the hand of the second runner who does the same thing. Bill, will you show us just what we are to do?"

Package Busting Relay—Eight Years and Up

Teams are in the same formation as in the preceding relay. The chairs, however, are unfolded and located just to the right of the leader of each team. One each chair are a number of empty paper bags. Thirty feet in advance of each team is a wastebasket.

DESCRIPTION.   "In this relay we find out which is the best bag busting team here tonight. On the chairs next to your leaders are a number of paper bags. On signal, the leader will pick up a bag, run to the wastebasket, blow up the bag, burst it, drop it in the wastebasket, and run back to the starting line. The second player does the same after the leader touches his hand. Let's see which team will finish first and who can produce the loudest 'pop.'"

Square Relay—Ten Years and Up

The players are divided into four teams. Each team is seated on the side of a square and faces a table in the center of the square as shown in the diagram below. The player sitting in the end seat at the left of each line holds some object such as a ball or beanbag.

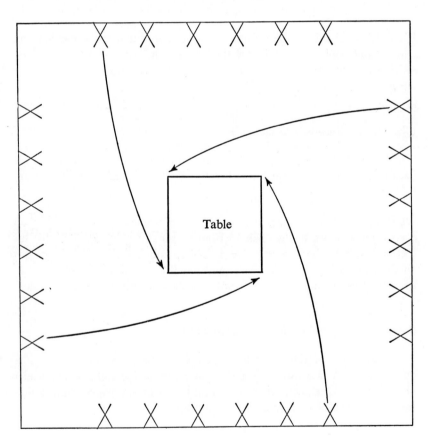

DESCRIPTION. "Let's watch Bill's team walk through this relay. When I give the signal John will pass the ball he is holding to Mary on his right, and she will pass it to the next player. Each player must handle the ball and pass it on. When Bill, at the far right of the line, get it he, carrying the ball, will walk as fast as he can around the table to his right and back to the chair where John is now sitting. The moment Bill starts his walk, however, each of you on his team must move one chair to the right, thus leaving the chair at the far left of the line vacant for Bill when he completes his walk. When Bill sits down he passes the ball to his right and the relay continues as before with each player walking in turn. When everyone has walked and the last player is seated, the race is over. Remember, now, there is no traffic officer at the table so be careful not to walk over one another."

LEADERSHIP SUGGESTIONS. Permit children and youth to run, but instruct adults to walk. Be sure to demonstrate with one team before starting the race. Suggest that each team constitute a cheering section for its runners.

BRAIN TEASERS

Brain teasers are interesting, enjoyable, and intriguing to many adults, but they have little value for youth. In general, I would restrict the use of brain teasers to small adult groups with a fairly high educational level. The leader must be very careful to avoid embarrassing anyone; don't call off individual scores or even insist that an individual give his answer to any particular question. The leader may ask for volunteers or he may divide the players into small groups which compete with one another on a team basis. In most instances, it is doubtful if any kind of competition is desirable.

The Shoe Salesman

A man comes into a store to buy a pair of shoes. He decides to purchase a pair costing $7.00 and presents a $20.00 bill in payment. The clerk lacks the proper change so he goes next door to another merchant and gets the $20.00 bill changed. He returns to his store, wraps up the shoes and gives the buyer his $13.00 in change.

A few minutes later, after the man had left with his shoes, the merchant next door rushes into the shoe store protesting loudly that the $20.00 bill is counterfeit. Upon investigation this is found to be true so the manager of the store refunds his $20.00. How much did the shoe store lose on the deal?

LEADERSHIP SUGGESTIONS. Give the various members of the group an opportunity to express their opinions. You will get several answers, but seldom the correct one. The store actually lost $20.00. Nothing was lost on the shoes since the store received seven good dollars for the shoes and the $13.00 in change was the next-door merchant's money, not the shoe store's. So, all that was lost was the $20.00 required to replace the counterfeit bill.

The Book Worm

Two books, volumes one and two, are standing on a bookshelf in the usual order. The covers of the books are each a quarter of an inch thick and the pages within each book are three inches thick. A bookworm eats its way from page one, volume one, to the last page of volume two. How far did he eat?

The answer, of course, is one-half inch since the worm eats only through the front cover of volume one and the back cover of volume two. The usual order for such volumes on a bookshelf is that volume one be on the left of volume two.

A Four-Way Puzzler

Give each person a blank sheet of paper and a pencil. Ask each player to draw a large X on his paper as shown below.

Description: "Now listen carefully. First I'll give you some hints for

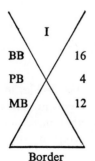

the solution of each problem and then I'll come back to the questions. In the top space of the X put a capital I. In the space to the right put the figures 16, 4, and 12. You're a bus driver with 16 passengers. At the first stop you let off 4 passengers and at the next stop you pick up 12.

At the bottom of the X draw a straight horizontal line. This line represents the boundary line between the United States and Canada. An airplane flying over the border crashes with ten survivors.

In the space to the left of the X write these three sets of initials: BB, PB, and MB. The initials stand for Baby Bull, Papa Bull, and Mamma Bull.

Now, let's go back to the top of the X. The first problem: next to the capital I write a small i with a dot above. Next problem: How old is the bus driver? Third problem: at the bottom of the X tell where you would bury the survivors of the plane crash. Last problem: The baby bull gets hungry. To which of the other two should it go?"

You will get many interesting answers, but few correct ones. The correct way to write a small i with a dot above is to place one dot above the other, for the small i already contains one dot. The answer to the second problem is the age of the player answering it since you specifically said, "You're a bus driver. . . . " The answer to the third problem is to be found in the general aversion to burying survivors. Most answers to the last problem will be wrong since we know there is no such thing as a mamma bull.

A Modern Intelligence Test

1. How many birthdays does the average man have?
2. Why can't a man living south of the Ohio River be buried in his home town?
3. If you went to bed at eight in the evening and set the alarm for nine in the morning, how many hours would you sleep?
4. Do they have a Fourth of July in England?
5. How many months have twenty-eight days?
6. What four words are on every piece of U. S. coin?
7. How many different species of animals did Moses take aboard the Ark with him?
8. How many outs in each inning of a baseball game?
9. A man takes a coin marked 500 B.C. to a bank. How did the banker know it was a fraud?
10. A man builds a rectangular house. Each side has a southern exposure. A bear walks by. What color is the bear?
11. Is it legal in Indiana for a man to marry his widow's sister?
12. A man has two U. S. coins in his hand that total 55¢. One is not a nickel. What are the two coins?
13. Two men are playing checkers. They play five games. Each man wins the same number of games. There are no ties. How do you account for that?

14. A woman gives a beggar 50¢. The woman is the beggar's sister, but the beggar is not the woman's brother. How come?
15. A doctor gives his patient three pills and tells him to take one every half hour. How long would the pills last?
16. How far can a dog run into the woods?
17. A farmer had 17 sheep and all but nine died. How many did he have left?
18. Divide 30 by ½ and add ten. What is the answer?
19. Take two apples from three apples. How many do you have?
20. A man enters a room with one match in his hand. In the room is an oil lamp, an oil heater and a wood stove. Which one does he light first?

Answers:
1. One. 2. Because he is alive. 3. One. 4. Yes, but they don't celebrate it. 5. All of them. 6. United States of America. 7. None, it was Noah. 8. Six. 9. In 500 B.C. no one knew it was B.C. 10. White, since only at the North Pole could all four walls of a house have a southern exposure and only polar bears are found there. 11. Not when he's dead. 12. A 50 cent piece and a nickel. One, the 50 cent piece, is not a nickel. 13. They are not playing each other. 14. The beggar is a woman. 15. One hour. 16. Halfway, because from that point on he is running out. 17. Nine. 18. 70. 19. Two. 20. The match.

Famous Characters

Friendly competition among small groups heightens interest in this game and embarrasses no one. The leader asks the question, "What persons or characters are associated with a Jawbone?" The first group to call out Samson scores a point. Other possibilities include:

1. A Log Cabin — Abraham Lincoln
2. A Wolf — Red Riding Hood
3. Bulrushes — Moses
4. A Moustache — Hitler
5. A Hatchet — George Washington
6. Wisdom — Solomon
7. Strength — Hercules
8. Airplane — Wright Brothers
9. A Spider Web — Robert Bruce
10. Many Wives — Henry VIII
11. An Apple — William Tell
12. A Kite — Franklin
13. A Whale — Jonah
14. A Silver Lamp — Aladdin
15. A Glass Slipper — Cinderella
16. The Armada — Sir Francis Drake

17. Cup of Hemlock — Socrates
18. Fiddle — Nero
19. Cleopatra — Antony
20. Falling Weights — Galileo
21. Pound of Flesh — Shylock
22. A Duel — Alexander Hamilton
23. A Looking Glass — Alice in Wonderland
24. A Cotton Gin — Eli Whitney
25. A Midnight Ride — Paul Revere

PENCIL AND PAPER GAMES

This type of activity has value provided it is properly conducted and provided the group is a homogeneous one with some college education. The college education may not be necessary to answer the questions, but it is doubtful if groups below this educational level will display much interest in the activity. Leaders should emphasize the play aspect of these games and refrain from creating any impression that a test of intelligence is about to be administered or that a contest for individual honors is to be conducted. Do not reveal individual scores.

Find the Partner

Distribute sheets to each player on which are mimeographed or dittoed the following latter parts of well-known phrases. Divide the group into teams of not more than eight players. Each team selects a scorer who records the answer agreed upon by the team. Allow a maximum of five minutes for this. The leader then calls out the correct answers and the team scorers determine their total score. A candy kiss for each member of the winning team might add to the fun of the occasion.

1. _____ and lightning
2. _____ and snow
3. _____ or perish
4. _____ or swim
5. _____ or die
6. _____ and hearty
7. _____ and roll
8. _____ and be merry
9. _____ and eggs
10. _____ and stripes
11. _____ and obey
12. _____ and dale
13. _____ and fortune
14. _____ and board
15. _____ and night
16. _____ and tucker
17. _____ and main
18. _____ and nail
19. _____ and fury
20. _____ to nuts

21. _____ and glove   26. _____ and fro
22. _____ and tongs   27. _____ and forth
23. _____ and chips   28. _____ and out
24. _____ and punishment   29. _____ and error
25. _____ and jury   30. _____ and gray

Answers:

1. Thunder	7. Rock	13. Fame	19. Sound	25. Judge
2. Ice	8. Eat, Drink	14. Room	20. Soup	26. To
3. Survive	9. Ham (or Bacon)	15. Day	21. Hand	27. Back
4. Sink	10. Stars	16. Bib	22. Hammer	28. In
5. Do	11. Love	17. Might	23. Fish	29. Trial
6. Hale	12. Hill	18. Tooth	24. Crime	30. Blue

Select Your Weapons

This is not the type of game to use with old ladies. The leader should be careful to select activities in which the participants are interested and are likely to display a fair degree of competence. Use the small-group plan of organization. Distribute to each player a copy of the following list of sports and a major item of equipment used in each. The object of this game is to match each sport with the equipment used in it. Each player contributes his thinking to the team effort recorded by the team's scorer. The leader should ask each team captain to notify him when the team has finished. When all are ready, the leader reads the correct answers and the winning team is announced with the proper ceremony.

1. Driver	—	Fishing
2. Shuttlecock	—	Gymnastics
3. Puck	—	Tennis
4. Foil	—	Curling
5. Cue	—	Golf
6. Net	—	Cricket
7. Agate	—	Shuffleboard
8. Reel	—	Croquet
9. Pelota	—	Badminton
10. Wicket	—	Ice Hockey
11. Racket	—	Horseshoes
12. Mallet	—	Archery
13. Horse	—	Fencing
14. Stake	—	Billiards
15. Quiver	—	Volleyball
16. Disk	—	Jai Alai
17. Stone	—	Marbles

Answers:

1. Golf	6. Volleyball	10. Cricket	14. Horseshoes
2. Badminton	7. Marbles	11. Tennis	15. Archery
3. Ice Hockey	8. Fishing	12. Croquet	16. Shuffleboard
4. Fencing	9. Jai Alai	13. Gymnastics	17. Curling
5. Billiards			

Famous Places or Things

This, too, is a matching game played in the same manner as the preceding game. The object of the game is to match each item on the left with its natural partner on the right.

1. Old Faithful	—	Oregon
2. The Louvre	—	Florida
3. The Acropolis	—	China
4. Empire State Building	—	Texas
5. Taj Mahal	—	India
6. The Pyramids	—	Yellowstone National Park
7. Carlsbad Caverns	—	Athens
8. Grand Canyon	—	London
9. Bryce Canyon	—	South Dakota
10. Independence Hall	—	Paris
11. Churchill Downs	—	New York
12. The Everglades	—	Rome
13. The Panhandle	—	California
14. Death Valley	—	Italy
15. Crater Lake	—	Arizona
16. The Badlands	—	New Mexico
17. Big Ben	—	Utah
18. Mt. Vesuvius	—	Philadelphia
19. The Great Wall	—	Louisville
20. The Colosseum	—	Egypt
21. The Alamo	—	San Antonio
22. The O K Corral	—	Tombstone

Answers:
1. Yellowstone National Park 2. Paris 3. Athens 4. New York
5. India 6. Egypt 7. New Mexico 8. Arizona 9. Utah 10. Philadelphia 11. Louisville 12. Florida 13. Texas 14. California
15. Oregon 16. South Dakota 17. London 18. Italy 19. China
20. Rome 21. San Antonio 22. Tombstone

Famous or Infamous Americans

Divide the group into small teams and give to each member a

copy of the material listed below. Team members pool their knowledge and the team scorer records the results by placing the proper number in the space on the right.

1. The Rail-splitter		——Sacajawea
2. The Rock of Chickamauga		——Hatfield, Leader of the Hatfield Clan in the Hatfield-McCoy Feud
3. The Cotton Gin		——Francis Marion
4. Old Hickory		——Thomas Jefferson
5. Old Fuss and Feathers		——William Jennings Bryan
6. The Silver-Tongued Orator		——Sam Houston
7. Stonewall		——Ethan Allen
8. The Pathfinder		——General Winfield Scott
9. The Little Giant		——Zachary Taylor
10. Scarface		——Abraham Lincoln
11. The Bird Woman		——Andrew Jackson
12. Mad Anthony		——General Wayne
13. The Raven		——J. C. Fremont
14. The Swamp Fox		——Jim Bridger
15. Hero of Fort Ticonderoga		——Tecumseh's Brother
16. Author of Declaration of Independence		——General George H. Thomas
17. Devil Anse		——Eli Whitney
18. Old Rough and Ready		——Al Capone
19. The Mountain Man		——Stephen A. Douglas
20. The Prophet		——General T. J. Jackson

Answers: 1. Lincoln 2. Thomas 3. Whitney 4. Andrew Jackson 5. Scott 6. Bryan 7. T. J. Jackson 8. Fremont 9. Douglas 10. Capone 11. Sacajawea 12. Wayne 13. Houston 14. Marion 15. Allen 16. Jefferson 17. Hatfield 18. Taylor 19. Bridger 20. Tecumseh's Brother

DRAMATIC FUN

No pretense is made of offering here a program of serious drama. Since total recreation programs usually are limited to a maximum of an hour and a half no extended period of preparation can be engaged in. Therefore, brief skits characterized primarily by pantomime and emphasizing fun and fellowship will constitute the major share of dramatic fun in social recreation. Care should be taken by the leader to avoid any type of presentation that may embarrass anyone or which can be considered cheap, vulgar, and in bad taste. Drama may be simple and still possess quality.

The widespread appeal of drama is revealed by the extent to which almost all people love to make believe. Both children and adults respond quickly and easily to dramatic stunts; charades; pantomimes; and story, ballad, and song dramatizations. Dramatic fun is one of the most delightful forms of recreation for both participant and spectator. Only a few suggestions are offered here since a later chapter deals more extensively with drama in recreation.

Parade of the Months

Divide the group on the basis of the months in which the members were born. Each group gets together to plan a skit designed to portray or symbolize something characteristic of their month. The leader then calls on each group to present its skit. Following each presentation, the audience is asked to identify the month. In general, that skit will be best which most clearly portrays a revealing feature of the particular month involved.

Some possible themes are:

January—Sing "Jingle Bells" or stage a snowball fight.
February—Pantomime cutting down a cherry tree or Lincoln splitting rails.
March—Kite flying, or simply march.
April—Stage some April fool jokes or dramatize April showers.
May—Dance around a maypole.
June—School is out.
July—Celebrate the Fourth.
August—A trip to the old swimming hole.
September—Back to school.
October—Halloween.
November—Thanksgiving.
December—Christmas.

Guess the Game

Divide into small groups not exceeding five or six players. Each group is given a few minutes to plan how it will act out the playing of a game. If time permits and the number of groups is small, permit each to present two games. After each presentation the audience attempts to identify the game that was presented. The leader should caution the audience to refrain from calling out the name of the activity until after the troupe has completed its act. Only highly organized games or sports should be presented. The leader should encourage the groups to present some sports that are not well-known in their particular section of the country. Examples might include curling, Jai Alai, yachting, water polo, squash, roque, ice boating, scuba diving, and mountain climbing.

Everyday Pantomimes

The group is divided into small troupes as in the preceding activity. Each group of actors selects two different common everyday activities and is given a few minutes to plan how it shall pantomime these. Clarity is an important quality sought. The audience guesses the activity following each presentation.

Possible activities include:

1. Milking a cow
2. Changing a tire
3. Dialing a telephone
4. Taking a shower
5. Playing a banjo
6. Mowing the yard
7. Spanking your child
8. Driving an automobile
9. Going to bed
10. Studying for an examination
11. Making out your income tax
12. Riding a horse
13. Climbing a ladder
14. Watching television
15. Scrubbing the bath tub

What Animal Am I?

Prepare in advance a number of slips of paper on each of which is written the name of a different animal. If the group is a small one, fifteen or less, and you feel certain no one will be embarrassed by an individual performance, give each person a slip; otherwise, follow the small-group plan as in previous presentations. Allow a short period of time to plan how one will imitate the actions of the animal assigned to him. Spectators will guess the name of the animal after the demonstration.

Suggested animals with some possible actions are:

1. Dog — Howl at the moon
2. Cat — Play with imaginary mouse, purr
3. Lion — Roar
4. Tiger — Pace back and forth, growl
5. Horse — Gallop
6. Rabbit — Hop and flop ears (hands at head)
7. Goat — Run and butt
8. Groundhog — Run into hole, then peer out
9. Squirrel — Climb tree, carry nut in mouth
10. Bull — Snort and paw ground

11. Gorilla   — Roar, strut, and beat chest
12. Bear   — Waddle, swaying head from side to side
13. Giraffe   — Eat leaves high on tree
14. Alligator   — Swim and snap jaws
15. Elephant   — Move ponderously, extend trunk for peanuts

Proverbs

Divide into small groups with from four to eight members. Ideally, not more than six groups should take part in this activity. As leader, you go from group to group giving each a choice of four or five proverbs. This procedure is preferable to the arbitrary assignment of one proverb by the leader. Allow time for the groups to plan their presentations, requesting each group captain to notify you when his actors are ready. Caution them that no talking is permissible; all must be in pantomime. When all are ready, the groups present, in turn, their proverbs. After each presentation the audience guesses the proverb. Permit no guessing until after the act is completed. Encourage hearty applause for each group.

In addition to the list of approximately thirty proverbs on pages 162-163 of this book, other possibilities are:

A word to the wise is sufficient.
All things come to him who waits.
Haste makes waste.
Easy come, easy go.
Don't count your chickens before they're hatched.
Two heads are better than one.
A stitch in time saves nine.
Absence makes the heart grow fonder
Paddle your own canoe.
If at first you don't succeed, try, try again.
A barking dog never bites.
A watched pot never boils.

Charades

Follow the small group plan of organization, preferably four to seven members. Each group decides for itself what it will pantomime—a word or the title of a story, play, book, motion picture, or song. Allow time for the group to prepare its skit. When all are ready each group, in turn, announces the general nature of its presentation and proceeds with the charade. After the charade has been completed, the audience attempts to guess the title or word pantomimed. The leader emphasizes that one of the outstanding characteristics of a superior presentation is clarity.

Groups should be encouraged to select their own words or titles to be pantomimed, but suggestions, such as those listed, sometimes are helpful in stimulating the creative processes.

Words:
        Automobile—ought-oh-mob-eel
        Aeroplane—Air-oh-plane
        Handkerchief—Hand-cur-chief
        Infancy—In-fan-cy
        Crocodile—Crock-oh-dial
        Cannibal—Can-eye-ball
        Heroes—He-rows
        Kingdom—King-dumb
        Masquerade—Mass-cur-aid
        Caricature—carry-cat-your
        Spinster—Spin-stir
        Eyelash—Eye-lash
        Cantankerous—Can-tank-er-us
        Parachute—Pair-a-shoot
        Parasite—Pair-a-sight
        Restitute—Rest-eye-toot

Book, Play, or Story Titles:

Little Women	*The Hound of the Baskervilles*
Gone with the Wind	*Antony and Cleopatra*
War and Peace	*Much Ado About Nothing*
Spartacus	*Crazy Horse*
A Midsummer Night's Dream	*The Coming Fury*
The Red Badge of Courage	*Drums Along the Mohawk*
For Whom the Bell Tolls	*All Quiet on the Western Front*

Song Titles:

"Down in the Valley"	"She'll Be Comin' 'Round the
"Row, Row, Row Your Boat"	Mountain"
"Cool Water"	"When the Saints Go Marching In"
"The Blue Tail Fly"	"On Top of Old Smoky"
"Don't Fence Me In"	"I've Been Working on the Railroad"
	"When You Wore a Tulip"

PROGRAMS FOR SPECIFIC GROUPS

This chapter has presented somewhat in detail, methods and materials involved in the conduct of programs of social recreation. Knowledge of the parts, however, is no guarantee that an individual can put them

together in such a manner that they will function harmoniously in relation to each other and in relation to the whole program. The purpose of
this section, therefore, is to give students an opportunity to see and analyze
two different types of programs planned for specific groups.

A Junior High School Club

Approximately thirty boys and girls of junior high school age will participate in a social recreation program for one hour and fifteen minutes.
The program will be held in a church gymnasium in the evening. The
members of the club know one another very well. The following program
will be presented:

1. Jungle Din
2. Coke Bottle Relay
3. Package Busting Relay
4. Hunters, Guns, and Rabbits
5. Chimes of Dunkirk (Folk-dance
   mixer)
6. Ping Pong Football
7. Ha Ha
8. This Is My Nose
9. Closing Song—to be chosen by
   the group

The party begins with Jungle Din not only because of the enthusiasm aroused by the game, but because the candy kisses hidden about the
gymnasium may be discovered by the youth if the game is not presented
first. The two relays and Hunters, Guns, and Rabbits are conducted in
sequence because they require the same line formation. The folk dance is
presented in the middle of the program provided there is no objection by
church officials. This, of course, is determined in advance. Ha Ha and
This Is My Nose are sitting games, but are characterized by enough action
to be popular with the energetic junior high school youth. No mixers are
used because the members of the club know each other well. Brain
teasers, pencil and paper games, and dramatic activities are not sufficiently
vigorous for this group.

A Parent-Teacher Association

This group anticipates an attendance of about 125 men and women
and has requested that a program be conducted in the school gymnasium
over a period of an hour and a half. The members are not well acquainted.
The following program is planned:

1. Fun Around the Clock
2. Grand March

3. Shock Relay
4. Hunters, Guns, and Rabbits
5. Circle Four Mixer
6. Squirrel in Trees
7. Square Dances—A. Take a Little Peek
                      B. Arkansas Traveler
8. Closing Song—"Good Night Ladies"

Since the members do not know each other well, a mixer, Fun Around the Clock, is conducted first. The mimeographed sheets will be distributed to the individuals as they enter the gymnasium from the auditorium where their meeting has been held. A very important factor influencing both the selection of activities and their conduct is the number of participants involved. The size of the group necessitates the selection of activities which can be conducted on a mass basis. Small group games are rejected for this program.

A grand march is conducted for three reasons: (1) it is fun; (2) a large number may participate; and (3) it finishes with the group in lines of 16 each in proper position for both the Shock Relay and Hunters, Guns, and Rabbits. The next activity, Circle Four Mixer, is both a good mixer and a highly popular party game. It ends with the group in position for Squirrel in Trees which is played at a walking pace and for no longer than three minutes. The program is concluded with the two square dances and a song.

Leaders may find that requests from community groups for social recreation leadership will become so numerous that they will be unable to meet the demand. Certainly each successful party motivates other groups to request a similar service. Many recreation departments have solved this problem by conducting social recreation leadership institutes for the preparation of volunteer leaders from churches, schools, and many other community agencies and organizations. Thus, the recreation department multiplies its efforts many-fold in the provision of expanded opportunities for all the people to participate in a type of recreation that emphasizes fun, friendliness, and social unity.

Selected References

Allen, Catherine L., *Fun for Parties and Programs* (Englewood Cliffs, N.J.: Prentice-Hall, Inc., 1956).

Burns, Lorell Coffman, *Instant Fun for All Kinds of Groups* (New York: Association Press, 1964).

Carlson, Adelle, *4 Seasons Party and Banquet Book* (Nashville: The Broadman Press, 1965).

Daly, Sheila John, *Party Fun* (New York: Dodd, Mead and Company, 1956).

Games for Quiet Hours and Small Spaces (10th ed.) (New York: National Recreation Association, 1954).

Harris, Jane, *File-o-Fun* (Minneapolis: Burgess Publishing Company, 1962).

Howard, Vernon, *Pantomines, Charades, and Skits* (New York: Sterling Publishing Co., Inc., 1959).

Johnson, June, *The Outdoor-Indoor Fun Book* (New York: Harper and Brothers, 1961).

Kraus, Richard, *Recreation Leader's Handbook* (New York: McGraw-Hill Book Company, Inc., 1955).

Mager, Sylvia K., *Games and Fun for Parties* (New York: Arco Publishing Co., Inc., 1958).

Mason, Bernard S. and Mitchell, Elmer D., *Social Games for Recreation* (New York: A. S. Barnes and Company, 1937).

The Recreation Program (rev. ed.) (Chicago: The Athletic Institute, 1963).

Tedford, Jack, *The Giant Book of Family Fun and Games* (New York: Franklin Watts, Inc., 1958).

Vannier, Maryhelen, *Methods and Materials in Recreation Leadership* (Belmont, Calif.: Wadsworth Publishing Company, Inc., 1966).

Chapter VIII

Sports, Games, and Outdoor Recreation

WE COME NOW to an activity that is common to children of all races and all times. The love of play as expressed through games is universal in the youth of all nations. Play is not simply play to the young child; it is serious business, dominating much of his life, absorbing most of his time and energy, shaping his social behavior, and contributing to his rapid growth demands.

Paralleling the growth and development of the child as he progresses toward maturity is an increase in the complexity of the games in which he participates. The more highly organized sports displace the loosely organized play of the young child. There is another difference between sports and games even more fundamental than the degree of organization. When children play games they quit when tired. The participant in a sport, provided he is truly an athlete, a competitor in the highest sense of the term, continues after he is tired, even to the point of complete exhaustion. Furthermore, frequently he undergoes long and arduous periods of training, requiring a high degree of self-discipline and self-denial, so that he may be capable of more intensive and more exhausting effort. An understanding of why he does this is of vital significance to leaders in recreation. What is the motivation that impels the athlete to forsake the easy and sedentary life for the vigorous and the exhausting? Can we discover the force that drives him unceasingly to seek excellence as an athlete when all about him people are willing to settle for mediocrity, or worse? What effect does this athletic spirit have upon a nation, and what happens to the life of a people when they no longer possess it?

These are vital questions that bear directly upon the welfare of both the individual and the nation. Leaders, worthy of the name, must have a deeper insight into the program of sports and games than simply a knowledge of what they are, their rules, basic skills, team strategy, how to teach them, and how to organize leagues and tournaments. These are the technical aspects of leadership and they represent competencies that are important, but if we stop here we are mere technicians, not leaders. Leadership must be eternally concerned with values; otherwise, it has no dominating significant purpose and is leading nowhere in particular.

LESSONS FROM HISTORY

No one can understand the significance of athletics in the lives of people and its impact upon a nation's culture unless he knows something of Grecian history. Our gymnasiums and stadiums, our athletics and Olympic games, trace their lineage to Greece. The Greeks were the only truly athletic nation of antiquity. It is not simple coincidence that some of the most notable eras in man's history—that, for instance, which produced the Parthenon—have been eras in which no gap existed between the appreciation of athletic excellence and the appreciation of esthetic excellence. Chief among the forces leading to the remarkable development of athletics among the Greeks was the desire to excel. This incessant pursuit of perfection dominated the Greeks as no other people have been dominated in the history of the world. Nor have any other people ever been so fond of competition which was not restricted to athletics, but entered into every aspect of their life. Contests were conducted in art, music, drama, poetry, sculpture, and oratory with such magnificent results that all civilized nations today are the richer for their incomparable Grecian heritage.

Individual excellence was the goal of Greek education and the ideal citizen was the man of wisdom and the man of action. History proves conclusively that when nations overemphasize the development of one aspect of man's nature to the neglect of the whole man, the results have been disastrous. Athens found the golden mean between the equally dangerous extremes of excessive specialization upon development of the physical only and the development of the intellect only. A sound mind in a sound body was their national goal and the means by which the early Greeks sought this goal were designed to promote the well-being both of the individual and of the state. Thus, there was no conflict in Athens between those who looked with favor upon athletics and those who emphasized the importance of the intellect. Plato expressed the Athenian point of view when he stated that the individual who is only an athlete is too crude, too vulgar, too much a savage; and he who is a scholar only is too soft, too effeminate. The ideal citizen is the scholar-athlete, the man of thought and the man of action.

War and the threat of war were major factors motivating participation in sports. The population of Sparta, during the eighth century, B.C., was composed of not more than 9,000 Spartans and approximately 250,000 subject people who were always ready to rebel. Sparta, of necessity, was an armed camp sitting on a powder keg with the fuse lit. The purpose of Spartan sports, in fact of all Spartan education, was to develop the man of action, the obedient, hardy, courageous, ruthless soldier wholly dedicated to the state and physically capable of defending it. In pursuit of this goal, the state assumed complete control of the lives of its citizens, from birth to the grave.

Today, it is easy to see the defects in the Spartan way of life. It was a narrow, brutalizing system that developed the bodies and neglected the minds; produced the one-sided athlete who cared not at all for music, art, literature, and philosophy; shaped human beings into obedient units of a mechanical fighting machine; and, as compared with Athens, made but a minor contribution to civilization and to human happiness. Sparta provides the best example in history of the tragic effects on human beings and on nations of an overemphasis on the physical to the neglect of the whole man.

There is another lesson we should learn from Sparta, a lesson that should never be forgotten. They knew what they wanted and they knew how to get it. We may not agree with their goal, but at least they had a goal, a clearly defined goal, and they were intelligent in the means by which they pursued it. Leaders who are skeptical of the degree to which sports may contribute to the development of the kind of citizen a nation desires will do well to ponder these words by Freeman:[1]

If we wish to see how far their education, in its best days, enabled them to prove true to their ideals, let us consider those 300 at Thermopylae waiting, with jests on their lips, for the onset of Oriental myriads, and remember that finest of all epitaphs, of which English can give no rendering, written upon their memorial in the pass in honour of their obedience unto death—

Go tell the Spartans, thou that passest by,
That here obedient to their laws we lie.

[1] Kenneth J. Freeman, *Schools of Hellas* (2nd ed.) (London: Macmillan and Co., Ltd., 1912), p. 34.

We recognize that sports, properly conducted, make a major contribution to fitness, to the culture of their time, and to the qualities of the ideal citizen as visualized by the nation. But there is another value inherent in competitive sports of vital importance to America although not generally perceived by most people. Gardiner calls it "the athletic spirit" which welcomes the contest, no matter how strenuous it may be, for the sheer joy of testing one's powers, of accepting the challenge because it is a challenge, and because the athlete loves a struggle. He further describes the true athlete and his motivation:[2]

The motive that turns his effort into joy is the desire to put to the test his physical powers, the desire to excel. It is not every people any more than every individual that feels this joy in the contest, in the effort. The athletic spirit cannot exist where conditions of life are too soft and luxurious; it cannot exist where conditions are too hard and where all the physical energies are exhausted in a constant struggle with the forces of man or nature. It is found only in physically vigorous and virile nations that put a high value on physical excellence.

America needs desperately a revival of the athletic spirit on a nationwide scale, a renaissance of the athletic ideal that will permeate every aspect of our lives. Athletics constitutes one of the last strongholds of the rugged life in a nation wherein the corrosive effects of luxury and soft living are threatening the welfare of both the individual and the state. The quest for excellence and the willingness to pay the price of greatness in terms of unremitting toil, self-denial, and self-discipline are almost nonexistent in the lives of many Americans who have accepted the easy option and mediocrity as their standards.

In the opportunity to cultivate the athletic spirit as it existed in ancient Athens lies one of the most vital of the challenges to the recreation leader.

THE ROLE OF SPORTS AND GAMES
IN RECREATION

No other aspect of recreation possesses the potentialities for good or evil that characterize the program of sports and games. In addition to the

---

[2] E. Norman Gardiner, *Athletics of the Ancient World* (Oxford: The Clarendon Press), p. 2.

values discussed in the preceding section, sports and games may contribute to health or they may undermine it; they may help a child grow in self-esteem and personal worth or they may destroy his self-confidence and acclimate him to failure; through the various teams, opportunities exist to help meet the need for acceptance, but they also may be the means by which a child experiences the bitterness of rejection. The child may learn to follow rules and respect law and order or he may learn cheating and a hatred of the law and officials; he may learn teamwork and coöperation or he may develop into a ruthless individualist who tramples upon the rights of others; he may derive great happiness from his play, provided the program fulfills its true function as a medium of enjoyable recreation, or, on the other hand, it may prove to be a source of bitterness if the pressures applied by adults make it impossible to lose and still have fun.

This Jekyll and Hyde characteristic of sports applies to the adult as well as to the youth program. There is dynamite in a municipal athletic program and explosions are always imminent. Recreation directors can recall numerous fights and other emotional eruptions on the athletic fields and in the gymnasiums, but seldom if ever remember battles among the dancers, musicians, actors, or arts and crafts participants. This is not a criticism of the program of sports and games, but only a reminder to leadership that strong emotional reactions will be evoked. This presents both a challenge and an opportunity—a challenge to operate effectively in a hazardous situation and an opportunity, especially with children and youth, to utilize for educational purposes these strongly emotionalized situations.

GENERAL RESPONSIBILITIES OF THE LEADER

Four general responsibilities must be assumed by the leader.

Establish the Goals

He must first determine the goals to be sought through the program of sports and games. In general, people participate because they have fun; they enjoy playing. Some will take part because the activity helps keep them fit; they feel better when they play. These are legitimate values and will suffice for the participant, but leaders will seek other goals as well.

Plan and Conduct a Program Designed to Achieve the Goals

The total sports and games program will consist of group games for younger children, individual and dual sports and games, gymnastics and stunts, and team sports or athletics. More than 120 of these activities are listed in Chapter 6 and many more will be found in the numerous books available on the subject. Leaders will find it helpful to review carefully the forces, factors, and principles presented in Chapter 6 that influence the planning of a comprehensive program of recreation. Of primary importance is the principle that calls for many and varied activities related to the needs, interests, and abilities of all the people. Older youth and adults, in harmony with the principle of involvement, should be invited to take an active part in planning and conducting the activities in which they are interested.

The leader who seeks constantly to advance the welfare of the individual and who understands the well-known concept of readiness, will select activities adapted to the abilities and interests of the particular age group involved. He will raise continually questions about the timeliness of the activity under consideration in the light of the child's total capacities. Is it economical to devote time and energy to a certain activity now or should it be postponed until the child is more mature? Judgments with respect to the appropriateness of activities will be made in terms of what is best for the participant rather than what is best for the spectators and the egos of parents.

Exercise a Teaching Function

The possession of motor skills is particularly important among children since they are a means to social acceptance and the development of a sense of personal adequacy and individual worth. When a child becomes fairly proficient at a game, he grows in self-confidence and a sense of security. If he lacks the game skills which children consider important, he is barred from the group or admitted grudgingly more as a hanger-on than as a full-fledged member with complete status.

One of the first duties of a leader who is concerned about the social adjustment and emotional well-being of children is to help them acquire the game skills that will unlock the door of social acceptance. This means that the leader must be a teacher. Instruction will include careful, detailed teaching in the area of skills as well as in team strategy; history of the game; rules; appreciations; and the social, moral, and ethical behaviors involved.

Improve the Program Through Continuous Evaluation

A constant effort will be made by the leader to improve the sports and games program in the light of values sought and the basic principles of program planning and of leadership. He realizes that the program is never finished, that it can always be bettered, and that complete satisfaction with it is a danger signal to be strenuously avoided.

THE LEADER AS A TEACHER

So vital is the teaching responsibility of the leader that it warrants special consideration at this point. Leadership is inextricably tied up with instruction. Leaders must teach both youth and adults how to play skillfully; help them to become proficient in games and sports; assist them to work coöperatively with others as members of a team; and adhere to high social, moral, and ethical standards in their play. The leader should understand, however, that much of his teaching must be informal, subtle, and indirect. He cannot use the direct and formal instructional methods frequently employed in schools except at the risk of losing the members of his group.

Man is a skill-hungry animal, but the lack of a high level of skill in games and sports among Americans is so prevalent as to constitute almost a national disgrace. With the exception of the members of the interscholastic athletic teams, the average high school graduate possesses very little skill in any sport. Many factors are responsible for this situation, among which are poor teaching; insufficient time, facilities, and supplies; and a failure to concentrate on one or two activities at the upper level of the senior high school. Too many teachers of physical education in our high schools are attempting to teach so many different activities that no student can become proficient in any of them. Trying to master everything, the student masters nothing. Lack of interest is a natural corollary of a lack of skill, so we graduate each year vast numbers of youth with no absorbing interest as a participant in any sport because they have very little skill in any sport.

The recreation leaders cannot assume the teaching responsibilities of the physical education teachers of America, but they can do everything in their power to supplement their efforts. They also should encourage the adolescent to concentrate on one or two sports that can be enjoyed throughout life and assist him with the best instruction of which they are capable.

In every activity one or more specific goals are sought. No activity is conducted without a purpose. The degree to which this purpose is attained generally depends upon how the leader guides the individual in relation to the activity. Skill, or the ability to perform effectively, usually is one value deemed important. Other values relate to a high level of social, moral, and ethical behavior. Still others may include health, fun, and happiness. Situations are arising constantly in our games and sports which are rich in opportunities for growth in skills and in desirable human behavior. If we, as leaders, know in advance what these situations are and how they may be utilized to produce the kinds of behavior desired, we can be far more effective than if we go into the activity blindly hoping that some teachable moments will appear, but never quite sure what they are likely to be or what we should do about them if they do occur. Leaders should understand that teaching opportunities exist throughout the entire period devoted to a game, but that frequently situations arise which are *uniquely* rich in value possibilities. It is with these unique moments or situations that we are primarily concerned in the following illustrations.

Drop the Handkerchief—Ages Five to Seven

Children are divided into groups of ten or twelve in circle formation facing the center of the circle. One child, holding a handkerchief, stands outside the circle.

RULES. On the signal go, the child with the handkerchief runs around the outside of the circle in a counterclockwise direction. At times he simulates dropping the handkerchief behind various children, but does not do so. Finally, after a very short period of time he drops the handkerchief directly back of a player, reverses his direction, and runs around the circle. The player, back of whom the handkerchief was dropped, picks it up and attempts to tag the player who dropped it before he can get back to the space vacated by the chaser. Whether the chaser is successful in tagging the runner or not, he becomes the new runner and the game continues as before.

TEACHABLE SITUATION. When any normal group of children plays this game almost invariably one or more specific situations arise which provide opportunities for the leader to strengthen the qualities of coöperation, sharing, unselfishness, and concern for the rights of others. Chasing and being chased are the two features of this game enjoyed most by the players. There is no fun just standing and waiting for the handkerchief to be dropped.

Many children love to be the center of attention. So, the leader may reasonably anticipate that at least one child will take the handkerchief and keep running around the circle and continue to do so until the leader stops play and calls the children around her. The discussion will go about as follows: "How do you like this game? How can we have more fun? What do you think we should do differently?" Some youngster will suggest that Johnny runs too long. "Oh, he does? How many of you think Johnny runs too long?" Every hand except one goes up.

The leader continues, "What happens when one person runs too long?" A child suggests, "The rest of us don't get to run at all." Through as simple an activity as Drop the Handkerchief, the leader teaches the children this basic truth—when some people get more than their share of the good things of a game others get less than their share; that the good things of life should be shared; and that each player should respect the rights of all the others. Thus, growth in social behavior takes place when the leader knows what she seeks, selects an activity in which this value resides, and conducts it with due regard to the quality of the experiences in which the children take part.

Conducting Drop the Handkerchief in such a manner as to achieve growth in social behavior in no way destroys the fun value of the game. More children have fun as each child shows greater regard for the rights of others.

Two Deep—Ages Five to Seven

A group of ten–twelve children stands in circle formation, facing the center of the circle, hands at their sides. Two players outside the circle formation are designed as runner and chaser. On signal, the chaser on the opposite side of the circle from the runner, chases the runner and attempts to tag him. At any time the runner may step in front of a player in the circle who then becomes the new runner since, at this point, the circle has become "two deep." Whenever the chaser tags the runner, the runner becomes the chaser.

RULES. The runner must not run very long before stopping in front of a circle player. The back child becomes the runner when a "two deep" situation occurs. The runner becomes the chaser whenever he is tagged. Players may run in either direction around, but not across, the circle.

TEACHABLE SITUATION. As in Drop the Handkerchief some runners may need to be reminded that others, too, wish to run and that they
should run for but a brief period of time before stopping in front of a
circle player. The leader should emphasize that the good player prefers
making a "two deep" to getting tagged. Some players become confused
when the runner stops in front of them, either standing as though paralyzed or chasing the chaser. The leader carefully will instruct each player to
be alert and to run instantly away from the chaser if the runner stops in front
of him. Since the chaser constantly is chasing fresh runners, it may be
desirable at times to have the newly active player become the chaser thus
giving the tired player an opportunity to stop in front of a circle player.

Brownies and Fairies—Ages Five to Seven

Divide the players into two groups, one known as brownies and the
other as fairies. The playing area is thirty–forty feet long and twenty–
thirty feet wide. Clearly marked lines designate the ends of the playing
area. For safety reasons these lines should be at least fifteen feet from
any obstruction such as a wall. The brownies stand on one end line facing
the fairies who stand with their backs to the brownies.

RULES. On signal by the leader, the brownies tiptoe quietly toward the
fairies. When, in the judgment of the leader, the brownies are close
enough to the fairies he calls, "Here come the brownies." The fairies then
chase the brownies back to their goal line, tagging as many as they can
before they reach it. All brownies who are tagged become fairies for the
next phase of the game. Then the brownies turn their backs and the
fairies approach them silently and the game continues as before. At the
conclusion of the playing period, the side with the greater number of
players is the winner.

TEACHABLE SITUATION. Some children, as in all tag games, will
refuse to admit they were tagged. Before the game begins, the leader should
emphasize the importance of children admitting instantly when they are
tagged. Immediately after the game begins the leader should praise the
children who acknowledge the tag and express disapproval of the behavior of those who fail to do so. Every effort should be made by the leader
to enlist the support of the group as numerous studies indicate that the
standard of behavior accepted by the group molds the behavior of its
members, at least while they are together.[3]

---

[3] For a more detailed discussion of the attainment of moral and ethical values
through recreation, the student is referred to pages 224-228.

The leader may anticipate that a few children will tag so vigorously as to cause runners to fall. This can be prevented by emphasizing a light touch and suggesting that everyone tag others as he, himself, would like to be tagged. The child who stays several steps back of the others as they approach their opponents constitutes a special problem. This is the type of youngster who wants all that anyone else gets from the game plus certain special advantages accruing only to himself. Good leadership will encourage these children to take the same risk as all the others and point out the unfairness of the head start they are claiming for themselves.

Run for Your Supper—Ages Five to Seven

The group stands in a large circle facing center and about arms' length apart. One child, the caller, runs slowly around the outside of the circle and suddenly stops between two children and calls, "Run for your supper." The two children between whom he stopped run in opposite directions around the circle. The runner who first gets back to his original position in the circle becomes the next caller and the game proceeds.

RULES. The caller may run around the circle no more than once before stopping between two players. Each runner must keep to his right in order to avoid a collision. The caller selects the winning runner.

TEACHABLE SITUATION. Some children may become so excited they run in the wrong direction or they run into the other runner because they forget to keep to the right. Leaders can help in the first situation by reminding the children when they start to run, to turn their backs on the caller. If they have trouble keeping to the right, the leader may ask all children to close their right hands and, when running, to keep to the side of the closed hand. It will be easier for the children if they walk, rather than run, the first few games.

Chinese Tag—Ages Eight and Nine

The children are scattered over the playing area. One child is "It." "It" starts chasing the children who run in all directions. When a child is tagged he must call, "I'm 'It,'" so that all the other children can hear him. The new "It," holding on with one hand to the part of the body tagged by the first "It," runs to tag another child.

RULES. "It" may tag any runner who becomes the new "It" and must call, "I'm 'It.'" The tagged player holds the part of the body tagged while running to tag another.

TEACHABLE SITUATION. Many children will run poorly and the leader should teach them how to run. They should be taught to point the toes straight forward with their weight on the balls of the feet when on the ground. The knees should be lifted high so that the upper leg is at least parallel to the ground. Some will make the common error of swinging the feet or knees sideways as they run. The hands should be loosely closed, not clenched. Arms should be bent at the elbows, forming a right angle, and should swing forward and backward from a position in which the hand is almost directly in front of the nose to where it is about even with the hip. Children frequently fail to use the hands at all and they often make the error of swaying the shoulders from side to side. The upper body is held straight and the entire body leans forward as far as possible without falling.

Some children may not admit it when tagged or they may push others instead of tagging them. Leaders should follow suggestions given in Brownies and Fairies. The leader invariably is plagued by the child who spoils the game by trying to be tagged rather than running away from "It." Various methods may be used to change his behavior. He may be kept out of the game for a while; social pressure from the group may be applied; or the leader may praise the children who are most difficult to catch and express disapproval of those who make a farce out of the game by trying to be caught.

In those instances where "It" is greatly handicapped in his running because of the location of the spot on the body he must hold on to, he may call on another child to help him catch someone.

Bull in the Ring—Ages Eight and Nine

The group joins hands in a circle. One child known as the bull is inside the circle. The object of the game for the bull is to break out of the circle and to avoid being caught after he escapes. The other children try to prevent the bull's escape from the circle and to catch him if he does escape.

RULES. The child who catches the bull becomes the new bull. The bull may not use his hands to pull or force his way out of the circle, but may duck under or separate the hands by running against them. Players may not use any parts of their bodies to block the bull other than hands and arms.

TEACHABLE SITUATION.   Some children may spoil the game by letting go of their hands intentionally and permitting the bull's escape. When this occurs the leader should establish a rule allowing all children to chase the bull except the two who were involved in his escape. A limited playing area should be established and the bull required to stay within this area while being chased. Sometimes the game is slowed to the point of boredom when the bull is unable to escape from the circle. The leader can remedy this situation by adding one or two bulls.

Dodge Ball—Ages Eight and Nine

Players are in two groups, one inside and one outside a circle about thirty feet in diameter. The boundaries of the circle should be clearly defined. The outside group attempts to hit the players inside the circle with a volleyball or large rubber ball. The players inside the circle may run and dodge in any manner possible.

RULES.   The ball must be rolled or thrown so as to hit players below the waist. Players rolling the ball must stay outside circle boundary lines. Players hit by a ball must join the throwers outside the circle and help hit the remaining players. If a player is hit above the waist or by a ball rolled or thrown by a child who has stepped across the circle boundary line, he is considered as not having been hit at all. When all players have been hit, the sides change.

TEACHABLE SITUATION.   Two situations constantly arise in this game which provide the superior leader with rich opportunities for constructive guidance in social and ethical development. There is constant temptation to cross the boundary line to get a better shot at a center player. The leader must not ignore this infraction of the rules. If he does ignore it, not only is the game less satisfactory, but he is contributing to development of the attitude that whatever you can get away with is all right. Before the game begins the leader should emphasize the importance of obeying this rule, pointing out that violating it is cheating and unfair to the other team, and that players who do violate it may be kept out of the game for a period of time. The leader should praise the players who obey the rule and express disapproval of those who disobey it.

A second situation which should be anticipated involves hitting players above the waist. A child may be seriously injured if struck in the face by a thrown ball. If the techniques suggested for the first situation prove ineffective here, leaders should eliminate all throwing and insist that the ball be rolled.

If the children have difficulty hitting the center players with one ball, a second, third, and even a fourth ball may be added in order to speed up the game.

THE LEADER AS AN ORGANIZER

The leader who is charged with the responsibility of organizing and administering a program of municipal sports will spend the bulk of his time and energy in attempting to solve the following problems:

1. Determining the scope and nature of the program.
2. Encouraging participation on a widespread scale.
3. Establishing an effective organization in which the participants share in planning and operating the program.
4. Securing adequate facilities, equipment, and supplies.
5. Financing the program.

Planning the Sports Program

The factors and principles that influence the planning of sports programs are no different from those that operate in the planning of all other phases of the program of recreation. Students, therefore, should review thoroughly the following materials before proceeding further with the problems involved in planning and operating a program of competitive sports:

1. Growth and development characteristics of the various age groups involved in the program—Chapter Three.
2. Principles of leadership—Pages 93-103.
3. Forces and influences affecting the program—Pages 112-125.
4. Principles of program planning—Pages 125-136.
5. List of games and sports—Pages 136-138.

The most important principle of program planning which should guide the leader is: *The program should consist of many and varied activities related to the needs, interests, and abilities of all the people.* Applied to the sports program, this principle means that leaders should:

(1) begin with activities in which people are interested and wish to participate; (2) provide only those activities that harmonize with the individual's needs, capacities, and potentialities; (3) offer an extremely broad and varied program so that everyone to whom such a program can be beneficial will be able to find some activity of interest and value. Activities for girls and women will be considered of equal importance to those for boys and men. The unskilled will not be neglected for the highly skilled nor will youth leagues and tournaments in baseball, softball, and basketball be permitted to crowd out shuffleboard, horseshoes, and volleyball for older adults. (4) Finally, the principle implies that program breadth and variety can best be achieved by starting with present interests of participants, but not stopping there. The superior leader will expand the interests of people by introducing them to new activities, by teaching, by demonstrating, and by other persuasive measures.

The National Recreation and Park Association reports a nationwide study[4] made during a recent year in which agencies were asked to indicate the activities they organized, supervised, or conducted for children and

Activity	Number of Agencies Reporting	
	Children	Adults
Baseball	2646	1348
Swimming	2422	2064
Softball	2313	2174
Tennis	2341	2011
Basketball	2507	1954
Horseshoes	1653	1238
Volleyball	1954	1653
Table Tennis	1681	1156
Badminton	1156	798
Ice Skating	1486	1185
Track and Field	1706	522
Shuffleboard	1100	880
Archery	1433	990
Touch Football	1681	603
Paddle Tennis	936	383
Golf	1323	1238
Tumbling and Gymnastics	1238	220
Fishing	1323	1046
Water Carnivals	716	330
Regulation Football	1156	245
Synchronized Swimming	936	245
Indoor Bowling	965	660
Roller Skating	493	245

[4] Donald E. Hawkins, ed., *Recreation and Park Yearbook 1966* (Washington, D.C.: National Recreation and Park Association, 1966), pp. 53–54

Activity	Number of Agencies Reporting	
	Children	Adults
Soccer	578	245
Boating	936	1046
Coasting	716	440
Ice Hockey	493	245
Snow Skiing	578	522
Handball	440	358
Tobogganing	550	493
Water Skiing	493	440
Winter Carnivals	163	163

adults. Games and sports, as in previous studies, led all other types of activities in frequency of mention, for both children and adults. Agencies reporting included both city and county authorities administering recreation programs.

Encouraging Participation

It is not difficult to persuade youth, especially boys, to participate in certain types of sports. The task becomes easier when physical education teachers in the schools are doing an effective job developing skills in a variety of activities. Recreation leaders should work closely with the physical education teachers, offering leagues and tournaments in those sports previously taught in the schools. However, the municipal sports program should not be limited to activities taught in school. For example, horseshoe pitching should be included as part of any comprehensive playground sports program although it is seldom taught in physical education classes.

Newspapers, television, and radio should all be utilized in publicizing the sports program. The following events are especially newsworthy: announcements of the openings of sports seasons; initial meetings of managers to form athletic leagues; sports offered for the first time; demonstrations or clinics by well-known sports celebrities; new records in track, swimming, and similar sports; unusual accomplishments by extremely young or very old participants; winning of a championship by a crippled youngster, and similar events of a human interest nature;[5] interviews with outstanding clergymen, judges, police officials, physicians, and others whose opinions are respected by the public, with regard to the values of the sports

---

[5] Leaders should be extremely careful to avoid any possible embarrassment to the persons about whom the story is written. The written consent of parents should be obtained before authorizing release of stories about handicapped children.

program; construction of new facilities; and, in the case of the newspapers, pictures of various teams and individuals in action.

The one basic need that all human beings constantly seek to satisfy is the need for personal adequacy or self-esteem. With many people, especially youth, this need is more easily and fully satisfied when successful performance results in recognition, status, and prestige acquired, at least partially, through adequate coverage by newspaper, television, and radio.

Establishing an Effective Organization

The principle of involvement directs a leader to provide opportunities for the players to share in planning and operating the sports program in which they are involved. It is imperative that this be done if the program of competitive sports is to be successful. The National Recreation Association lists five types of sports groups which have proved effective as the machinery for coöperative action:

1. The *single-sport association,* composed of teams, leagues, clubs or players in a particular sport, such as a municipal softball, basketball or tennis association.
2. The *commission,* more or less representative of the players in a particular sport and appointed to administer city-wide competition in it.
3. The *federation* or association, concerned with a variety of sports or the total city-wide program; in some cases this is a federation of the associations formed around a single sport.
4. The *association* concerned with sports for a limited section of the city's population, such as an industrial athletic association or women's sports association.
5. The *club,* composed of players in a particular sport sponsored on a city-wide basis, such as an archery or hiking club.[6]

A combination of the single-sport association and the commission has proved to be the most successful plan in the author's experience. In adult softball for example, the association-commission plan includes the following features:

1. All players elect five to nine persons to serve for one year on a commission.
2. Among the numerous responsibilities of the commission are:
   A. Serves as spokesman for all participating groups and individuals.
   B. Establishes all rules, policies, procedures, and standards relating to softball. These include rules on eligibility, player conduct, contracts,

---

[6] National Recreation Association, *Community Sports and Athletics* (New York: A. S. Barnes and Company, 1949), p. 33.

releases, postponements, determination of championships, entry and protest fees, length of season and number of games, awards, and type of equipment and supplies.

  C. Acts on all protests and other disputes.

  D. Amends the constitution and by-laws.

  E. Approves schedules.

  F. Assists the department in the selection, training, assignment, and supervision of umpires.

  G. Determines the types of leagues to be established and helps ensure equality of competition within each league.

3. The superintendent of recreation, or the supervisor of athletics, serves as secretary-treasurer of the commission, but is not a member of the commission.

4. Important committees of the commission will deal with such matters as officials, schedules, protests, and changes in the constitution.

5. The commission works coöperatively with recreation department personnel and in harmony with departmental philosophy, policies, and regulations. It is neither a figurehead nor a completely autonomous body.

EQUALITY OF COMPETITION. Equality of team strength is a vital factor in the successful operation of competitive sports. Interest on the part of both players and spectators is heightened by keen competition and is killed by its absence. Therefore, leaders should make every effort possible to ensure that teams and individuals are evenly matched.

Among the steps aimed at producing equality of competition are:

HANDICAPPING. Golf is a sport in which handicaps are easily determined and applied. A player turns in his scorecards over a period of time, signed by himself and those with whom he played. His best ten scores, of the last twenty-five, are used to establish his handicap. This is done by determining his average score, subtracting par, and taking 80 percent of the difference. For example, if his average among the ten scores is eighty-two, and par is seventy-two, the difference is ten; and 80 percent of ten is eight, which is his handicap. He should continue to turn in his scorecards throughout the season and a handicap committee will change his handicap as his scores warrant.

An effective method of handicapping horseshoe pitchers is to determine the average number of ringers a player pitches in fifty shoes. If a pitcher averages twenty ringers in fifty pitches he will average sixty points in ringers since a ringer counts three points. Sixty is his handicap. The pitcher who averages twelve ringers has a handicap of thirty-six. He will be given twenty-four points at the beginning of a fifty-shoe match against the better player. All handicaps are subject to change as the ringer averages change throughout the season.

CLASSIFICATION ON BASIS OF ABILITY. This method involves two important steps: (1) classification of leagues as open, closed, or semi-open; and (2) evaluating team strength in light of past performances by players.

Open leagues permit teams to sign the best players in the community no matter where they work or to what organizations they belong. Teams in semi-open leagues generally represent a business or industrial organization, a church, club, or some other group involving definite membership. The managers of these teams vote to determine the number of "outside" players each team may sign—frequently five or seven out of a total roster of fifteen or twenty. Organizations sponsoring teams in closed leagues restrict their players to bona-fide members or employees. Where more than one league in each classification exists, these leagues may be rated on the basis of relative strength. Members of the commission governing the sport can be very helpful in appraising the strength of teams and assigning them to the proper league. A few managers usually exist in every city who try to get their team into a weak league so they may be assured of a championship.

League classification for softball in Sheboygan, Wisconsin in a recent year was:

Classic Industrial	Junior A (19 years and under)
Church and Fraternal 12" Slow Pitch	Junior B (16 years and under)
12" or 16" Slow Pitch (35 years and over)	Walther (18 years and under)
CYO Junior (19 years and under)	Girls (high-school age and over)
CYO Cadet (16 years and under)	

A different type of classification for basketball is used in Milwaukee:

League	Classification
Muni-Ace	Open — Top caliber
Major AAA North	Open — Above average
Major AAA South	Open — Above average
Major AAA Central	Open — Above average
Major AA North	Open — Average
Major AA South	Open — Average
Commercial	Employees of Firm

CLASSIFICATION ON BASIS OF AGE. As indicated above, Sheboygan uses this method of ensuring equality of competition for youth and older adults. Many cities limit the number of players under a specific age who may play with any team in its slow-pitch league. As the number of older persons continues to increase, age as a basis of classification will be utilized more and more. St. Petersburg, Florida, has a Three-Quarter Century Softball Club.

For playground competition in such sports and games as baseball, softball, volleyball, croquet, horseshoes, paddle tennis, and croquet golf, many cities classify players on an age basis. Madison, Wisconsin, uses three age divisions: midgets, under twelve years; juniors, twelve–fifteen years; and seniors, fifteen–eighteen years. No uniform national classification plan is desirable, but leaders should be guided in the establishment of their plan by one major consideration: the age range within a group should be sufficiently narrow so that youth in approximately similar stages of development will compete with one another. Where the range is too great the younger players often will be unable to make the teams. Where they do compete against considerably older opponents their lack of success prevents attainment of the goal for which all human beings strive—a sense of personal worth and self-esteem. Furthermore, they are far more likely to be injured in certain types of activities than if they were competing against players their own age.

PLAYER CONTROLS.   Most of the troubles that plague leaders of competitive sports are those which involve people rather than things. Many of their potential difficulties can be prevented by the establishment of tested routine procedures for purposes of efficiency and control. These procedures should be in writing, frequently incorporated in the by-laws of the constitution governing the sport, and distributed to all players, managers, sponsors, officials, and all others directly involved in the activity.

The exact procedure to be followed in adding or releasing players must be defined carefully and scrupulously carried out. Players should be required to sign contract cards in duplicate. The original is filed in the office of the department of recreation while the team manager keeps the duplicate. Lima, Ohio, stipulates that a softball team shall consist of not more than fifteen players and that player additions and releases must conform to the following regulations:

1. All players must sign contracts.
2. A player on one team may not play on another team until he procures a release from his manager.
3. No player may play on more than two teams in one season, nor return to his original team.
4. In all cases of dispute between the manager and a player seeking his release, the Softball Commission shall decide the dispute.
5. The released player may not play with another team until the second scheduled game for this team following his release.

Leaders should discourage players from moving about from team to team. When a player signs a contract he is both legally and morally

"Old" Horace Mann Bldg.
719 N. Jameson

(RECREATION OFFICE COPY)

Phone CA 9-6761
or CA 3-1646

LIMA DEPARTMENT OF RECREATION
Player's Contract

Name..Employer..............................

Address... Phone No..........................

I hereby agree to play... for
(Name of Sport)

.... in the ....League
(Name of Team)

during the 196.............season.   Date Filed

I further agree to abide by the Rules and Regulations of the Lima
Department of Recreation and the Constitution and By-Laws of the
Commission governing the sport mentioned above, and to return to my
sponsor, on demand, all equipment issued to me.

Signed ....

For Players under 21 years of age: ....
(Parent or Guardian Signature)

As manager of the above team, I have this .... day of ....,
196..........., duly signed the above player.

Signed..
(Manager's Signature)

"Old" Horace Mann Bldg.
719 N. Jameson

(MANAGER'S COPY)

Phone CA 9-6761
or CA 3-1646

LIMA DEPARTMENT OF RECREATION
Player's Contract

Name.. Employer..............................

Address...Phone No..........................

I hereby agree to play... for
(Name of Sport)

.... in the ....League
(Name of Team)

during the 196.............season.   Date Filed

I further agree to abide by the Rules and Regulations of the Lima
Department of Recreation and the Constitution and By-Laws of the
Commission governing the sport mentioned above, and to return to my
sponsor, on demand, all equipment issued to me.

Signed..

For Players under 21 years of age:..
(Parent or Guardian Signature)

As manager of the above team, I have this .... day of ....,
196..........., duly signed the above player.

Signed..
(Manager's Signature)

Form 1. Player's contract

obligated to play with this team throughout the season. Situations do infrequently arise which justify a transfer, but forced releases should be kept to an absolute minimum.

LIMA DEPARTMENT OF RECREATION

Release Form

Date..

I, Manager ....Team,

of the.. League, hereby release

.... from contract to play with the above

team as provided in the Constitution and By-Laws of the Lima Softball Association.

(Signed) ....

Release Effective..

Form 2. Release form

FACILITY CONTROLS.   An important responsibility of leadership is the issuance of practice permits for the use of ball diamonds, tennis courts, gymnasiums and similar facilities. The exact procedure an individual should follow in securing a permit should be stated in written form and copies should be made available to all interested parties. When a team wishes a permit to practice softball the manager may call the department office and request the reservation of a specific diamond. If this diamond is available, the secretary checks it off on the master list of diamonds for that day and hour so there will be no possibility of a conflict in its use. She then fills out the permit form and either mails it to the manager or holds it until he calls in person. Permits should be issued no more than one week in advance and where there are not sufficient diamonds, a team must use one permit before it can secure another.

OFFICIALS.   An important factor in any program of competitive sports is the quality of the officiating. Incompetent officials breed protests, arguments, fights, injuries, player unrest, and spectator criticism. Leaders must

DEPARTMENT OF RECREATION
Lima, Ohio

Diamond and Gym Permit

Date........................

The...........................
is hereby given permission to use...........................
Date of Permit...........................
Hours of Permit...........................

.... Director of Recreation

All teams or persons using city or school property agree to abide by Rules and Regulations of the Board of Education and the Recreation Board of the City of Lima, Ohio.
(OVER)

Date ....
Name...........................
Facility ....
Date of Permit...........................
Hours of Permit ....

Form 3. Facility permit (regulations appear on reverse side of form)

210

solve the problem of securing men and women who know the rules, have developed some competency in the art of officiating, and who are willing,

REGULATIONS

1. No one is allowed on floor without gym shoes.
2. All athletic teams using diamonds or gym floors must furnish their own equipment, such as basketballs, volleyballs, softballs, etc.
3. The use of tobacco in any form is absolutely prohibited on any school property or city ball diamonds.
4. Teams using gym floors for practice must have at least five and no more than 14 players on floor.
5. Spectators may not attend practice sessions in school gyms.
6. The janitor is responsible to the recreation department for the enforcement of the above rules.
7. We reserve the right to refuse or recall permits.
8. Ball diamonds must not be used if wet.

for only nominal compensation, to call the plays and take the abuse which fans, players, and managers in this country too frequently heap upon the sports arbiter.

Officials should be paid for their work and participate in both a pre-season and an in-service training program. In some cities the selection, training, assignment, and supervision of officials are under the jurisdiction of the chairman of the committee on officials of the sports association. Funds for the compensation of officials in adult contests generally are derived from team entry fees and gate receipts.

Leaders should issue detailed written instructions to officials covering such items as the procedure involved in assigning officials to games, reporting of scores, wearing apparel, game equipment and supplies, officiating techniques, handling of protests and disciplinary cases, pay schedules and time cards, inclement weather, and coöperation with recreation personnel in charge of facilities.

LEAGUES AND TOURNAMENTS. Among the competencies of importance to leaders is a knowledge of the strengths and weaknesses of various methods of organizing competition and skill in their use.

SINGLE ELIMINATION TOURNAMENT. This is the least desirable tournament because one half of the competitors are eliminated after their first contest. However, when time is limited this is the best type of tournament as it can be run off quickly.

Steps in arranging a single elimination tournament are:

1. Determine the number of entries.
2. Determine the number of byes.
3. Draw the tournament bracket and locate the byes.
4. Draw for positions.
5. Place the teams or players in their respective positions.

Chart 1 represents a single elimination bracket with eight teams participating and no byes.

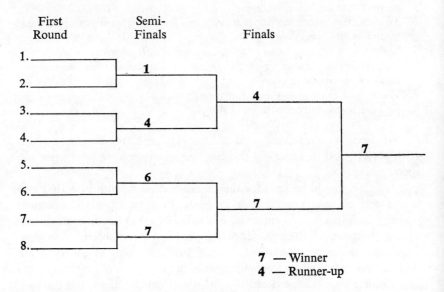

Chart 1
Single Elimination Tournament

The number of games required to determine a winner is always one less than the number of contestants entered.

Three minor complications may arise which add to the complexities of tournament planning and operation: (1) the "seeding" of entrants; (2) the determination of "byes"; and (3) the selection of a consolation champion.

Let us assume that a tennis tournament is to be conducted. The tournament should be planned so that the superior players do not eliminate one another early in the tournament, but meet in its latter stages.

If two entries are seeded, one is placed at the top of the upper bracket and the other at the bottom of the lower bracket. Thus, the two seeded entries in Chart 1 would occupy positions one and eight. If the four best players are seeded, the third generally is placed at the top of the lower bracket, position five, and the fourth at the bottom of the upper bracket, position four. The four best players, however, usually are seeded only in a bracket of sixteen; eight, when there are thirty-two entries. In a sixteen-player tournament the four seeded players would occupy first, eighth, ninth, and sixteenth places. Where byes are necessary, the seeded players get them in the order of their ranking. Seeding should be practiced only when the previous record of the contestant warrants.

Byes are necessary whenever the number of entrants is not a perfect power of two, such as four, sixteen, thirty-two, sixty-four. Their purpose is to guarantee an even number of entrants for all tournament rounds beyond the first, thus eliminating the unfair advantage accruing to a team provided with a bye and a lengthy rest in the middle of a tournament. All byes, therefore, must be placed in the first round. The number of byes is determined by subtracting the number of entrants from the next higher power of two. If six players are entered, subtract six from eight which is the next higher power of two. This leaves two, which is the number of byes. In Chart 2, the total number of entrants is eleven. Subtracting eleven from the next higher power of two, which is sixteen, leaves five byes. All byes should be distributed as evenly as possible throughout the upper and lower brackets; if the number is uneven, one more should be placed in the lower bracket. Unless certain entrants are seeded, each player draws a number and the luck of the draw determines who gets the byes.

CONSOLATION ELIMINATION TOURNAMENT. This type of tournament permits each team to play at least twice and, for this reason, is preferable to the single elimination. The most common type of consolation tournament is that in which all losers in the first round, instead of dropping out of the tournament, continue play in a straight elimination schedule culminating in a consolation champion. A consolation tournament for eight teams is shown in Chart 3.

DOUBLE ELIMINATION TOURNAMENT. In this type of tournament no competitor is eliminated until he has lost two games or matches. After losing a game in the winner's bracket, he continues play in the loser's bracket. If he goes through the loser's bracket undefeated, he meets the winner of the winner's bracket for the tournament championship. Thus, an entrant may still win the tournament championship after losing one game or match. In this respect the double elimination tournament differs from the consolation and is superior to it. However, it requires considerably more time than does the consolation tournament. Furthermore, the winner of the loser's bracket must play six games to win the tournament championship while the winner of the winner's bracket must play but five, and this additional game frequently weighs heavily against the team involved.

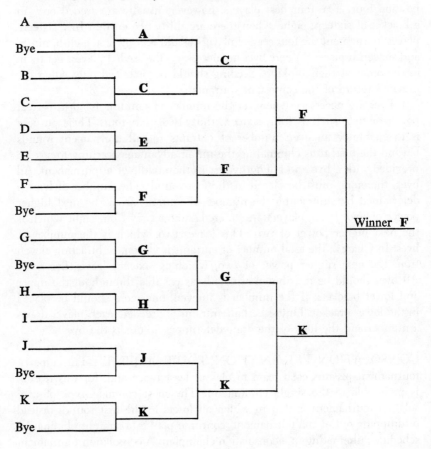

Chart 2
Single Elimination Bracket for Eleven Teams

Chart 4, on page 216, illustrates the draw for a double elimination tournament with eight entries. Leaders should understand two intricacies of this type of tournament: (1) if the winner of the loser's bracket defeats the winner of the winner's bracket, an additional game must be played, since no team is eliminated until it has lost two games; and (2) losers in the semi-finals of the winner's bracket must "cross over" and play winners in opposite loser brackets. For example, D plays F rather than B, thus preventing the possibility of a team being defeated in the first game of the winner's bracket and in the second game of the loser's bracket by the same team.

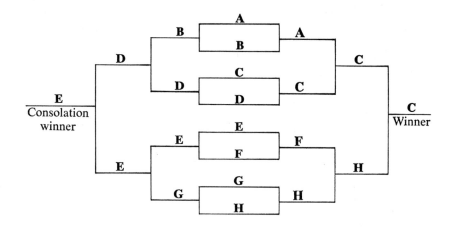

Chart 3
Consolation Tournament for Eight Teams

LEAGUE OR ROUND ROBIN TOURNAMENT.   This is the fairest way of determining a champion, as it provides for each contestant to play each of the other contestants at least once. The league schedule in many sports may require each team to play two or more games with each opponent. This is the most commonly used form of organization and is especially popular with such sports as softball, baseball, basketball, volleyball, and horseshoe pitching. League operation is most effective with six or eight teams.

Leaders should be thoroughly familiar with this simple method of arranging a schedule. If eight teams are involved, write half the numbers *down* in the left column and the other half *up* in the right, or parallel, column. Since all teams have drawn a number they are automatically paired for the first day of play with the number opposite their own. To determine the remainder of the schedule, rotate all numbers down in the left column and up in the right except No. 1 which remains stationary at all times. The top number in the right column is moved each time immediately beneath No. 1 and the bottom number in the left column is moved over to the bottom of the right column.

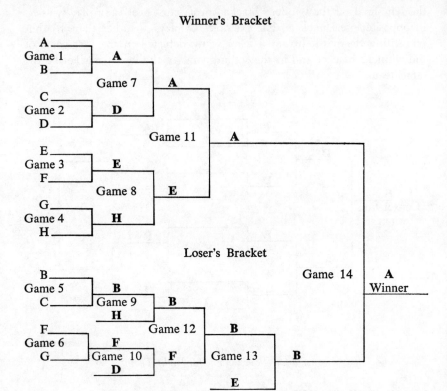

Chart 4
Double Elimination Tournament for Eight Teams

The following schedule for an eight-team league illustrates how the above plan operates.

1st Date	2nd Date	3rd Date	4th Date	5th Date	6th Date	7th Date
1–8	1–7	1–6	1–5	1–4	1–3	1–2
2–7	8–6	7–5	6–4	5–3	4–2	3–8
3–6	2–5	8–4	7–3	6–2	5–8	4–7
4–5	3–4	2–3	8–2	7–8	6–7	5–6

If, for example, each team is scheduled to play each of the other teams three times throughout the season, the three different dates may be placed above each set of games, thus eliminating the necessity of repeating the schedule. The home team may be designated by proper manipulation of the numbers and a statement in the schedule to this effect: "The team listed first in the schedule is the home team for the first and third rounds of play and is the visiting team during the second round." In accordance with this statement, Team 3, as listed above, is the home team three times the first round, four times the second round, and three times the third.

A very successful technique for maintaining a high level of interest among all teams in the league throughout the season and thus reducing forfeits to a minimum is the "round" system of play. Teams begin to lose interest during the latter half of the season if they have lost so many games there is no possibility of their winning the championship. Under the round plan of competition an eight-team league, in which teams play once a week over a season of fourteen weeks, will play two rounds. The winner of the first round will play the winner of the second round for the league championship.

A six-team league playing once a week over a fifteen-week season will play three rounds and a total of forty-five games. Each team will play fifteen games, or five games per round. If there is a different winner in each round the three teams meet in a single elimination tournament for the league championship. If Team A should win two rounds and Team B one round, Team B must defeat Team A twice to win the championship.

No matter how many games a team may lose during its first two rounds, this plan of competition keeps open the door of hope to its members who reassure one another with the promise, "We'll get them in the third round." But a team that loses its first ten games under the straight season plan has no possibility of winning and frequently forfeits its remaining games.

Securing Adequate Facilities, Equipment, and Supplies[7]

One of the most important responsibilities of a leader is to help groups carry out effectively the measures leading to achievement of their goals. A team cannot achieve its goals without facilities, equipment, and supplies. The leader, therefore, must help the group acquire these essential factors in the successful operation of a competitive sports program.

---

[7] For detailed suggestions on the construction and maintenance of sports areas the student is referred to:

George D. Butler, *Recreation Areas—Their Design and Equipment* (New York: The Ronald Press Company, 1958).

M. Alexander Gabrielsen and Caswell M. Miles (eds.), *Sports and Recreation Facilities for School and Community* (Englewood Cliffs, N.J.: Prentice-Hall, Inc., 1958).

Participants in National Facilities Conference, *Planning Facilities for Health, Physical Education and Recreation* (Chicago: The Athletic Institute, Inc., 1956).

Properly constructed and maintained facilities attract participants and facilitate the development of a high level of skill and interest in play. On the other hand, tennis courts overgrown with grass, ball diamonds with infields undragged for weeks, horseshoe courts with holes in the ground where a putty-like clay should be, and shuffleboard courts with uneven surfaces and partially obliterated lines, repel would-be players and create a bad public image of the recreation department. Leaders should seek excellence in facilities as well as in program for the two are inseparable. Unfortunately, there is a general tendency to demand excellent facilities for the more popular activities, such as baseball, basketball, football, softball, and track, but to be satisfied with mediocrity and worse in facilities for such sports as horseshoes, volleyball, archery, gymnastics, and handball. It is probable that less than ten percent of the recreation departments of this country have constructed batteries of official horseshoe courts and maintained them properly, or even possess official volleyball nets. The lack of skill and interest in these and similarly neglected sports is a direct measure of the failure of recreation leaders to provide excellent facilities. It can hardly be expected that a boy will become fired with a driving desire to achieve a high level of superiority in the art of horseshoe pitching through months of constant practice with a pair of rusty, unmatched mule shoes, pitched into a hole, at pieces of pipe driven into the ground at varying angles and heights.

It is generally false economy to purchase the cheapest supply and equipment items as the cheapest often lacks durability and may prove ultimately to be the most expensive. Furthermore, the cheapest protective equipment may provide inadequate protection and shoddy game supplies lower both the quality of play and the degree of satisfaction enjoyed by the players. No infallible rule will apply in all cases, but the leader should hesitate to purchase either the cheapest or the most expensive items unless the weight of available evidence impels him to do so.

Financing the Program

Common practice throughout the United States provides funds for operating the competitive sports program from two major sources, taxes and fees. Construction and maintenance costs of facilities, such as ball diamonds, tennis and horseshoe courts, gymnasiums, and football fields, as well as the costs of the general supervision provided by the recreation department, generally are met through tax funds whether the participants are youth or adults.

If the use of a facility necessitates an expenditure of funds by the recreation department beyond normal, routine costs these additional expenses usually must be paid by the participating teams. Milwaukee charges for use of a baseball diamond for a game if: (1) the diamond is located on an area not under regularly scheduled leadership at the time of day for which the permit is granted; and (2) the diamond is used after 6:00 P.M. whether the lights are used or not.

The charge for an unlighted diamond under the above conditions is $10.00 for a three-hour limit and $15.00 for a lighted diamond. For softball diamonds under similar conditions and for a two-hour limit, the charges are $6.00 and $8.00.

Equipment and supplies for children and youth are purchased from tax funds by the recreation department, with the exception of fielders' gloves in baseball and softball, and players' uniforms. Uniforms frequently are furnished by sponsors. Some cities charge entry fees to teams comprised of children and youth and some do not. Milwaukee makes no charge to its boys' evening softball leagues playing on the summer playgrounds provided volunteer umpires are used and no trophies awarded. When trophies are awarded, a fee is charged to defray the cost of the trophy. The Milwaukee policy in baseball is to charge a franchise fee of $15.00 per team in their high-school and cadet leagues plus a forfeit fee of $5.00; the midget league franchise fee is $12.00. Team fees are used primarily to help pay costs of officiating and trophies.

It is almost universal practice to charge adult teams an entry fee sufficient in amount to cover all costs of officials and awards. In addition, in such sports as softball and baseball, they must provide their uniforms, bats, gloves, and protective equipment worn by the catcher. Many cities require them to furnish the game balls also. Where admission is charged, the gate receipts may be used to help pay league operating costs. In Madison, the baseballs for the adult night leagues were purchased from gate receipts and, after one game, were turned over for use in the youth leagues.

Milwaukee collects a $50.00 entry fee from adult teams in its Triple A baseball league, $35.00 from its top softball teams, $25.00 from basketball, and $15.00 from volleyball. The Milwaukee policy on fees and charges may be summed up as follows: "The adult and teen-age participants should accept some of the financial responsibility where the individual (1) receives special instruction, (2) is given priority use of facilities, or (3) is provided with special equipment."[8]

---

[8] *Fees and Charges* (Milwaukee: Department of Municipal Recreation and Adult Education, Milwaukee Public Schools).

TEAM SPONSORS. No discussion of financing sports competition would be complete without a reference to team sponsors who carry a large share of the financial burden. Many groups of young men and women would have difficulty paying the full cost of a season of athletic competition were it not for the important financial contributions made by sponsors. Many of these individuals and organizations sponsor teams simply because they like sports; others, because of real or imagined advertising benefits accruing from having their name connected with a team.

The recreation leader has a number of important responsibilities to carry out in relation to this general problem of sponsorship. They are:

1. Prohibit the sponsoring of youth teams by business firms that represent or advertise alcoholic beverages, tobacco, or other products which would be in bad taste or morally indefensible for youth to publicize.
2. Protect the sponsors against players who deliberately try to "gouge" them for everything they can get—free drinks, free meals, more equipment, entertainment, trip expenses.
3. Assist the sponsor, when necessary, to recover the uniforms provided players. A player who refuses to return his uniform to the sponsor may be barred from all further participation in department activities.
4. Furnish the sponsor with an estimate of the legitimate anticipated expenditures for the season and, at least in the case of youth teams, hold rigorously to this estimate. Some years ago, in Madison, Wisconsin, the director of the junior baseball program personally secured the sponsors for the 54 teams in the leagues by assuring them that the caps and shirts for the players would cost a certain specified amount and no more. He collected the sponsors' contributions, purchased the caps and jerseys, and distributed them to the teams. No team could approach its sponsor for any additional wearing apparel nor could the boys have worn it even if he had provided it of his own free will. The sponsor knew that when he made his original investment he would not be asked to make another that year. Sponsors are not difficult to secure under these conditions, but they quickly lose any desire to sponsor teams when they are looked upon as legitimate prey by unscrupulous players and managers.

FOUR CHALLENGES TO LEADERSHIP

Life would be much simpler if the choices to be made in solving problems that confront us could be between right and wrong. Unfortunately it is not that easy. Our trouble begins when a choice must be made between a mixture of right and wrong, a combination of good and evil. In each of the following challenges to leadership this combination exists. There undoubtedly is both good and bad in highly organized competitive sports for children. There is value in conformity and there may be injurious effects from conformity. Competition and coöperation are neither wholly good nor wholly bad. The purpose of this section is to help the student of leadership understand the issues involved and suggest some guidelines for arriving at intelligent decisions.

The Challenge of Diversity

We are a nation of conformists in many respects. Our tendency to conform extends even to participation in sports. Children and youth, particularly, are motivated powerfully by the desire for group approval. The emotional well-being of children depends in large measure upon their acceptance into the groups of their choice. Acceptance by one's peers requires a willingness to "go along with" the group, to dress like the group, talk like it, and participate in the sports considered important by the group. The relative importance of a sport to an adolescent generally is measured in terms of its status value which, in turn, is determined by the number of spectators that view it. The result of all this is the creation of an aristocracy of sports in America, a hierarchy of activities, in which honor, glory, and renown are accorded the favored few capable of making the football, basketball, baseball, and track and field teams. The mass of youngsters, less endowed with athletic ability, have two choices: (1) to go out for the "minor" sports, which, of course, can't be very important or they wouldn't be called "minor"; or (2) to become a spectator and make no effort to become an athlete.[9] As a result of their unwillingness to accept a subordinate role in an athletic-class-conscious society, in which they are denied the satisfaction of experiencing a sense of dignity and personal worth, many hundreds of thousands of young people prefer the role of spectator to that of "third class" athlete.

The secondary schools and colleges of America have contributed materially to the development of an athletic elite by placing almost exclusive emphasis, in many instances, upon only the highly skilled participants. They have neglected the relatively unskilled youth. Our recreation leaders are the inheritors, rather than the creators, of this tragic situation, but they should do all in their power to remedy it by:

---

[9] See pages 130–132 for a more detailed presentation of this point of view.

1. Guiding some children and youth into the unusual, or "unpopular," types of sports, provided they appear to be fitted for them. Don't try to force all children to become football, baseball, basketball, or track participants. Encourage originality and individuality in sports participation.
2. Encouraging everyone to accept the point of view that every sport is "major" to the person who participates in it, that there are no "minor" sports, and that respect for a human being includes an acknowledgement of the worth of the specific athletic activity which he enjoys.
3. Stimulating participation by everyone, at the highest possible level of skill, in at least one team sport and one individual or dual sport. Many different activities must be offered and every effort made to popularize and glamorize those activities not so fully invested with status value. It is of interest and of some value to note here that the record of the United States in Olympic competition will be improved not by further concentration upon a few sports, but rather by an intensification and distribution of our efforts over a wide variety of sports.[10]
4. Developing a high degree of skill in at least one individual sport not engaged in by the masses, acquiring a teaching competency in several, and utilizing both assets to lead others into these new interests.
5. Influencing administrative officials to meet the same high standards in facilities, equipment, and supplies for all sports that they now meet so frequently only for the most popular sports.

The Challenge of Balance

Competition, and coöperation, must not be carried to extremes. Too much competition can be destructive to human personality. When beating someone becomes a supreme objective of life, defeat, especially frequent defeat, results in a devalued self-esteem, a depreciated sense of personal worth, a deterioration of human dignity, and a developing sense of inadequacy and failure. Furthermore, excessive competition tends to limit one's feeling of identification strictly to his own small group. Combs points out:[11]

The survival of our democratic society depends on an increasing number of responsible and trustworthy persons who have the capacity for identification with their fellow men. They recognize that we live in a tremendously inter-

---

[10] A typical program of Olympic sports is that prepared for the 1968 Games in Mexico: basketball, boxing, canoeing, cycling, equestrian sports, fencing, field hockey, gymnastics, modern pentathlon, rowing, shooting, soccer, swimming, track, volleyball, water polo, weight-lifting, wrestling, and yachting.

[11] Arthur W. Combs, "The Feeling of Identification," *Perceiving, Behaving, Becoming—Yearbook 1962* (Washington, D.C.: Association for Supervision and Curriculum Development, 1962), pp. 165, 166.

dependent and coöperative society which requires members who think well of each other, who trust each other, and who see their stake in others . . . . . . This is not to imply that all competitive experiences are destructive. Competition between groups in a friendly atmosphere may very well foster coöperative behavior within groups. If such experiences in coöperation increase an individual's feelings of identification, then they can be of value. However, if coöperation within a group is achieved at the expense of hostility toward a much larger segment of mankind, even competition between groups needs to be questioned.

All games are coöperative efforts first and competitive struggles second. The members of a team must first coöperate or there is no team, only a collection of individuals. They must coöperate with their leader or coach, the officials, with one another, and with the other team, at least to the extent of putting in an appearance at the time and place agreed upon and abiding by the rules of play.

Just as too much and too intense competition should be avoided so also should the leader avoid the other extreme of too little competition, for to do so is to deny the nature of man. Huizinga believes that competition is the very essence of play:[12]

The urge to be first has as many forms of expression as society offers opportunity for it. The ways in which men compete for superiority are as various as the prizes at stake. Decisions may be left to chance, physical strength, dexterity, or bloody combat. Or there may be competitions in courage and endurance, skillfulness, knowledge, boasting, and cunning . . . The competition may take the form of an oracle, a wager, a lawsuit, a vow or a riddle. But in whatever shape it comes it is always play, and it is from this point of view that we have to interpret its cultural function.

Directives for the leader seem to be definite and clear:

1. Provide a broad program of competition in both team and dual sports, but do not pressure anyone into it.
2. Make every effort to ensure equality of team strength so that everyone may experience a reasonable measure of success.
3. Teach children and youth that beating someone is not as important as playing the game skillfully, and that the good sportsman obeys both the letter and the spirit of the rules. Also emphasize that the opposing players are not enemies, but friends, without whose coöperation no game would be possible.
4. Encourage participation in relatively non-competitive activities, such as bicycling, hiking, roller skating, skiing, fishing, riding, archery, and target shooting.

---

[12] Johan Huizinga, *Homo Ludens—A Study of the Play Element in Culture* (Boston: The Beacon Press, 1950), p. 105.

The Challenge of Moral and Ethical Values

Appearing and reappearing throughout the pages of this text is a continuous emphasis on the vital importance of moral and ethical character in the citizens of a democracy and the inescapable responsibility of recreation departments, in coöperation with other institutions of society, to make their fullest possible contribution to the attainment of these values. The significance of a moral basis for human behavior is expressed by the Educational Policies Commission:[13]

No society can survive without a moral order. A system of moral and spiritual values is indispensable to group living. As social structures become more complex, as the welfare of all depends increasingly upon the coöperation of all, the need for common moral principles becomes more imperative. Especially in a society which cherishes the greatest possible degree of individual freedom, the allegiance of the individual to commonly approved moral standards is necessary. No social invention however ingenious, no improvements in government structure however prudent, no enactment of statutes and ordinances however lofty their aims, can produce a good and secure society if personal integrity, honesty, and self-discipline are lacking.

In other words, we must not confuse shadow with substance for laws are no substitute for personal integrity nor coercion for self-discipline. "If there are not developed in men some inner moral restraints strong enough to control their impulses toward power and brutality, the alternative appears to be the rule of the strong over the weak, of the few over the many, of the despot over the subject."[14] Furthermore, as we gain increased power over things we realize ever more clearly that unless our advances in the physical sciences are matched by equal progress in the social sciences —in the area of human relationships, ideals, moral values, self-understanding, and self-discipline, the results can be complete extinction of the human race.

Detailed consideration of the responsibility of leaders to conduct activities in such a way as to achieve moral and ethical values is undertaken at this point because sports and games are particularly rich in these values. Here the child chooses how to behave in situations that are natural, often emotionalized, and frequently involve moral choices among competing courses of action. To accept the premise, however, that moral

[13] Educational Policies Commission, *Moral and Spiritual Values in the Public Schools* (Washington, D.C.: National Education Association of the United States, 1951), pp. 3–4.

[14] *Ibid.*, p. 11.

values reside in our sports and games and that leaders should seek to attain them is no guarantee of success in their pursuit. There is nothing automatic or accidental about the achievement of moral values. They must be planned for just as carefully, and sought as deliberately, as we plan for the development of individual game skills or team strategy.

FOUNDATIONS FOR ACHIEVING MORAL AND ETHICAL VALUES. Exactly how leadership should function in the effective pursuit of moral and ethical values is by no means fully understood. Considerably more research is needed to throw light on the many complexities related to this problem. However, certain conclusions and basic points of view seem to be reasonably well established:

1. The basic requirement for the development of moral and ethical values through recreation is a sincere belief on the part of all leaders that the matter is of the highest importance and that it is a mutual responsibility of the department of recreation and its leaders to seek these values in coöperation with other institutions and members of the community.

2. There are no neutral experiences. Every experience a child has in the sports program either adds to or subtracts from the quality of his character. No part of the child stays away from the playground or the community center. Children are affected as complete organisms by their experiences in sports and games and no aspect of their growth and development can be ignored by the successful leader.

3. Moral and ethical values are more effectively achieved if they permeate the entire program of recreation and are sought as normal, natural outcomes of the recreation experience.

4. Values originate in experience. Values may be good or bad. The quality of the values which accrue from participation in sports depends largely upon the number and the quality of the experiences. The development of moral and ethical people is best promoted through experiences in which these values exist and in which the participants learn to make proper moral choices among alternative courses of action.

5. The task of the leader is to help provide the experiences in which these values reside; to identify the values; bring them into consciousness; analyze them; lead children to make intelligent choices among conflicting courses of action and to see the possible results of one course as weighed against another. "As a result of making many choices in concrete behavior situations under proper guidance, generalized attitudes are formed and dependable behavior patterns are established."[15]

_____
[15] Ellis F. Hartford, *Emphasizing Values in Five Kentucky Schools* (Lexington: University of Kentucky, 1954), p. 8.

6. The influence of the group in shaping the moral and ethical behavior of its members is very powerful. This is especially true of small, intimate groups during the time its members are together. Insofar as the schools are concerned Jones points out that, "It is impossible to say how much contribution is made by teacher-pupil relations and how much by class-pupil relations, but if we consider these two together we have the two factors in the school situation which are most clearly related to character development."[16] However, a study by Jones indicates that while group morale may result in a child suddenly showing improved character responses it does not necessarily follow that such conduct will continue if the group influence is removed. This means that provision should be made, whenever possible, for prolonged exposure "to such conditions to allow the gains to become integrated into individual standards and habits."[17]

7. Knowledge about desirable moral conduct does not increase the probability that an individual will practice it.

8. The earlier a child is influenced toward moral conduct, the earlier does he begin to develop his own controls and evolve his own sense of values.

9. Desirable character responses are most effectively motivated when the child experiences satisfaction from moral and ethical behavior and dissatisfaction from undesirable conduct. Approval of the group, the leader, and self-approval appear to be the most valuable forms of motivation.

10. Transfer of moral behavior from the sports situation to other situations beyond the playground, the athletic field, and the gymnasium must be effected, otherwise such behavior has but limited value. A number of studies justify the conclusion that in developing honesty, for example, the child must be led to practice honesty in a variety of situations, to be consciously aware of the honesty factor in each of these situations and to respond in a desirable manner to this generalized concept, to see relationships among the situations, and to progress away from the specific and in direction of the general. All this is essential if transfer is to take place.

HOW THE LEADER FUNCTIONS. As an illustration of how a leader seeks moral values and their transfer, let us take the situation described on page 80, of the softball centerfielder who dived for a line drive, rolled over, and came up with the ball in one hand. When asked by the umpire if he had caught the ball his reply was that he had trapped it. Here is an experience rich in moral values provided the leader functions in somewhat the following manner:

---

[16] Vernon Jones, "Character Development in Children—An Objective Approach," in *Manual of Child Psychology*, Leonard Carmichael, (ed.) (New York: John Wiley and Sons, Inc., 1946), p. 729.

[17] *Ibid.*, p. 728.

1. As soon as possible, following completion of the game, the leader should sit down with the boys, all of them analyze the situation, and determine the other courses of action the centerfielder could have taken. He, of course, could have told the umpire he caught the ball, and lied, or he could have said, "You're the umpire, you call it," and been evasive. The third possibility was the one he adopted—telling the truth.

2. Each course of action should be discussed thoroughly in terms of its possible results as weighed against each of the other courses of action. Just what would have happened if Bill had lied to the umpire and told him he caught the ball? No one except Bill would have known about it so what difference would it have made? If Bill's team had won the game would they really have won it? How would the lie affect Bill, if at all?

3. The boys must make a moral judgment with respect to the correct action as they view it. Did Bill do the right thing? If so, why? If not, why not? Arriving at a decision is not enough; the reasons underlying the decision are vital also. If we may assume that the boys agreed with Bill, the leader should supplement their approval by his own praise since the possibility of Bill's and the other boys' repeating his action is enhanced by the feeling of satisfaction derived from the approval of the leader and the group.

4. Almost all writers in the area of character education agree on the vital importance of identifying the trait or value and seeking to generalize with respect to it. There is not much value to be derived from this specific situation if Bill and his teammates learn only that it is desirable to tell an umpire you trapped the ball, when you trap it. The leader points out that Bill told the truth, a mark of a gentleman and a good citizen. He states that honesty means uprightness and fairness. Thus, the boys begin to see that what Bill did is a good thing and that people describe it by the words "truthful" and "honest."

   This is the beginning of generalization. The complete process requires that Bill and his fellows experience a large number of situations in which the terms "truthful" and "untruthful," "honest" and "dishonest" are applicable. Unless the boys are able to identify the honesty element in a variety of situations and respond to this generalized concept, their concepts will be an unorganized and unintegrated collection of "do's" and "don'ts" applicable only to the specific situations in which they have had experiences.

5. The final step is the evolvement of a system of values, based on moral and ethical principles, which invests life with meaning, purpose, and significance. These values furnish a guideline for human conduct, a means for determining what is good, what is bad, what is right, and what is wrong. In essence, they are a philosophy of life, a foundation and an expression of character. The individual possessing such a philosophy is not dependent upon social approval to provide the satisfactions for his conduct. He is never insensitive to social approval,

but one measure of his maturity is the degree to which his actions are in harmony with his ideals. The truly great leader will seek to develop in youth that type of character which finds its basic satisfactions and motivations not in rewards and punishments originating from without, but in ideals and values generated from within.

The Challenge of Suitability

Competitive athletics for children has been one of the most controversial issues confronting recreation leaders during the past fifteen years —an issue which frequently has generated more heat than light and resulted more in a rehearsal of the prejudices of those involved in the controversy than in an honest endeavor to arrive at an intelligent solution to a professional problem.

The first step in the solution of any problem is to define the problem. We are concerned here with highly organized, highly competitive games for boys between the ages of eight and twelve years, in which major emphasis is placed by the leadership on winning; in which considerable pressure to win is applied by parents and other adults; and which may culminate in the determination of district, state, regional, or national championships. We are not questioning the desirability of competition as an essential factor in the development of boys in this age group, provided this competition meets certain standards.

The recreation leaders of this nation, as professional people, must take a position on this matter and defend it. Are we in favor of this kind of competition for children? Are we opposed? What valid reasons do we have for our stand? It is not enough to say that if the recreation department does not provide such competition, some other agency will do so and, therefore, we had better get involved and see that the job is done right. This is no argument for professional people to advance. What would we think of a doctor who said, "If I don't give my patient this harmful drug he very likely will get it elsewhere so I'd better see that he gets it under good supervision." Presumably we are better qualified to plan and conduct sports programs fitted to the needs and abilities of children than anyone else in the community, with the possible exception of the physical education people. The community has a right to expect guidance from us on controversial issues of this nature.

The intelligent approach to a problem of this nature is through research on the effects of highly competitive sports on children. Unfortunately research in relation to this problem is quite incomplete. We know a great deal more about the effects of competition on junior high school youth than we know about its effects on children under 12. The valid medical information we do have indicates that the incidence of injury to the tissue and skeleton of the pre-adolescent child in competitive activities is negligible; that in reality the chance occurrence of damaging or retarding type injuries is not a factor to be considered in the support or elimination of competitive programs for this age group; and that circulatory disturbances to the heart, blood vessels, and lungs is not a factor in favor of curtailing or discontinuing sports participation by people at any age provided they have normal hearts. Therefore, assuming that leaders insist on thorough pre-competitive medical examinations to ensure normalcy, the weight of medical evidence is in favor of competitive programs properly conceived and intelligently conducted.

We need the answers to questions other than those dealing with the medical aspects of intensive competition before arriving at any final conclusion. Such questions as the following are highly significant:

1. What are the values we seek for children of this age through a program of sports and games?
2. Is highly organized competition the best way to attain these values?
3. Is the child ready, physically, psychologically, and socially for this kind of experience?
4. Is it economical to spend time, energy, and money in teaching an eight-year-old boy to play baseball or should we wait until he is more mature?
5. Is the welfare of the child considered to be of paramount importance? Is this the real reason why the activity is being conducted? Or are we more concerned with victory, promoting a sport, advertising the town, and inflating the egos of parents?
6. Will the boys spend so much time and energy on this one activity that they will fail to participate in the many rich experiences they should have at this age when interests are so varied and skills so easily developed? Should not specialization be delayed a few years?
7. Has this type of play lost the simple, spontaneous, casual, happy-go-lucky characteristics which real play for children of this age should possess? Has fun been replaced by grimness and happiness by seriousness? Can a boy make mistakes in his play and still have fun?
8. Are eight- and nine-year-olds psychologically ready for highly organized team competition? Can they withstand the pressures generated by the imposition of adult standards, publicity, cheering crowds, championships, awards, travel, and "high-powered" coaches?
9. If victory becomes the measure of success will not the poorer players withdraw from sports participation because of the sense of failure and personal inadequacy engendered by their inability to win?
10. Will the promotion of this activity for the highly skilled boys result

in the neglect of other boys not sufficiently skilled to participate in the league?

11. What are the effects of a fiercely competitive activity on highly sensitive children who are not yet ready emotionally for experiences in which ultimate success can be enjoyed by only a few?

12. Are there any sound reasons why well-prepared leaders in a community recreation program should subject themselves and their players to arbitrary regulations imposed by a national organization wholly unfamiliar with local problems? In short, if a community is going to operate a program of baseball for youngsters, why can't the recreation department do the job itself without getting involved with a highly organized national organization?

In the absence of conclusive research on highly controversial problems, we should turn for help to the considered judgment of professional leaders as a basis for program planning. Four significant statements bearing upon the question of competitive sports for children of elementary school age have been issued during recent years by the following groups:

1. National Conference on Physical Education for Children of Elementary School Age. Thirteen national organizations and agencies were co-sponsors of this conference. Consultants included pediatricians, a growth and development specialist, a psychiatrist, and doctors of physical medicine.

2. The Joint Committee on Athletic Competition for Children of Elementary and Junior High School Age, comprised of representatives of the American Association for Health, Physical Education, and Recreation; the Society of State Directors of Health, Physical Education, and Recreation; the Department of Elementary School Principals; and the National Council of State Consultants in Elementary Education.

3. National Conference on Program Planning in Games and Sports for Boys and Girls of Elementary School Age.

4. Committee on School Health of the American Academy of Pediatrics.

All four groups agreed, in general, on the following:

1. Children of this age need a broad and varied program under competent leadership.

2. All activities should take into account the age and developmental level of the child. Furthermore, extreme care should be taken to match children with others who are of corresponding maturity and ability.

3. Tackle football and boxing should not be included in the program.

4. Competitive programs should be restricted to neighborhood and community levels. State, regional, and national tournaments, bowl, charity, and exhibition games are not recommended.

5. Competition is an inherent characteristic of growing, developing children. Its value depends largely upon the quality of the leadership.
6. Highly organized, highly competitive programs should be avoided.
7. Communities should look to their professionally prepared recreation leaders and physical educators for leadership.
8. Adequate medical supervision should be provided for all children participating in a competitive athletic program.
9. The program should include all of the children participating on many teams in numerous sports. This is not the place to emphasize a star system.
10. The competitive sports program should yield both educational and recreational results.

Recreation agencies throughout the United States report that games and sports lead all other recreation activities in popularity among both children and adults.[18] Various national sports associations estimated the number of bowlers, during a recent year, at 27,500,000; fishermen, 32,000,000; swimmers, 33,000,000; hunters, 20,000,000; golfers, 8,525,000; tennis players, 7,300,000; water skiers, 5,100,000; snow skiers, 5,000,000; archers, 8,000,000; and softball players, 22,500,000. Many other millions compete in basketball, baseball, volleyball, and numerous other sports and games. But there are also many millions who are not participating in any sport. The causes of their non-participation may be lack of time, money, facilities, skill, interest, or any one, or several, of many other factors. The challenge to leaders in this area of recreation is twofold; (1) plan and conduct present activities in such a manner as to achieve all the values which the program of competitive sports should yield; and (2) expand the opportunities for participation so that the lives of an ever-larger number of people may be enriched by the sports experience.

OUTDOOR RECREATION

Traditionally, the outdoors has been an important part of American life—first as a wilderness to be conquered, then as a source of inspiration and recreation. The value of going into the outdoors to refresh the spirit and body has been understood by men since Biblical times. However, it is only recently in this century that Americans, closely confined by a highly

---

[18] Donald E. Hawkins, ed., *Recreation and Park Yearbook 1966* (Washington, D.C.: National Recreation and Park Association, 1966), p. 53.

complex civilization, have begun developing a deeper appreciation of the outdoors to be used for the purpose of recreation.

The basic goals to which outdoor recreation contribute are the same as those for all recreation as presented in Chapter Four. And yet there is a uniqueness which characterizes outdoor recreation. This uniqueness lies in the fact that this area of recreation is based on, or has significant contact, with nature. The program should not be a duplication of the regular city recreation program transplanted to the woods or outdoor setting. The program should consist of activities that can best be done in the out-of-doors.

The Program

The outdoors with its lore, history, beauty, color, and natural resources provides the program's background and substance. The sphere of outdoor recreation program possibilities is extremely varied. A program might include camping, fishing, hunting (gun or bow and arrow), hiking, snow and water skiing, boating, horseback riding, mountain climbing, and picnicking. The use of snowmobiles is the most recent activity being enjoyed out-of-doors.

In this setting it is possible to promote an understanding of conservation, to study the stars, to collect original craft materials, to study Indian lore, or to study and experience the beauty of nature or to participate in the wonders of the out-of-doors. Each individual can find many experiences that will broaden and fulfill his life.

Values

The outdoor recreation program is recognized as having some unique values that should be experienced by everyone.

1. Experience adventure—the outdoors is a healthy and practical setting for adventure programs.
2. Develop an appreciation of the out-of-doors and nature—experience a real kinship with the earth.
3. Learn resourcefulness and develop skills—survival, accident prevention, first aid, cooking, shelter construction, axe and tool craft, and any particular skill needed for each activity (for example, making a fishing pole, learning the technique, getting the bait, then fishing).
4. Develop responsibility—a chance to be independent, out on one's own, to develop initiative, to meet certain problems and difficulties, and to work with a group.

Leadership

Under good leadership, outdoor recreation should become a most fruitful experience for everyone. The recreation leader has most of the skills and knowledge necessary to conduct the outdoor recreation program. It would be desirable in most cases if leaders had more preparation and experience in the selection and care of outdoor equipment, in stimulating and motivating participants toward discoveries and reasoning about nature, in outdoor living skills, in knowledge concerning the out-of-doors, and in being constantly alert regarding safety precautions.

Wherever possible, people should be given an opportunity for direct first-hand experiences outdoors. Catching a large trout, sliding down a glacier, climbing a new peak, and hiking through spectacular mountains are enjoyments of body and spirit that cannot be translated into words.

Selected References

Andrews, Gladys, Saurborn, Jeannette, and Schneider, Elsa, *Physical Education for Today's Boys and Girls* (Boston: Allyn and Bacon, Inc., 1960).

Bucher, Charles A., *Foundations of Physical Education* (Saint Louis: The C. V. Mosby Company, 1968).

Combs, Arthur W., "The Myth of Competition," *Childhood Education,* 33, No. 6, 1957, 264.

Cook, Walter L., *Lifetime Sports: A Guide for Instruction and Administration* (Washington, D.C.: National Recreation and Park Association, 1968).

Danford, Howard G., *Recreation in the American Community* (New York: Harper and Brothers, 1953).

Hartley, Ruth E. and Goldenson, Robert M., *The Complete Book of Children's Play* (New York: Thomas Y. Crowell Company, 1957).

Hawkins, Donald E. (ed.), *Recreation and Park Yearbook 1966* (Washington, D.C.: National Recreation and Park Association, 1966).

Hess, Lewis A., "Competitive Athletics for My Son?", *Childhood Education,* 31, No. 9, 1955, 441.

Huizinga, Johan, *Homo Ludens—A Study of the Play Element in Culture* (Boston: The Beacon Press, 1950).

Joint Committee on Athletic Competition for Children of Elementary and Junior High Age, *Desirable Athletic Competition for Children* (Washington, D.C.: American Association for Health, Physical Education, and Recreation, 1953).

Loughmiller, Campbell, *Wilderness Road* (Austin, Tex.: The University of Texas Press, 1965).

Mitchell, Viola and Crawford, Ida B., *Camp Counseling* (4th ed.) (Philadelphia: W. B. Saunders Company, 1966).

Mulac, Margaret, *Games and Stunts for Schools, Camps and Playgrounds* (New York: Harper and Row, 1964).

National Recreation and Park Association, *Federal Assistance for Recreation and Parks* (Washington, D.C.: National Recreation and Park Association, 1967).

National Recreation Association, *Community Sports and Athletics* (New York: A. S. Barnes and Company, 1949).

Oberteuffer, Delbert, *Physical Education* (rev. ed.) (New York: Harper and Brothers, 1956).

The Recreation Program (Chicago: *The Athletic Institute*, 1963).

Reichert, John Lester, "Competitive Sports Before the Teens," *Today's Health*, 35, No. 10, 1957, 28.

Scott, Harry A., *Competitive Sports in Schools and Colleges.* (New York: Harper and Brothers, 1951).

Skubic, Elvera, "Studies of Little League and Middle League Baseball," *The Research Quarterly*, 27, No. 1, 1956, 97.

van der Smissen, Betty and Knierim, Helen, *Recreational Sports and Games* (Minneapolis: Burgess, 1964).

Chapter IX

Music and Dance

JUST AS THE professional leader discovers his goals for recreation in general on both the level of the individual and the level of society, so, too, will he find compelling reasons for emphasizing the arts not only because of their vital significance to the individual, but also because of what they contribute to the national culture.

'TO FEED THY SOUL'

The basic goals to which the arts contribute are the same as those for all recreation presented in Chapter 4. And yet there is a uniqueness which characterizes the arts simply because they *are* the arts and constitute the heart of our national culture. We need to be fully aware of their significance both to the individual and to the nation. Let us see, first of all, what the arts mean to us as a people.

If we are concerned with the judgment of history with respect to the quality of our society we have but to compare Athens with Sparta to determine the part played by the arts in shaping that judgment. The Spartans, confronted by enemies on all sides and by the necessity of keeping in subjection many times their number of slaves, abandoned completely the pursuit and patronage of the arts. The arts were sacrificed to national survival. The Spartan code produced hardy, vigorous, courageous, highly skilled, disciplined, brutal soldiers, and nothing more. They possessed the endurance of supermen and the artistic sensitivity of oxen. Sparta drowned her potential virtues in militarism and no nation mourned her fall. Durant speaks her epitaph, "Today, among the scanty ruins of that ancient capital, hardly a torso or a fallen pillar survives to declare that here there once lived Greeks."[1]

Hardly a day's ride away from Sparta the Athenians were building a civilization so magnificent in its varied cultural aspects that every nation of the world today is the richer because of its incomparable legacy. What has Sparta to offer that will compare with the philosophy of Socrates and Plato, the sculpture of Phidias and Praxiteles, the drama of Euripides and Sophocles, or the poetry of Pindar?

One factor which threatens our national culture is the extent to which we are becoming a nation of viewers and listeners rather than participants in cultural activities. It is much easier simply to turn a dial and listen to music on television or radio than to create our own music. Let the music professionals handle all the creative activity while the public passively listens! But the well-springs of music in this nation will dry up unless music becomes the province of the amateur who, in the final analysis, creates and maintains a cultured society. The arts, in a democracy, belong to everyone and everyone has a responsibility to contribute to the national culture and to support it. Should the arts be any less a community responsibility than are health, welfare, and fire protection? Can the most highly industrialized nation in the world refute the charges of materialism and lack of culture so frequently made against it? Can we, as a nation, return to the spirit of this ancient maxim?

> "If of thy mortal goods thou art bereft,
> And from thy slender store two
> loaves alone to thee are left—
> Sell one, and with the dole
> Buy hyacinths to feed thy soul."

The quality of our civilization will be determined not only by our wealth, our machines, and our commercial or scientific genius, but also by our ability to express creatively or artistically the deeper meaning of life as we envisage it.

TOWARD A MUSICAL AMERICA

Among the many advantages of music as a leisure activity, the following seem most important:

---

[1] Will Durant, *The Life of Greece* (New York: Simon and Schuster, 1939), p. 87.

1. It is universally accepted as a highly desirable activity.
2. It can be enjoyed alone or in a group.
3. Music appeals to all ages.
4. Its cost ranges from nothing to whatever one wishes to pay.
5. It helps to create friendships and a sense of unity.
6. It provides emotional release and relaxation.
7. Of all the arts of communication, music is one of the most expressive.
8. A wide range of skill from the neophyte to the master is possible with a high degree of enjoyment accruing at each level.
9. It brings into the lives of people an element of refreshing beauty.
10. Music contributes to a developing sense of personal adequacy by providing reassuring experiences of success.
11. Music contributes to one's cultural development.
12. It contributes to the morale of both the individual and the group.

MUSIC IN RECREATION

The latest Yearbook by the National Recreation and Park Association[2] provides some indication of the scope and nature of the music activities sponsored or conducted by public recreation departments. Band concerts led all other types of music activity for both children and adults. Agenices reporting included both city and county authorities administering recreation programs.

Activity	Number of Agencies Reporting	
	Children	Adults
Band Concerts	936	965
Choral Activities	716	716
Festivals	412	302
Informal Instrument Groups	688	330
Music Shows	660	412
Orchestral Concerts	493	468

The different types of music groups functioning under the auspices of recreation departments are numerous and varied. Frieswyk[3] reports on a recent study conducted by the National Recreation and Park Association which revealed 165 different types ranging from skiffle bands to symphony orchestras. To list just a few groups or activities:

---

[2] Donald E. Hawkins, ed., *Recreation and Park Yearbook 1966* (Washington, D.C.: National Recreation and Park Association, 1966), p. 55.

[3] Siebolt Frieswyk, "The Performing Arts as Recreation," *Recreation*, June 1960, p. 257.

Accordion Bands
Adult Quartets
Band Concerts
Children's Choir
Choral Groups
Combos for Dance Accompaniment
Creative Music for Children
Drum and Bugle Corps
Folk Singing
Glee Clubs
Group Singing
Guitar Lessons

Harmonica Bands
Kazoo Bands
Listening Groups
Minstrel Shows
Music Festivals
Old Fiddlers' Clubs
Orchestra Groups
Playground Music and Festivals
Rhythm Bands
String Quartets
Variety Shows
Ukulele Groups

All music activities, no matter how numerous, can be classified as listening, singing, or playing, and no program is complete which fails to concern itself with all three phases. In providing opportunities for all the people to enjoy these three phases of music and develop their innate musical capacities, recreation departments should accept the following responsibilities:

1. Provide opportunities for all ages and all levels of musical taste to experience the pleasure of listening to music through such media as recordings, radios, television sets, concerts, and recitals.
2. Encourage community singing in both small and large groups and stimulate the organization of all kinds of choral groups.
3. Sponsor the organization of instrumental ensembles through provision of supervisory leadership and the necessary facilities, such as rooms for rehearsals and auditoriums for concerts.
4. Furnish instruction for those individuals who wish to learn to play an instrument or to sing and who have had no such opportunity previously.
5. Build a file of talented musicians in the community and encourage them to offer their services on programs of a civic service nature.
6. Help mobilize the musical resources of the community both human and physical.
7. Work harmoniously with other agencies in a common effort to conduct such city-wide activities as music festivals, operas, concerts, and show-wagon projects.

LEADERSHIP THROUGH LISTENING EXPERIENCES

Leaders have a strong belief in music as a vital and most enjoyable phase of recreation, but have a deep and almost chronic sense of their own inability to conduct it effectively. Music, to most of them, has become a kind of mysterious jungle through which no one can find his way unless he is technically skilled in the solution of such enigmas as musical notation, music reading, how to chord songs, and all the other secrets involved in the term "musical symbols." Their feelings of insecurity, incompetence, and self-distrust are further accentuated when they view the broad area of instrumental music against the background of their own inability to play anything at all.

You may not be able to teach the technical aspects of music, but your common sense, ingenuity, and zeal can overcome your lack of musical skills so that there will always be something you can do musically for both children and adults. The provision of a listening program, which helps the participant find beauty and enjoyment in music, is within your ability even if your musical skills approximate zero.

Responsibilities of the Leader

The first responsibility of the leader is to provide the facilities and equipment for listening: This involves securing record players, radios, and television sets of high quality and the rooms in which they can be used effectively. These rooms should be characterized by good acoustics, provided with comfortable chairs, and lend themselves to informal listening by individuals and small groups. Every community center should have one or more of these rooms. Even on the playground where no indoor facilities may be available, the versatile leader will find a quiet corner where the listening program may be held.

Provide a variety of high quality music to be heard: This may be done through recordings, radio, television, concerts, recitals, and demonstrations by your musician friends invited to your playground or community center.

It is desirable to plan regularly scheduled programs of recorded music, beginning with records that possess an immediate appeal interspersed with some which have a more lasting appeal. Do not spend your limited funds on "popular" music since most of it won't be popular very long. Encourage the children to bring some of their own recordings of recent song hits, if this seems desirable.

The listening program for children should include some instruction designed to heighten their interests and deepen their understandings. They should be told the name of the composer and enough about the music they are listening to for purposes of identification. As leaders we can help expand the child's world to include an acquaintanceship with some of the creative artists who contributed such beautiful music for the delight of their minds and hearts. We can lead them to an increasing realization that composers expressed themselves through their music in ways that can be recognized. This is why you can identify immediately a Strauss waltz and why you will hear people say, "I've never heard this before, but it sounds like Mozart to me." Furthermore, we have a professional responsibility to help children to be selective and discriminating, to be able to distinguish between excellence and mediocrity in the midst of an overwhelming amount of music of questionable taste and value to which they are exposed constantly by recordings, radio, and television. This is one opportunity to teach children to prefer excellence to mediocrity.

Nye recommends that recordings for children possess some of the following characteristics:[4]

1. There can be active physical response to the music.
2. The mood is distinct.
3. The melodies heard are song-like.
4. The tone quality is beautiful.
5. The music tells a story.
6. Aspects of the music relate to the experience and interest of children.
7. The selection is short (because the attention span of these children is brief).

Establishment by the leader of a record library through which music lovers may borrow or rent records is an important facet of a listening program. Some people can't afford to buy all the records they would like to hear just as they cannot afford to buy all the books they would like to read. Thus, the record library meets the same need in music that the conventional public library does in literature.

It is recommended that leaders, in their efforts to build the best possible record libraries, consult both the school music specialists and qualified individuals in their local record shops. Any attempt to list here the compositions which should be secured would be of little value since new and improved recordings are appearing constantly.

Listening to music through the medium of recordings is but one phase of a total listening program. The leader should arrange concerts and recitals which give pleasure to the audience and an opportunity for the performing musicians to be heard. An earnest effort should be made to discover the soloists, choral groups, and instrumental groups that are

<hr>

[4] Robert Evans Nye and Vernice Trousdale Nye, *Music in the Elementary School* (Englewood Cliffs, N.J.: Prentice-Hall, Inc., 1957), pp. 122–123.

in every community and encourage them to contribute their talents in concert halls, on the playgrounds, in the community centers, in the parks, and at other places where people may enjoy them. This implies that the leader must be familiar with the musical resources of the community, maintain a file of musical talent, and work harmoniously with all individuals and organizations in the community in a common effort to provide the broadest possible program of quality music.

Encourage all ages to participate in the listening program: One effective means of motivating children to listen to good music is to invite a musician to visit your playground or community center and play for them. He might also be asked to tell how he first became interested in music, where he studied and for how long, what music has meant to him, and some of his most interesting experiences.

The leader should keep the public informed about music programs planned for the community. This will include quality programs scheduled on radio, television, in schools, churches, community centers, concert halls, and in parks and on playgrounds. The information may be disseminated by means of announcements over radio and television, posters, notices on bulletin boards, and articles in newspapers.

THE LEADER DEVELOPS A SINGING PROGRAM

In Chapter 5, we learned that among the various types of leaders were (1) the leader who works directly with people as they participate in recreation activities on the playground or in the community center, or elsewhere; and (2) the administrative leader whose role is primarily an executive one involving planning, organizing, and administering. The most important responsibility of the administrative leader is to provide the conditions within which the activity or group leader can function on a high level. The student should keep in mind, therefore, that certain of the responsibilities listed below are primarily those of the recreation administrator, some belong to the activity leader, while others are joint responsibilities shared by both.

Responsibilities of the Leader for the Total Singing Program

The first responsibility of leadership is to determine just what its responsibilities are in the development of a singing program. This involves defining or establishing the scope and nature of the program and then identifying the tasks to be performed.

The most important of these responsibilities are:

1. Encourage and assist individuals and groups that wish to sing without assuming direct responsibility for them.
2. Develop a broad program of vocal music within the department of recreation for which direct responsibility is taken.
3. Organize and conduct community singing both as an important recreation activity in itself and in connection with family night activities on the playgrounds or in community centers, parties, meetings, camp programs, dinners, hikes, and other appropriate occasions.
4. Discover those individuals capable of teaching your staff members how to be good song leaders. Frequently these persons may be recruited from the ranks of the professional musician.
5. Build a file of singers in your community and enlist their talents in a program of community service.
6. Secure the services of specialists to direct the choral groups.
7. Provide the facilities, such as rehearsal rooms and auditoriums, for both the choral and informal singing groups.
8. Provide opportunities for the choral groups to give public performances. These opportunities may be discovered in connection with the recreation program as well as in relation to the schools, civic organizations, and various kinds of public meetings. Competition among choral organizations, if not overdone, will be helpful here.
9. Maintain a good library of song books, song sheets, song slides, and choral music. Leonhard[5] recommends that the leader seek expert advice in selecting these materials; that for community singing he should select one or more song-book titles and secure a sufficient number of copies for regular use plus at least one copy of all the better song books; and for the choral program he should furnish two or three choral collections with enough copies so that each singer may have one.

Among the better song books of value to the recreation leader are:

1. Daniel, Oliver, *Round and Round and Round They Go* (Evanston, Ill.: Summy-Birchard Publishing Company, 1952).
2. Spaeth, Sigmund Gottfried, *Sigmund Spaeth's Song Session* (New York: Remick Music Corporation, 1958).
3. Wilson, Harry Robert, *Sing Together with Harry Robert Wilson* (New York: Consolidated Music Publishers, Inc., 1956).

---

[5] Charles Leonhard, *Recreation Through Music* (New York: A. S. Barnes and Company, 1952), p. 86.

Choral Singing

Very few leaders in recreation will possess the specific musical competencies which one must have to be successful in the direction of choral groups. However, all leaders should know what this phase of the music program includes, why it is important, and what is involved in its conduct.

Choral singing refers to the highly organized singing of groups which come together for the sole purpose of singing and which rehearse regularly under the leadership of a competent director. Major emphasis is on excellence in singing with a view to performing in public. Among the various types of choral organizations are the mixed chorus, men's glee club, women's glee club, and small singing ensembles, such as men's quartet, mixed quartet, women's quartet, and women's trio. Barbershop quartets are included here.

Major responsibilities of the administrative leader who seeks to develop a program of choral singing include the provision of competent directors, adequate facilities, supplies, and equipment, ample opportunities for public performances, and the encouragement which stems from a sincere belief that choral singing is a vital part of a program of recreation.

The Art of the Song Leader

We are concerned here not with polished performances by groups organized for the express purpose of singing, but with helping informal groups enjoy the intensely rewarding emotional experiences which result when people sing together. Effective leadership in group and community singing is an artistic accomplishment which ranks high among the special competencies of the recreation leader.

The most practical solution for the non-singing leader is the use of records. Many beautiful songs for children are available in record form and are extremely effective in motivating the singing of children. Children can bring records from home to supplement those provided by the department. Play the record through so the children may hear the whole song. Don't try to teach it part by part and don't emphasize musical facts, fundamentals, or technical competence. Your purpose is not to develop competent vocalists, but to bring to your children the joys and satisfactions in singing.

Let the children sing with the record whenever they feel like it. It might be well to allow them to interpret the music first through bodily movement and then through singing. Even though you may not sing well, you can usually stimulate the children's singing by using your own voice to pick up the tune.

Many musically unskilled leaders have enlisted the aid of parents and others to play the piano or some other instrument, or to lead their various groups in singing. Enthusiasm, interest, and ingenuity may be no substitute for musical competence, but they do offer real compensatory values.

The leader plans ahead: Adequate preparation for community singing involves careful and detailed advanced planning. The leader should:

1. Prepare a program comprised largely of songs familiar to the members of the group.
2. Select songs which will not offend anyone, especially racial, religious, and national groups.
3. Select songs appropriate to the age of the group. Senior citizens prefer the old songs while teen-agers like more modern music.
4. If the occasion warrants, select songs that have a common theme. For example, a selection of Irish songs would be appropriate for St. Patrick's Day.
5. Provide for variety in your program with many different types of songs.
6. When selecting your songs, take into consideration the educational level, musical tastes, social, economic, and other relevant characteristics of the group.
7. Provide satisfactory accompaniment; piano, if possible. The leader and the pianist should be near one another.
8. Furnish the group with the words of all songs through the media of song books, song slides, or song sheets.
9. Plan to invite the members of the group to suggest a few of the songs.
10. Prepare to inject some friendly competition into the singing. One half of the group may sing against the other half or the women may compete against the men.
11. Plan to end the program before the interest begins to lag.

The leader directs singing: Enthusiasm and self-confidence are two of the most important characteristics of the successful song leader. The best song leaders the author has known were complete extroverts, extremely enthusiastic about singing, and highly successful in transferring their enthusiasm to others. They were capable, but not great singers themselves. They differed in many respects, but they also were alike in many ways. For example, in general they used the standard conducting gestures although they avoided excessive arm waving and often used no motions at all.

The skillful use of hand, head, and body motions as visual aids to singing helps get the group off to a good start, indicates the tempo, interprets the song with respect to its degree of vigor, helps the leader to avoid dominating children's singing with his voice, and assists in bringing out the beauty in voices by indicating long sustained tones and their appropriate release.

TYPES OF SONGS

The success of community singing depends more upon the leader and the songs than upon any other factors. The types of songs which have proved to be especially popular for community singing are described below. Some leadership suggestions also are included.

Action Songs

These are songs which evolve an action response and usually are more popular among children and youth than among adults. The group should be given ample time to learn the song before "actions" are introduced. The leader should not permit the movements to become stereotyped. Creativity may be stimulated by dividing the children into small groups each of which works out its own way of acting out the song. Examples of this type of song are "This Old Man," "She'll Be Comin' Around the Mountain," and "John Brown's Baby."

Folk Songs

The rhythm and melody of these songs are simple and basic because they have grown out of the needs, aspirations, and the culture of the people. They play upon the heartstrings of people as they sing of personal emotions and heroic deeds. They deal with the raw materials of life and are a vital part of our musical heritage.

The bewitching melodies of "On Top of Old Smoky," "The Blue-Tail Fly," "I'm A-leavin' Cheyenne," "Down in the Valley," and countless others have an irresistible appeal because they are rooted in the lives of the common people. Alan Lomax, whose contributions in the

area of folk music are truly monumental, tells us what our folk songs
mean to us:[6]

So, slowly, our folk songs grew, part dream and part reality, part past and
part present. Each phrase rose from the deeps of the heart or was carved out
of the rock of experience. Each line was sung smooth by many singers...
until the language became apt and truthful and as tough as cured hickory.
Here lies the secret of their beauty. They evoke the feeling of the place and
of belonging to a particular branch of the human family. They honestly
describe or protest against the deepest ills that afflict us—the colour bar,
our repressed sexuality, our love of violence, and our loneliness. Finally,
they have been cared for and reshaped by so many hands that they have
acquired the patina of art, and reflect the tenderest and most creative impulses
of the human heart, casting upon our often harsh and melancholy tradition
a lustre of the true beauty.

Many of our folk songs tell a story of the people who made and
sang them and the song leader should learn these stories and relate
them to the group in his introductory remarks. For example, "Down in
the Valley" is a lament of the mountaineer from the Smokies who, when
sent to the state penitentiary at Raleigh for moonshining or some other
crime, suffered so deeply as he was shut off from the wind, the stars, and
the sky of his beloved mountains.

Hymns and Carols

Hymns are religious songs in praise or honor of God while carols
are Christmas songs or hymns. Most of these songs have been written
expressly for performance by congregations in religious services. These
inspirational and religious songs must, of course, be led and sung in a
manner that harmonizes with their sacred themes.

Examples of this kind of song are "Beulah Land," "Onward Christian Soldiers," "God of Our Fathers," "Silent Night," and "Oh, Come
All Ye Faithful."

Popular Songs

Most "popular" songs are not popular very long. They usually are
light in character and temporary in nature. The leader will be wise not

---

[6] Alan Lomax, *The Folk Songs of North America* (Garden City, N.Y.:
Doubleday and Company, Inc., 1960), p. xxviii.

to spend much time or money on them. They appeal more to adolescents than to adults. If you teach them at all, try to use some of the better ones. A very few have been of sufficiently high quality to withstand the test of time. Two examples of these are "The Bells of St. Mary's" and "My Wild Irish Rose."

Rounds

Rounds are songs in which the singers, divided into two or more groups, enter at equal intervals of time and achieve a harmonious result. For example, "Row, Row, Row Your Boat" is normally sung by adult groups in four parts. One group begins alone, at the beginning; a second group begins just as the first starts singing the song through a second time; the third group begins when the first starts its third round; and the fourth group starts singing when the first begins its fourth round.

Small children cannot master round singing in four parts. The leader, therefore, should provide for these to be sung by small children in only two parts instead of the customary three or four. Too often this type of singing sacrifices quality for volume when each group tries to "drown" out the others in what has degenerated into a vocal combat. The leader can prevent this by emphasizing beauty and harmony in contrast with trying to see which group can sing the loudest. Examples of well-known rounds are "Three Blind Mice," "Row, Row, Row Your Boat," and "Are You Sleeping." These very familiar rounds are sometimes sung so often as to become boresome. The good leader will introduce other excellent but not so familiar rounds, such as "Oh, How Lovely is the Evening," "A Spanish Cavalier," "White Coral Bells," "Sweetly Sings the Donkey," "Canoe Song," and "Kookaburra."

Spirituals

The singing of spirituals—so deeply moving, so intensely emotional—reflects the tragedy of the black people in some songs and their eternal optimism in others. Throughout their spirituals they have affirmed their faith in a personal God and their passionate belief that some day justice would triumph and an end would come to their sorrow and shame.

The noble beauty of their songs, the depth of feelings they express, and the magnificent quality of their singing have combined to make the occasions intensely emotional experiences never to be forgotten. The white man may imitate the black man in the singing of his spirituals, but can never equal him. Some of their finest spirituals are "Jacob's Ladder," "When the Saints Go Marchin' In," "Roll, Jordan, Roll," "The Old Ark's A-Moverin,'" and "Swing Low, Sweet Chariot."

Patriotic Songs

This type of song includes "The Star Spangled Banner," "America," "America the Beautiful," and the "Battle Hymn of the Republic." Youth should be taught and adults reminded of the conditions which motivated the writing of these songs. Love of country is a desirable goal of the recreation leader and one of the most effective ways of achieving it is through songs of this nature.

Songs of Sentiment

Most of these songs express the love of one human being for another although a few deal with one's attachment for a state or region. They are more popular with older adults than with children or youth. They include "My Old Kentucky Home," "When You and I Were Young, Maggie," "Silver Threads Among the Gold," "Way Down Upon the Swanee River," "Love's Old Sweet Song," "In the Gloaming," and "Carry Me Back to Old Virginny."

This classification is by no means a complete one. Many excellent songs do not fit within any of the above categories. The major purpose of the listing is to give the beginning song leader some conception of the great variety of songs and thus influence him to enlarge his repertoire and increase his competencies.

THE LEADER AND THE INSTRUMENTAL PROGRAM

Unless the leader is a music specialist, his responsibilities in the instrumental program will be largely administrative since active leadership with instrumental groups requires a musical competency considerably beyond that of most playground and community center leaders. The organization of a rhythm band and the teaching of one or more of the easy-to-play instruments may lie within his scope of ability.

In bringing instrumental music to young and old, the leader is concerned with two different groups; those who have never played before and those who have. In order to meet the needs of both groups Leonhard recommends that the recreation department offer elementary class instruction in playing instruments and sponsor the organization of instrumental ensembles.

Certain highly significant facts should be presented here as they are definitely related to intelligent leadership in this phase of the musical program. The United States Office of Education reports that during the decade of the 50's the public secondary schools of the nation sponsored 35,000 orchestras and 50,000 bands. The American Music Conference estimates that there were 43.9 million amateur instrumentalists in the country at the end of 1967, and the proportion of youngsters was 17.1 million in the 4-to-21 bracket to 26.8 million adults. It is logical to assume that from this vast reservoir of musical talent recreation departments would have an inexhaustible supply of adults clamoring for an opportunity to continue their participation in music. Unfortunately the assumption appears to have no factual foundation. Thorne reports:[7]

It is regrettable that of over four million students participating in school bands and orchestras comparatively few of them, if present patterns continue, will choose to take advantage of the very thing this experience should do, perpetuate musical participation into adult life as a continuing source of enjoyment and satisfaction. The best estimate from available figures indicates that 16 out of 17 instrumentalists stop playing when they leave school, either selling their instruments or putting them to rest in the attic.

One of the reasons for this tragic burial of one's talents, according to Thorne, is the few cities and towns which provide the opportunities for adults to continue their instrumental music experiences. She places the major share of the blame on the school music people, however, for their emphasis on professionalism in music, although knowing very few would become professionals, and for their concentration on bands and orchestras, both of which require considerable skill. A corollary of this is the school's emphasis on classical music when the students' interests are elsewhere and condescending and even disdainful attitude which it frequently takes toward all instruments "other than those that fit into he traditional band or orchestra."

Even where recreation departments are providing opportunities for former high school and college students who have had band and orchestra experience, they frequently seek out only the more advanced players and neglect the less skilled and the beginner.

---

[7] Marie Thorne, "The Case for the Informal Instruments," *Music Journal*, October 1961, p. 75.

Classes for Beginners

In light of the above facts, the twofold nature of the recreation department's responsibilities becomes clear. One of these responsibilities is to provide an opportunity for the beginner to learn to play a musical instrument; the other is to provide opportunities for those who know how to play to continue to enjoy, and further improve, their musical skills.

Many recreation departments offer instrumental classes for beginners with the length of the course depending on the type of instrument. Classes in the recorder, autoharp, ukulele, or harmonica may extend over a period of only four to six weeks, while the time devoted to the more difficult orchestra and band instruments will be considerably longer.

Leaders should encourage more extensive participation in the use of the informal or folk instruments, such as the mandolin, harmonica, ukulele, accordion, banjo, and guitar. Don't let anyone belittle these instruments or those who play them as constituting a kind of second-class musical citizen. Thorne points out that, "The informal instruments have always been the vehicles through which people have poured out their hearts through their folk music," and she raises a vital question: "Who is to say that the person who has taken Beethoven to his heart via the mandolin regards his music with any less reverence or relish than the one who does so with a violin?"[8] The creation or toleration of a class consciousness is as indefensible in music as it is in sports or any other area of recreation.

Among the many advantages of the informal instruments the following rank high:

1. They are easy to learn.
2. They are inexpensive.
3. Emphasis is on the music rather than on the highly technical or mechanical aspects of its creation.
4. They are musically sound and enjoyable.
5. They are easily portable.
6. Most are accurate in pitch and soft in tone.
7. Their informality harmonizes with the nature of the recreation situation.

Opportunities for Continuing Musical Experiences

The recreation department should sponsor the organization of instrumental ensembles through which the members of school music groups may further their education and enhance their enjoyment of music during the

---

[8] *Ibid.*, pp. 77–78.

summer months and by means of which "alumni" instrumentalists may continue their musical experiences.

DANCE IN RECREATION

Many excellent books on dance are available to the recreation leader who wishes to increase his competencies in this most delightful and deeply satisfying performing art. Most of the professional literature on dance has been written primarily for the teacher and includes a fairly large number of dances described in considerable detail.

There is no intent to duplicate these books here, a few of which are listed at the end of this chapter. A book which professes to treat the subject of leadership in recreation on a broad scale must not attempt to explore in depth any particular activity area, otherwise it will quickly assume the proportions of an encyclopedia. We are concerned in this section with a brief inquiry into the part which dance has played in the history of man; the contributions it makes to the enrichment of life; the place it should occupy in a program of community recreation; the responsibilities of the leader for its operation; and how superior leadership functions through this particular medium in an effort to achieve the goals of recreation.

The Origins of Dance

Dancing probably is the oldest of the arts, presumably preceding man himself. Turkeys, birds, and apes engage in recognizable dance forms and processes. Terry points out that,[9]

. . . dance commences with life itself and that its history is as old . . . as living matter.

It is safe to assume that early man danced first out of sheer physical exuberance, perhaps next in connection with courtship and lastly in terms of ritual. A fourth dance purpose might be found in the need of or desire for communication, a communication based upon gesture and mimesis.

Through tribal dances existing to this day, we can guess that when man emerged from the stone age era and arrived at a neolithic culture, he had ritual dances for every important occasion: for marriage, for birth, for circumcision, for propitiation of the gods, for illness, for war and, in fact, for any occasion requiring the aid of magic, of increased powers, of dedication.

---

[9] Walter Terry, "History of Dance," *The Dance Encyclopedia* (New York: A. S. Barnes and Company, 1949), p. 239.

No art provided primitive man with as diversified and complex a vehicle of expression as the dance for he developed it from the simple prancing and preening of the animal into a thousand forms touching every aspect of his communal and individual existence.

Dancing rivaled music in popularity among the Greeks although it was quite different from our own. Men were rarely brought into contact with women through the medium of dance. Rather, it was an artistic exercise revolving around religion, athletics, war, and every major event of life and every season or festival of the year. Dance contests, usually involving choral song, were emphasized.

The dance as an art disappeared with the decay of Roman civilization and continued to sleep for centuries under the dominance of the Christian church which looked upon it as provocative of immorality. But even the opposition of the church could not abolish the folk dances of the people. Medieval moralists might condemn the dance as an invention of the Devil, but dancing was practiced by nearly all the people. The French and Germans especially were fond of the dance and created many folk dances through which they celebrated their numerous festivals and victories.

Two distinct forms of the dance gradually evolved over the years. Under the auspices of the nobility, the dance assumed a dignified, refined, and stylized form eventually leading to the ballet, the gavotte, and finally to the waltz, polka, and mazurka. A further development involved its introduction into the theater and its practice by professional dancers. Dance among the common people, on the other hand, was simple, vigorous, unrestrained, highly expressive, and spontaneous.

In early America, dance, along with all other forms of recreation, was opposed by the Puritans. The South, however, was more liberal and enjoyed square dances, the waltz, and some English folk dances. Most of our recreational dancing today consists of folk, square, and social, or ballroom, dancing. When the emphasis is placed on good fellowship, fun, and an enjoyable, happy experience for all, folk and square dances will command the enthusiasm of large numbers of people for they are a part of the good life, one of the most ancient forms of communal joy.

The Values We Seek

Let us limit our discussion of values in dance to pointing out how dance can be sufficiently vigorous to contribute to fitness. By adding to the joy of living and providing for the release of tension, dance assists in the maintenance of mental health. As an individual grows in his ability to dance well, he enjoys success in his constant search for personal adequacy, thus gaining status and self-esteem. Such social values as respect for others, concern for their welfare, coöperation for the common good, and the acquisition of certain social graces may all accrue from the dance, especially the folk dance. Finally, through folk dancing an individual may grow in understanding and appreciation of the culture of his own country and that of others. When a leader teaches a dance of another nation to a group of American children or adults he is under obligation to use this dance as a means of deepening their understandings and appreciations of the cultural heritage of that nation.

The dancer, himself, takes part for the sheer fun of dancing—he seeks no other goals. The dance is an end in itself. The leader too, must appreciate the vital significance of enjoyment and happiness as outcomes of the dance, but he will seek multiple values as in all other areas of the recreation program.

A MAJOR COMMITMENT

A recreation department has two outstanding responsibilities with respect to a program of dance: (1) the provision of opportunities for its people to enjoy the dance skills and interests developed in school, home, or elsewhere; and (2) instruction in the rhythmical skills and social behaviors related to dance provided this instruction has not been secured through some other agency. Recreation leaders seldom find it necessary to teach people how to read because the schools meet this responsibility, but dance literacy is by no means as universally achieved.

Many recreation departments offer classes in various kinds of dance. Pasadena provides an instructional program in twenty-seven elementary schools, a dance workshop, and ballroom dance instruction at five junior high schools. During a recent summer, Denver provided instruction in tap dancing in twenty schools over a period of approximately two months with classes meeting once a week for two hours a day. Classes in modern dance also were offered at three centers for elementary, junior, and senior high school boys and girls over a six-week period. Flint, Michigan, conducted classes in tap and social dance at thirty different locations. Milwaukee, in a recent year, taught 4,018 boys and girls in ballet, ballroom, tap, folk, and square dance classes with a total attendance of almost 30,000. In addition, more than 1,600 adults were enrolled in ballroom,

Latin-American, ballet, square, and modern dance classes. Newark, New Jersey, conducted dance classes or dances at fifty-two playgrounds or community centers. Ballet, social, folk, square, tap, and modern dance were emphasized with a number of dance festivals presented in various sections of the city during the summer playground season.

The extent to which departments of recreation provide opportunities for people to dance is indicated by the following data collected by the National Recreation and Park Association.[10] Agencies reporting included both city and county authorities administering recreation programs.

Type of Dance	Number of Agencies Reporting	
	Children	Adults
Ballet	660	163
Folk	632	716
Modern	632	192
Rhythms	412	82
Social	1018	936
Square	990	1100

A total of 3,142 local governmental units—cities, counties, towns, villages, and school and park districts—were included in this report. Since many reported their program included more than one type of dance for both children and adults, it is evident that many communities offer no opportunities whatsover in dance or failed to indicate these opportunities in their report.

Types of Dances

Several different types of dances are conducted by recreation departments, but social, square, and folk are the most popular. Rhythms for younger children also are emphasized.

RHYTHMS. Rhythms, or rhythmic activities, involve movement through which a child expresses himself creatively to music. The term *fundamental rhythms* relates to such basic natural movements as walking, running, skipping, hopping, sliding, and galloping. Other movements in which the arms, legs, head, and trunk are involved, but the body is not moved from one place to another, include bending, stretching, swinging, swaying, twisting, turning, striking, pushing, pulling and lifting. Combinations of these activities also are included.

---

[10] Hawkins, *op. cit.*, p. 55.

When the child, exercising his imagination, interprets to music his ideas with regard to the actions of animals, such as camels, elephants, horses, and rabbits or of such characters as giants, fairies, dwarfs, and witches, he is engaging in *interpretive rhythms*. Creativity is released when children are stimulated, encouraged, and influenced to explore, to originate, and to discover various ways of expressing themselves through a variety of movement forms.

Leaders will emphasize fundamental rhythms, or the basic dance movements, with all children of elementary school age while interpretive or creative rhythms will be limited primarily to younger children, ages six to eight years.

FOLK DANCE.   Folk dance is to dance what folk music is to music. It is an art form in movement which originated out of the everyday life of the common man and through which he expressed his convictions about religion, work, war, play, and the various customs and rituals of the people. Centuries old, most of these dances have lost their original meanings and today are engaged in simply because they are one of the most enjoyable of all human activities.

SQUARE DANCE.   Square dancing is a popular form of American folk dance in which four couples participate in quadrille formation. It traces its parentage to the New England Quadrille and the Kentucky Running Set. The former originated in France and the latter in the low country of England and Scotland. The child of this union is the American square dance with its own unique characteristics.

SOCIAL DANCE.   Social dance is also referred to as ballroom dance. It is an outgrowth of the European folk dance, but rose above its plebeian origin when dancing masters refined, stylized, and dignified it for the nobility. Today teen-agers usually prefer the rock and roll and novelty dances while adults participate more generally in the less vigorous and more conservative dances. The senior citizen prefers waltzes and fox trots danced to the old time tunes with which he is familiar.

NO SUBSTITUTE FOR PLANNING

One of the leader's chief responsibilities in the area of dance is to provide opportunities for youth and adults to enjoy the dance skills and interests which they have developed. This means that the leader must work effectively with members of the group in planning and conducting a series of dances. Successful dances do not come about by accident; they are the result of careful, detailed, intelligent, and coöperative planning in which nothing is taken for granted.

Let us assume that you are a leader in a community center working with an upper teen-age organization of several hundred members and that you are planning your first dance. What are some of the most important things you should do?

In the first place, involve as many youngsters in the planning as possible. Create the feeling that this is *their* dance and that its success depends primarily upon their own efforts. The *principle of involvement* should constitute one of your major guides throughout this activity. Establish the following committees and help them to understand and carry out their responsibilities: publicity, decorations, finance, facilities, refreshments, music, hospitality, special entertainment, and clean up.

COMMITTEE RESPONSIBILITIES

1. *Facilities.* This committee is responsible for securing a place to hold the dance and for such equipment items as a public address system, stage and chairs for the orchestra, lighting arrangements, and seating facilities for those who wish to sit out a dance. Care should be taken to select an attractive place, neither too large nor too small. Nothing has a more deadly effect on a teen-age dance than a large dance floor with a small number of dancers. Teen-agers prefer congestion to wide-open spaces at their dances.
2. *Decorations.* The work of this committee is extremely important. Senior high school youth are interested in the proper "night club" atmosphere for their dances and the decorations committee attempts to create such an atmosphere by the ingenious use of fireproofed crepe paper, soft, colored lights, and balloons. By these means the committee transforms a plain, almost drab, gymnasium or large room into a fairyland of color with the all-important "atmosphere" so vital to the success of the dance. Whenever a special theme is selected for a dance, the committee carries out this theme in its decorations.
3. *Publicity.* The publicity committee is responsible for the preparation and release of all information related to the dance. This may involve newspaper articles, bulletin board notices, posters, announcements before school and other groups, mailing announcements to members, and even radio and television appearances. The significance of this

committee is indicated by the fact that many youth groups have discovered that the interest and attendance of their membership vary directly with the adequacy of their publicity.

4. *Finance.* This committee must determine what the dance will cost and how these expenses may be met. A budget will be prepared after consultation with the other committees. Major expenditures will include the orchestra, decorations, publicity, and possibly rental, refreshments, and custodial services. The amount to be charged each dancer will then be determined in light of the total estimated expenditures and the anticipated number of dancers. Too high a dance fee will limit attendance and defeat the purpose of the dance.

5. *Music.* If an orchestra is to be secured, this committee selects it and makes all arrangements with regard to costs, type of music to be played, starting and closing times, intermissions, and all other matters involving music. If records instead of a "live" orchestra are to be used, the committee selects the records, sees that they are available, and coördinates its efforts with those of the Facilities Committee to ensure provision of the minimum essentials for effective recording, calling, singing, and speaking. These will include: a turntable, at least one speaker, one microphone, tone control for both microphone and speaker, and volume control. A variable speed turntable is desirable for records of all speeds, as are separate tone control for microphone and phonograph, separate volume control for each, outlets for more than two speakers and two microphones, and a monitor speaker for the caller in case of a square dance.

Members of the group attending the dance can easily be persuaded to contribute to the pool of records for the evening by sharing with others their own favorite dance records. Adhesive tape may be used to identify these records. The committee should keep track of the records that are favorites with youth and those that are not well liked.

6. *Hospitality.* This committee welcomes all members as they enter the building and tries to make them feel wanted throughout the evening. Committee members watch for those who appear to be less fully accepted than others and, unobtrusively, assist them to meet a number of the more popular youth.

7. *Refreshments.* This committee is unnecessary where the department of recreation operates a regular snack bar service. Where such a service is not offered, the committee decides what refreshments are desirable, in what quantity, how much shall be charged for each item, and makes arrangements for use of a kitchen or other facility from which to sell the refreshments. The committee also orders all items, secures the workers to sell them, and renders a complete financial accounting following the dance.

8. *Special Entertainment.* The group may wish some type of entertainment during intermissions. It is the responsibility of this committee to

secure the amateur talent for any floor shows that are conducted. The committee should make a survey of all amateur talent available, maintain an up-to-date file of such talent, and draw upon it on such occasions.

9. *Clean Up.* The function of this committee is indicated by its name. Much of its work may be of a preventive nature—cautioning and persuading the dancers against littering the dance floor, restrooms, and other areas used. It should work closely with the refreshments committee since refreshments, improperly controlled, are a major source of trouble for any clean-up committee. Soft drinks should be dispensed in paper cups rather than in bottles and should be drunk at tables provided for this purpose and within a prescribed area. No refreshments of any kind should be permitted on the dance floor.

The clean-up committee should meet with the building custodian in advance of the dance and have a definite understanding with respect to the nature of its responsibilities and the policies under which the group is expected to operate.

The personnel of all committees function under the general supervision of the leader. Good leadership involves youth to very great degree in the planning and operation of its dances, but if anything goes wrong the leader, not the youth, will be held responsible by his superiors. Therefore, the leader must work with all committees, advising, stimulating, encouraging, and sometimes criticizing. During the dance, the leader moves around the dance floor, making his presence felt by all but not interfering unless there is cause. He tries to get action on improper conduct in an unobtrusive manner without calling attention either to himself or the dancers involved.

THE LEADER AS A TEACHER

Large numbers of people in this country, both young and old, either cannot dance at all or dance so poorly that they are embarrassed by their lack of skill and, for this reason, drastically limit their participation.

The complete playground and community center program, therefore, will offer opportunities for all age groups to learn to dance. Many departments of recreation are unable financially to employ a dance specialist. Whatever dance instruction is offered generally must be through the regular leaders who cannot possibly be experts in all areas of recreation. However, they can develop the competencies essential to providing a limited program of instruction in rhythms and folk dances for children, a few simple square dances, and social dances for youth and adults. It is the purpose of this section of our text to offer some suggestions to the novice dance leader; the dance specialist neither needs our help nor will he find any in these pages.

The leader's teaching responsibilities are threefold: (1) to help the learner develop the skills essential to effective and satisfying experiences in dance; (2) to assist the learner to acquire and practice the social graces associated with dance; and (3) to help him understand and appreciate dance as a vital part of the culture of nations.

Learning the Basic Skills for the Folk Dance

Dance, like basketball, has its basic fundamentals in which some degree of skill must be developed before the activity can be a highly enjoyable one. The first stage in learning a folk dance requires the development of skill in the fundamental movements of walking, running, leaping, jumping, hopping, skipping, galloping, and sliding. Certain combinations of these movements, such as the *step-hop*, must be learned as the second stage. A third stage involves mastery of certain basic folk dance steps. The *schottische*, based on the step and step-hop, is an example as is the *waltz* which consists simply of two walking steps covering ground while the third is a closing step. The fourth and final stage is to learn the folk dance itself which is based on one or more of these basic folk dance steps. The Swedish Clap Dance with its emphasis on the polka step is an illustration of a folk dance based on a fundamental folk dance step.

1. *Walk.* The walk may be in any direction, with an even rhythmic transfer of weight from one foot to the other; the toe touches the floor first, followed by the ball of the foot. Various rhythms may be used with the walk.
   Record: Folkraft 1440
2. *Run.* Similar to a fast walk, the run may be performed to various rhythms and in any direction. Both feet are off the floor at one time.
   Record: Folkraft 1441A
3. *Jump.* A spring off the floor, with the toes last to leave and first to touch the floor. The take-off may be from one or both feet, but the landing should be on both feet with a slight knee bend to absorb the shock.
   Record: Folkraft 1441A
4. *Leap.* The individual springs off the floor from one foot and lands on the other with a slight knee bend throughout the entire movement.

Performed to an even rhythm, the leap is similar to a slow run when done in moderate tempo and either height or distance may be emphasized.

Records: Folkraft 1441 A — 3/4, Folkraft 1442 B — 4/4 Folkraft 1443 A — 3/4

5. *Hop*. A spring off the floor on one foot, landing on the same foot. The ball of the foot first touches the floor with a slight bend of the knee. Even rhythm.

Record: Folkraft 1442B

6. *Skip*. Uneven rhythm. The skip is a combination of the walk and hop performed on the same foot, alternating feet on each beat. It is performed to 2/4 or 6/8 time, two skips to a measure, "hop—step, hop—step."

Record: Folkraft 1441B

7. *Slide*. The movement is sideward and the rhythm uneven. If the slide is to the left, the left foot slides to the left in constant contact with the floor, followed by the right foot in a quick closing step. As the right foot completes the closing movement, it assumes the body weight thus freeing the left foot for a continuation of the slide. The slide is performed to 2/4 or 6/8 time, two slides to a measure.

Record: Folkraft 1442A

8. *Gallop*. The movement is forward with uneven rhythm. The same foot continues to lead followed by a quick close of the other foot. The action is vigorous with knees elevated. The gallop is performed to 2/4 and 6/8 time, two gallop steps to a measure.

Record: Folkraft 1442A

BASIC DANCE STEPS. Five basic steps constitute the most important fundamental elements in folk dancing today. These steps are the two-step, polka, schottische, waltz, and mazurka. In learning these steps Kraus recommends that the learner,[11]

... listen to the music, analyze and clap its rhythm, and then, slowly and carefully, learn the step pattern. This is usually done moving slowly in a forward direction, *without* partners. Only when the basic footwork has been learned do dancers take partners, learn to move in other directions, or turn as couples. Then they are ready to do a simple folk dance making use of the step they have learned.

TWO-STEP. Step forward on the *left* foot, close with the *right* foot so the ball of the right foot is next to the heel of the left. Transfer the weight to the right foot and step left again. Repeat, beginning with the

---

[11] Richard Kraus, *Folk Dancing* (New York: The Macmillan Company, 1962), p. 21.

right foot. As a basic step of folk dancing, the two-step is danced in 2/4 time in the following style:

Count:	1	and	2	and	1	and	2	and
Cue:	step	close	step	(hold)	step	close	step	(hold)
Footwork:	left	right	left		right	left	right	
Rhythm:	quick	quick	slow		quick	quick	slow	

The two-step is found in all dance forms and is the basis of the fox trot, a ballroom dance, although it has been adapted to the slower and smoother 4/4 time with an accent on the first and third beats.

After learning the two-step in a forward direction, it should also be learned as a sideward and backward movement.
Record: Folkraft 1444

POLKA. The polka, a couple dance originating in Bohemia, is characterized by a lively step with an uneven rhythmic pattern performed in 2/4 time. It is very similar to the two-step, except that the "step—close —step" of the two-step is preceded by a quick little hop. Thus, the style is:

Count:	1	and	2	and	1	and	2	and
Cue:	hop-step	close	step	hop	step	close	step	hop
Footwork:	right-left	right	left	left	right	left	right	right

Leaders should teach the two-step before teaching the polka, as the former is the foundation of the latter.
Record: Folkraft 1446A

SCHOTTISCHE. The schottische consists of three steps and a hop, usually performed in 4/4 time with a smooth, even rhythm. It may be done forward, sideward, backward, or with a turning movement. The practice pattern is:

Count:	1	2	3	4	1	2	3	4
Cue:	step	step	step	hop	step	step	step	hop
Footwork:	left	right	left	left	right	left	right	right

When danced to lively 2/4 tunes, the schottische step is considerably bouncier and frequently appears as three running steps and a hop.
Record: Folkraft 1445

WALTZ. The waltz is a smooth, graceful step done to 3/4 time in even rhythm. It consists of three walking steps, the first two of which cover ground while the third is a closing step. The first step is forward, the second to the side, and the third is a closing step. The pattern follows:

Count:	1	2	3	1	2	3
Cue:	step	step	close	step	step	close
Footwork:	left	right (side)	left	right	left (side)	right

Much of the beauty of the waltz is derived from the constant turning movement which is an outstanding characteristic of this extremely popular dance step. Therefore, the leader must not only teach the step in its simplest form, but also must teach the continuous right-face turn. As a preliminary step to teaching the complete turn, the leader should teach a quarter turn using the box waltz pattern:

Count:	1	2	3	1	2	3
Footwork:	step	step	left	step	step	right
	forward	right	closes	right	left	closes
	left	to	to	backward	to	to
		side	right		side	left

Kraus recommends that the continuous right-face turn be taught as follows: [12]

Facing a side wall each dancer steps backwards on his left foot, toe turned in, and turning right (1). He steps to the side with his right in the line of direction (2). He closes left foot to the right (3) completing a half turn. He then steps forward with the right foot, toe turned out (1), sideward in the line of direction with the left (2), and closes the right foot to the left (3), completing the full turn.

After practicing this individually, dancers practice as couples with the boy following the above instructions while the girl, in the initial movement, steps forward with her right toe turned out.
Record: Imperial 1036; World of Fun M110

MAZURKA. The mazurka basically involves these three movements: a forward step with one foot and a closing step with the other, followed by a hop on the closing foot. On the hop the free foot is lifted, the knee bent, and the foot swung back near the other ankle. The step is done in 3/4 time with a strong, even, three beat rhythm. The accent is on the second beat. The pattern is:

Count:	1	2	3	1	2	3
Cue:	step	close	hop	step	close	hop
Footwork:	left	right	right	left	right	right

[12] *Ibid.*, p. 29.

The same foot continues to lead throughout a series of mazurka steps except when some other action intervenes.

Record: Folk Dancer MH-1018A; Educational Dance Recordings FD-3

Acquiring the Social Graces

A dance is far more than mastering a technique of moving the body in a rhythmic manner and in harmony with one's partner. A dance is a matter of dress, of conversation, of extending an invitation, of accepting or politely refusing, of proper conduct on the dance floor, of skill, of courtesy, of being a gentleman, of being a lady, of enjoying refreshments, of regard for others, of knowing and practicing the social graces. It is an educational, as well as a recreation medium of rich potentialities and the leader should realize as large a return as possible on his investment of time and energy in this activity. It is an important function of leadership to teach youth the social graces, or acceptable code of behavior, which encompass the dance in this country and which add so greatly to its enjoyment. There is little cultural value in an activity engaged in by crude, vulgar, and discourteous participants.

Among the most important of the social graces or aspects of social behavior which the leader should teach in association with the dance are the following:

1. Each dancer should be concerned at all times for the feelings of the other dancers.
2. The gentleman invites the lady to dance. She always accepts unless circumstances beyond her control prevent, in which case she does not accept an invitation from another gentleman for the same dance.
3. Each dancer thanks the other at the conclusion of the dance.
4. A gentleman precedes a lady on their way to the dance floor.
5. Whenever a lady is not dancing, a gentleman should invite her to dance rather than stand on the sidelines or "cut in."
6. Each person should be neatly dressed in clothing that is appropriate for the occasion. It is well to determine in advance what is "appropriate." When in doubt, it is better to choose the more conservative dress.
7. Dancers should progress with the traffic, not against or across it. Generally, all movement is in a counterclockwise direction. Faster or more vigorous dancers should dance near the periphery of the group.
8. A gentleman wishing to dance with another gentleman's lady, should first request permission from the lady's partner and then, if permission has been granted, from the lady herself.
9. No dancer should attempt to teach new steps to another at a ballroom dance.
10. A gentleman never leaves a lady on the dance floor at the conclusion

of a dance. He may escort her to where she was sitting when he invited her to dance, introduce her to another gentleman whom he
knows, or, if she desires, take her to a group of her friends.
11. Any form of behavior that draws the attention of the group to you or
your partner should be avoided.
12. In square dancing:
    a. One should not leave a square to join another group.
    b. If unaccompanied, the gentleman should take the nearest lady for
    a partner.
    c. Each individual assists his partner in swings and couple turns by
    balancing pull against pull.
    d. Introduce yourselves and be friendly to the others in the set.
    e. Help the beginners in a set if you can do so unobtrusively and
    without embarrassing them. Do not offer assistance unless reason-
    ably certain it will be welcomed.
    f. If you know nothing about square dancing, don't attend a dance
    unless specific invitations have been extended to beginners.

Understanding Square Dance Terms

Students are referred to certain dance books at the end of this
chapter for detailed instructions related to the fundamental figures and
extensive terminology of the square dance. However, some of the most
common of these terms are described below.

Square. Four couples form a square with each couple facing the
center of the square. The lady is on the man's right. Couples are numbered counterclockwise around the square with couple one having its
back to the caller. Couples one and three are "head couples"; couples two
and four are "side couples." The lady to the left of each man is the
corner lady, to the right is the right-hand lady, and directly across the
square is the opposite lady.

Shuffle. The shuffle is the basic step used in square dancing. The
feet remain lightly in contact with the floor as the dancer moves forward
transferring his weight from the ball of the boot to the heel.

Allemande. The caller designates this figure as "allemande left" or
"allemande right." On "allemande left," corners join left hands, turn
each other around, and return to place. On "allemande right," the man
joins right hands with the lady on his right, turns her around once, and
returns to place.

Balance. Partners face, join inside hands, take two steps backward
and bow, then two steps forward to the original position.

Balance and swing. Balance as above, then swing your partner once
around with a waist swing.

Break. Release hands.

Circle. All dancers join hands in a circle and move left or right as the call indicates. Circle left if the direction is not indicated.

Do-Si-Do. Partners face one another; advance, passing right shoulders. Step to the right and, without turning around, move backward to starting position.

Forward and back. Take four steps into the center and four steps back to place.

Grand right and left. Partners face, grasp right hands, and pass right shoulders. Moving forward they give the next person their left hands and pass left shoulders. They continue in this manner around the circle, ladies moving clockwise and men counterclockwise, until they meet, whereupon they promenade home unless the call directs them to continue the Grand Right and Left back to home position.

Honor partner or corner. Ladies curtsy and men bow to partner or corner as call designates.

Ladies chain. Two ladies move toward each other, join right hands and pass right shoulders. Each lady then gives her left hand to the opposite man who puts his right arm around her waist and turns her once around counterclockwise. Ladies return to partners who turn them around to original position.

Pass right through. Two couples face, move toward each other, each dancer passes right shoulders with his opposite, and continues forward to execute the next call.

Promenade. Each man holds his partner's right hand in his right and her left hand in his left, with his right arm crossed above her left arm. The lady is to the right of the man. Couples move counterclockwise around the circle.

Right hands across. Men or ladies, as the caller designates, join right hands in the center and turn clockwise.

Right or left hand swing. Partners join right or left hands and swing around clockwise.

Two hand swing. Partners join both hands and shuffle once around clockwise. Elbows are held close to the body.

Waist swing. The man's right arm is around the lady's waist with her left hand and arm resting on his upper arm and shoulder. Man's left arm is raised sideward and he holds lady's right hand in his left. Couples turn clockwise.

Buzz step or pivot swing. Partners take position described above. The lady leans back against the man's right hand; right feet are side by side. Dancers turn clockwise by stepping on the right foot and pushing with the left which is placed slightly behind and close to the right. The right foot is the pivot foot and remains in contact with the floor while the left foot simulates the action involved in pushing a scooter.

Twirl. This is a square dance turn in which the man holds the lady's right hand in his right hand and turns her clockwise in place under her own right arm.

Steps in the Teaching Process

Since no two dances are identical, the techniques involved in their presentation will differ to some extent. However, dances also are characterized by many similarities which justify the establishment of several steps in the instructional process which, in general, apply to the teaching of all dances.

1. Place the group in formation for the dance.
2. Name the dance, give its nationality, and present briefly any interesting information about it that will add to the children's cultural appreciation and understanding. Don't talk too long; some of this material can be presented later.
3. Relate this dance, if possible, to dances previously taught. Such relationship may include common nationality, similar steps or figures, identical formations, and kindred ideas expressed.
4. Play some of the music so the dancers can catch the enthusiasm and spirit which the music alone can impart to them. Furthermore, this will give them some idea of the character and speed of the music. Clap out the beat.
5. Stand where you can best be seen by the largest number. If a circle dance, stand to one side alomst as a part of the circle rather than in the center of the circle.
6. Break the dance into natural segments or units. Demonstrate the first unit slowly without music and with your back to the group. For example, the first unit in Gustaf's Skoal is simply walking four steps forward and four steps backward, first by the head couples and then by the side couples.
7. Teach the group to walk slowly through this first unit without music. The leader may clap, count, sing the words, or call out verbal cues. In some dances it may be desirable to teach the boys' and girls' parts separately and combine them later after they have been practiced. Difficult steps may be practiced individually and without regard to formation.
8. Repeat the first unit with the music.
9. Teach all other units in the same manner.
10. Review the entire dance slowly without music.
11. Demonstrate the entire dance with music. This may be done by some

of your advanced dancers or by you and one of your more skilled youngsters.

12. All dancers participate in the complete dance with music. It may be desirable for you to assist them by means of verbal cues.
13. Correct errors common to the group first then and give whatever individual help is necessary. Do not embarrass the individual who is having difficulty by staging "private" lessons with the rest of the group as a critical audience.
14. Arouse the group's enthusiasm for the dance by being enthusiastic yourself.

FOLK DANCES AND MIXERS

This section presents ten folk dances, mixers, and square dances simple enough for most children of elementary school age. Several possess sufficient appeal to popularize them among both youth and adults. Our purpose here is not to offer a comprehensive list of dances, but rather to give a few illustrations of how leadership functions through this particular recreation medium.

Bingo—Children and Adults

American
Bingo is a delightful dance and social mixer. Its simplicity and exuberant melody popularize it among all age groups. A number of variations exist.

FORMATION: Double circle, partners side by side, hands joined, girl on the right.

PART ONE: All walk counterclockwise around the circle singing,

> A big black dog sat on the back porch
> And Bingo was his name.
> A big black dog sat on the back porch
> And Bingo was his name.

PART TWO: All join hands to form one large, single circle, girl on boy's right. The dancers continue to walk counterclockwise singing,

> B - I - N - G - O; B - I - N - G - O; B - I - N - G - O
> And Bingo was his name.

PART THREE: Partners face each other and join right hands, calling out "B" on the first chord. Each dancer passes on to a new person, in a Grand Right and Left Figure, joining left hands, calling "I" on the next chord; continue, joining hands with a third person and shout "N"; on to a fourth person with the left hand, shouting "G." Joining right hands with the fifth person, shout "O" even more vigorously than on any previous letter, and swing once around clockwise.

Repeat the dance from the beginning.

SUGGESTIONS TO THE LEADER. Younger children have a problem of differentiating between the right and left hands and feet. The leader will find that it pays to work on this problem a few minutes before engaging in Bingo. A game, such as Simon Says, will prove helpful in which the leader says, "Simon says right foot up" and the children follow directions.

Younger children also will be quite confused on the Grand Right and Left in Part Three if they have never done it before. These directions should be helpful: "Shake hands with your partner. Now take one step forward and shake left hands with the person behind your partner. Take one more step forward and shake right hands with the next person." It is best to walk slowly through this movement many times, calling out "right hands," "left hands," before trying it with music.

Emphasis should be placed on the fact that unless everyone does his part, no one can have any fun.

Record: RCA Victor LPM 1623

Gustaf's Skoal—Children and Adults

Swedish Quadrille

"Skoal" is a Scandinavian word used in toasting someone's health. Part One of the dance is performed with a stately, even exaggerated, dignity as the dancers represent the ladies and noblemen of the court. In Part Two they banish their inhibitions and dance in an enthusiastic, gay, and lively peasant fashion.

The dancers may sing these words or they may dance without words:

Part One.

A toast we pledge, to Gustaf who is brave and true,
A toast we pledge, to Gustaf brave and true.
A toast we pledge, to Gustaf who is brave and true,
A toast we pledge, to Gustaf brave and true.

Part Two.

> Fa-la-la-la-la-la-la-la-la,
> Fa-la-la-la-la-la-la-la-la,
> Fa-la-la-la-la-la-la-la-la,
> Fa, la, la.
> Fa-la-la-la-la-la-la-la-la,
> Fa-la-la-la-la-la-la-la-la,
> Fa-la-la-la-la-la-la-la-la,
> Fa, la, la.

FORMATION: This is a simple square dance with four couples.[15]

PART ONE:

Meas. 1–4: Head couples, with inside hands joined and free hands on hips, walk forward three steps singing the words, bow on the fourth count to the word "pledge," and then walk four steps backward to place.

Meas. 5–8: Side couples do the same figure, singing the second line.

Meas. 9–16: Repeat action from the beginning.

PART TWO:

Meas. 17–24: Side couples form arches by raising inside, joined hands. Head couples take four skips forward, drop hands, turn away from each other, face the nearest arch, join inside hands with the opposite person, and skip under the arches with four skips. Releasing hands, all clap their own hands, return to original positions, join both hands with their partner and swing once around with four skipping steps. All of this action in Measures 17–24 requires sixteen skipping steps.

Meas. 25–32: Side couples repeat action with head couples forming the arches.

SUGGESTIONS TO THE LEADER. Teach children the song before attempting the dance. Also teach that the last step backward in Part One is a closing step. Clap out the rhythm of the sixteen skipping steps before skipping with the music. These steps may be practiced by each dancer working by himself about the gymnasium and out of formation. Couples forming the arches should pull as far apart as possible and raise their joined hands high so ample room will be provided the skippers.

Records: RCA Victor LPM 1622; Folkraft 1175; Educational Dance Recordings FD-1

Csebogar—Children and Youth

Hungarian Circle Dance

The word "csebogar" means the "beetle."

---

[15] See page 264 for description of the "square" formation.

FORMATION: Dancers form a single circle, facing center, with hands joined. Girl on partner's right.

PART ONE:

Meas. 1–4: Slide eight steps to the left.

Meas. 5–8: Slide eight steps to the right.

PART TWO:

Meas. 1–4: All take three steps toward the center of the circle, raise arms, and stamp on the fourth count. Take three steps backward, lower arms, and stamp on the fourth count.

Meas. 5–8: Partners face, hook right elbows, raise left arms sideward and swing clockwise once around with eight skips.

PART THREE:

Meas. 1–4: Partners face each other in a single circle, both arms extended sideward with hands joined. Take four slow step-draw steps (step-close) sideward toward the center of the circle, starting with the boy's left and the girl's right foot. Do not transfer weight on the last step. Arms move up and down in a rocking motion in this figure.

Meas. 5–8: Four step-draw steps sideward away from center.

PART FOUR:

Meas. 1–4: Partners take two step-draws to the centers, and two out, as above.

Meas. 5–8: Right elbow swing again with eight skips as in Part Two, Meas. 5–8.

SUGGESTIONS TO THE LEADER.   Do not permit any jerky movements designed to break the circle on the sliding steps. Leaders may find it desirable to teach the two-hand swing before advancing to the elbow swing which is more difficult. If the dancers have had no previous experience with the step-draw step, teach it before introducing the dance and practice it with individuals before attempting it with partners.

Records: RCA Victor LPM 1624; Folkraft 1196; Educational Dance Recordings FD-1

Swedish Clap Dance—Klappdans—Ages Ten and Up

Swedish Couple Dance or Mixer

FORMATION: Double circle, partners side by side with girl on right, inside hands joined, facing counterclockwise. Free hands on hips.

PART ONE:

Meas. 1–8: All take eight polka steps forward, starting with the hop on the inside foot, swinging the joined hands backward, and turning to face partners. On the "step-close-step" of the polka step, swing the arms forward and turn back to back.

PART TWO:

Meas. 9–16: Dance four heel-toe polka steps forward, starting with outside foot. Place heel of outside foot forward (1 and), touch toe of same foot in back (2 and), then advance one polka step forward, starting with hop on inside foot (measure 10); repeat with inside foot. Repeat all of above action with the heel-toe polka danced four times.

PART THREE:

Meas. 17–20: Face partner in double circle, hands on own hips. Boys bow as girls curtsy; both clap own hands three times.

Repeat bowing and clapping.

Meas. 21–24: Partners clap each other's right hand, then own hands, then partner's left hand, then own hands again.

Turn self once around in place and stamp three times.

Meas. 25–28: Bow or curtsy to partner, then shake right forefinger at partner three times in a "scolding" gesture.

Repeat, shaking left forefinger at partner three times.

Meas. 29–32: Repeat clapping and turning action of measures 21–24.

Repeat entire dance.

SUGGESTIONS TO THE LEADER. This is the most difficult of the dances listed above and necessitates slow and careful teaching. Teach and practice both the polka and heel-toe polka steps without partners at first and without music. Then practice the polka step with couples at first without turning face to face and back to back. The verbal clue for the heel-toe polka is "heel, toe, hop-step-close-step." The clapping part of this dance can be very confusing and requires careful practice at first without music. Records: Folkraft 1175; RCA Victor LPM 1624

Glow Worm—Children and Adults

American

This is one of the simplest of couple mixers involving no complicated figures and only a walking step.

FORMATION: Couples in a double circle, facing counterclockwise, with ladies to right of men in promenade position.

Meas. 1–2: All promenade around the circle with eight walking steps.

Meas. 3–4: Drop hands, partners face each other; each walks backward four steps away from one another, then forward four steps toward new partner on the right.

Meas. 5–6: Do a do-si-do with new partner and return to place with eight walking steps.

Meas. 7–8: Join both hands with this partner and swing clockwise for eight counts, or once around.

Repeat dance from the beginning.

SUGGESTIONS TO THE LEADER. Two dance terms should be reviewed here and the action practiced before attempting this mixer. These terms are "do-si-do" and "two hand swing," both described in a previous section of this chapter entitled *Understanding Square Dance Terms*. Record: RCA Victor LPM 1623

Norwegian Mountain March—Ages Ten to Twelve

Norwegian

This dance symbolizes three mountain climbers with the one in advance representing the guide.

FORMATION: The dancers are in triangle formation with the "guide" in front and the other two slightly behind, all facing counterclockwise. These two stand side by side with inside hands joined, and outside hands joined with the "guide."

PART ONE:

Meas. 1–8: Starting on the right foot, take a total of twenty-four steps or eight waltz steps, accenting the first count of each measure. On the first beat of each measure, the guide turns slightly toward the advanced boot and looks back at the two climbers behind him.

PART TWO:

Meas. 9–10: The two climbers form an arch with their inside hands while the guide waltzes backward under the arch. The climbers waltz in place.

Meas. 11–12: The dancer on the left, moving clockwise, dances across and under the guide's right arm in two waltz steps. The others dance in place.

Meas. 13–14: Dancer on the right, in two waltz steps turns in place under own right arm.

Meas. 15–16: Guide dances in a right-face turn under his own right arm, so that group is in original position.

Meas. 17–24: Repeat Part Two.

SUGGESTIONS TO THE LEADER. The waltz step must be practiced at some length before this dance can be enjoyed. Teach it first without the music; do it slowly. Then speed it up considerably until it is almost a running step as this tempo is necessary to fit the music. Practice the waltz with the music as individuals before joining hands in the actual dance. One word of caution: As the second dancer waltzes under her own right arm, her hand and the guide's must be held loosely or she will be unable to make the turn.

Records: RCA Victor LPM 1622; Educational Dance Recordings FD-1; Folkraft 1177

Ten Pretty Girls—Youth and Adults

American

This is a couple dance, originating in the Southwest, and may be done as a threesome mixer with the center person moving forward each time.

FORMATION: This dance will be described as a couple dance with the opening formation a double circle of couples facing counterclockwise, inside hands joined, free hands on waist. Actually, any number of dancers may form a line with hands joined or behind each other's backs.

PART ONE:

Meas. 1–2: Each person taps the left toe twice, diagonally forward left. Cross the left foot back of the right and step on it; step sideward right on the right foot; cross the left foot in front of the right and step on it. Pause.

Meas. 3–4: Repeat the above action in reverse, beginning with the right foot.

PART TWO:

Meas. 5–6: Starting with the left foot, take four strutting (walking) steps forward.

Meas. 7: Swing the left leg forward vigorously and lean backward; then swing the left leg backward and lean forward.

Meas. 8: Do three stamps in place—left, right, left.

Repeat entire dance starting with the right foot. If desired, the man may move forward to a new partner on his three stamping steps while the lady moves three steps backwards.

SUGGESTIONS TO THE LEADER. The "grapevine" step which must be executed in Part One, Measures 1–4, probably will be new to the dancers and may present a problem unless slowly and carefully taught. Teach it without music first and practice it as individuals.

Records: RCA Victor LPM 1624; MacGregor 605; Folkraft 1036

Virginia Reel—Youth and Adults

American

This is probably the most popular of the "contra" or "longway" dances. While it is looked upon as perhaps the most typical of American dances, its origins are to be discovered in England.

FORMATION: Two parallel facing lines, preferably with six couples.

PART ONE:

Meas. 1–8: Both lines walk forward three steps, bow or curtsy to partner, and then walk backward to place. Repeat this action.

Meas. 9–16: All walk forward, join right hands with partners, swing once around clockwise and return to place. Repeat this action with left hands joined, turning counterclockwise.

Meas. 17–24: Same action as above with both hands joined, turning once clockwise. All walk forward and do-si-do.

PART TWO:

Meas. 1–8: The head couple in each set slides down between the couples to the foot of the set in eight slides, and then back to place in eight slides.

Meas. 9–16 (Repeated): The head couple hooks right elbows, turns once and a half around clockwise, then separates and goes to opposite line (man to ladies' line and lady to man's). Head gent turns second lady once around with a left elbow hook as head lady does same with second gent. They meet each other in the center again and turn with a right elbow hook once around. They then proceed to the next person in the opposite line and turn as before. They continue this "reeling" action until all have been "reeled." They then join both hands, after swinging half-way around, and slide back to the head of their lines.

PART THREE:

Meas. 1–8: The head couple turns to the outside and, followed by the others, walks to the foot of the set.

Meas. 9–16 (Repeated): The head couple, upon reaching the foot of the set, joins hands to form an arch. The others, now led by the second couple, advance beyond the head couple, turn, join hands, slide through the arch, and back up where the set was originally, only now the second couple has become the new head couple. The original head couple is now the foot couple.

The dance is repeated until each couple has had an opportunity to be the head couple.

SUGGESTIONS TO THE LEADER.   There are no difficult steps to learn in this dance, but a number of different figures may make it necessary for the leader to call in advance what is about to take place. Common calls are:

Part One: Meas. 1–8: "Forward and back."

Meas. 9–12: "Right hand around."

Meas. 13–16: "Left hand around."

Meas. 17–20: "Both hands around."

Meas. 21–24: "Do-si-do."

Part Two: Meas. 1–8: "Reel the set."

Part Three: Meas. 1–8: "Cast off to the foot."

Meas. 9–16: "Form the arch and pass through."

Records: RCA Victor LPM-1623 (without calls); RCA Victor LE-3002 (with calls); Folkraft 1249

Take A Little Peek

This simple square dance is popular among both young and old. The call, with some variations, is:

First couple out to the right of the ring

'Round that couple and take a little peek

(Partners divide and peek around the second couple.

Lady peeks right, gent peeks left.)

Back to the center and swing your sweet

(First couple swings)

Around that couple and peek once more

(Couple once again peeks around couple two)

Back to the center and circle four

(Couples one and two join hands and circle once around to the left)

Lead to the next.

The first couple repeats this action with the third and fourth couples.

The call is repeated with the second, third, and fourth couples in turn leading the dance.

Record: RCA Victor LE-3000

Oh, Johnny

This may be danced in the regular square formation or with all dancers in a large single circle in which case it serves as an excellent mixer.

Oh, you all join hands and circle the ring

(Circle moves to left)

Stop where you are and you give her a swing
    (Swing your partner)
Now swing that girl behind you
    (Gent swings girl on his left)
Go back home and swing your own if you have time
    (All swing their partners)
Do-si-do 'round your own
    (Do-si-do around your partner)
Now you all run away with your sweet corner maid
    (Promenade counterclockwise with corner lady who becomes
    your new partner)
Singing Oh, Johnny, Oh, Johnny, Oh!
Continue until record is completed.

Records: Folkraft 1037; Imperial 1099. Neither record is with calls.

Selected Record Sources

Educational Dance Recordings, Inc., P. O. Box 6062, Bridgeport, Connecticut.

Dance Record Center, 1159 Broad Street, Newark 2, New Jersey.

Folk Dance House, 108 West 16th Street, New York 11, New York.

The Folk Shop, 161 Turk Street, San Francisco 2, California.

Many of the records you will wish to use can be found at your local dealer.

Selected References

Music

Baird, Forrest J., *Music Skills for Recreation Leaders* (Dubuque, Iowa: Wm. C. Brown Company Publishers, 1963).

Daniel, Oliver, *Round and Round and Round They Go* (Evanston, Ill.: Summy-Birchard Publishing Company, 1952).

Frieswyk, Siebolt H., "Music's Place in Recreation," *Music Journal,* XVIII, No. 1, 1960, 34.

Kaplan, Max, *Music in Recreation* (Champaign, Ill.: Stipes Publishing Company, 1955).

Leonhard, Charles, *Recreation Through Music* (New York: A. S. Barnes and Company, 1952).

Lomax, Alan, *The Folk Songs of North America* (Garden City, N.Y.: Doubleday and Company, Inc., 1960).

"Music is Recreation," *Recreation,* LIV, No. 5, 1961, 243.

Nye, Robert, *et al., Singing with Children* (Belmont, Calif.: Wadsworth, 1962).

Rosenberg, Martha, *It's Fun to Teach Creative Music* (New York: Play Schools Association, 1963).

Spaeth, Sigmund Gottfried, *Sigmund Spaeth's Song Session* (New York: Remick Music Corporation, 1958).

Wilson, Harry Robert, *Sing Together with Harry Robert Wilson* (New York: Consolidated Music Publishers, Inc., 1956).

Dance

Andrews, Gladys, *Creative Rhythmic Movement for Children* (Englewood Cliffs, N.J.: Prentice-Hall, Inc., 1954).

Czarnowski, Lucille and McKay, Jack, *How to Teach Folk and Square Dances* (1965 Tenth Avenue, San Francisco 22, Calif., 1953).

Hall, J. Tillman, *Dance!* (Belmont, Calif.: Wadsworth, 1963).

Harris, Jane A., Pittman, Anne, and Waller, Marlys S., *Dance A While* (Minneapolis: Burgess Publishing Company, 1964).

Hawkins, Alma, *Creating through Dance* (Englewood Cliffs, N.J.: Prentice-Hall, 1964).

Holden, Rickey, *The Contra Dance Book* (Newark, N.J.: American Squares (Dance Record Center), 1956.

Hunt, Paul and Underwood, Charlotte, *Calico Rounds* (New York: Harper and Brothers, 1955).

Kraus, Richard, *Folk Dancing* (New York: The Macmillan Company, 1962).

———, *A Pocket Guide of Folk and Square Dances and Singing Games for the Elementary School* (Englewood Cliffs, N.J.: Prentice-Hall, 1966).

Kulbitsky, Olga and Kaltman, Frank L., *Teacher's Dance Handbook* (Newark, N.J.: Bluebird Publishing Company, 1959).

Waglow, I. F., *Social Dance for Students and Teachers* (Dubuque, Iowa: Wm. E. Brown Company, 1953).

Chapter X

Drama and Arts and Crafts

THE RECREATION LEADER who seeks some higher purpose, some deeper meaning and significance, than the pleasure of the moment in a dramatic skit or the amateur efforts of a crafts club can find it in his dual role of creator and transmitter of the cultural heritage of mankind. Every generation is but a link in the chain of human progress, bound to all other generations only when it acquires, contributes to, and passes on the best of its cultural heritage. Civilization is never guaranteed to any generation; it is not inborn. The cultural inheritance of the race, accumulated over many millions of years and contributed to by billions of people, must be acquired anew by every generation. One of the greatest challenges to the recreation leader is to convey the best of our cultural heritage to the present generation, thus strengthening the ties that bind our civilization to the great civilizations of the past, and to preserve for future generations all that is of cultural value for them in our own.

THE BEGINNINGS

Drama is one of the performing arts. It is the expression of thought or feeling in a form that seems beautiful to us because it captures some significant aspect of life and holds it momentarily for our lingering enjoyment or leisurely understanding. It also may arouse or release life's tensions. Like all the other arts it is unnecessary in that it is not essential to survival, but it is precisely the unnecessary things that differentiate civilized man from the savage and the animal. Drama, therefore, may be called one of the "noble superfluities" of life.

How did drama begin? The determination of all prehistoric origins involves an element of guesswork, but it is probable that drama evolved from a union of music, song, and dance. Much of primitive dance centered upon imitation of the movements of animals and men and later on the mimicry of actions and events. Savage tribes played a drama of death and resurrection as well as sacrificial and festival ceremonies closely related to, or involving, religion. Durant suggests that, "In like manner a thousand forms of pantomime described events significant to the history of the tribe, or actions important in the individual life. When rhythm disappeared from these performances the dance passed into the drama, and one of the greatest of art forms was born."[1]

During the Golden Age of Greece, drama reached heights never before attained in the history of the world. Outdoor theaters, seating many thousands, were constructed throughout the Greek world, but the major tragedies and comedies were first played in a theater of stone built by the Athenians on the southern slope of the Acropolis about 500 B.C. and dedicated to the god Dionysus.

Only men could aspire to be actors, a role much honored in Greece although disdained in Rome. In all kinds of plays the actors wore a mask, fitted with a resonant mouthpiece of brass so his voice might carry better. The quality of such playwrights as Aeschylus, Sophocles, Euripides, and Aristophanes, combined with the excellence of their actors, gave to Greek drama at this period of their history a grandeur which lends further proof to the conclusion that "great nations have always been characterized by great art."

PRESENT STATUS IN RECREATION

A study conducted by the National Recreation and Park Association[2] reveals the extent and nature of drama in community recreation programs during 1965:

---

[1] Will Durant, *Our Oriental Heritage*. New York: Simon and Schuster, 1954, p. 89.

[2] Donald E. Hawkins, ed., *Recreation and Park Yearbook 1966* (Washington, D.C.: National Recreation and Park Association, 1966), p. 55.

	Number Reported By Cities and Counties	
Activity	Children	Adults
Community Theater	522	603
Creative Dramatics	688	192
Festivals	412	302
Pageants	412	245
Puppets and Marionettes	522	82

The number of departments conducting drama is not particularly impressive when we realize that almost 3,000 governmental units were included in the study and that many were counted more than once as they reported activity in several phases of dramatics. Nevertheless, it is just as important to know in what direction we are going as it is to know where we are at any one time. Remarkable progress has been made in community drama since the turn of the century. Approximately 120,000 nonprofessional stage productions are put on annually, many cities are providing more adequate facilities for all types of drama activity, both indoor and outdoor, and the Association of the Junior Leagues of America alone sponsored, during a recent year, 1,903 performances which reached almost a million children.[3]

A realistic appraisal of present status is essential if further progress is to be made. Musselman's appraisal, while limited to creative dramatics, applies also to other phases of drama and focuses attention upon the real essence of the problem—leadership:[4]

From the limited sources of information concerning creative dramatics for children and youth, it seems quite evident that it is still regarded as a "sometime thing;" that it is found primarily in summer playground programs; that confusion concerning its nature is still prevalent; that leadership is scarce and frequently nonspecialized; and that its scope as a continuing activity is not generally understood.

Leadership is the primary problem. There are over eight thousand recreation leaders employed full time, year 'round, in public recreation. However, there are over 76,000 leaders in all, the difference being primarily in the vast number of summer playground leaders used for seasonal work. These playground leaders are primarily college students, who may or may not have had any training in any form of drama.

---

[3] National Recreation Association, "Drama is Recreation," Recreation, February 1962, pp. 77–78.

[4] Virginia Musselman, "Creative Dramatics in Recreation Programs," in Children's Theatre and Creative Dramatics, Geraldine Brain Siks and Hazel Brain Dunnington, eds. (Seattle: University of Washington Press, 1961), p. 194.

Approximately forty different forms of drama are reported by recreation departments, but all fall into one of two categories—formal or
informal. Formal dramatics involves a written script, lines to be memo-
rized, a director who interprets the play and directs action, emphasis on
staging and costuming, with major consideration given to the entertainment of an audience and its reaction to a finished product. Children's
Theatre, Little Theatre, and Community Theatre are all media for the
production of formal dramatics.

Informal drama is an inclusive term designating all forms of im-
provised drama: dramatic play, story dramatization, impromptu work
in pantomime, puppet and shadow plays, and all other extemporaneous
drama in which emphasis is placed upon the participant. It is not concerned with preparing people to become actors, nor in creating plays for
an audience. The leader is a guide rather than a director. Since this
informal drama is created very largely by the players themselves, the
term *creative dramatics* is used interchangeably with it.

It is not the purpose of this chapter to explore deeply the many
problems involved in formal play production, nor to atempt the task
of professional preparation of drama specialists. We propose to deal primarily with informal drama because we believe that the relatively
untrained leader, with some assistance, can offer rich, meaningful, and
creative experiences to children, youth, and adults through these types
of activities.

TO BELIEVE IN MAKE-BELIEVE

When we place drama under the spotlight of our goals for recreation it is easy to believe deeply in the values of "make-believe." For no
other area of human activity offers richer opportunities for personal
fulfillment and growth in certain qualities of the good citizen in a democratic society.

Drama opens doors, extends horizons, and sets the imagination free.
In creative dramatics, a child can be anything or anyone he wants to be.
The timid boy can be a brave hero and the plainest little girl can be a beau-
tiful princess. Ribicoff reports on the "magic carpet" qualities of drama:[5]

Asked what the theater had given him, the actor, Howard Lindsay, answered:
"It has been my education. Where else could I have traveled so far? I have

---
[5] Abraham Ribicoff, "The Theater as a Teacher," *Recreation*, December 1961,
p. 516.

been in the streets of Corinth when Jason and Medea were throwing harsh words at each other. I was at Aulis when the Greek fleet sailed to Troy. I was in Mycenae when Orestes came back to kill his mother Clytemnestra. I have been in the drawing rooms of Lady and Lord Windermere of London. And I shouldn't forget to say, I have ridden into Western towns with the James brothers. Where else could I have done things like that?

Creative dramatics is a group art through which a collection of individuals may become a team by sharing responsibility, hard work, interest, enthusiasm, and happiness. As the various members of the group grow closer together in sympathy and understanding, and as they learn the great lesson of coöperation, the social values inherent in the drama experience become readily apparent.

Appreciation of one of the great art forms of the world should be an outcome sought by leadership. The child should be helped to recognize, appreciate, and acquire a taste for beauty and excellence, thus developing a life-long interest in and love for drama.

Surely one of the greatest values which should accrue from creative dramatics is the degree to which it makes life more intense and more meaningful—the extent to which it illuminates some basic truth or principle. When a child simply reads or is told a story which involves human emotions, he always is out on the periphery of the situation. He reads *about* it; he is told *about* it. He himself does not *experience* it. But when he plays the part of the individual involved, he *becomes* that person and suffers or exults with him.

In "The Bishop's Candlesticks," for example, only by *becoming* Jean Valjean can a child truly plumb the depths of human emotions and begin to understand the bitterness which lacerates the souls of those whom society has condemned and rejected. And this understanding, faint though it may be, is a step toward a deeper insight into one of the most vital of all human emotions—compassion for those less fortunate than we.

And, finally, drama is fun. It adds to the richness and enjoyment of living; it is a part of the good life. Heckscher believes that the public happiness depends primarily upon

. . . the participation in a common life which is recognized as being enriched, which is known to be illuminated and made coherent, by the forms of art. The challenge in this realm crowns all others, for except as it is met, the citizens of freedom will in decades to come fail of the rewards which make democracy, and make freedom itself, worthwhile.[6]

[6] August Heckscher, *The Public Happiness* (New York: Atheneum, 1962), pp. 292–293.

CREATIVE DRAMATICS

As indicated earlier in this chapter, creative dramatics is an inclusive term embracing all forms of drama in which the emphasis is upon creativity, originality, imagination, and informality. Beginning with the dramatic play of little children, it also includes original pantomines, charades, story dramatization, creative plays, and hand puppets and marionettes, provided the children make them and improvise the dialogue. Throughout all facets of the program the welfare of every child is of paramount importance. This kind of drama is for everyone, not just the talented few.

Dramatic Play

This is the make-believe of young children, the very essence of life to them. It is delightful fun, a way of learning, a means of social adjustment; it is a cushion against defeat and frustration, a device for reliving familiar experiences and preparing for those yet to come; it is a technique for extending one's horizons, of removing the limitations of time and space, of promoting identification with any character or situation that comes within the scope of the imagination.

In his dramatic or imaginative play, the child relives experiences with which he is familiar and explores new ones. A trip to the zoo today provides material for dramatic play tomorrow as the children re-enact the whole delightful experience. They lumber along like the elephants, pace back and forth like the tigers, imitate the roar of the lion, and clamber about as did the monkeys.

A major responsibility of the leader in dramatic play is to discover activities in which the children are interested and then guide them into these dramatic play experiences. Much of imaginary play comes from the children's experiences. A trip to a railroad station, a hospital, a fire station, a post office, or a museum can provide a wealth of material for dramatic play among children five to seven years of age. Mother Goose is a rich storehouse for the leader in search of rhymes and jingles with dramatic merit.

There is almost no limit to the possibilities for dramatic play. One example will indicate the opportunities for spontaneous group pantomime made possible by an imaginative leader. It is a beautiful afternoon on a summer playground. The leader remarks, "What a beautiful day! What would you like to do on a day like this?" Every child will have a suggestion. One would like to go on a picnic, another to the zoo, a third would like to go fishing. One boy wishes to go to a ball game with his father while a girl may prefer going to the beach.

The leader allows the children to choose and the group votes in favor of a picnic. Then the leader asks, "What are some of the things you would like to do at the picnic?" Suggestions include wading in the brook, skipping stones in the water, climbing trees, catching butterflies, fishing, picking dandelions, and building a fire. The leader, attempting to create the proper mood, says, "What a wonderful place for a picnic! For a few moments, let's each one of us do what he wants to do most."

After each child has engaged in his own individual pantomime, the leader may guide them into group dramatic play by saying, "It's rather warm, but Jimmy seems to have cooled off by wading in the brook. Let's all take off our shoes and stockings. Be careful when you step into the water because some of the stones are slippery and other are sharp. Let's all look for a crawfish."

The alert and creative leader will include dramatic play experiences as a part of the daily program for his children. These make-believe experiences will arise out of the interests and activities of the children themselves.

Pantomime

Pantomime is a process by which one expresses thought and feeling through bodily action. It is the foundation of all dramatic expression and is especially vital in creative dramatics for young people. Pantomime is to drama what passing, shooting, and dribbling are to basketball. It lies at the heart of dramatic play, is the basis of characterization, and may be engaged in for itself alone purely as relaxation and recreation. The leader who is desirous of including creative dramatics in his program of recreation must develop some competency in the handling of pantomime. Furthermore, certain activities involving pantomime, such as charades, have considerable social recreation value and should be included in the total program whether or not they lead on to higher levels of dramatic accomplishment.

Pantomime constitutes a major share of the imaginative play of younger children. It may be introduced to older children in a number of ways:

1. The leader may ask the children, "How many things can you say without using your voice?" This question elicits such answers in pantomime as "My head aches," "I'm hungry," "yes," "no," "I'm sleepy," and "goodbye."
2. A second step might be to remind the children that the Indians used to talk to members of other tribes entirely through sign language which was largely pantomime. The leader then suggests they all be Indians and say only by pantomime such things as, "My mother would like to have you come over tonight for supper;" or, "We had a fire in our house yesterday and the firemen came and put it out."
3. Lease and Siks[7] recommend make-believe trips and seasonal activities as providing excellent material for pantomime. A trip to a farm where everyone helps the farmer with his work might involve feeding chickens, hunting eggs, pitching hay, hoeing corn, milking cows, chopping wood, and feeding the pigs. Or an imaginative re-enactment of last winter's experiences in the snow sets the stage for a snowball fight, rolling snowballs, building snowforts and defending them, skating, and skiing.

   From these examples, it is apparent that beginning pantomimes for children should be kept simple, should be fun, and should involve large muscular movements.
4. The leader may combine pantomime with the elements of a game, thus adding a new dimension of fun to the activity. This mildly competitive activity involves the division of children into groups and allows each group to guess what another group is pantomiming. It is best to start with the simple and easy activity and progress step by step up the ladder of difficulty.

   We might begin with pantomimes involving the senses. One group peels a banana and eats it. Another pops some popcorn, salts and butters it, then eats it with a great deal of pleasure. Another group smells something delicious, decides to track it down, and discovers a pumpkin pie in the oven. Still a fourth picks up a fluffy little kitten and strokes it softly.

   The second step leads us to pantomiming certain bodily conditions as they affect us in our normal activities. These might include catching a ball with a sprained finger, walking in an extremely tight pair of shoes, trying to study with a toothache, and walking to school when the weather is below zero.

   The third step is more difficult as it calls for emotional expression. One group is asleep and is awakened by a noise in the middle of the night. Its members must register fear solely through pantomime. Another is angered by a persistent and evasive mosquito as it attempts to sleep. You are a member of a third group and a pet dog which you

---

[7] Ruth Lease and Geraldine Brain Siks, *Creative Dramatics in Home, School, and Community* (New York: Harper and Brothers), 1952, pp. 55-57.

love dearly has just been killed by an automobile; or you have just looked at your report card and discovered you received all A's.

Step four brings us to characterization, which means that we now are ready to be someone different from ourselves. The leader may introduce characterization by becoming some type of person from everyday life who is well-known to the chidren, such as the school janitor sweeping the floor, a policeman directing traffic, a bus driver collecting fares and driving his bus, a fireman holding a hose and directing a stream of water into a burning building, or mother making a telephone call. The children guess who the leader is characterizing and then are given an opportunity to present other characterizations.

Lease and Siks recommend that efforts at characterization begin with characters from reality and progress to make-believe characters from fairyland and Mother Goose. They point out that:

It is truly a thrilling experience for eight-year-olds to become sly old witches, mischievous goblins, wicked kings, dancing fairies, bold giants, stately princes and princesses, and other fairy tale folk. If children learn how to get under the skin of a new character from the very first meeting, they will always put forth their best creative efforts.[8]

Mother Goose is a treasure house of delightful material for characterization as are other favorite stories for children. Among their most popular characterizations are:

Goldilocks awakened by the three bears.
The king in his counting house, counting out his money.
Little Miss Muffet frightened by a spider.
Old King Cole calling for his pipe, bowl, and fiddlers.
The Knave of Hearts stealing the queen's tarts.
The queen in the parlor eating bread and honey.
The maid hanging out the clothes.
The three little kittens crying because they lost their mittens.
Old Mother Hubbard going to her cupboard to look for a bone.

Characterization should be fun and it should emphasize thought and feeling rather than technique. For example, if the children are preparing to be the king as he counts out his money, the leader may say, "If we are going to be a king, we must think and feel like a king. Who can tell us how a king feels that is different from how the ordinary man feels? How does having so much money make him feel? What do you suppose he is thinking as he counts his money. Now let's be this king and feel like he does."

As the children act out their concepts of royalty, the leader remembers the importance of praise as a motivational technique and comments with enthusiasm on the excellence of their presentations.

5. Charades is a fascinating game in which a word or a series of words is acted out in pantomime by one group while others guess.

_____
[8] Ibid., p. 60.

Frequently titles of books, songs, or motion pictures are pantomimed.

One popular version of charades is played in this manner. The
group is divided into teams with not more than five players on a team.
Each team sends one representative to the leader who gives him a slip
of paper on which is written a title of a book, song, or movie. He
looks at his slip, hurries back to his group and begins to pantomime
the title. As soon as his group guesses the correct title, they stand up,
shout out the title, and remain standing until all have finished. Score
is kept on the basis of the time required to guess the title. The winning team is the one that has the lowest total time for five games.
Five games are played so that each player may have an opportunity
to act out a title. A maximum of two minutes is allowed for each
presentation, except that the last group to finish is permitted but
fifteen seconds more than the next to last group. Thus, one slow
group cannot hold up the other groups for longer than fifteen seconds.

The actor first indicates whether the title is that of a book, song, or
movie and then holds up as many fingers as there are words in the
title. If the group fails to guess the first word, he holds up two fingers
to show that he is going on to the second word. Small words may be
indicated by holding the thumb and forefinger close together. A timekeeper is needed if scoring is on a time basis.[9]

SHADOW PLAYS, PUPPETRY, AND MARIONETTES

All three of these terms can be summed up in the one word, "puppetry," since marionettes are string-controlled puppets which are worked
from overhead, and shadow plays frequently involve the use of shadow-
puppets which are flat figures operated by rods or wires against a trans-
lucent screen illuminated from behind.

Few aspects of drama can compare with puppetry in popularity with
children. When children make their own puppets, design and construct
the costumes, build the stage and scenery, and create and produce their
own plays, a natural union of crafts and drama takes place in a truly
creative setting. As indicated by Anderson,[10] in addition to stimulating the
imagination and offering a valuable release, puppetry combines five creative projects into one:

---

[9] Students are referred to pages 181–184 for additional pantomime games and
charades which have proved popular with various age groups.

[10] Muriel Anderson, "Making Hand Puppets," *School Arts,* March 1962, p. 18.

1. *Sculpture*—when the children shape and fashion the heads of their puppets of papier-mâché.
2. *Fashion design*—when they make the costumes for their puppets and attempt to design costumes which harmonize with the character of the particular puppet. This also involves the harmonizing of colors.
3. *Writing*—the preparation of the script for the show.
4. *Staging*—building the stage, painting the backdrop, making curtains and other properties.
5. *Speech*—which involves rehearsing and putting on the play.

In the initial stages of puppetry the leader should not be too ambitious. It is best to begin with a simple story or make up your own play with no more than two or three characters. Many folk and fairy tales make excellent puppet plays. Be sure that there is plenty of action as puppets are most effective when they are doing things. Make them fight, run, jump, or push.

STORY DRAMATIZATION

Story dramatization is the activity most frequently implied by the term *creative dramatics*. It is one of the most desirable activities on playgrounds and in community centers because: (1) it is highly enjoyable; (2) it is a natural outcome of the story-telling period; (3) no equipment is required; (4) it may be used effectively either indoors or out; (5) the same children need not be present from day to day; and (6) the length of time devoted to the activity at any one period is completely flexible.

We are under no illusions that we possess the ability to devise a short cut to superior leadership in creative dramatics. However, we know from years of experience that the typical playground leader must work with such a wide variety of activities that it simply is impossible for him to be highly competent in all, or even in a majority of them. For this reason, it seems best that we limit ourselves at this point to a simple, concise listing of the most important steps or leadership techniques involved in helping children and youth enjoy the creative experiences inherent in story dramatization.

Role of the Leader

The leader is a guide, not a director. One of the fundamentals of leadership in creative dramatics is acceptance of the point of view that a major function of the leader is to stimulate the imagination, encourage creativity, and motivate the growth of children from within. This is best done, not by domination and dictation, but by skillful questions, suggestions, and discussion.

The leader, working with the children, selects stories of literary quality based on the interests and abilities of the group. The success of story dramatization depends in part on the choice of material. Not all stories lend themselves equally well to creative drama. A story may be superior as literature for children and be entirely unsuitable for dramatization because it lacks certain qualities essential to playmaking.

Among the most important criteria by which a story should be judged for its dramatization potentialities are:

1. The story should be interesting to the children and be well liked by them.
2. The story should possess literary quality. A common criticism of recreation leaders is directed at the poor quality of our playground and community center drama. Much of this criticism is valid. There are so many beautiful and well-written stories from which to choose that there is no possible justification for us to use trite or crude materials.
3. The plot should be simple and involve strong emotional conflict. Too many incidents, episodes, or situations before the climax is reached dissipate interest.
4. The story should provide plenty of opportunity for interesting action. A story lacking in movement will prove uninteresting to children who quickly exhaust its possibilities and become bored and restless.
5. The characters should seem real to the children and should be clearly defined. At least they should possess one definite characteristic, otherwise children will find it extremely difficult to identify with them. For example, a child always prefers to be one of the mean sisters in *Cinderella,* the kindly and deeply compassionate bishop in *The Bishop's Candlesticks,* or the angry and envious queen in *Snow White and the Seven Dwarfs,* rather than essay the role of some drab, colorless, and obscure character.
6. Dialogue should be interesting, brief, and natural.

The leader will achieve more satisfactory results in story dramatization by utilizing the best of children's stories selected in light of the above criteria than he will by attempting to have children create original plots. Only leaders who have a thorough understanding of dramatic elements and play structure should attempt the latter.

A few stories of outstanding quality, judged in terms of the above criteria, are:

CHILDREN FIVE TO SEVEN YEARS

The Elves and the Shoemaker	Grimm
Goldilocks and the Three Bears	Robert Southey
Little Miss Muffet	Mother Goose

Old King Cole...Mother Goose
The Queen of Hearts......................................Mother Goose
Sing a Song of Sixpence..................................Mother Goose
The Three Billy Goats Gruff.............................George Dasent
Three Little Kittens..Eliza Follen

CHILDREN EIGHT AND NINE YEARS

Cinderella..Charles Perrault
Roads..Rachel Field
Rumpelstiltskin...Grimm
The Shepherd Boy and the Wolf................................Aesop
The Sleeping Beauty..Grimm
Snow White and the Seven Dwarfs..............................Grimm
The Three Wishes.................................Olive Beaupré Miller
The Town Mouse and the Country Mouse.........................Aesop

CHILDREN TEN AND ELEVEN YEARS

The Boy Knight of Reims.............................Eloise Lownsbery
The Emperor's New Clothes..................Hans Christian Andersen
Johnnie Appleseed.............................Emily Taft Douglas
The Stone in the Road...................................._____
William Tell...James Baldwin
The Wise People of Gotham................................_____
Robin Hood's Merry Adventure with the Miller...........Howard Pyle
The Enchanted Shirt.......................................John Hay

YOUTH TWELVE TO FOURTEEN YEARS

The Bishop's Candlesticks..............................Victor Hugo
The Nuremberg Stove..............................Louise de la Ramée
Rip Van Winkle....................................Washington Irving
Tree of Freedom....................................Rebecca Caudill
A Christmas Carol..................................Charles Dickens
The Moor's Legacy.................................Washington Irving
Abe Lincoln's Other Mother.......................Bernadine Bailey
The Christmas Apple..................................Ruth Sawyer

The leader establishes an environment conducive to creativity. Creativity, like any fragile plant, flourishes only in soil prepared especially for its growth. Freedom is one of the most important elements supporting a climate of creativity for the act of creation cannot be forced. Children must be free to make choices, to exercise meaningful judgments, to give rein to their imaginations without fear of caustic criticism. The leader does not confuse freedom with license nor domination with guidance. He does have standards and goals, but they are within the reach of the children.

Creativity is nurtured most effectively when every child feels wanted, liked, accepted, and able.

Even as simple a procedure as seating the children in a circle so they may face one another, rather than in formal rows, has value in stimulating a climate for creativity.

The leader tells the story in a manner to stimulate the interests and imaginations of the children. Careful preparation is the key to successful storytelling. Reading a story to the children and memorizing it are equally ineffective. The leader should read the story several times and become thoroughly acquainted with the plot, the action, and the characters before attempting to tell it to the children. He should tell the story aloud several times for his own benefit as one important step in his preparation.

The leader and children plan the scenes and action. After the story has been told to the children and they decide they wish to dramatize a play of their own based on it, the children and the leader carefully analyze the story. To stimulate discussion, the leader may ask several questions.

In considering *The Bishop's Candlesticks,* for example, they will discuss such questions as: What kind of man was the bishop? Who was Jean Valjean? What did he look like? Where had he been for the past nineteen years? How did he feel? Why did he steal the silver? Who were the gendarmes? How did they act? Why did the bishop give Jean Valjean the candlesticks? How did Jean Valjean react to the bishop's gift?

The leader guides the discussion, but does not insist on any particular conclusions. The children determine both the number and the nature of the scenes, probing and analyzing each one and playing them several times. After each scene has been fully explored and dramatized, the children discuss the action, plot, and characterization. Suggestions for improvement are made and changes in cast may be effected. Then, the scene is dramatized again and re-evaluated. When all the scenes have been played, re-played, and evaluated, they are put together in sequence and the entire play is presented. The play is never looked upon by anyone as being finished because in creative dramatics improvements may be made at any time.

The leader guides the children in characterization and casting. The leader and the children discuss the characters. How does Jean Valjean look when he enters the bishop's home? Someone shows how he looks. Someone else shows. There is discussion and possibly revision. How do the gendarmes act when they bring Jean Valjean back to the bishop? Someone shows how they act. Others make suggestions. Other characters enter into the discussion. How did they look; how did they feel; and what did they do? Why? Let's try some of the parts now. In every instance, if a child is going to be Jean Valjean it is his special responsibility to make the other children *see* and *feel* Jean Valjean. The chief reason why costumes, stagesettings, and properties should be eliminated, or at least subordinated to the acting is because they affect his role before he has a chance to say a word.

The leader guides the children in evaluation. Children are encouraged to evaluate their plays from every possible standpoint because this is one of the best ways of realizing excellence in the plays they create. Constructive criticism is not ignored but the leader should understand that praise is the most powerful single factor in the development of a child's faith in himself and in spurring him on to the highest achievement of which he is capable.

FROM CHARADES TO SHAKESPEARE

A look at some of the community drama programs conducted by recreation departments across the country reveals a wide variety of activities, both formal and informal, ranging from charades to Children's Theatre, simple pantomime to puppets, and story plays to Shakespeare.

Dramatic activities conducted by the Department of Public Recreation of Kenosha, Wisconsin, center primarily around the Kenosha Little Theatre and the Summer Children's Traveling Theatre. The Kenosha Little Theatre has operated under the sponsorship of the Department of Public Recreation for more than two decades. The Little Theatre is financially independent of the Department insofar as these expenditures are concerned: all public performance costs including the printing of tickets, director's salary, rental of costumes, royalty fees, and similar items.

The Department provides all secretarial help and is responsible for the fiscal management of the Little Theatre. The Director of Public Recreation serves as treasurer. In addition, the Department provides all rehearsal and stage facilities with no cost to the Kenosha Little Theatre except nominal custodial costs incurred in connection with the use of public school buildings at the time of public performances for which admission is charged.

The Kenosha Little Theatre averages four public productions a year, consisting of one musical production and three strictly dramatic productions. Among the plays or musical programs presented in recent years are "The Fourposter," "Send Me No Flowers," "South Pacific," "Breath of Spring," "The Miracle Worker," and "Carousel." The cost of admission is kept very low—an adult season ticket is only $3.00 while students are admitted to the four productions on a $2.00 season ticket.

One of the most amazing features of the community theatre or little theatre movement in this country is the vast amount of work done by volunteers who love the theater so deeply that they are willing to devote hundreds of hours of dedicated effort each year to its promotion. Many of these people have no desire to be actors or actresses. They simply want to be a part of the theater and they are willing to serve in any capacity. They build scenery and paint it; construct properties; serve as stage hands and prompters; sell tickets; act as ushers; publicize the plays—even sweep the stage. These are the people who constitute the real strength of adult amateur drama in the United States. In Kenosha, the director of the Little Theatre is the only paid individual connected with the program.

The Summer Children's Traveling Theatre utilizes a specially constructed four-wheel stage trailer for its performances. The actors are youth of junior high school age organized into two separate casts, one of which gives morning performances while the other presents afternoon plays. A performance is presented at each playground in the city.

The Milwaukee Municipal Recreation Department places major emphasis on the dramatic arts for both young and old. Creative dramatics constitutes an important aspect of the program for children on the summer playgrounds and in the community centers. The Department issues helpful mimeographed materials to its leaders dealing with such topics as *Creative Dramatics*—what it is and how to introduce it; *Material for Dramatization*—a twenty-three page bulletin which compiles a list of outstanding poems and stories for creative dramatics; another bulletin entitled *Dramatic Play and Pantomimes*; and a number of formal plays for children and youth completely mimeographed.

The highest level of formal drama for youth is represented by the Junior Milwaukee Players, an organization for junior and senior high school youth interested in drama. A School of the Theatre is a part of this organization with classes held once a week in acting, make-up, voice, dance, body movement and coördination.

The adult program of drama reaches its peak in the Milwaukee Players, a community theater organization. Over many years, this organization with its hundreds of performing and supporting participants has played to thousands of people, awakening or refining skills and appreciations, on the one hand, and contributing to knowledge, understanding, and enjoyment on the other. Typical productions presented within recent years include: "The Circle," "Taming of the Shrew," "Macbeth," "My Sister Eileen," "Madwoman of Chaillot," "Blythe Spirit," "On the Town," and "Twelfth Night."

For more than thirty years, School of the Theatre has provided instruction in the theatre arts as a part of the total program of adult dramatics. The Department of Municipal Recreation maintains a close relationship with all high school graduates who were active either in drama or music while in school and seeks to interest them in continuing to participate in these activities. The Department also maintains a complete costume bureau from which its various drama groups may requisition at any time.

LITTLE THEATRE AND CHILDREN'S THEATRE

Some adult amateur dramatic groups are known as little theatres, some as community theatres, while others, such as the Milwaukee Players, identify themselves by other names. Regardless of their names, their functions are about the same: (1) to give those with a vital interest in the theatre, both actors and supporting participants, an opportunity to further this interest under superior leadership; and (2) to produce plays of high quality for the enjoyment and artistic appreciation of the audience, so that drama, which has expressed fundamental human needs and aspirations since the dawn of civilization, may become an essential part of the lives of an ever-increasing number of people.

The term *Children's Theatre,* as generally used, refers to an international movement, in which plays, written by playwrights, are presented by living actors for child audiences. The players may be adults, children, or a combination of the two. Its purposes have been repeatedly stated: "(1) to provide worthwhile and appropriate entertainment for young audiences, and (2) to promote individual and social growth through experience in the dramatic arts."[11]

In the United States, children's theatre is a twentieth century movement with the first significant children's theatre founded in 1903. Mitchell reports on the number of adult groups producing today: "In the United States more than 1,200 units, largely amateur, produce from one to four plays annually for children. More and more community groups, 200 high schools, and at least 220 colleges are producing.[12] Growth of the movement in the area of higher education is especially significant when we note that only one university, Northwestern, was producing plays for children three decades ago.

---

[11] Nellie McCaslin, "History of Children's Theatre in the United States," in *Children's Theatre and Creative Dramatics,* Geraldine Brain Siks and Hazel Brain Dunnington, eds. (Seattle: University of Washington Press, 1961), p. 26.

[12] Albert O. Mitchell, "Children's Theatre Produced by Adult Groups," in *Children's Theatre and Creative Dramatics,* Geraldine Brain Siks and Hazel Brain Dunnington, eds. (Seattle: University of Washington Press, 1961), p. 33.

ARTS AND CRAFTS

A considerably larger number of recreation departments conduct varied programs in arts and crafts than in music and drama. The most commonly offered arts or crafts activities for children, according to a recent survey by the National Recreation and Park Association, in order of frequency of mention, are: papercraft, clay modeling, leathercraft, weaving, drawing, painting, woodwork, metalcraft, ceramics, needlecraft, and plastics. The five most popular activities among adults are ceramics, painting, leathercraft, drawing, and needlecraft.[13] Students should understand that while studies of current practice possess value by revealing what people are now doing, they do not necessarily indicate what people would prefer doing. This should be kept in mind as we discuss activities that do appear on the above list and others that do not.

THE VALUES WE SEEK

Anyone who has made a careful examination of the professional literature in arts and crafts will find a close philosophic kinship existing between the highest aims of this literature and the values sought by recreation as discussed in Chapter 4 of this book. This, of course, is as it should be because the higher a profession rises in the discovery of its aims, the more do these aims become the common property of all. Let us determine how arts and crafts may contribute to the development of personal adequacy, or individual fulfillment, and to social growth and democratic citizenship.

On the level of the individual, the recreation leader is concerned with helping each participant to become the kind of person he is capable of becoming. Everyone wants to see himself, and to have others see him, as able, successful, wanted, liked, and accepted. Every human being has a certain degree of creative ability. Unused, this quality, like any other, becomes dwarfed and atrophied. One of our most important goals, therefore, should be to foster, through arts and crafts, the growth and development of the creative potentialities of both young and old. A feeling of deep

---

[13] Hawkins, *op. cit.*, p. 55.

personal accomplishment and enhanced self-esteem results as the individual expresses this creative impulse in the production of some work of art,
something of his own creation. For arts and crafts, as one of the finest
examples of human expression, represents mastery over both materials and
self, and accompanying this sense of mastery are self-confidence, dignity,
personal worth, and the respect of others which normally is associated with
artistic accomplishment.

There is happiness and joy in creative accomplishment. These are
outgrowths of participation in an activity in which certain human needs
are satisfied. No scientific measuring devices are needed to reveal the joy
in a child's heart as a puppet head comes into being as a result of his creative accomplishment, or the quiet happiness of an aged couple as they
work side by side on a common activity in a community center crafts program. Some share of this happiness frequently is derived from the beauty
which art brings into otherwise drab and ugly lives. Another contributing
factor is the absence of the competitive element with its emphasis upon
beating someone, and the sense of failure and defeat when one is beaten.
In this program everyone works at his own ability level and all are winners; there are no losers.

Arts and crafts contribute to mental health by providing a means of
relaxation and an escape valve for tensions, in a troubled, frustrated, tension-ridden, and neurotic world. Perhaps no man ever carried any heavier
responsibilities than did the late Winston Churchill during World War II.
Many men would have broken under the strain. Let him tell how art
helped him to carry the load:[14]

Painting is complete as a distraction. I know of nothing which, without exhausting the body, more entirely absorbs the mind. Whatever the worries of
the hour or the threats of the future, once the picture has begun to flow
along, there is no room for them in the mental screen. They pass out into
shadow and darkness. All one's mental light, such as it is, becomes concentrated on the task. Time stands respectfully aside. . . .

Among children who have a tendency to exhaust themselves in active,
vigorous play, the arts and crafts period can be one of the most valuable
allies a leader has in his efforts to bring some degree of serenity into an
otherwise hectic day.

One further value of art was presented earlier in this chapter. Art is
a universal language, a kind of poetry without words, by which all men
can speak to one another of beauty, appreciation, freedom, and friendship.

---

[14] Winston S. Churchill, *Painting as a Pastime* (London: Odhams Press, Limited, 1948), p. 31.

When the Mona Lisa made her famous visit to the United States, no interpreter was needed to convey her message to the people of this country.

METHODS MUST HARMONIZE WITH ENDS

The existence of certain values in arts and crafts activities is no guarantee of their attainment. The decisive factor is the quality of the experience and this is determined in large part by the leadership. We learned in Chapter 5 that an individual may be an effective leader in one situation and quite ineffective in another. The qualities and competencies of the leader must be relevant to the particular situation or problems to be solved. This means that the superior leader in arts and crafts, working through a unique medium, and in situations sometimes possessing unusual features, must understand the problems he faces and command the competencies required for their solution.

Methods must be compatible with the ends sought. Development of the creative potentialities of children and youth can best be realized when the leader emphasizes original thinking, planning, and doing. When he assigns projects and utilizes craft kits, patterns, stereotyped cut-outs, hectographed outlines, numbered painting sets, and coloring books, he blocks the creative powers of youngsters and reveals nothing but their ability to imitate and conform. Art experiences should represent a deep, personal involvement by the participants. No such involvement is possible when the nature of one's participation is comparable to the experience of assembling the parts of a jigsaw puzzle.

At the other end of the scale is the "laissez-faire" type of leader who just hands out supplies and expects the participants to create out of a vacuum. The effective, creative leader plays an active, not a passive, role. One of his first responsibilities is to establish a wholesome climate for creativity; an informal, pleasant atmosphere within which a sympathetic and understanding leader encourages originality, and stimulates everyone to seek excellence at his own level of ability. This kind of leader understands the necessity for some direction and a constructive approach if there is to be any progress beyond the level of mediocrity, but he does not judge youth by adult standards.

Guidance is a major function of the good leader. He provides a variety of activities and, as far as possible, permits freedom of choice with respect to selection of activities in order that each person may engage in that which is most meaningful to him. He gives help when needed, but he does not interfere or do a child's work for him for he knows that when this occurs the child no longer feels that the project is his own. His guidance may include: (1) helping the child select the materials and tools suited to his ability; (2) providing inspiration through trips to a zoo, farm, or fire station; (3) assisting him to define his problem and acquire the information and skills needed for its solution; and (4) rekindling his enthusiasm when it begins to die out. He is especially alert to help the child with a special problem: the one who hides his work or throws it away because he is ashamed of it; the child whose lack of confidence and self-reliance impel him to lean too heavily on the leader; or the one who never seems to complete anything, wasting his energies, his time, and the supplies.

The leader provides the necessary materials, supplies, equipment, and facilities. He is an initiator, provider, encourager, and motivator. He emphasizes creativity, the personal satisfaction and joy of doing, rather than perfection of the product. He helps everyone to realize success as early and as frequently as possible. He praises children for work well done, but withholds praise unless it is merited. He neither asks a child, "What is it?," nor laughs at his efforts, no matter how inferior they may be.

The leader refrains from offering any awards or promoting contests. He motivates primarily through praise and the display of finished products. The display or exhibit is very important as it gives recognition to every child and contributes to his developing sense of personal adequacy. *Every* child's work should be shown with the display arranged in such a manner that no indication of preference is indicated. Since each child is different and the work of each child is different, the leader must judge each product by an individualized set of standards. It is not desirable to equate mediocrity with excellence, but these are relative terms as used here; that which is excellent for one child may be mediocre for another. If a child has done the best of which he is capable, then the accomplishment is significant to him and should be of equal significance to his leader.

Some Special Problems

When a leader is able to anticipate problems he is in a better position to solve them than if he comes upon them suddenly and completely unprepared. The playground leader particularly, in many situations, may be confronted by one or more of the following difficulties:

1. Lack of adequate facilities, equipment, and supplies. All of his arts and crafts activities may have to be carried on out-of-doors. This has some

advantages, but noise, wind, softball games, and many other distractions simply add to his problems. He may have an insufficient number of work tables and no chairs at all. There may not be enough tools or supplies for everyone who wishes to take part. There may be inadequate storage space for the supplies, equipment, and partially completed articles. Of course, where school or other public buildings are located on areas used for summer playgrounds, a room in these buildings frequently may be utilized by the arts and crafts group. However, many playgrounds must be operated with no more than an extremely small shelter house for storage of supplies or with no indoor facilities at all.

The superior leader who is not easily discouraged and who is determined to provide for his children the best possible program of arts and crafts under these circumstances will:

A. Select those activities which can be carried out successfully within his limitations.
B. Mobilize the resources of the home. Many parents will be willing to furnish certain materials and supplies. If a hotplate is needed at a certain stage in the process, the child may do this work at home. Also, if the playground has insufficient storage space, partially completed projects may be kept at home.
C. Utilize scrap, native, and inexpensive materials to supplement the more costly types. This should be done even if cost is not of major importance because these materials enrich the program in many ways as will be indicated later in this chapter.
D. Charge a small fee to cover only the costs of the materials which become the property of the child upon completion of his product. This is common practice and is sound public policy. Materials purchased by public funds should not become the private property of individuals until they have reimbursed the community to the extent of their cost. This policy imposes upon the leader an obligation to keep these costs within range of the ability and desire of the children to pay.

2. A wide age range of participants. While the art teacher generally will work with one grade level at a time, the recreation leader may have youngsters from six to sixteen in his group. The pressure of other activities will not permit more than one daily period for arts and crafts. What is he to do? The solution may lie in the woman leader taking the younger children while he takes the older ones; or she may take the younger children and girls while he takes the older boys. Also, some of the older girls may be used as assistant leaders to help with the very young children.
3. The problem of time. A typical playground program involves all ages, young and old, and a wide variety of activities. Where is a leader to find time for a rich and meaningful program of arts and crafts? The answer to this problem is relatively simple—if he believes in the worth of the program, he will find time for it. The neglected activities in a recreation program are those toward which the leader is apathetic.

THE PROGRAM IN ARTS AND CRAFTS

Art is the creation of beauty. Beauty may be produced or expressed in many different ways. When beauty is expressed through dance, music, and drama we refer to the activities as the *performing arts*. When beauty is created through the media of drawing, painting, sculpture, ceramics, photography, and clay modeling, we use the term *arts and crafts*. The term *arts* is a general term which includes all of these creative activities. *Crafts* are a part of the total art program and consist of all those creative activities "involving skillful work with three-dimensional materials to produce an expressive and sometimes useful form or product."[15]

Students are referred to page 138 for a listing of a number of arts and crafts activities.

Space will permit us to discuss how leadership functions through but a few of these activities.

Drawing

Drawing is one of the basic fundamentals of any art program, but it should never be limited simply to ordinary drawing with crayons or pencils. The drawing program should include a sufficient variety of experiences to command the interests of children and provide opportunities for experimentation. Among the materials used will be colored chalk, crayons, charcoal, felt pens, perhaps pencils on a limited basis for older children, various kinds of paper depending on the drawing medium used, brushes, tempera paints, fixatives, and some etching tool such as a compass or old pen point.

SCRIBBLE DESIGN.   The first step in a child's early atempts to draw is known as the scribble stage. This stage is characterized by the child's discovery that he can make marks on a paper with crayons and that it is fun to do so even though the scribbles are meaningless. He should be praised for his efforts with no attempt made to hurry him into controlling the direction of his lines.

As the child grows in his ability to control his lines, the scribble may become the basis for a colored design. Materials needed will be crayons

---

[15] Thelma R. Newman, "Is It Art or Craft?," *Arts and Activities*, May 1962, p. 35.

and newsprint or 12″ × 18″ drawing paper. Teach the child to start at the edge of the paper with black crayon, go to the top, down to bottom, and over to the outer edge in his scribble. This produces a large scribble which makes the second step an easy one. The entire page should be filled in. In between the scribble lines made by the black crayon will be open spaces. These should be colored in by different colored crayons. Both varied colors and textures may be used to add contrast to the design. Stimulate the imaginations of the children by asking them to look *into* their scribble drawings in an attempt to find realistic objects, such as animals, flowers, and people.

As the child develops the ability to produce recognizable symbols such as a human figure, the leader should understand that this is a great step forward for him and should encourage him with sincere praise. He should also remember that there is no one "correct" way of drawing anything and that the uniqueness of a child's drawing is its most important quality.

CRAYON ETCHING.   Crayon etching is an interesting and enjoyable method of producing line drawings. Each child is given a piece of smooth, white paper which he covers completely with a coat of crayon in a light color. He may use a single color or several different colors, even occasionally blending two colors. Over the top of these light colors he puts a surface coating of black crayon, or he may use a coating of black tempera paint after adding a small amount of soap to make it adhere to the crayon. The child draws his picture by scratching through the black surface of the paper, thus exposing a myriad of colors previously applied with crayon. Any sharp, pointed instrument, such as the tip of a compass, an old pen point, or the tip of a pocket knife will serve as an etching tool.

CRAYON RESIST.   This type of activity involves a combination of India ink or tempera paint with crayon. After the drawing has been made heavily with crayon, paint over it with India ink or a dark tempera color. This frequently converts a mediocre drawing into a rich and exciting picture. The quality of the picture may be improved still further by using crayon again after the first application of water color and continuing to alternate the two.

Painting

Children enjoy painting experiences above all other types of art activity. Young children are especially free and natural painters since they are not shackled by the fears and inhibitions which handicap the older artist.

The leader who is concerned with the answer to the question, "How do I teach a child to paint?," should ponder carefully Erdt's reflections on this problem:[16]

There is no definite answer. Creative work is not taught like the multiplication table. The teacher can only provide the motivation, circumstances, materials, time, and appreciation that make a happy, creative experience possible for children. Evaluations of painting are based on the maturation of the group. It is right and proper for a young child to have a strip of blue across the top of his paper for the sky and to have the sun in a corner if this is the way he wants it to be. For the teacher to criticize his natural way of working is to run the risk of upsetting the balance, color, and repetition in a composition and to impose adult standards on the child's work.

There are no blueprints providing rigid, inflexible guidelines to success in any type of creative activity. The leader, however, must not make the mistake of believing that since this is true, there is nothing of any particular significance for him to do. Every area of human activity has its disciplines, its knowledges, its competencies, and its restrictions. Children should acquire an understanding of the materials and the tools used in painting and develop some skill in their manipulation. The leader not only teaches these technical aspects of painting, but, as in drawing, he provides a climate conducive to creativity; he is a provider, an originator, a motivator, a guide.

Two kinds of paint are used with children: opaque tempera paint and transparent water colors. The leader should begin with tempera and advance to water colors with the older children. Be sure to provide a good quality brush. Half-inch and three-quarter-inch bristle brushes are best for tempera. Teach the child to hold the brush firmly, but not tightly, about where the ferrule and handle are joined. Tempera painting may be done on many different kinds of surfaces; wrapping paper, colored construction paper, natural and colored newstock, cardboard, wood, and cartons.

The leader should guide children into the development of the following good work practices: wearing suitable clothing, aprons, or an artist's smock made from a man's discarded shirt with most of the sleeves cut off; wiping off the brush against the edge of the paint container; washing the brushes at the end of the day and placing them upright in a jar to dry; hanging up the paintings overnight to dry; and helping the leader and the other children to clean up after the art period is over for the day.

---

[16] Margaret Hamilton Erdt, *Teaching Art in the Elementary School* (rev. ed.), (New York: Holt, Rinehart and Winston, Inc., 1962), pp. 195–196.

Painting with water color should be reserved for children about nine or ten years of age and older because it requires more practice than tempera painting and it brings a new activity into their art experiences. A No. 10 camel's-hair brush should be provided. Also, water color or waterproof marking pens may be used, particularly by younger children. As with tempera paintings, children should be encouraged to use large, free movements. Beginners should not be concerned with detail. Under no circumstances should pencil outlines be made preliminary to painting. If a child feels the necessity of some guide lines, teach him to block out the large areas of his painting with a brush and light color.

Water-color painting may be done on wet or dry paper and both Manila and white water-color paper may be used.

WATER COLOR ON WET PAPER. A quick wash of the paper is preferable to a heavy soaking. Paint directly on this wet paper encouraging the colors to blend in a fuzzy manner. These rich color blendings and soft edges are the unique outcomes of this particular technique. This child will learn from experience just how wet his paper and how thin his paint should be for best results.

FINGER PAINTING. Finger painting is easy and provides a valuable art experience for young children. Unless it is handled effectively, however, it can be a messy and unpleasant experience. The painting may be done on the floor or on tables, but in either case clean newspapers should be spread out over an area large enough to protect the floor or tables. The children should wear aprons and roll up their sleeves.

Finger painting should be done on a good quality paper with a slick surface. Regular paper for this purpose, glazed shelf paper, or butcher paper may be purchased. Other necessary supplies or equipment include the paint, a bucket of water for washing hands, and a sponge or two for wetting the paper.

The paint is a slippery, water-base paint which can be purchased wherever other school paints are sold, or you can make your own. Hoover recommends the following recipe costing about 20 cents and providing about one and a half pints, sufficient for approximately thirty children:[17]

One 12 oz. box of Faultless starch (or other cold water starch)
An equal quantity of soap flakes (such as Ivory or Lux)
Two cups of cold water
Powder paint for coloring

------

[17] F. Louis Hoover, *Art Activities for the Very Young* (Worcester, Mass.: Davis Publications, Inc., 1961), p. 41.

Mix together the starch and soap flakes. Slowly addd the water while stirring.

Mix and beat until it reaches the consistency of whipped potatoes. Add powder or tempera paint to get the desired color, keeping in mind that dark colors show up more effectively than light colors in final paintings.

You will find it desirable to give a demonstration provided this is a first experience for the children. Emphasize how much fun it is and that they need have no fear of getting their hands in the paint. Wet the paper, place a spoonful of paint in the middle, and begin to spread it evenly over the paper. Encourage the children to use large and free motions while painting, utilizing open hands, closed fists, sides of their hands, lower arms, and knuckles. Both hands should be used together or alternately. In short, *finger painting* is totally inadequate as a term descriptive of the parts of the body involved in the painting because far more than the fingers are used.

Since large, sweeping hand and arm movements are emphasized, children should be encouraged to concentrate on design, motion, landscape, beaches, deserts, and clouds rather than on pictures. One advantake of this medium is that children may wipe out their mistakes or change their designs at any time and start over again without any waste of materials.

When thoroughly dry, finger paintings frequently are so badly curled they are difficult to display. This can be corrected by pressing them on the unpainted side with a warm iron.

ORIENTAL SCROLLS OR SODA-STRAW PAINTING. This is a fascinating activity which appeals to young and old. You will need some India ink or black tempera thinned, Manila paper, colored crayon, and soda straws. Drop a small dot of India ink in the center of the paper. Each child then takes a soda straw and blows through it, moving the ink into various lines and shapes. The straw does not touch the ink; children should be cautioned also against sucking through the straws. The paper may be turned as necessary to keep the design developing in the direction desired. All kinds of designs and abstractions will appear from gaunt, ghostlike trees to spider webs, and every conceivable object and idea in between. After these designs cover the paper, they are allowed to dry. Then, the child, using crayon, outlines the trees, animals, birds, butterflies, or abstract shapes which his imagination permits him to see. Blowing the ink is lots of fun, but this second stage of the activity has the greater creative value.

Papercraft

Papercraft appears more frequently in the arts and crafts programs conducted by public recreation departments than does any other single activity. This popularity is due very largely to these facts: (1) it is inexpensive; (2) it offers a wide range of creative experiences adaptable to many different age levels; and (3) many of the articles can be completed within one or two periods.

Almost every imaginable kind of paper can be used from the plain and practical to the fancy and glamorous: newsprint, corrugated paper, sandpaper, shelf paper, merchandise wrappings, and discarded greeting cards; charcoal, water-color, metallic, wood-grained, and marbleized papers. Even wallpaper can serve a useful purpose. You will also need several pairs of scissors with sharp points, preferably a pair for each child. Pinking shears and a stapler will be helpful although not essential. A paper cutter is needed, but no child should be allowed to use it because of the safety factor. Wallpaper paste and an all-purpose white glue are needed for pasting. Glitter glue painted on the paper with the glitter sprinkled over it adds to the glamor of Christmas decorations. Small seeds, shells, beads, and similar tiny objects can be used to decorate paper and cardboard in the same manner. Cellophane tape is useful in joining papers.

PAPER SACKS. Paper sacks are useful in making masks and animals. There are two kinds of masks; those worn over the head and those carried on a stick. The first step in making a head mask is to place the sack over the child's head, locate the spots for the eyes, nose, and mouth and mark them with chalk. The child then cuts out the holes. Hair can be made of yarn, raveled out rope, steel wool, twine, crochet cotton made into braids or tufts, a cut-up mop, or paper. Whatever material is selected, it is pasted on the head along with oversize ears. The sack is finally decorated with tempera paint, the more hideous the better. A stick mask is constructed by pasting on the eyes, nose, and ears, stuffing the sack with paper, and mounting it on the end of a stick.

Children about seven and eight years of age love to make paper sack animals. Steps in their construction include: (1) collect a large amount of shredded packing paper for the "insides" of the animals, mailing tubes for their legs, large sacks for the bodies, and small ones for the heads; (2) stuff the large paper sack with shredded paper; (3) fold over the ends of the sack and glue then together; (4) construct the head from a small sack in the same manner; (5) fasten the head to the body with pins or sew it

on with a darning needle and cotton string; (6) punch four holes in the
body for the legs and insert the mailing tubes. Glue these to the body
with strips of paper; (7) cut a tail and ears from other paper and glue
them in place; and (8) paint appropriate markings on the body with
tempera.

PAPER SCULPTURE. Paper sculpture is the art of manipulating
paper into a three-dimensional effect. The design, size, and background
for the sculpture must first be determined and the type of paper selected
accordingly. Remember that your design must stand away from the
background and that it must have height, width, and depth. To achieve
this three-dimensional effect requires some skill in cutting and joining
pieces as well as curling paper with scissors, fringing, and cutting spirals
from circles.

Newhoff describes the experiences of a group of junior high school
boys and girls in making heads and necks of paper. The students used a
sheet of construction paper 12" x 18" for the heads. If they failed to find
the exact complexion desired, they colored white paper with water color,
rolled the paper into a cylinder and stapled it together. A piece about two
inches deep was cut for the neck and fastened in place. Slots were cut for
placement of the nose which also was made from paper. The nose was
made with tabs for insertion in the slots. The eyes, lips, eyebrows, ears,
and other features were cut from construction paper, colored, and pasted
in place. Hair was cut from colored paper or tinted by hand. The children
made curls by cutting thin strips of paper, joined at the top, and curling
them by running them around a closed scissors. Hats, hatbrands, and
other decorations were cut from paper; scraps of feathers, and other appropriate materials were attached with glue where necessary.[18]

PAPIER-MÂCHÉ. Papier-mâché is a craft developed in France and
the words mean "mashed paper." The processes are simple with no definite rules to follow. Among the many interesting objects which can be
made from papier-mâché are trays, bowls, masks, puppet heads, toys,
both animal and human figures, piggy-banks, and relief maps.

Two methods my be used in the papier-mâché process. One is the
pulp method in which paper, generally old newspaper, is torn into small
pieces, soaked in boiling water, and stirred until the mixture becomes a
pulp. For one and a half sheets of newspaper, mix two heaping table-
spoons of flour with cold water. Add one cup of boiling water. If boiling

---

[18] Theresa Newhoff, "Try Creating with Paper," *School Arts,* November 1962,
p. 32.

water is not available a papier-mâché pulp may be made by soaking bits of torn paper in unheated water and allowing it to stand overnight until the paper is soft and pulpy. Add the flour and water mixture to the paper pulp after draining off the excess water. The pulp is then squeezed into whatever shape is desired. This method is suitable for making small figures, puppet heads, raised decorations, and relief maps since it is handled very much as one would handle clay. However, the *pulp method* is not as commonly used as the *strip method*.

The *strip method* involves the use of strips of paper, dipped in wallpaper paste, and then applied to the mold or form. If you wish to remove the mold after completion of the article, it will be necessary to grease it with lard of Vaseline before applying any strips of paper. Some prefer to soak the strips of paper in water for about 30 minutes so they can be shaped more easily. After the article has been built up to the size desired by the application of layers of paper on top of each other, it may be finished with paint, varnish, or any other decoration.

Small children should be limited in their early papier-mâché experiences to simple, bulky figures, such as chickens, pigs, ducks, rabbits, and mice. The procedure is relatively simple and consists of (1) forming the main body of the animal or bird by stuffing pieces of newspapers into small paper bags; (2) forming the general outlines of the head through the use of smaller wads of newspaper; (3) taping the head to the body by one-inch-wide strips of newspaper, dipped in wallpaper paste, running across the head and down along the body. Attach additional parts of the body, such as wings, tails, legs, ears, and nose in a similar manner. The entire figure is then built up with strips of newspaper which have been dipped into the paste. A final cover of torn paper toweling may be added to provide a better painting surface. The figure should be allowed to dry for a few days and then painted.

BALLOON MASKS. Mattil describes a fascinating activity for youth from about eleven to fifteen years—the use of balloons as a base for masks. Each youngster should bring a balloon which, when inflated, is somewhat larger than his head. He first covers this inflated balloon with three or four layers of papier-mâché and puts it aside to dry. Only after the foundation is dry and hard can the boys and girls develop the type of mask desired.[19]

The round shape could easily become a lion or a bear or a person or a pumpkin. Using the standard methods of papier-mâché making earlier described, the children can develop whatever creature they wish from this basic

[19] Edward L. Mattil, *Meaning in Crafts* (Englewood Cliffs, N.J.: Prentice-Hall, Inc., 1959), pp. 100–101.

shape. After this has dried sufficiently and has hardened, the teacher, using a razor blade or X-acto knife, must cut a hole in the bottom of the mask large enough for the child to slip his head through. The balloon may then be removed. When the mask fits, openings made for visibility can be easily disguised in the painting of the mask. This kind of mask would probably be best decorated with a good quality of poster paint or tempera paint, and finally decorated with bits of scrap materials.

The strip method of utilizing the papier-mâché process is commonly used in constructing the heads of hand puppets. This procedure is described on the preceding page.

Printing

Printing is a process which enables an individual to reproduce the designs which he creates. Muddy footprints on the newly-scrubbed kitchen floor are a demonstration by the child of the fundamentals of printing, although not likely to be appreciated as such by the mother.

One of the many advantages of printing as a part of the arts and crafts program is the wide variety of activities which vary so greatly in degree of difficulty. Thus, they provide a graduated series of creative experiences suitable to the abilities of everyone. The ways of making prints are almost endless. They include fingers and palm of hand; sponges; carved blocks of wood and linoleum; vegetables, such as potatoes, carrots, and turnips; etched and scratched metals; a string in paint; oil paint and water on glass; silk screens; lithograph crayon on stone; and inked green leaf; spool, button, or box; a cork; eraser—all these and many others provide opportunities for constant experimentation in and enjoyment of a rich variety of processes.

It is impossible to describe all of these approaches to printing so we shall discuss in detail only a few of the lesser-known ones which seem to offer the greatest possibilities in the recreation situation. The printing medium may be printer's ink, water soluble ink, tempera paint, or water colors. Finger tips, brayers, brushes, and sponges may be used to apply the medium to the printing surfaces, or, as in the case of potato printing, an ink pad may be used and the potato pressed down on it. The paper should be fairly absorbent, such as Manila and construction paper although experiments should be tried with other kinds.

FINGER AND SPONGE PRINTING.   Finger printing is the first step in printing for young children and involves little more than dipping a finger tip in tempera paint and pressing it on paper. An attractive pattern results when several colors are used. The child now moves on to sponge printing which also is very simple. A fine-grained sponge is cut into small pieces. Rub a moistened piece of sponge over a pan of water-color paint or dip it in tempera paint. Press the sponge on the paper with varying degrees of pressure each time as this will determine the size and shape of the spots. A separate sponge will be needed for each color. Prints made with the fingers and sponges serve as attractive book covers and mats.

IMPRINTS WITH MATERIALS. Potatoes, carrots, turnips, cabbages, radishes, boxes, spools, and strings can all be used in printing. String or yarn can be glued to an oatmeal carton, rolled through paint or ink for a single impression on the carton itself, then the carton can be rolled on paper for repeated impressions. Potatoes and other vegetables can be cut with simple designs and used for printing. Young children should not attempt to cut a design into the surface of the vegetable after it has been cut in half, but should use the total surface as the printing shape. Variety may be attained through size, color, the use of different vegetables, and overlapping shapes.

Older children should be taught how to cut the vegetable with a smooth, direct cut clear through at one stroke; how to cut a simple design in the smooth surface after first tracing it on the vegetable with a pencil or nail; and how to hold the knife perpendicular to the vegetable and cut around the design from the outer edge (always cutting *away* from oneself), thus leaving a smooth edge around the design. They should learn to press the vegetable on an ink pad moistened with tempera, showcard paint, or any water soluble inks; to print experimentally a few times on scrap paper until they determine the amount of paint or ink needed to make a smooth print; and, finally, to print the design on white drawing paper, Manila paper, colored construction paper, brown wrapping paper, or newsprint. After some skill has been developed, the children may make placecards, a poster, decorations on costumes, a border design on a napkin or tablecloth, or Christmas cards.

A very similar activity is known as *soap printing* in which designs are cut into a large bar of soap.

Weaving

Weaving is a valuable, primitive, and creative craft which stimulates the imagination and possesses a natural appeal for all children and many adults. The author remembers that several years ago one of the community centers in Madison, Wisconsin, fell heir to a large loom. It was

the most popular single piece of equipment in the entire center. Everyone
wanted to use it.

There are many values in weaving, including a great deal of fun.
In addition, because of the importance of weaving in our early culture,
it has historical significance for children which should be made clear to
them by the leader. The principle of program integration is emphasized
when the children make and operate their own looms.

The leader should understand and interpret to the children these
common terms used in relation to weaving.

Loom: The frame on which warp can be stretched.
Selvage: The two edge threads of the warp.
Shuttle: A wooden or metal device on which yarn is wound. It carries the
filler "weft" through the warp.
Warp: The vertical or lengthwise threads on the loom.
Web: The finished cloth.
Weft: The horizontal threads which cross the warp.
Yarn: Any kind of thread.

MAKING THE LOOMS.   Many kinds of looms exist and looms can be
made from many different types of objects. For example, looms have been
constructed on the tops of paint boxes, from pieces of cardboard, soda
straws, hollow macaroni, oatmeal boxes, small cards, and wooden frames.
Manufactured looms generally used by children are the jiffy loom for
weaving pot holders; the waffle loom on which table mats are made; and
the harness loom for weaving mats, scarfs, and other small articles.

Since the recreation leader is more concerned with the process than
the product, with the quality of the experience and its effect on the individual than with any material outcomes, it seems highly desirable to
make the looms. This enlarges the weaving experience, makes it more
meaningful, and, incidentally, reduces its costs.

The making of two simple looms will be described. A cardboard
loom may be constructed from a heavy piece of cardboard about
12″ x 16″ in size. The two 12″ ends should be notched about every
one-quarter inch so that the warp threads may be strung the length of the
cardboard and under the notches. After the vertical warp threads have
been strung, the weft or horizontal threads may be added. The weft yarn
may be wound around a tongue depressor, or wooden ice cream stick,
which will serve as a shuttle. On this simple loom a beautiful tapestry
may be woven.

A wood frame loom also is easily constructed from ¾″ x 1⅜″
pine. The two shorter strips comprising the top and bottom of the loom
are 12″ long and the two longer side strips 14″ long. All four strips are

sanded and then the two end strips are placed on *top* of the side strips and nailed securely at each of the four corner joints.

Mark off dots at one-half-inch intervals down the center of the two end strips. Drive one-inch finishing nails halfway into the wood in the center of each dot. Slant the nails outward so the warp threads will not slip off. The loom is now ready to be warped. For young children who have not had previous weaving experience, a space of one inch between threads is desirable at first. This should soon be reduced to one-half inch.

TECHNIQUE OF WEAVING. Among the numerous articles which one can weave are belts, mats, tapestries, pot holders, samplers, napkins, bags, coin purses, pillow tops, scarfs, ties, and small rag rugs. The materials used in weaving are determined by the nature of the article being woven. For example, heavy wool strips of cloth, colored cotton goods, and muslin can be used for rugs; yarns and lengths of old stockings for table mats, purses, and rugs; and desirable cords or strips of plastic material for belts. Since warp is subjected to more wear during the weaving process than is weft, it should consist of material which will not break easily. Cotton, wool, and linen threads are most satisfactory with nylon, silk, chenille, hemp and binders' twine also used. The standard filler materials, or weft, are linen and wool, but cotton rug-roving, cloth strips, bamboo sticks, flower stems, dried lily leaves, wheat, corn, and oat straw, pine needles, cattails, barks, and grasses are also used.

The leader should remember that an activity which is too easy lacks challenge and interest, while one which is too difficult is equally unattractive because it fails to meet man's basic need for self-enhancement. An individual can't feel able and successful in an activity so difficult that he experiences nothing but failure. Weaving ranges in difficulty all the way from the simple, rudimentary ins and outs of paper weaving by young children to the highly technical aspects of the craft involving color, design, and many other problems encountered in creating such dramatic tapestries as the present-day Navajo Indian Rugs made in our own country.

Paper is an excellent material with which to teach young children to weave. They can make their own mats by folding the paper in the middle across the short way and cutting with scissors from the fold to within an inch of the two open ends. The mat becomes the loom and the cut strips are the warp. If a paper cutter is available, the leader should cut the weft strips for young children and permit them to select their own colors and widths from the variety of widths cut.

The leader then demonstrates for these youthful weavers. Choose two colors of paper, perhaps one light and one dark color. Using one slip of paper, show how the fingers lead the paper through the warp strips—over one and under one, over one and under one. When the entire strip has been threaded across the mat, or loom, push it down to one end of the mat as far as it will go. Be sure that an equal length of each weft strip extends beyond the mat on each side. Alternate colors of your weft strips. Also be sure that each time you start across the warp strips with a new weft strip you go *over* the strip you went *under* before, and *under* the strip you went *over* before.

Gibson points the way toward progression in paper weaving:[20]

(1) The mat may be cut with wide and narrow strips, or with rhythmic, sweeping curves. . . . (2) The individual weaving strips, which I suggest should usually have straight, parallel sides, may be cut with some wide, some narrow, some very wide, some very narrow, ranging from an ⅛″ to 2″ in width. (3) Ends of woven strips may be cut flush with mat or left as decorative fringe.

Paper weaving can serve as a logical introduction to other forms of weaving. When children first advance from paper to yarn, a heavy cotton rug yarn ¼″ thick is recommended. Purchase several colors, including black and white, and cut it into strips about four inches longer than the width of the loom, thus leaving two inches on each side of the loom. When the loom is completely filled up to the nails, lift the weaving off the loom, or, if this is not possible, cut it off. Cut the fringe evenly and stitch the edges flat on a sewing machine or by hand, or they may be bound with ribbon or bias tape. The ends of the warp can also be tied with slip knots pushed up close to the weaving provided they are long enough.

It is good leadership to teach older children to make a crayon drawing of any color pattern planned in advance of the actual weaving. A more uniform pattern may be secured by putting in a strip of colored weft at one end of the loom and repeating with the same color at the other end and continuing in this manner until the weaving is completed. If a design is to be woven into the center of the article, put this in first and weave the remainder of the article around this central design. Be sure to keep an even tension by avoiding too tight a pull on the weft as the weaving proceeds. Teach the children to experiment with a variety of weaves. They should vary the simple over and under weave with over two and under two and then reverse as they come back through the warp for a basket-weave effect. The weft color also may be varied to create stripes and the materials intermixed to secure varying textures.

---

[20] Ellery L. Gibson, "New Ins and Outs of Paper Weaving," *School Arts.* September 1962, p. 22.

A careful choice of yarns of harmonious colors and interesting textures followed by the overlapping and interlacing of threads in plain weave will result in artistic design effects of great beauty.

Modeling

The term *modeling* is used here in its broadest sense to include both modeling and sculpturing. We are concerned with the process of producing designs or sculptured forms with some type of plastic material. These forms are three-dimensional in nature in contrast with the two-dimensional characteristics of drawing and painting. It is precisely this three-dimensional quality of modeling which adds variety to the arts and crafts program, enriches it, stimulates the imaginations of children, and provides opportunities for many to succeed where previously, in the two-dimensional arts, they were frustrated and ineffective. As Mattil puts it, "The teacher may watch a child struggle indefinitely trying to draw a figure with legs crossed but who might immediately solve this problem when working in clay simply by lifting one leg and crossing it over the other."[21]

Many new and different materials may be used in modeling. Each is a new experience and a new challenge, calling for the participant to vary his approach and his mode of expression as the material with which he works changes. Among the three-dimensional materials used in modeling are clay, a salt ceramic, wire, toothpicks, soda straws, soap, paraffin, Zonolite-cement mixture, plaster, wood, Zonolite-newspaper pulp mixture, metal foils, papier-mâché, styrofoam, sawdust and wheat paste, and even spaghetti. Let us see how the leader functions in relation to a few of these materials.

CLAY. Two kinds of clay are used for the modeling program: (1) a non-hardening substance known as plasticene or plastilene; and (2) common earth clay. Each has its advantages and disadvantages. Plasticene is more difficult to work with, but it can be used over and over again as it does not harden. Where emphasis is on the process and the child, and where the individual forms no attachment for the product, the possibility of reusing the material numerous times has considerable economic significance. Common earth clay may be purchased in dry or moist form in amounts from 50 to 500 pounds. This dry clay flour may

---

[21] Mattil, *op. cit.,* p. 9.

be mixed with water in small amounts without removing it from the plastic bag. Let the clay age for a few days after being mixed before you use it. Keep it in an airtight crock or garbage can with a tight-fitting lid. Since earth clay always shrinks during the drying process, no type of armature may be used to strengthen any part of the figure under construction. Shrinking clay over non-shrinking framework results in the clay breaking into many pieces. This limits the group to modeling only squat, compact figures when using earth clay.

Mattil[22] recommends a salt ceramic as an excellent substitute for clay. If the playground or community center does not provide the equipment needed for its production, it can easily be made by the mothers in their homes. One cup of table salt, one-half cup of corn starch, and three-quarters cup of cold water are mixed in the top part of a double boiler. The heat is turned on, the stirring continues, and in two or three minutes it reaches the consistency of bread dough. At this point, place it on wax paper or aluminum foil and allow it to cool; then knead it for a few minutes. It is now ready for use. If desired, it may be stored for several days by wrapping in wax paper. Its many advantages are (1) it hardens to the consistency of stone; (2) it is easily painted; (3) it permits the use of any type of armature since it does not shrink when drying; (4) it has greater durability than unfired earth clay; and (5) it is clean.

There is no "right" way of clay modeling, especially with younger children. Some may construct the different parts of the body—head, arms, legs—separately and then attach them to the central portion of the body; others may prefer to start with a ball of clay and squeeze out the peripheral sections. Let them use whichever method they prefer. Under no circumstances should they copy a model made by the leader or anyone else, for then, what should be one of the most satisfying and creative of art experiences is reduced to the level of an imitative exercise of busywork, completely devoid of all creative value.

Probably very few recreation departments will be able to provide kiln for the firing of their clay models, but the objects made may be permitted to harden by drying in air. Unfired models may be painted with tempera or water color if some decoration is desired. Level the base of your models by rotating them on coarse sandpaper; then scratch the child's initial into the clay.

Erdt[23] describes the modeling of a thumb and finger bowl by children six to eight years of age using earth clay. A child takes a small

22 Ibid., p. 12.
23 Erdt, op. cit., pp. 245–246.

portion of clay and shapes it into a ball. The thumb and fingers are worked into the center of the ball hollowing it out and shaping the walls of the bowl. The walls are kept thick. Paint on a decoration with engobe while the clay is still moist. Engobe consists of color pigments added to clay that is mixed with water to the consistency of cream. Set the bowl aside to dry. When completely dry, rotate the base of the bowl on sandpaper and initial with the child's name.

Puppets

Puppetry is highly popular among children six to twelve years of age. Hand puppets are more suitable for younger children while older youngsters generally prefer string marionettes. Puppetry provides an admirable opportunity for the integration of drama and crafts with the children constructing their puppets and then manipulating them in their plays. Many different kinds of puppets can be constructed, from the simple paper bag puppet to the much more complicated papier-mâché type. Among the most common types of materials are the shoe box, light bulb, styrofoam, paper bag, potato, mitten, sock, papier-mâché, bean bag, sawdust paste, and milk carton.

The recreation leader should be fully competent to teach children how to construct a few of these different kinds of puppets in his arts and crafts program. Let's begin with one of the simplest—a paper-bag puppet. One of the advantages of small paper bags lies in the fact that their varied shapes, sizes, colors, and textures make them wonderfully suited to use as fist puppets. No matter what you do to them, it only enhances their textural effects. A squeezed surface becomes facial wrinkles; a rumpled midsection resembles a potbelly; and a distorted top is a perfect double chin. Twist off part of the bag for a head and you have a gnarled old witch. A very small candy bag forms a bulbous nose; an upcurling slip of black paper pasted under the nose provides a villainous-looking mustache; and steel wool, yarn, or raffia are perfect for hair.

Shoebox puppets also are easy to make and attractive when completed. The bottom of the box becomes the front of the puppet. Cut a two-inch hole in one end of the box through which the puppet's paper-bag neck will be thrust. Its head, arms, and legs also are made from brown paper bags. Stuff a five-pound bag half full of scrap paper, shape it into a ball, and put a rubber band around the neck. Form the feet or shoes by cutting a paper bag in two lengthwise and stapling the top of each half to the box. The other ends are the feet. Shape the hands and feet with scissors. Paint features on the head and add crepe paper, steel

wool, or yarn hair. A coat, vest, and tie may be drawn on the box with
crayon. Slip the neck through the neck hole, place the puppet on your
lap, grasp the paper-bag neck, and tip the head as you carry on a conversation with your creation.

Puppets made of discarded light bulbs and papier-mâché are inexpensive and intriguing. You will need a discarded bulb, wallpaper
paste, newspaper, and tempera paints. Tear the newspaper into strips
3½" x ½". Dip strips into paste and place on bulb. Continue until the
entire surface is covered by four thicknesses and then set the bulb aside
to dry. Break the bulb after the papier-mâché is thoroughly dry and carefully remove the broken glass and filament from the head. Make a paper
collar and paste it at base of neck to hold the puppet's garment. Wrap a
piece of cardboard about 3" wide around your forefinger and tie it
with string or use a rubber band to keep it from unrolling. Insert this
tube into neck of puppet and wedge it tightly in place with shredded
paper mixed with paste. After drying this will enable you to control
movements of the puppet's head.

Mitchell[24] tells how to construct papier-mâché puppets at the upper-
grade and junior high levels. Form a ball of crushed newspapers the size
of the puppet head and attach it to a cardboard cylinder by means of
paper strips and paste. Form a small wad of paper and fasten it on for
the nose. If you are making a rabbit or a clown, paste together several
layers of paper for the ears. Paste several layers of small, torn strips of
paper over the entire head and then cover with small pieces of paper
toweling in about the same manner as you would shingle a roof. Be sure to
cover all rough places. Small, twisted ropes of paper toweling can be
added for mouths and eyebrows. Also, one or more of these small ropes
should be fastened at the bottom of the neck cylinder to hold the puppet's
clothes on. The papier-mâché head becomes so hard that it is almost
impossible to fasten clothing to the head. Paint the head a skin color,
shellac after it is dry, and glue the yarn hair on. Use simple gathered
pieces of cloth for the clothes, leaving holes for the fingers so gestures may
be made.

Natural and Scrap Materials

Two excellent reasons exist for the use of natural and scrap materials: (1) they cost little or nothing; and (2) they not only enrich the

---

[24] Jean O. Mitchell, "Seven Kinds of Puppets," *School Arts,* March 1958, pp.
17–18.

program, but they involve the children in an exciting adventure centering around hunting, discovery, and heightened appreciation of the resources in their own environment.

Possibilities are almost limitless. A listing of scrap materials alone would be voluminous. To name just a few—discarded paper bags, scrap lumber from the lumber yard, odd pieces of metal and plastic, aluminum foil, old wire, newspapers, egg shells, used light bulbs, cork, glass, leather, buttons, tin cans, fabric scraps, and boxes of all kinds. Empty cardboard boxes and cartons are everywhere, waiting to be picked up and converted into whatever the child's imagination can conceive. We used discarded ice cream cartons by the hundreds in making Japanese lanterns to be carried in our annual lantern parade. Drug store owners were glad to get rid of them.

So extensive are the possibilities in the field of nature crafts that entire books have been written on the subject. Pods, seeds, galls, and acorns can be used in making earrings, pins, dangle bracelets, and curtain pulls. The horns of animals may be converted into buttons, pendants, rings, pins, napkin rings, and belt buckles. Large pine cones may be transformed into grass gardens by sprinkling grass seed and then dirt into the crevices, setting the cone upright in a saucer of water, and keeping it damp. Smaller cones may be sprayed with white or gold paint and used as decorations during holidays. A gold-sprayed cone, with a wide-spread paper tail and paper head, makes an excellent miniature turkey gobbler for Thanksgiving decorations.

Nuts sliced into thin discs and shellacked, varnished, or lacquered make attractive buttons and bracelets. Dried cattail leaves can be woven into mats, any short piece of branch will make a whistle, and leaves may be used in spatter printing and plaster casting.[25]

SPATTER PRINTING.   Spatter printing is a simple process, quick, inexpensive, and fascinating. It involves the spattering of small particles of paint onto paper on which has been placed a small, flat object such as a leaf, weed, grasses, or other native materials. More than one object may be used on a single piece of paper and the child should be encouraged to arrange his materials to form an attractive design. Additional supplies needed are a small amount of tempera paint, a discarded toothbrush, and a knife or a small piece of wire screening.

Place a small amount of paint on the toothbrush. Hold the wire screening about six inches above the paper and paint over it with the

---

[25] For an excellent summary of what to use, what to make, and how to make it, students are referred to: "Crafts with Natural Materials," *Recreation*, March 1959, p. 104.

brush. Small flecks of paint are thrown or spattered onto the paper as the brush snaps from wire to wire. Since the paint cannot touch the paper under the leaf or other object, a design is created of this object. After the paint dries, the child removes the object. If a screen is not available, a knife blade may be pulled across the top of the brush thus causing the bristles to spatter paint down on the paper.

Inadequate funds is no justification for a narrow, limited program of arts and crafts. The superior leader is ingenious, creative, resourceful, and imaginative. He accepts a lack of funds not as an excuse to do little or nothing, but rather as a challenge to utilize his unique qualities in providing for his people the best possible program of arts and crafts.

Selected References

Drama

Batchelder, Marjorie, *The Puppet Theatre Handbook* (New York: Harper and Brothers, 1947).

Baumol, William J. and Bowen, William G., *Performing Arts—The Economic Dilemma* (New York: The Twentieth Century Fund, 1966).

"Drama Is Recreation," *Recreation,* LV, No. 2, 1962, 75.

Durland, Frances Caldwell, *Creative Dramatics for Children* (Yellow Springs, Ohio: The Antioch Press, 1952).

Feiler, Jane A., "Let's Give a Puppet Show," *Arts and Activities,* 50, No. 2, 1961, 11.

Howard, Vernon, *Pantomimes, Charades, and Skits* (New York: Sterling Publishing Co., Inc., 1959).

Lease, Ruth and Siks, Geraldine Brain, *Creative Dramatics in Home, School, and Community* (New York: Harper and Brothers, 1952).

Siks, Geraldine Brain and Hazel Brain Dunnington, eds., *Children's Theatre* 1958).

———— and Dunnington, Hazel Brain, eds., *Children's Theatre and Creative Dramatics* (Seattle: University of Washington Press, 1961).

Ward, Winifred, *Drama with and for Children* (Washington, D.C.: U.S. Department of Health, Education, and Welfare, 1960).

————, *Playmaking with Children* (2nd ed.) (New York: Appleton-Century-Crofts, Inc., 1957).

Arts and Crafts

Amon, Martha Ruth and Rawson, Ruth Holtz, *Handcrafts Simplified* (Bloomington, Ill.: McKnight and McKnight Publishing Company, 1961).

Bale, R. O., *Creative Nature Crafts* (Minneapolis: Burgess Publishing Company, 1959).

Benson, Kenneth R., *Creative Crafts for Children* (Englewood Cliffs, N.J.: Prentice-Hall, Inc., 1958).

Erdt, Margaret Hamilton, *Teaching Art in the Elementary School* (rev. ed.) (New York: Holt, Rinehart and Winston, Inc., 1962).

Hoover, F. Louis, *Art Activities for the Very Young* (Worcester, Mass.: Davis Publications, Inc., 1961).

Mattil, Edward L., *Meaning in Crafts* (Englewood Cliffs, N.J.: Prentice-Hall, Inc., 1959).

Reed, Carl and Orze, Joseph, *Art from Scrap* (Worcester, Mass.: Davis Publications, Inc., 1960).

Roukes, Nicholas, *Classroom Craft Manual* (San Francisco: Fearon Publishers, 1960).

Wankelman, Willard, Richards, Karl, and Wigg, Marietta, *Arts and Crafts for Elementary Teachers* (Dubuque: William C. Brown Company, 1954).

Two magazines, each published monthly except July and August, carry excellent articles on all kinds of arts and crafts. They will be of great assistance to leaders seeking to improve themselves in this area of recreation. The magazines are:

Arts and Activities, published by the Jones Publishing Company, 8150 N. Central Park Avenue, Skokie, Illinois, 60076.

School Arts, published by Davis Publications, Inc., Printers Building, Worcester, Massachusetts, 01608.

Chapter XI

Leadership for Senior Citizens

RECREATION LEADERS SHOULD not forget that there is a crisis of maturity which is as real and as normal as the "storms" of adolescence. In fact, the elderly and teenagers share many of the same problems of alienation and isolation and the same needs to establish and maintain values, dignity and meanings in life.

All too often, aging brings a lowering of self-esteem against which many an old person fights like the devil with every mental and intellectual resource he can muster at a time when, inevitably, there is a loss of vitality, vigor, looks and sexual potency. Quite naturally, an older person resents his loss of productivity and his dependency on others.

Cultural factors are at work, too. The old person of today lives in the midst of a go-go generation in which everyone is urged to think young rather than to think wise and youth is worshipped as a virtue. Small wonder that some older persons may become obsessed with a sense of being discarded; most of them do at one time or another, and a few to the point of acute depression and psychosis.

Few aspects of American life should more deeply disturb the student of recreation than the present roleless character of the aged. Here is one of the two most rapidly growing segments of our population; more than 18 million souls, over five times the number in 1900, with a predicted total of at least 32 million in the next forty years when it will exceed 10 percent of our population; an impressive record for half a century of contributing to the greatness of the nation; deeply sensitive men and women born into a work-oriented society and shaped by its system of values; human beings whose happiness depends in large measure upon satisfaction of the universal need to be needed, to be accepted, wanted, liked, and to play a useful role in society. Representing a vast wealth of experience accumulated over the years and the sound judgments that accompany it, this is the group to whom life is still precious, but, for whom life frequently lacks meaning, significance, vitality, and happiness because we not only fail to honor the aged in our society, but we deprive them of any definite place in the economic and social structure thus inducing social isolation, emotional and financial insecurity, and loss of status.

GOLDEN AGE—FACT OR FANCY?

The effectiveness of leaders who work with the aged will depend partially upon their intimate and detailed knowledge of this segment of our people.[1] The years beyond sixty-five are euphoniously referred to as the Golden Years, implying a kind of paradise on earth, a modern Valhalla in which all old people live out the twilight of their lives in a quiet sort of perennial happiness, enjoying all the things they have always wanted to do, but never had the time to do until now. It's a very pretty picture, but is it true?

For some people it probably is. The principle of individual differences applies to senior citizens as to all human beings and no doubt the retirement years do constitute a Golden Age to some people as they spend their leisure in a way that adds to the meaning and contributes to the fulfillment of life. These are the people who are free from the corrosive anxiety induced by financial insecurity; who have continued to be active and have maintained a keen interest in the world about them; whose health is good and social competence high; and whose emotional security is fortified by the maintenance of stable and intimate relationships that are regarded as good in themselves and not as inferior substitutes.

Such people are in the minority. Facts derived from a number of studies of the aging cast considerable doubt upon the unalloyed happiness supposedly characterizing this period of life and dull the halo which gives it the name of Golden Age. Let's take a look at the facts, not simply to dispel any illusions, but to enable us to understand better these senior

---

[1] Students are referred to pages 52–56 for a detailed list of characteristics of the aging and their implications to recreation leadership.

citizens so that we may be more effective as we work with them in our leadership role.

Statistics show that senior citizens are not at all healthy as a group, either mentally or physically. Thus, irregularity in attendance because of illness is a constant factor of significance in conducting their recreation programs. As the older person declines in vigor he tends to participate in less active and less competitive phases of recreation. The part played by hobbies in his life will depend upon whether or not he enjoyed strong hobby interests early in life, for how a man spent his leisure at thirty and forty is an important factor in determining how he spends it at age sixty-five.

The basic psychological needs of senior citizens are the same as for anyone at any age; to be wanted, accepted, liked; to experience a sense of usefulness, of importance, and the emotional security that accompanies perception of oneself as being able and adequate and the realization that others also perceive you in this way. A number of factors undermine the position of the aging in American society, some of which are inherent in the nature of the aging organism while others have their origins in the culture of a work-oriented society.

Declining physical abilities frequently are a source of dismay and emotional disturbance especially to the individual who had always experienced a considerable degree of ego satisfaction from this aspect of his life.

Loneliness is one of the most persistent and universal afflictions of the aging. Kuhlen describes a common tragedy:[2]

In old age with loss of spouse, friends, and associates through death, there is continued decline in companionship, but especially for women who are more likely to survive their husbands . . . The frequentcy of social isolation in old age, even in situations such as a well-run old people's home and a hospital ward where many others are *physically* present, is surprising. These losses in old age are especially serious because of the probable importance to good adjustment of being able to achieve a sense of significance, of worth, and of belongingness through relating to other individuals and groups.

Seventy-five percent of older people live with their own families in their own homes, 15 percent in their own homes either alone or with non-relatives, 4 percent live with non-relatives, but not in their own homes, 3 percent in institutions, and 3 percent in hotels and rooming houses. Barron points out:[3]

---

[2] Raymond G. Kuhlen, "Aging and Life-Adjustment," in *Handbook of Aging and the Individual,* James E. Birren, ed. (Chicago: The University of Chicago Press, 1959), pp. 857–858.

[3] Milton L. Barron, *The Aging American* (New York: Thomas Y. Crowell Company, 1961), p. 36.

The social isolation implied in many of the above domestic arrangements of the aged produces not only feelings of loneliness, bitterness, and a loss of meaning and purpose in life, but also suggests one of the important bases of financial hardship and insecurity in old age: the lack of family support.

Compounding still further the isolation of older people and its corollaries—a growing sense of uselessness, loneliness, loss of status, and bitterness—are such factors as the loss of a job, and work-friends, elimination of family responsibilities, and abandonment of membership in clubs and other organizations because of reduced income. Thus, the years ahead, particularly for the individual who is not prepared or educated for old age, frequently represents an uncharted and frightening vacuum characterized by a corrosive anxiety over the apparent meaninglessness of existence except as a marking of time until death. Life has shrunk to one dimension only—length—and the individual cut loose from the anchors of his life is thrown back on his own inner resources which often prove inadequate to the task.

Gerontologists are becoming increasingly convinced that the lack of social integration is a vital causative factor in mental disorders of the aging. About one third of all persons admitted to state mental hospitals for the first time are sixty years of age and over while the median age of all psychotic first admissions is approximately sixty-one years. It once was assumed that these mental disorders in old age were the inevitable result of a senescent organism. A number of recent studies, however, support the growing belief that the kinds of social relations experienced by the aged are a crucial factor in their mental health.

A study in England by Lewis and Goldschmidt sought to determine the common social causes of disorders necessitating the placing of aged persons in mental hospitals. They found that "failure to retain a place in the community, to be a member of a family, to have an appreciated share in the life of some household or working group has been common in patients studied."[4] Their conclusion was that the basic underlying sociogenic factor in disorders of mental health was a lack of social integration.

Lang, reporting on the income of all senior citizens, whether heads of families or not, states that, "In 1958, three out of five men and women over sixty-five received less than $1,000 in money income."[5] Thus, large numbers of our senior citizens are relegated to the financial sidelines for the opportunity in modern America to live a comfortable, secure, and well-rounded life on less than $1,000 a year is limited indeed!

[4] Aubrey J. Lewis and H. Goldschmidt, "Social Causes of Admissions to a Mental Hospital for the Aged," *Sociological Review*, July 1943, pp. 86-98.

[5] Gladys Engel Lang, ed., *Old Age in America* (New York: The H. W. Wilson Company, 1961), p. 10.

Contributing still further to the second-class citizenship status of the aged in our society is our general attitude toward old people. We honor youth, vigor, beauty, and work in America none of which is descriptive of the aged. We look upon old age as a disaster and old people as objects of pity. They occupy no clear-cut role as distinctive individuals who still count for something in the community. The United States is not the best country in which to grow old, as indicated by Barron's startling contrast between the role of the aging in Western civilization and in North Burma:[6]

. . . in many so-called "primitive" tribes, aging is much less a social problem than in the Western industrial world. Among the Palaung of North Burma, for instance, the aged receive great homage and live happy lives. No one dares step on the shadow of an older person for fear incalculable harm will come. Such an honor is it to be old that as soon as a Palaung girl marries she is eager to appear older than she actually is. The older a woman becomes, the greater the honor she can expect to receive.

The amount of money and energy expended by American women to create an illusion of a youth that no longer exists is a fair indication of how we look upon old age in this country.

LABORERS WITHOUT LABOR

Among the psychological forces or stresses that play a centrally important part in the lives of senior citizens, particularly men, are those which society imposes directly upon them by forcing them to retire from their jobs. Our American society places a high value on work or employment and denies in large measure any rewards or recognitions for those no longer active in the labor force. For more than three hundred years we have dedicated ourselves to an almost fanatical belief in the innate goodness and importance of work. The inevitable corollary to the worship of any concept is contempt for its opposite. A society dedicated to war will despise peace and if it values beauty it will detest ugliness. Although confronted by automation and other factors that are freeing us increasingly from the fetters of labor we still look upon total leisure not as a state of bliss, but as a kind of condemnation to a reduced role devoid of worth, dignity, meaning, respect, and status.

---

[6] Barron, *op. cit.*, p. 25.

Human beings in part are the products of their environment; they are shaped and fashioned by the ideas, ideals, attitudes, and other forces operating in their society. Thus, the senior citizen in this country must be seen as an individual who has been exposed for sixty-five years or longer to the influences of a work-oriented society in which leisure and recreation have been considered a waste of time. Released suddenly from work opportunities about which his value system revolves, and confronted by the necessity of "wasting" time in leisure activities, the psychological impact of the guilt feelings which result may be acute. Even where a sense of guilt may not exist the retired employee misses the routine of work, the sense of usefulness, of importance, and of individual worth. Josephine Lawrence perceives that work in our society has meaning beyond the making of a living as revealed by this passage:[7]

That was what Munsey Wills missed most—the sense of orderly procedure, the pattern for getting through a day . . . There was no substitute for work. It wasn't enough to feel oneself useful, at least not if one's life was small and unimportant. Then it became necessary to be thought useful by others, necessary to stand approved in other eyes. If you had a job, you had your self-respect —it was as simple, and as difficult, as that.

We can understand, therefore, why the senior citizen is reluctant to accept retirement, a fact that can be verified by several sets of statistics. For example, a recent survey of more than two million workers sixty-five years of age and over who were eligible for federal old age insurance benefits revealed that about 40 percent were not receiving these benefits. All but a few of these people had chosen to stay on the job or had returned to work after having experienced the disillusionment of retirement. Many, however, have no choice. They don't retire at sixty-five—they are kicked out. In 1960, about 60 percent of the male population over sixty-five and 90 percent of the female population over sixty-five were not in gainful employment. All indications point toward further expansion of the volume of unemployment for senior citizens. Wolfbein and Burgess show a decrease from 58.3 percent in 1930–31 to 41.4 percent in 1950–51 in our economically active male population sixty-five years and older, and conclude, "The...trend in all countries of Western culture shows a continuing decline in the proportion of the economically active of those above pensionable age. There is no evidence of the emergence of counteracting factors."[8]

[7] Josephine Lawrence, *The Web of Time* (New York: Harcourt, Brace and Company, 1953), pp. 227, 238.

[8] Seymour L. Wolfbein and Ernest W. Burgess, "Employment and Retirement," in *Aging in Western Societies*, Ernest W. Burgess, ed. (Chicago: The University of Chicago Press, 1960), p. 73.

Phair indicates that progress in our treatment of the aged has not proceeded very far beyond the level of primeval man.

OLD MEN*
In savage tribes where skulls are thick,
And primal passions rage,
They have a system, sure and quick,
To cure the blight of age.
For when a native's youth has fled,
And years have sapped his vim,
They simply knock him on the head,
And put an end to him.

But we, in this enlightened age,
Are built of nobler stuff.
And so we look with righteous rage
On deeds so harsh and rough.
For when a man grows old and gray,
And weak and short of breath,
We simply take his job away
And let him starve to death.
—George E. Phair

The evidence indicates that large numbers of our senior citizens constitute a society of laborers without labor in a nation that exalts work over leisure. The vital implications of this unique and tragic situation must be understood by the recreation leader if his work with the aged is to be effective. For no matter how much we may do for them through the provision of recreation activities, their major problem remains unsolved until our society discovers for them a significant role and accords to them the respect which they deserve, but do not at present receive.

GUIDELINES FOR LEADERS

Highly skilled leadership is basic to the successful conduct of a program of recreation for senior citizens. In general, the same fundamental principles and techniques of leadership that apply to all other groups prove equally effective with the aged. However, a leader may be successful with youth or young adults and be unsuccessful with this group since some specialized knowledge, skills, and techniques are essential.

*Tony Won's Scrapbook, Reilly and Lee Company, 1933.

A number of leaders who have had several years of experience with the aged agree that it requires more skill and ability to work with this age group than with any other. Many of the behavior problems with which the leader must contend have their origins in the lonely and unhappy roles forced upon the aged in our society. The leader who knows some of the most vital facts of gerontology and geriatrics, in addition to the information provided in the preceding sections of this chapter, will understand these old people and be extremely patient with them. He knows that their desire to follow a routine, their sensitivity to criticism, and their resentment of change stem chiefly from a deep-seated sense of insecurity. Relatively minor problems assume a significance out of proportion to their importance. The leader must have patience with their little quirks and peculiarities, understand their characteristics, needs, aspirations, and heartaches and bring to his assignment a deep compassion, sympathy, and humility. In addition, he must develop the capacity to understand their problems and the leadership skills to work with them effectively in the conduct of a broad program of recreation that will challenge their abilities, restore their sense of individual worth, build new friendships, and create a new happiness that will endure throughout the twilight of their lives.

Among the most important leadership suggestions or techniques applicable to senior citizens are the following:

1. Invite the participants to take an active part in planning and carrying out their own activities. The professional leader should not dominate these people.
2. Provide a broad and varied program for all senior citizens—all races, creeds, economic levels, and both sexes. Activities should be planned for those who are well and those who are sick; those who live in their own homes and those who live in institutions; and those who are retired and those who are working.
3. Create a friendly, congenial environment in which these people will feel secure, wanted, accepted, able, and liked. Treat them as responsible adults, however, rather than as children.
4. Take into consideration the unique limitations of old age and adjust your program accordingly.
5. Also take into consideration the individual's education, economic status, and recreational experiences and skills. The likes and dislikes of the participants are important factors in program development.
6. Do not permit the more aggressive members of the group to dominate the others.
7. Provide the type of physical facilities appropriate to the abilities of the group. For example, a meeting room on the third floor of a building without an elevator is wholly undesirable.

8. Impose no dues or assessments that might restrict membership.
9. Provide numerous opportunities for individuals to achieve recognition, self-esteem, and social approval.
10. Emphasize enjoyment, congenial companionship, fun, and happiness. A high degree of skill in the activities comprising the program is relatively unimportant.
11. Provide instruction whenever desirable in those activities in which the individuals lack sufficient skill to engage with any degree of satisfaction.
12. Allow no sudden changes in the program or procedures unless requested or approved by the members.
13. Invite and persuade members to participate, but put no pressure on them to do so.
14. Play no favorites, avoid controversial issues if possible, and do not be disturbed by complaints.
15. Encourage members to advance beyond the lowest level of programming—that of simply being entertained—to the higher levels which involve creative participation and the rendering of service to the group and then to the community.
16. Invest community service activities with significance, purpose, and a promise of satisfaction to the participants. For example, "needlework" is a vague and nebulous term, but "sewing for hospital patients" conveys a strong and immediate appeal. "Stuffing envelopes" implies a kind of busywork of little consequence whereas "preparing the campaign mail" for the Cancer Society involves the responsibilities and dignity of a worthwhile community service.
17. Provide some activities that extend over a considerable period of time, challenge the continued interest and devotion of the participant, possess long-term holding power, and serve psychologically as work substitutes. This is the kind of activity to which the individual can return again and again, as he formerly could to his work, and with which he can identify himself in an inherently satisfying manner.
18. Remember that their feelings of inferiority and inadequacy stem primarily from loss of status and the special disabilities of old age. Help them achieve what they need so deeply—affection, understanding, appreciation, security, and a sense of worth and usefulness.

INTERESTS AND ACTIVITIES

The development of a program of recreation for senior citizens will be affected by the same general forces, influences, and principles that shape a program for any age level. Major differences between a program of recreation for senior citizens and a program for adolescent youth will be reflected not so much in the types of activities as in the preferences expressed within these types, preferences influenced largely by factors related to age. For example, both groups like music, but they prefer different songs; both will take part in games, but shuffleboard will be more popular among the aged than among youth. We are primarily concerned at this point with the task of identifying these unique interests and leisure activities that appear to possess the greatest possibilities for enriching the lives of senior citizens.

Social Activities and Special Events

The most popular leisure activities in which senior citizens participate are those of a social nature in which emphasis is placed on friendliness, fun, sociability, companionship, and belonging. Informality is preferred to over-organization as it encourages relaxation, provides a leisurely tempo, and assists the individual to forget his worries and anxieties. A minimum of competition builds for group solidarity and morale. The aged enjoy the opportunity just to sit around, relax, and talk. Planned activities or weekly meetings are important to them, but should not be permitted to constitute a major part of the total program. This indicates the need for facilities of a "drop-in" nature. In addition to the more extensive and highly organized facilities utilized by Golden Age Clubs, which include both men and women, "drop-in" centers for older men only have proved extremely valuable. Milwaukee has opened a number of these centers in their playground field houses from 9:30 A.M. to 3:00 P.M. daily except Saturday and Sunday, provided leadership for them, and sponsored such activities as card playing, horseshoe pitching, croquet, and bowling. They are called "XYZ" Clubs for men only; the "X" stands for extra, the "Y" for years, and the "Z" for zest.

More than 120 municipal playgrounds and parks in Los Angeles are provided with recreation clubhouses where, in many instances, special facilities for the enjoyment of senior citizens are located. Among these special facilities are bowling greens, tables for card games, horseshoe, shuffleboard, roque, and boccie courts.

The oldsters love to play cards, especially euchre, 500, whist, cribbage, sheepshead, canasta, and rummy. Some cities conduct city-wide tournaments in several of these games. They enjoy playing for small prizes generally purchased from a fund created by assessing each player not more than 25 cents for each evening's play. The leader should not permit any fee to become so large that it restricts participation, nor should prizes become so costly as to mar the sociability of the event.

Parties of all kinds are extremely popular. These people especially love the monthly party honoring the members whose birthdays occur during this particular month; the special wedding anniversary dates of members such as the Silver and Golden Wedding Anniversaries; and special days such as Mother's Day, Father's Day, Halloween, Valentine's Day and various state and national holidays. Since they like to eat together, a potluck supper or some other form of providing refreshments usually is a feature of their parties. At their birthday parties, the honored guests sit at the head table, are serenaded with appropriate songs, blow out candles on the birthday cakes, have their pictures taken, and enjoy the special entertainment that follows the dinner. At times rather elaborate candle-lighting ceremonies add to the dignity of the occasion. An event of this nature has considerable news value and may provide the central theme for a news story, with pictures, in the local press.

At all times the leader must keep in mind that some individuals will feel shy, uneasy, and socially incompetent. They will want to take part in the program, but lack the confidence to do so. They have seen themselves as unable and unaccepted all their lives. They may be helped by a leader who is friendly, relaxed, avoids giving rapid directions necessitating quick decisions, responses, and judgments, and who so conducts an activity as to enable the most inept person to enjoy immediate success.

Travel movies, colored pictures, some comedy, and an occasional educational film seem to be most popular with the aged. Among the sources of such films are air, bus, and train lines and other commercial and industrial concerns. Outside speakers and entertainers may contribute to the program provided what they have to offer is related to the needs and interests of the audience. The senior citizen will not fake an interest in something that bores him and he is quite likely to let the speaker know he is bored. The leader, therefore, who plans a lecture series should be guided by the principle of involvement and select only those topics and speakers agreed upon by a program committee comprised of older people. The Department of Municipal Recreation and Adult Education in Milwaukee sponsors lectures to meet expressed interests. Among the subjects recently discussed were:

> Design for Living in the Golden Years
> The Senior Citizen Takes Stock
> Don't Be Afraid to Grow Old
> Food and Nutrition
> Security in the Later Years

Fitness after Sixty
Three-Generation Family
Forum on Aging

Speakers included nutritionists, doctors, psychiatrists, and medical specialists. The experience of Milwaukee also indicates that "Armchair Travel" is a popular activity among senior citizens. People whose hobby is traveling and who take pleasure in sharing their films and colored slides with others often present fascinating travel talks.

A special event known as Recognition Week is a high point of interest to senior citizens in Milwaukee. A week in May is set aside during which the city honors its senior citizens. Special programs are held in the various Golden Age Clubs honoring all members eighty years and older. Charters are presented to those groups in existence for a period of five years.[9]

Bulletins or newspapers, containing a variety of news items about the members, human interest stories, letters, and original songs and poems are issued at regular intervals. The bulletin provides both a means of communication among the members and a form of recognition. They love to see their names in print and the leader, understanding their need for status, prestige, and recognition, will utilize the bulletin, partially at least, for this purpose.

Music

The senior citizens like music, but it must be music with which they are familiar. There is no artificiality about them; they will not pretend to like something they don't like just for the sake of being considered "cultured." Group singing of the old songs is always popular and many of their home talent programs center around the music theme. Leaders should discover the favorite songs of the members, mimeograph them, distribute them to all who are interested, and then use this list as a basis for developing a program of informal group singing that emphasizes social values, friendships, and creation of a feeling of group solidarity.

Among the favorites compiled by the senior citizens in one city are:

"Long, Long Ago"   "When You Wore A Tulip"
"The More We Get Together"   "Old Mill Stream"
"While Strolling Through the Park   "In the Good Old Summertime"
    One Day"   "Santa Lucia"

---

[9] *Golden Age Clubs, A Handbook of Information.* Milwaukee: Department of Municipal Recreation and Adult Education, Milwaukee Public Schools.

"By the Light of the Silvery Moon"   "Home on the Range"
"Dinah"   "Whistle While You Work"
"I Want A Girl"   "Long, Long Trail"
"Auld Lang Syne"   "When Irish Eyes Are Smiling"
"She'll Be Comin' Round the   "Moonlight Bay"
    Mountain When She Comes"   "When It's Springtime in the Rockies"
"Smiles"   "'Til We Meet Again"
"Peggy O'Neil"   "Let's All Sing Like the Birdies Sing"
"Daisy Bell"

One important function of the leader is to discover those individuals who possess musical talent and encourage them to use it in entertaining their own club members as well as other senior citizens who may be shut-ins. The leader should keep a file of those who have either vocal or instrumental talents. In the area of instrumental music there may not be enough musicians to form orchestras or large band units within a single Golden Age Club, but small social or square dance bands may be formed to provide the music for their own functions.

In Milwaukee, the All-City Chorus, composed of members from the Golden Age Clubs, meets once a week just for the joy of singing together and to prepare programs for public presentation from time to time. The climax of each year is the "Gay Nineties Show" which includes variety and stunt acts as well as music. This production draws capacity houses at each presentation.

Many cities make it possible for senior citizens to enjoy at reduced rates concerts sponsored both by professional musical organizations and by the municipal recreation department. Many gift tickets also are made available.

Dance

Most senior citizens enjoy greatly their old time dances although a few do not know how to dance. For these, and others who wish to improve, the leader should provide instruction in dancing. Care should be taken to exclude spectators as these older people are quite sensitive about their lack of skill.

The waltz, schottische, two-step, and other old ballroom dances are popular, as is square dancing. Some square dances are too strenuous and too complicated for this group and should be avoided. The music must not be too fast. Williams[10] suggests the following squares for senior citizens:

---

[10] Arthur Williams, *Recreation in the Senior Years* (New York: Association Press, 1962), p. 76.

Virginia Reel   Forward and Back
Quadrilles   Lady Round the Lady and Gent Solo
Hinky-Dinky, Parlee-Voo   Promenade the Outside Ring
Oh, Susanna   Take a Little Peek
Life on the Ocean Wave   Old Gray Bonnet
Around That Couple and Swing at   The Wheat
    the Wall   Anicka
Darling Nelly Gray

Techniques of successful leadership include: (1) being alert for signs of fatigue; (2) in teaching a new dance use a set of more highly skilled volunteers to learn the dance and then distribute the couples among other sets as assistant teachers and demonstrators; and (3) where women predominate, as they generally do, let those who take the part of men wear paper hats.

Arts and Crafts

Among the most important factors a leader must take into consideration when working with senior citizens in arts and crafts are:

1. Physical deficiencies of old people, such as impaired vision, declining vigor, and slowed reaction time indicate the desirability of avoiding crafts of a fine or intricate nature that may strain the eyes, tax the strength, or demand rapid or highly coordinated movements.
2. Arts and crafts provide a rich opportunity for creative self-expression, a basic need throughout life.
3. Many older adults lack skills in this area of recreation and since they are not highly disposed to engage in activities with which they have had no previous experience, leaders must give them special encouragement and assistance if the spark of creativity is to be rekindled.
4. The activities must be purposeful and significant to the older individual and avoid any implications of being mere "busywork."
5. The financial limitations of older people indicate the desirability of using some free or inexpensive materials, at least in the initial stages of the program.
6. Grouping, as a means of facilitating participation, should be on the basis of skills.
7. Special facilities for arts and crafts should be provided whenever possible.[11]

A number of cities conducting extensive programs for senior citizens report that arts and crafts groups have particular appeal to women probably because many of them are already skilled in such home crafts as

---

[11] Students are referred to pages 295–297 for a detailed discussion of the values of the program of arts and crafts.

knitting, sewing, cookery, and weaving. Long Beach reports that their crafts media range from pine needle basketry to handiwork with copper and rock mosaic. Classes meet at twelve recreation centers throughout the city. The Milwaukee program emphasizes sewing, wood-working, drawing, lettering, knitting, crocheting, toy making, and furniture repairing.

Other activities popular among senior citizens include weaving, leathercraft, metalcraft, plastics, quilting, pottery, painting, papercraft, textile printing, and candle making. In every instance, the program should be based on the needs and interests of the participants.

Drama

The part played by drama in the lives of older persons must be considered from two points of view—that of the active participant and that of the spectator or member of the audience. Its values range from casual entertainment to creative satisfaction and individual fulfillment. Drama in the total program of recreation for the aged generally will assume a position of lesser importance in terms of numbers interested and time devoted to it than will such types of activities as music and social recreation, but the ardor of its devotees will be unmatched.

Simple pantomimes, charades, skits, dramatic stunts, and dramatizations are popular. The individual who possesses some dramatic ability and is willing to use it in entertaining others is always in demand and contributes not only to enriching the leisure hours of his friends, but greatly enhances his own sense of personal worth. Drama can be integrated with other activities, such as birthday parties and certain types of special events, thus contributing still further to the impressiveness of these ceremonies. The annual "Gay Nineties Show" produced by the Golden Agers in Milwaukee combines drama and music into a fascinating production attracting many thousands of people.

Typical of the special steps taken by various cities to make it possible for senior citizens to enjoy various dramatic productions are the efforts in Milwaukee where several downtown theaters have promoted special matinee performances of a number of outstanding productions and invited senior citizens for a nominal fee. On occasion, bus trips are made to nearby cities so the aged may attend stage presentations of "The Music Man," "My Fair Lady," and similar productions, also at special prices. Two downtown theaters sponsor a Golden Age Movie Club permitting adults sixty years of age and over to obtain without charge a membership card that entitles them to see, at any time, the featured attraction at either theater upon presentation of their card and payment of a fifty-cent fee.

Sports and Games

Many different kinds of recreational games are popular. Men who hesitate to venture into creative activities frequently make their entrance into post-retirement recreation through participation in such games as shuffleboard, lawn bowling, horseshoe pitching, croquet, roque, quoits, billiards, pool, darts, chess, checkers, and giant checkers. Dominoes and bingo for inexpensive prizes, which often include free tickets to concerts, movies, and radio or television shows, attract large numbers. Bathing, swimming, walking and even bicycle riding have their devotees.

In Long Beach, California, as in most of the senior centers throughout Florida, interest in shuffleboard reigns supreme, partially because the game appeals to the women as well as to the men. Approximately 800 senior citizens participate regularly at thirty-six courts divided among four locations in Long Beach. Shuffleboard tournaments lie at the heart of the program of all senior citizens' clubs in Florida. The All States Friendship Club of Coral Gables, Florida, not ony conducts numerous tournaments among its members, but operates many invitational meets involving players from cities as far as 200 miles away. Anyone who questions the competitive spirit and the playing skill of the aged have only to observe the rabid shuffleboard fan in action, particularly the Florida variety.

Leaders, of course, should remember that activities must not be too vigorous or the aged will not participate. It is in shuffleboard and games of a similar nature, in which emphasis is placed on skill and finesse rather than on strength, speed, or endurance, that the older person re-establishes his faith in himself. There is considerable ego support in the discovery by a seventy-year-old that he can defeat a man forty years younger than he.

Camping and Outdoor Recreation

Senior citizens love to travel, explore new places, see new sights, and enjoy the especially close comradeship that characterizes these trips. Care must be exercised in the selection of sight-seeing routes, destinations, and in keeping costs at a minimum as members must pay their own expenses. Golden Agers in Milwaukee visit such major points of interest as the Wisconsin Dells, the observatory at Lake Geneva, the lace mills at New Glarus, and the airport at General Mitchell Field. They sing to their heart's content while the bus rolls along, browse around in quaint little gift shops, and relax over their inexpensive meals in pleasant and attractive surroundings. Trip days are always looked forward to with keen anticipation and reflected upon long afterwards with happy memories.

Trips for senior citizens have become one of the most attractive activities on their program in Long Beach. In its initial stages this activity included fewer than 100 persons making but one local trip a month. Now, almost 2,000 club members schedule an average of one trip each week and venture as far afield as Hawaii, Mexico City, and the Canadian Rockies. The attitude of those who participate in these trips is best summed up in the words of one member: "To one who no longer drives, who has a limited income, who is not always aware of nearby attractions, and who is most apprehensive about venturing any distance alone, these 'Golden Tours' which we share have been, and are, a genuine blessing."

Picnics also are popular as they bring into the lives of the aged an element of variety and change that add zest to life. The leader must not make the mistake of believing that because of their relative simplicity picnics require little or no planning. No activity involving the transportation, feeding, and recreation of a number of people operates automatically. In planning for a picnic, the necessary committees should be established. An overall planning committee will be supplemented by such other committees as site, transportation, food, publicity, and program. The picnic site should not be so far away as to be expensive, exhausting, or too time-consuming to reach. It should provide adequate shelter in case of inclement weather, cooking facilities, a sufficient number of picnic tables and benches, restrooms, shade, parking, and the level area needed for the planned program. A first-aid kit should be available at all times and the leader be skilled in its use.

Camping for senior citizens is in the pioneering stage at the present time. A number of cities are enthusiastic over its possibilities and are experimenting with it, but because of inadequate camp facilities and certain other factors only limited programs have been offered to date. The extent to which senior citizens are interested in camping is revealed by a study in Atlanta, Georgia, which showed that 14.4 percent of the total number of respondents who could get about without help would avail themselves of a camping service, if offered. Thus, approximately 8,076 aged persons in metropolitan Atlanta wanted to go to camp, but less than 1 percent of the camping service needed for senior citizens was being met by the community at the time of this study.[12]

The Atlanta Parks and Recreation Department conducts a week-long camping program for approximately fifty senior citizens each year. The cost to each camper is $16.00.

In Milwaukee, through the coöperation of the United Community Service, the Salvation Army, and the Department of Recreation, a num-

[12] Senior Citizens Leisure Time Subcommittee, *Senior Citizens Committee Report* (Atlanta: Metropolitan Atlanta Communty Services, Inc., 1959), p. 7.

ber of Golden Agers have been able to spend a happy week at the Salvation Army Camp. The ages of those who attend range from sixty to ninety-one years. The old people enjoy a variety of activities—fishing, boating, swimming, horseshoes and other games; talent shows in the evening, and singing under the stars.

In an effort to extend camping opportunities to a larger number of older persons, leaders frequently have found it necessary to defray part of the costs through community groups. However, they should prevent the stigma of social welfare from enveloping the camp project.

Hobbies

Hobbies, unlike music, sports and games, and arts and crafts, do not constitute a specific type of leisure activity. On the other hand, every category of leisure interest may yield a rich harvest of hobbies. The variety of hobbies pursued by human beings is almost unlimited. There are approximately 25,000 button collectors alone in this country and more than 15 million stamp collectors, probably the most popular hobby of all.

The majority of older people who pursue meaningful hobbies began cultivating them early in life. Birren points out that, "... it is interesting to note that hobby activities decline consistently from late adolescence through middle adulthood. Only after age fifty do hobby activities seem to increase until a person reaches the early seventies. Thereafter, as could be expected with the diminution of sensory functions, they decrease again."[13]

This revitalization of interest among the aged in hobbies, previously enjoyed years ago, indicates that leaders should encourage this interest in every way possible. Milwaukee operates two hobby workshops in different parts of the city where senior citizens, in addition to enjoying the creative satisfaction of making things, also take pride in displaying the finished product at community exhibits and hobby shows. An all-city Golden Age Hobby Show is conducted every other year by the recreation department and features crocheting, embroidery, knitting, sewing, weaving, woodworking, leathercraft, dolls, collections, and antiques. Ages of entrants range from sixty to ninety-three years. A center area is devoted to live demonstrations where hobbyists are seen practicing their hobbies. The daily newspapers and weeklies coöperate by featuring the event and two of the larger department stores provide window display space for exhibits throughout the week prior to the show. Participation certificates are awarded to all who take part in the show, but the element of competition is eliminated entirely.

---

[13] Birren, *op. cit.,* p. 321.

Community Service

Every normal human being, and the senior citizen is no exception, is motivated strongly by the need for self-enhancement. He needs to feel important, and a sense of worth, prestige, and status in a work-oriented society is attained most effectively through work that is recognized as being of value to society. The right to continue to work at paid employment is denied many of the aged because of forced retirement policies. Two vital reasons exist which make it imperative that ways be found by which the older person, who considers himself no longer important or of use to anyone, can meet this need: (1) because the satisfaction of this basic human need is essential to his own personal welfare and happiness; and (2) because society cannot afford to waste the vast resources represented by the tremendous pool of skills, experiences, and judgments inherent in the manpower of our senior citizens. This point of view is expressed by Dr. Joy Elmer Morgan, President of Senior Citizens of America:[14]

There is immense unused talent among persons who have been forced to retire in their 60's which should be directed to the service of the community.

Think what it would mean if each older person would make himself master of one community problem and without thought of pay, give himself to working toward its solution.

A first step toward giving of oneself in services truly community-wide in nature is the accomplishment of simple tasks within one's own senior citizens' group, the completion of which advances the welfare of the group. One learns to walk before he runs. The degree to which the members are involved in contributing their best efforts toward enriching the life of the group is both a measure of the strength of the group and its significance to the individual. The democratic leader seeks to make himself increasingly unnecessary and he succeeds only as the members achieve a high degree of self-direction. Some of the responsibilities the members can assume include:

Welcoming and greeting regular and new members
Preparing and serving refreshments
Keeping attendance records
Washing dishes and cleaning up
Recording all money contributions and disbursements

---

[14] *Rocky Mountain News,* July 8, 1962, Denver, Colorado, p. 10.

Serving on various club committees
Producing, folding, addressing, and mailing the club bulletin
Planning special programs
Helping with decorations
Addressing envelopes for birthday and illness cards
Serving as ushers or hostesses
Visiting sick members

Milwaukee reports that "Even the shyest person will be encouraged if he or she has something definite to do," and "When the club members find something to do in the group which brings them recognition, they have a tendency to cling to their responsibilities."

When the senior citizen goes beyond the confines of his own group, his opportunities for community service are extended immeasurably. Among the significant contributions which senior citizens frequently make to their communities are the following:

Reading to the blind
Visiting the sick
Surveying the recreational needs of the community
Participating in the Friendly Visitors Program, the Community Chest, the Anti-Tuberculosis Association (filing X-Ray Charts), mailing envelopes for the Easter Seal Society, and assisting the Red Cross
Collecting and repairing clothing
Sending CARE packages
Making tray favors for hospitals
Repairing children's books and toys
Staffing information booths
Serving as traffic-crossing guards
Assisting in the city library
Making gifts for orphans or needy children
Providing entertainment to institutional groups
"Adopting" certain children in a children's home and sending them cards and gifts
Delivering hot chocolate, cookies, and doughnuts to volunteer workers in a city beautification program
Serving as nurses' aides in a hospital program
Serving for the Crippled Children's Easter Seal Camp

The aged are beginning to discover that one way of rendering some socially useful service and achieving status in the community is through united political action. As they increase in numbers and become more dissatisfied with their lot, there is every reason to anticipate that they will seek relief through the ballot box. Oakland, California, reports that persons fifty and older constituted 37.5 percent of their population of voting age in 1960 and predicts it will reach 42.2 percent by 1980. At least two national organizations of senior citizens already have begun to mobilize nationwide pressure on Congress to enact programs favorable to them.

The aged have as much right as any other segment of our population to function actively as a part of our political society. However, we must recognize that people generally become more apathetic, conservative, and hostile to change and new ideas as they grow older. Our nation cannot afford a new and disruptive minority, bitter, frustrated, in love with the past and afraid of the present and the future. Wilensky describes the danger:[15]

> The common picture of the aged as apathetic and conservative may be accurate. But as with the apathetic everywhere, they stay on the sidelines of community controversy only until something triggers them off. In Northampton, Massachusetts, normally apathetic older people (who were also less educated and more science resistant) were easily mobilized to defeat a fluoridation plan . . . . Their free-floating aggressions can be turned against everything from new residents to suspect library books, from school-bond issues to fluoridation of the water . . . . The aged must be seen as a peculiarly potent pool of extremism; apathy and activism may, in the end, be blood brothers.

A vital goal of the recreation leader who works with the aged, therefore, must be to help them remain alert, progressive, and active participants in the broader aspects of our community, state, and national life.

THE GOLDEN AGE CLUB

One of the fastest growing phases of recreation in America today is the senior citizen program. In a survey of over 1,000 programs for senior citizens, it was found that 218 were centers and 803 were clubs.[16] Most of the centers were open at least five days a week and nineteen were open seven days a week.

Throughout the nation the most popular plan of organization for the conduct of recreation for the aged is the senior citizen or Golden Age

---

[15] Harold L. Wilensky, "Life Cycle, Work Situation, and Participation in Formal Associations," in *Aging and Leisure*, Robert W. Kleemeier, ed. (New York: Oxford University Press, 1961), p. 239.

[16] Jean Maxwell, *Center Project, Report No. 15* (New York: National Committee on Aging.)

Club. In Milwaukee there are forty Golden Age Clubs, involving 3,000 members, sponsored by the recreation department with about ten others in the suburbs and private agencies. The Atlanta Department of Parks and Recreation sponsors nineteen Golden Age Clubs with 975 members. The Senior Citizen Association of Los Angeles County estimates that in Los Angeles the 180 senior citizen clubs have a total membership in excess of 23,000, or nearly one-sixth of the total population over sixty years of age.

In most cities, the club is a simple organization, inviting to membership all men and women who meet the age requirement which differs from city to city. The minimum age limit in Milwaukee is sixty; in Atlanta and Pasadena, fifty; in Coral Gables, Florida, it is forty. The membership fee also varies widely. There is no charge for membership in Milwaukee; policies differ from club to club in Atlanta—those charging a fee range from ten cents to twenty-five cents a month; annual dues are $2.00 in the Pasadena Senior Center; Coral Gables residents pay $7.00 a year and non-residents an additional $10.00 per family. Milwaukee issues a membership card for identification purposes. An attractive club pin is available for a nominal fee. A member may belong to one club only.

Most clubs have a professionally prepared leader who carries the greater share of responsibility for organization and program, but his work is gradually lessened as the group adopts a simple constitution, elects officers, and appoints committees that grow in ability to plan and direct their own activities. The club is the organizational instrument through which the activities and purposes previously discussed in this chapter are conducted and realized.

The Atlanta clubs meet twice a month; the Milwaukee, weekly. Where a special building or center exists exclusively for use by the aged they may drop in almost any time of day. The Pasadena Senior Center is open daily throughout the week from 9:00–5:00 and on weekends from 12:00–5:00. A typical meeting consists of informal visiting, group singing, introduction of guests, announcement of birthdays, and presentation of new members. Committee reports are given, followed by special announcements, reading of correspondence, and new business. After the business session, a social hour usually follows consisting of cards or other games; a special program involving music, drama, movies; or a speaker is presented. Refreshments of coffee, cake, and ice cream generally conclude the evening. Members achieve a feeling of independence and self-sufficiency by placing their voluntary contributions in a box for this purpose.

A club's constitution should be kept as simple as possible. It usually consists of the following articles:

Article   I. Name.
Article   II. Object.
Article   III. Membership.
Article   IV. Management or officers.
              This article usually lists the personnel of the executive com-
              mittee and other committees.
Article   V. Meetings.
Article   VI. Quorum.
Article   VII. Amendments.

The by-laws present in greater detail data with respect to membership, dues, duties of officers and how they shall be elected, powers and
duties of the executive committee, meetings, order of business, amendments, standing committees, and guests. The standing committees in one
club include a card committee, a committee on dances, one on food,
publicity, and activities. In addition, the Sunshine Committee is responsible for sending cards to members who are ill and flowers for funerals.

The larger cities establish the administrative machinery for effecting
a high degree of coördination among the various clubs. The Milwaukee
All-City Council is composed of two representatives from each of the
Golden Age Clubs. This Council serves as a planning and steering committee for such all-city activities as picnics, bus trips, concerts, card
tournaments, hobby shows, and entertainments. The Council meets once
a month with the Director of the Golden Age Clubs and frequently several
club leaders.

Caught in the Backwash

The critics of Golden Age Clubs and their programs are not numerous, but they are articulate. Mulac advances to the attack:[17]

Golden age clubs and senior centers and such programs are admittedly aimed at
helping those caught in the backwash of progress. These are stopgap programs,
emerging measures, and relief aid to the victims. Until we find better methods
of alleviating the misery of time-surfeited, leisure-sick people, they are helpful.
We should not lose sight of the fact that they are, at best, relief programs.

She further criticizes the clubs because they segregate on the basis of
age, attract only the needy, arouse pity, and stimulate the "do-gooder and
maternal tendencies of certain types of leaders. As a result," she con-

---

[17] Margaret E. Mulac, *Leisure—Time for Living and Retirement* (New York:
Harper and Brothers, 1961), p. 28.

cludes, "the general picture of a golden age club is one of sadness and defeat to those on the outside."[18]

Barron supports Mulac when he charges:[19]

. . . they apparently have met the needs of only a small proportion of the aged, for many are not attracted to the golden age clubs and centers. Some are reluctant to join because of the "welfare" sponsorship of some of the clubs; others are too independent to want to be organized into clubs; and still others think the activities are too childish and otherwise meaningless for older people like themselves. And lastly, despite all the publicity about these clubs and centers, there are many aged who do not know about them and who have not been properly motivated to take advantage of them.

We have listed the above criticisms because we believe students of recreation leadership should be aware they exist. We shall make no attempt to answer these criticisms in detail because most of them have already been answered in this chapter. For example, to say that senior programs attract only the needy is hardly a valid criticism when we remember that 60 percent of the aged have an income of less than $1,000 a year. Nor should a club be condemned because it presents a picture of "sadness and defeat to those on the outside." Of far greater importance is how the members themselves see the club and the program. Typical of the reactions of many members of Golden Age Clubs are these from Milwaukee:

"Last year I lost my wife. I am now living with my son and his family. They try to be kind, but their friends are young and I am only in the way. In my Golden Age Club I take part in activities with folks my own age and am happy."

"There is never a dull moment at our club. Here we get a chance to meet new folks and be happy together."

"I look forward to the monthly birthday parties, with ice cream and cake. One of the happiest days of my life was when my club helped me celebrate my eighty-fifth birthday. I never really had a birthday before."

Perhaps the critics are not really criticizing the clubs as much as they are criticizing a society that so far has refused to recognize the total problem and attack it intelligently. Programs of recreation relieve the bitter loneliness of the aged, contribute to their health and happiness, provide defenses against boredom, involve them as contributors to the well-being of the community and the nation, and add to their self-respect and personal dignity. They do not, cannot, and never were intended to provide a substitute for work and the status role accompanying it. The time may

[18] *Ibid.*, p. 178.

[19] Barron, *op. cit.*, pp. 201–202.

come in America when the aged will have had so much practice in the leisure arts before retirement that leisure will not constitute the problem after retirement which it now presents. But this time has not yet arrived. We still live in a work-oriented society and have not yet discovered the secret of extracting from our leisure activities the satisfactions formerly found in our work. The problem of retirement will be solved when this secret is discovered, but until this time arrives the best minds of the nation should address themselves to the vital task of finding for the aged a significant role in our society.

Selected References

Baley, James A., "Recreation and the Aging Process," *The Research Quarterly*, 26, No. 1, 1955, 1.

Barron, Milton L., *The Aging American* (New York: Thomas Y. Crowell Company, 1961).

Birren, James E., ed., *Handbook of Aging and the Individual* (Chicago: The University of Chicago Press, 1959).

Bortz, Edward, *Creative Aging* (New York: Macmillan, 1963).

Burgess, Ernest W., ed., *Aging in Western Societies* (Chicago: The University of Chicago Press, 1960).

Donahue and others, eds., *Free Time—Challenge to Later Maturity* (Ann Arbor: The University of Michigan Press, 1958).

Kleemeier, Robert W., ed., *Aging and Leisure* (New York: Oxford University Press, 1961).

Lang, Gladys Engel, ed., *Old Age in America* (New York: The H. W. Wilson Company, 1961).

Mulac, Margaret E., *Leisure—Time for Living and Retirement* (New York: Harper and Brothers, 1961).

The Nation and Its Older People—Report of the White House Conference on Aging (Washington, D.C.; U.S. Department of Health, Education, and Welfare, 1961).

National Council on the Aging, *Centers for Older People* (New York: The National Council on the Aging, 1962).

Phelps, William Neal, "Our Senior Citizens," *The Journal of Educational Sociology*, 31, No. 2, 1957, 117.

Tibbitts, Clark, ed., *Handbook of Social Gerontology* (Chicago: The University of Chicago Press, 1960).

Tibbitts, Clark and Donahue, Wilma, eds., *Aging in Today's Society* (Englewood Cliffs, N.J.: Prentice-Hall, Inc., 1960).

Williams, Arthur, *Recreation in the Senior Years.* (New York: Association Press, 1962).

Woods, James H., "How to tell a Good Golden-Age Club," *Recreation,* 46, No. 9, 1953, 522.

Chapter XII

Leadership for the

Handicapped

PEOPLE DIFFER FROM each other in a variety of ways—physically, intellectually, socially, and emotionally. In most cases, such differences are of little significance. However, some differ so greatly that they have become known as a special group referred to as the "handicapped." One of the most widely-used definitions for a handicapped person is "one who cannot play, learn, work, or do the things other children of his age can do; or is hindered in achieving his full physical, mental and social potentialities; whether by a disability which is initially mild but potentially handicapping, or by a serious disability involving several areas of functions with the probability of life-long impairment."[1]

Recreation leaders are mostly concerned with two types of handicapped individuals: (1) persons who have a physical disability such as a crippling condition, deafness, or blindness; and (2) persons who have intellectual limitations and to whom we usually refer as mentally retarded.

INTERESTS AND ACTIVITIES

The changing attitude of the public toward handicapped persons is one of the most significant social trends of the second half of the

---

[1] *Conference Proceedings,* Golden Anniversary White House Conference on Children and Youth (Washington, D.C.: 1960), p. 381.

twentieth century. Indifference and rejection are giving way to collective concern and positive action.

Directors of recreation programs are changing their attitudes regarding their responsibility for serving these individuals. Because of this change in attitude, the recreation programs have extended the range of their provisions to include activities which meet the needs of the handicapped.

The handicapped individual or person is first a human being. But he is, notwithstanding, a person with differences. To meet the needs of the handicapped, recreation programs may have to provide transportation, a bus with a lift, buildings without stairs, ramps, and adaptations of many activities which in some cases might require extra leaders and personnel.

The handicapped have both the same needs as do their peers and some different needs pertinent to their particular handicap. The recreation program must help meet both needs in the effort to bring the handicapped to the maximum of their developmental potential, and to prepare them adequately for a full life as we do for normal persons.

The development of a program of recreation for the handicapped will be affected by the same general forces, influences, and principles that shape a program for any age level. Major differences between a program of recreation for the handicapped and a program for other groups will be reflected not so much in the types of activities as in the ways these activities are adapted to the needs of each individual or group of individuals. We are primarily concerned at this point with the task of identifying these unique adaptations of activities in order that the lives of the handicapped may be enriched.

The handicapped individual needs friends, family fun, a chance for games and sports, social parties, camping, dramatics, music and dance, arts and crafts, and a chance to try his wings in adventurous ways. If recreation is necessary for the normal individual, then it is also necessary for the handicapped. It is realistic to admit that a handicap may keep a person from certain activities, but until he has tried he will not know how much he can do or how much pleasure a new venture may bring. There is no kind of recreation activity that some handicapped person has not enjoyed.

The following are examples of some activities which have been enjoyed.

MARATHON. A man in a wheelchair in Tucson, Arizona, wheeled through the whole twenty-six miles, 285 yards of a marathon. "The real reason I'm doing this is to prove that just because someone is in a wheelchair, it doesn't necessarily mean he's handicapped and can't compete with other people. He was a fifteen-year-old and a four-sport letterman at Elkton, Minnesota, High School when polio attacked his legs. Today, at thirty-one, he does just about everything but walk and run, thanks to his realization that the world of sports and physical activity isn't only for those who are 100 percent able.

TRACK. A fifteen-year-old sophomore who has been blind since birth ran the forty-yard dash for a High School in Portland, Maine. In his first start, he was clocked at 7.7 seconds. The winning time was 5.2. He stayed in his own lane by holding in his left hand a metal ring which slid along a light guide rope. He was caught, a couple of strides beyond the finish line, by his coach.

FISHING. Because of the thoughtfulness of a group of Portland, Oregon, fishermen, there is an area on Oregon's Deschutes River where trout fishermen who are confined to wheelchairs have special facilities. Three miles north of the community of Maupin a paved road leads to a parking area by the river. From there, a ramp slopes gently to a wooden platform where seven stalls for wheelchairs are set up.

SWIMMING, SKATING, AND BOWLING. Like most fourteen-year-olds, a girl in Slatedale, Pennsylvania, likes to roller skate, ice skate, bowl, ride a bike, and swim. But for her doing these things represents a real achievement because she is blind.

FOOTBALL. When Oregon School for the Deaf football players go into a huddle they show the play's signs rather than tell them. Their reactions have become so good they now have the highest scoring high school football team in Oregon. The team plays eight-man football.

BAND. Blind since birth, a sixteen-year-old member of the Braintree, Massachusetts, High School drill team marched to the sound of the band during football games. She kept in position by counting the exact number of steps needed to go one way, then the exact number of steps she would move in another direction before turning again. During the difficult maneuvers, her drill team friends whispered directions to her.

GOLF. A totally blind golfer says he considers it a bad day for him if he shoots over 95 for a round of golf, and he "blows his stack" if he takes more than thirty-eight putts. He has won the National Blind Golf Championship fourteen times and the international title eight times.

OLYMPIC GAMES FOR THE DEAF. Three Colorado athletes competed in the eleventh International Games for the Deaf in Belgrade,

Yugoslavia during the summer of 1969. More than 1,000 deaf athletes competed in the World Games for the Deaf from thirty-eight countries. The U.S. team was composed of 120 athletes.

NATURE. A forest trail for the blind was dedicated in Colorado's White River National Forest September 17, 1967. The Braille Trail was a unique first in the Nation, and the sixth trail of this type opened in New Mexico in 1968. A nylon cord was stretched from post to post to guide the sightless visitors. The blind are encouraged to compare the smooth bark of the fir with the rough, scaly bark of the spruce. Near an old tree stump, the braille sign suggests that they feel the old stump and with sensitive fingers, count the annual rings to tell how old the tree was when cut.

PARALYMPICS. The Stoke Mandeville Games held annually at Stoke Mandeville Hospital, Aylesbury, England, began in 1948 as a modest competition in archery involving twenty-six paralyzed ex-servicemen and women from the Second World War. In succeeding years competitions in wheelchair basketball, javelin throwing, putting the shot, table tennis, fencing, weightlifting, and swimming were added to the initial competition of archery. In 1952, the Games became an international sports event by the arrival of a team of paraplegic war veterans from The Netherlands.

SOCIAL. The Recreation Education Department of Colorado State College, Greeley, Colorado, the Department of Special Education at Colorado State College, the Public Schools Special Education Program, and the Greeley Recreation Department jointly sponsor dances for physically and mentally handicapped teenagers. One of the participants remarked: "I have never had so much fun in all my life." Another girl told her teacher at class the next day that her parents were taking a trip to Florida but if there was another dance, she was going to ask them to leave her at home so that she would be able to go to that dance. Another girl stated, "Three different boys asked me to dance with them."

COMPETITIVE SPORTS. Physically disabled students at the University of Illinois have been prime movers in the proper development of skilled competitive sports throughout the nation since the war. The current activity program includes wheelchair football, wheelchair basketball, wheelchair bowling, wheelchair table tennis, wheelchair fencing, wheelchair cheerleading, wheelchair square dancing, adaptive swimming, bowling for the blind and semi-ambulatory, as well as activities in lesser organization and social-recreational events.

GUIDELINES FOR LEADERS

It is a necessity that leaders in handicapped recreation programs first become acquainted with the physically and mentally normal individual within our society. It is difficult, if not impossible, to understand the handicapped individual without first understanding the normal. Basic concepts of understanding that have been presented throughout this text are essential to the leader who ultimately will be a recreation leader working with the handicapped. Thus, the program of educating the recreation leader of the handicapped should become a program that is essentially an extension of basic preparation for the general recreation program for normals of all ages.

Some important leadership suggestions are applicable to the handicapped:

1. The socializing value of recreation for the handicapped must be realized. The strongest of all the needs of the handicapped is to be in social groups. Social opportunities are a must.
2. The handicapped person has to grow up the same way a normal person grows up.
3. The handicapped person has the right to participate in any activity in order to receive some type of satisfaction and enjoyment.
4. The handicapped person must have an opportunity to succeed.
5. Wherever possible, keep the handicapped with a normal group. Don't segregate them from society.
6. The handicapped must learn to live with his disability. Let him do for himself as much as possible.
7. Take the positive rather than the negative approach. Look at the handicapped in terms of what they can do rather than concentrating on what they cannot do.
8. Since many handicapped persons (especially the mentally retarded) have short attention spans and are easily distracted, the leader must have plans for a variety of activities during their leisure time.
9. Leaders who work with the handicapped may have to adapt recreation activities to suit the abilities and limitations of each individual.
10. Many handicapped individuals have poor manual skills which restrict the expression of their creativity. However, the fact that, a person's skills are poor does not minimize their value for him.
11. In working with the handicapped the leader must demonstrate freely (except with the blind), speak clearly, and make sure everyone understands.

12. Patience, a sense of humor, and ingenuity are invaluable in working with the handicapped.
13. If at all possible, invite the participants to take an active part in planning and carrying out their own activities. The professional leader should not dominate these people.
14. Create a friendly, congenial environment in which these people will feel secure, wanted, accepted, able, and liked. Treat them as human beings.
15. Remember that their feelings of inferiority and inadequacy stem primarily from their special disabilities. Help them achieve what they need so deeply—affection, understanding, appreciation, security, and a sense of worth and usefulness.

Selected References

"Activity Program for the Mentally Retarded," *The Journal of Health, Physical Education, Recreation*, April, 1966.

Council for Exceptional Children and American Association for Health, Physical Education, and Recreation, *Recreation and Physical Activity for the Mentally Retarded* (Washington, D.C.: American Association for Health, Physical Education, and Recreation, 1966).

Daniels, Arthur S. and Davies, Evelyn A., *Adapted Physical Education* (2d ed.) (New York: Harper & Row, 1965).

Pomeroy, Janet, *Recreation for the Physically Handicapped* (New York: Macmillan Co., 1964).

"Programs for Handicapped," *The Journal of Health, Physical Education, Recreation*, October, 1968.

In developing a camp program for the mentally retarded, the following agencies may be contacted:

Joseph P. Kennedy Jr. Foundation, 719 13th Street, N.W., Washington, D.C.

National Association for Retarded Children, 420 Lexington Avenue, New York, New York.

National Society for Crippled Children and Adults, 2023 West Ogden Avenue, Chicago, Illinois.

Chapter XIII

Evaluation in Recreation

THE FRENCH PHILOSOPHER Voltaire once said, "If you would speak with me, define your terms." It is important that all leaders have a common understanding of what evalution means as a basis for appreciating its significance to recreation and utilizing it in the improvement of all phases of the department's work.

WHAT IS EVALUATION?

Throughout this book we have emphasized constantly that leaders should seek certain important goals or values in everything they do—that activities are the means which, properly conducted, should lead us to these ends or values. But how do we know if we have succeeded or failed in achieving the goals we set out to achieve? We find this out through evaluation. The word "evaluation" is derived from the word "value" and refers to the process of determining the extent to which we have attained the goals formulated and accepted by the department, the participants, and the leaders. Evaluation should tell us whether or not we are getting results; whether progress is being made in the direction we desire to go.

The process of achieving worthwhile results in recreation involves five vital steps:

1. Determining the goals.
2. Selecting the activities through which these goals may be attained.
3. Conducting these activities in harmony with good leadership practices.

352

4. Using evaluation to determine the extent to which the goals are being realized.
5. Making improvements based upon results of the evaluation.

Evaluation may be a simple or a highly complex process depending upon the circumstances and the insights and research competencies of the persons involved. It may be as elementary as expressing one's judgment with respect to the quality of a workshop by answering a number of questions about its various aspects. On the other hand, evaluation may include an intensive study of leadership, program, environment, administration, finance, and the effects of the recreation experience on the growth and development of children, as well as the social, moral, and ethical behavioral changes effected. It may also attempt to determine the degree to which recreation contributes to satisfying the one basic human need, the developing of personal adequacy. In assessing the impact of recreation on the individual a variety of evaluative techniques or devices may be utilized, such as anecdotal records, observational methods, questionnaires, inventories, interviews, check lists, rating scales, tests, personal reports, projective methods, case studies, cumulative records, sociometric methods, self-appraisal, post-meeting reaction sheets, and measures.

Some Basic Points of View

An understanding of the meaning of evaluation in the broadest sense will include acceptance of the following:

1. Evaluation must start with a clear statement of the goals of recreation and seek to determine the degree to which these goals are being realized.
2. Evaluation is a continuous process.
3. Evaluation is a means and not an end. The ultimate purpose is improvement of the work of the department of recreation.
4. Evaluation includes both objective and subjective devices.
5. Evaluation is a coöperative process. If possible, all persons affected by it should share fully in its conduct.
6. Evaluation is concerned both with results and with the means or the methods used in attaining the results.
7. Evaluation provides information helpful in improving public relations.
8. Self-analysis is an important aspect of evaluation.
9. Evaluation is concerned with why the program is successful or not and with what changes should be made to improve its effectiveness.
10. Evaluation is basic to every human endeavor. All human beings are constantly being evaluated with respect to the quality of their contri-

butions. The patient evaluates the doctor, the client judges the quality of his lawyer, parents praise or condemn the teacher, and, even on the golf course, a player is rated in relation to par or his competitors, or both.

WHY WE NEED EVALUATION
IN RECREATION

Evaluation in recreation, at least insofar as determining what happens to people as a result of participating in leisure activities, is almost nonexistent and its discussion constitutes a blind spot in the literature of our field. The attendance figure represents the sole measure of success in most communities. The number of people who take part in our programs is extremely important as an index of their popularity, but we should be even more concerned with what happens to these people as a result of their participation. Evaluation should seek the answer to this question.

Very few people engaged in community recreation are making serious efforts to evaluate their programs or their practices. The community which supports the recreation department, however, has a proper concern that its program pays adequate dividends on the investment. As competition for the tax dollar increases in intensity, communities will demand more and more factual evidence to justify the costs involved.

Additional benefits of evaluation include the following:

1. The morale of the staff is improved as evidence accrues that goals are actually being attained. Leaders have a very real regard for the quality of the department with which they are connected and proof of that quality is an extremely important factor in the development of professional morale.
2. A higher quality of recreation will result from an effective program of evaluation.
3. Recreation will make greater progress toward full professional status as it presents more conclusive proof of the extent to which it attains valuable goals.
4. As evaluation focuses the spotlight on strengths and weaknesses, data essential to long-range planning are made available.
5. Staff members are motivated to do better work when they know they are going to be evaluated.
6. We live in a society of accelerated change and complexity. As society changes so must our programs and our methods change if we are to keep up to date. Recreation needs continuous evaluation if we are to

understand these social, cultural, and technological changes and their implications for the recreation leaders of America.

7. Participation by leaders in evaluation increases their sensitivity to the importance of goals in recreation and the means by which they may be achieved.
8. Evaluation improves public relations as parents and other members of the community share in carrying out the program of evaluation.
9. Leaders grow professionally as they participate in the evaluative process.

OBSTACLES TO EVALUATION

If evaluation is so important in recreation why have we failed to conduct programs of evaluation? Is it because we don't recognize its importance? The author does not believe this is a major reason for our lack of energy as evaluators. Many superintendents of recreation to whom he wrote shortly before beginning work on this chapter emphasized the importance of evaluation, deplored their failures in this area of endeavor, and expressed an earnest desire for help.

One factor retarding evaluation in recreation is the nature of the recreation situation. Teachers in our schools can administer tests and carry out other evaluative procedures whether the pupils want to take part or not, but the recreation leader must depend entirely upon voluntary participation and the word "test" generally repels rather than attracts volunteers. The evaluation of results in recreation has been limited also by a lack of evaluative techniques appropriate to the situation and by a dearth of investigators competent to handle those techniques which are appropriate.

The problem of evaluation in recreation is further complicated by the fact that in considerable measure we deal with the intangibles of life. There is little difficulty in evaluating a child's ability to run the 50 yard dash, as a stop watch and norms for this event and age are all that are necessary. But how do you measure the joy in his heart as he crosses the finish line ahead of all the others? Can the pleasure which art gives us be objectively measured like so many yards of cloth? All human beings want to be liked, accepted, to be able, and successful. Will your scales record this kind of growth as though it were so many pounds of butter? Can your check lists encompass the happiness of a group of teenagers as they sit around a campfire and the leader explains to them some of the mysteries of the heavens? Will all the rating scales in the world suffice to record the beauty of a sunset on the Grand Teton or a perfectly executed aria from *La Traviata?* Or what evaluative device would you use to measure the bitterness of social rejection or growth in moral behavior? But these are the very essence of life, the truly great things in human experience, the factors which shape our personalities.

We are faced with a number of very real obstacles in our efforts to evaluate recreation, but their existence does not excuse us for doing nothing. An airplane could never fly were it not for the opposition provided by the air. Where exact measurements cannot be obtained, judgments must suffice. Progress in evaluation will be made as individual leaders and departments win small victories in this badly neglected area of recreation. Two such "victories" in the form of specialized studies indicate that certain values of recreation can be appraised and they point the way toward additional investigations:[1,2]

1. A study of residents in two cottages in a home for older persons revealed that persons who participated in group activities such as card playing, shuffleboard, pool, pinball, and horseshoe, had on the average a much higher 'happiness score' than individuals who engaged only in activities like walking, reading, sewing, embroidery, and listening to radio and watching television. This clearly indicates that group activities assist in personal adjustment and promote happiness.
2. A study of groups of persons attending a day center for older people in New York indicates that visits to health clinics were reduced by 50 to 70 percent in the period after attending the center, as compared with a like period before joining. This would seem to show that participation in organizational activities moderates excessive concern about bodily ills, real and imaginary.

HOW TO EVALUATE
THE TOTAL PROGRAM

Leaders may evaluate their programs by using criteria prepared by national agencies or by establishing their own evaluative criteria based upon the values they deem important. The coöperative self-evaluation

[1] Ernest W. Burgess, "Social Relations, Activities, and Personal Adjustment," *American Journal of Sociology,* January 1954, pp. 352–360.

[2] Ruth S. Cavan and Others, "Personal Adjustment in Old Age," in *Aging in Today's Society,* Clark Tibbitts and Wilma Donahue, eds. (Englewood Cliffs, N.J.: Prentice-Hall, Inc., 1960), p. 303.

plan, which involves preparation of evaluative criteria as well as its application, is recommended for the following reasons:

1. The greater the degree of involvement by leaders in all phases of the evaluation, the more rewarding does the project become.
2. Criteria prepared for a specific community by persons who are involved in the program will possess greater relevancy and be used with more enthusiasm and effectiveness than if prepared by individuals unfamiliar with the local situation.
3. Leaders will not feel they are being inspected and criticized when they share in a coöperative enterprise.
4. Self-evaluation strengthens the ability of all individuals involved to think together critically and constructively, a quality basic to continuous progress in recreation.

All aspects of a department of recreation's operations are related and these interrelationships must be taken into consideration by the evaluators. For example, when you evaluate the program of a community center you must also evaluate the leadership because two centers may have identical programs and yet achieve quite different results because the leadership of one is effective and that of the other is not. The student, however, will find it much simpler to approach the problem of evaluation on two levels—program and leadership—remembering at all times their extremely close relationship.

First Steps

A department must decide first of all what it wishes to evaluate. Instead of attempting to evaluate all phases of its work in terms of all of its goals, it may decide to concentrate its efforts on finding out what contribution the program for the aged is making to the mental health of these people. Or the staff may expand this qualitative project to include a quantitative analysis of the total number of aged in the community, the percent of these eligibles participating in the program for senior citizens, the regularity and intensity of their participation, the reasons why they do or do not participate, and a tabulation of their likes and dislikes with respect to the present program. One department recently chose to evaluate its program in terms of the extent to which it was meeting the needs of its young adults; another, the handicapped. A third conducted an intensive investigation to determine what results were being achieved in helping children and youth meet the need for acceptance.

These five steps are basic to any effective evaluation regardless of whether breadth, depth, or both be the major characteristic of the project.

1. Prepare a clear statement of the goals you seek through the recreation program. This is fundamental to all evaluation as the major function of evaluation is to determine the extent to which you are achieving your goals. A special committee on values, goals, or philosophy may be charged with this responsibility, but the entire staff should have an opportunity to contribute to the final statement. Members of the lay public also should be invited to serve on this committee.
2. Interpret these goals, whenever possible, in terms of the behavior of people, especially of children and youth. Let us assume that one of your goals is strengthening the quality of coöperation in children and youth. You would then identify, in many different recreation situations, the kinds of behavior that indicate progress toward attainment of this specific goal. In crafts, for example:
   A. Willingly shares with others the use of equipment and supplies.
   B. Helps clean up after the craft club meets.
   C. Assists others less capable than he.
   D. Contributes to the common pool of scrap or inexpensive craft materials.
3. Provide the kinds of recreation situations or experiences which lead to the established goals. This means simply that if you seek to strengthen the quality of coöperation in young people you must provide activities in which their coöperative, or non-coöperative, behavior may be studied.
4. Observe the behavior of the participants in terms of the previously prepared list of behaviors suggested in Item 2, above, in an effort to determine progress toward achievement of the goals.
5. Analyze results of your study, attempt to discover basic causes for your failures and successes, and make the changes in your program which seem to be indicated. Further study to determine the effectiveness of the changes instituted should result in additional refinement of the program.

Evaluative Criteria

It is good practice in evaluation to use as many techniques as possible; simple appraisal methods should be supplemented by the use of scientific instruments provided the department has the personnel skilled in their use. The preparation and application of evaluative criteria upon which to base one's observations is one technique in which all members of a department, as well as participants in the program, should share. This device involves the preparation of questions designed specifically to determine how effective the program is in terms of goal attainment. Every activity is placed under the spotlight of the criteria and judged accordingly. Criteria valid for a teen-age program may not be valid when applied to a program for senior citizens. Furthermore, questions directed to leaders may not be appropriate for participants. However, many questions do apply to the total program and to leaders and participants as indicated by the following list:

1. Is the program sufficiently broad in scope to provide a wide range of choice for everyone in the community regardless of age, sex, race, ability, or any other differences?
2. Are adequate opportunities offered the participants to share in planning and operating the program?
3. Is the participant given an opportunity to grow psychologically by experiencing success repeatedly rather than suffering constant failure?
4. Does the program include activities sufficiently vigorous to develop organic power or fitness?
5. To what extent does your program provide opportunities for participants to be of service to the community?
6. To what degree does your program encourage family participation?
7. Are the creative abilities of the participants challenged?
8. Do the participants have fun?
9. What are the most popular activities? The least popular? Why?
10. Does the program consist of activities in which reside the values you feel are important?
11. Are individuals encouraged to expand their recreational interests as well as continue in those in which they are now competent?
12. Are activities provided in which interest may persist over many years?
13. Do your activities possess educational as well as recreational value?
14. Is excellence in all phases of your program sought in preference to mediocrity?
15. Is the integrated program emphasized whenever possible?
16. Is the program sufficiently flexible to permit adaptation to varying situations?
17. Do your activities contribute to mental health by providing socially acceptable outlets for pent-up emotions?
18. Are adequate opportunities offered for each individual to grow in self-esteem and personal adequacy, to be recognized, to be somebody?
19. Is there an opportunity for every individual to become a member of a group of importance to him, to be accepted, to be a part of something bigger than himself?
20. Does the program include some activities characterized by adventure and an element of danger?
21. Are the unskilled given an opportunity to develop skill in the activities of their choice?
22. Is respect for human beings cultivated in your program?
23. To what degree does the individual grow in the ability to coöperate for the common good as a result of participating in your activities?
24. What contribution are you making toward developing in children and youth respect for both the letter and the spirit of the law?
25. Does the program strengthen the moral fiber of children and youth?

26. Are the activities suited to the age level of the group?
27. Does the activity cultivate a spirit of friendliness and group solidarity?
28. Does the program offer opportunities for the development of leadership qualities in the individual?
29. Are program goals selected on two levels—the level of the individual and the level of society?
30. Does the program encourage the development of the individual within a framework of social and moral purpose?

These evaluative criteria may be used in various ways. The questions may be answered in the form of a questionnaire both to the staff and, with minor changes, to participants. Or the staff may be divided into small groups which discuss each question carefully and render a group judgment. Other evaluative techniques should be used, such as interviews, observation methodology, anecdotal records, attendance and registration records, case studies, and sociometric methods.

EVALUATING GROWTH TOWARD INDIVIDUAL FULFILLMENT

One of our most important goals is development of the individual to the highest possible degree primarily through assisting him to meet the basic human need for personal adequacy. One aspect of this need is the need to be accepted, to be a member of a group, to be liked, wanted, and respected by one's peers. There is no bitterness to compare with the bitterness of social rejection. If the recreation leaders of this nation were successful in nothing else than the identification of the rejected children and youth in our society; determined the causes of these rejections, and assisted these youngsters to change their behavior so as to remove these causes; and thus enabled these lonely, disliked, and embittered children to gain a measure of happiness, popularity, acceptance, and social effectiveness, they would make a contribution of vital significance to our democratic society.

Sociometry appears to offer more to the recreation leader in the solution of this particular problem than any other of the scientific evaluative techniques and its effective utilization does not require an expert in research. Sociometry is a method of studying the organization of groups and of identifying the popular persons, the lonely, the disliked, the cliques, cleavages between subgroups, and general patterns of group integration or disintegration.

Values of the Sociometric Technique

The leader who understands and has developed some competence in the use of the sociometric test will discover a number of specific purposes for which the device is especially useful in a recreation setting.

1. *Improving the social adjustment of the individual.* Although the test itself is not a socialization device, its most extensive use in recreation has been as a measure of an individual's social acceptance since it determines the extent to which he is accepted by his peers. The ability of an individual to attain status among his peers is vital to his happiness, his total personality development, his mental health, and his social effectiveness. But the leader must know who needs help before he can give it.

Sociometry provides the basic information with respect to patterns of rejection and attraction among the group members which the leader needs as a starting point for his efforts to help each individual who needs help. After the lonely, the unpopular, and the disliked have been identified and guidance measures carried out over a period of time designed to improve their individual and group status, retests will provide objective evidence of the extent to which desirable behavior changes have been effected through the recreation experience.

The values of the sociometric test in the improvement of the social adjustment of human beings is not limited to those individuals who have adjustment difficulties. Gronlund points out that the identification of leadership potential and assisting individuals "in the development of this potential ability is equally as important as helping the isolate or rejectee gain status." This "popular leader" identified by the sociometric test has the personality and social skills basic to leadership, but frequently lacks other leadership competencies. Helping him develop the skills necessary for actual leadership in recreation situations should be of vital concern to leaders and recreation administrators alike.[3]

2. *Improving group relations.* For the leader who is concerned with improving human interrelationships in recreation, sociometry reveals valuable clues basic to effective guidance, group organization, and whatever therapeutic measures may be necessary to correct socially ineffective situations. On the surface one group may look very much like all other groups. But a group resembles an iceberg in that nine-tenths of its emotional climate and prestige relations are beneath the surface, hidden from the leader yet powerful in effect and dominating in action.

---

[3] Norman E. Gronlund, *Sociometry in the Classroom* (New York: Harper and Brothers, 1959) p. 14.

Most of us live, work, and recreate in groups of one kind or another. Friction, tension, ill-will, cleavages, hostility, and various types of interpersonal conflicts exert a vicious disintegrative effect disrupting the efficiency of the group and impairing the personality development of the individual. Sociometry probes beneath the surface of group life bringing out into the open numerous clues to this underlying network of interpersonal relations.

3. *Improving the organization of groups.* In general, a social group is most effective when composed of individuals who like one another and prefer to associate with each other. Thus, their energies are not dissipated in hostile and aggressive behavior. Clubs, committees, and various other groups are likely to be more productive, coöperative, and happier in whatever they are doing if they are chosen, partially at least, on the basis of sociometric choices. Even an athletic team, selected entirely on the basis of skill, may not win many games if the players dislike one another and fail to work together for the common good. For as Todd puts it, "... the purpose of sociometrics is to effect the release of the greatest amount of social energy within the group for coöperative action by objectively identifying the social forces in the group and then arranging the most harmonious and productive combinations within it."[4]

How to Construct and Apply the Test

Let us assume for purposes of illustration that you are a leader of a group of fifteen children ranging in ages from ten to twelve years. How do you build and use a functional choice test? The purpose of this test is to find out who wants to be with whom in certain specific situations. The nature of this choice situation is extremely important. If it is the right kind of situation the test will provide the information the leader needs; if it is not, the information revealed will have but superficial and fleeting value. Important characteristics of these choices are:

1. The choice should be general rather than specific in nature. For example, it is better to ask them to name three children with whom they would like to play rather than with whom they would like to play softball, as the softball situation provides too limited a basis for social interaction.
2. The choice must be meaningful to the individual making it; it must involve something he really wants to do.
3. The choice situation must be a realistic and highly probable one. Asking children to choose associates for field trips when such trips are seldom conducted will have little value.

---

[4] Frances Todd, "Sociometry in Physical Education," *Journal of Health, Physical Education, and Recreation,* May 1953, p. 23.

4. The choice situation should be such that individuals can choose each other for the same activity thus revealing mutual relationships.
5. The choice should be accompanied by the leader's promise that the child's wishes insofar as possible will be taken into account in arranging the groups.

The first sociometric test should be given only after children have had an opportunity to become acquainted with each other, otherwise their choices are meaningless. The number of choices to allot the individuals is determined partly by their ages, but mainly by studies which show that five choices enable the leader to satisfy more fully the desires of the members to be placed with two or more of their chosen associates. Children from six to eight years of age should be limited to three choices while five is recommended for older children and youth.

When explaining to the children what is to be done do not use the word "test." Simply explain to them that during the next several weeks they will be playing a number of group games and that you would like to have their help in arranging groups that play best together. They can do this by writing on the 3 x 5 card you have given them the names of five children they would like to play with. As a general practice, asking children to list the names of those they do *not* want to play with is not recommended as it heightens tension and stimulates hostility. Additional instructions should include the following:

1. They may choose anyone in the group.
2. Their choices will be kept confidential.
3. Each child will be placed in a group with at least two of his choices if at all possible.
4. They should make all five choices.
5. The groups will be arranged on the basis of their choices within the next three days.
6. Their own names should be written at the top of the card.

This entire procedure should take less than five minutes.

Analyzing the Results

Analyzing the results is a fascinating process somewhat comparable to a detective searching for clues at the scene of a crime. But the trained detective will discover and interpret clues that the average individual never sees. We must know how to handle the rich store of information recorded on the cards and what to look for, otherwise the data will prove of little use to us.

THE MATRIX CHART. A matrix chart is a simple tabulation form giving a total picture of all children's preferences and all positions in the group. The following suggestions will facilitate construction of the chart:

1. Alphabetize and number children's cards.
2. List the names in alphabetical order down the left side of the sheet with the boys' names appearing first.
3. Number the children consecutively from top to bottom and do the same across the chart.
4. Draw a heavy line both horizontally and vertically between the boys' and the girls' names so that choices between the sexes may be easily identified.
5. A diagonal line drawn from the upper left-hand corner of the chart to the lower right-hand corner cuts through the squares that are unused since the children do not choose themselves.
6. A vertical column may be provided at the left of the names in which to summarize choices of the same and opposite sex.
7. Two horizontal summary columns are provided at the bottom of the chart in which to record the total number of choices received by each child and the mutual choices received.

A detailed analysis of the data presented in the matrix chart reveals the following:

1. Bill A. and Alice B. are the stars of the group, a star being an individual who receives a large number of choices on a sociometric test. Bill received nine choices and Alice eight.
2. Hope S. is the only isolate. She was not chosen by anyone.
3. Rudi D. and Ron R. received but one choice each. They are termed neglectees as a neglectee is one who receives relatively few choices.
4. The number of mutual choices is fairly evenly distributed except in a few cases.
5. Only fourteen of seventy-five choices went to members of the opposite sex.

THE SOCIOGRAM. Important and valuable as the matrix chart is in providing a quick and easy interpretation of sociometric data, it is a first step only and should be supplemented by a sociogram. The sociogram is a graphic picture which identifies cliques, pairs, threesomes, and gangs, as well as the wanted and unwanted child.

The diagram on which the data are plotted is constructed as follows:

1. Draw four concentric circles.
2. A vertical line through the center of the diagram separates the sexes.

Matrix Chart

Choices Given				Children Chosen														
OS	SS	Name		1	2	3	4	5	6	7	8	9	10	11	12	13	14	15
2	3	Bill A.	1			③		①			2	5		④				
0	5	Bob B.	2	3		⑤		2	①		④							
1	4	Dick C.	3	③	④				2		①		5					
0	5	Rudi D.	4	2	5	3		1	④									
2	3	Nick F.	5	①		5					②				3			4
1	4	Len K.	6	5	①		④				3	2						
1	4	Ron R.	7	1	5			3	2				4					
1	4	Sam T.	8		④	①		⑤		2		3						
0	5	Alice B.	9										③	⑤	1		②	④
0	5	Grace K.	10									②		③	④		⑤	①
1	4	Helen M.	11	②								③	①		5			4
2	3	Lora P.	12						5		4		③				1	2
0	5	Hope S.	13									2	1	5	4			3
1	4	Betty T.	14	4								①	③	5				②
2	3	Ruth W.	15	3							2	④	⑤				①	
John Tracy (Leader)		Choices Received	SS	6	5	5	1	5	4	1	5	5	5	3	3	0	3	5
			OS	3	0	0	0	0	1	0	2	3	2	1	1	0	0	1
		Mutual Choices	SS	2	3	3	1	2	2	0	3	4	5	2	1	0	3	3
			OS	1	0	0	0	0	0	0	0	0	0	1	0	0	0	0

OS = Opposite Sex SS = Same Sex O = Mutual Choice

3. The numbers along this vertical line indicate the number of choices for each child located within this particular circle; for example, within the circle marked 4 will fall all children receiving no more than four and no less than two choices.
4. Place the boys to the right of the vertical line and girls to the left with mutual choices located near one another and joined by a solid line.

Plotting only mutual choices keeps the sociogram fairly simple. Eliminate crossed lines whenever possible.

The advantages of the sociogram over the matrix chart are clearly evident. All the patterns of relationship are outlined in a conspicuous manner. Reciprocated and unreciprocated choices are defined; the popular and the unpopular stand out clearly. The two stars (numbers 1 and

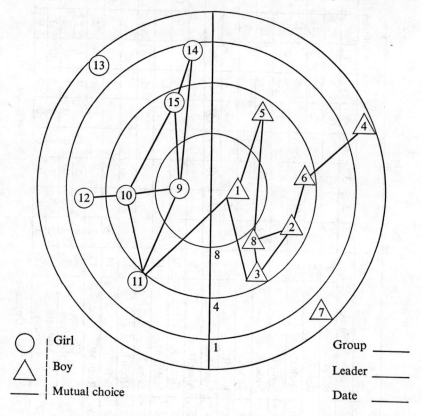

Sociogram of Choices of Play Companions

9) are located in the center of the sociogram. The girl (number 9) has four mutual choices while the boy (number 1) has three. Note that he does not choose the next most popular boy (number 8). Could this be because he resents the possible competition for group leadership he senses in number 8? The two stars (1 and 9) apparently have no desire for each other's play companionship. What are the basic reasons for their leadership positions? Are they actually leaders and is their influence on the group wholesome?

Girl number 13 and boy number 7 received no choices on the sociometric test, and boy number 4 received only one choice. Why are these youngsters isolated or neglected? How can the leader determine the causes of their unpopularity and what can he do to help them become liked and accepted? This is an imperative responsibility of the superior leader. If we know the factors that motivate children's sociometric choices we are well along the road toward understanding why certain children are not accepted. Gronlund throws light on this important problem:[5]

In general, children who are highly chosen by their peers on a sociometric test tend to be more intelligent, to have higher scholastic achievement, to be younger in age, to have greater social and athletic skill, to participate more frequently in sports and social activities, to have a more pleasing physical appearance, to have more social and heterosexual interests . . . than children who receive few or no sociometric choices from their peers. Sociometric choice patterns also indicate that children tend to choose as associates those children whose ability, skill, and interests are similar to their own or are slightly higher. Too great a deviation from the other group members on any personal characteristic seems to contribute to lower sociometric status on the part of the deviant.

Reasons for the rejection of children by their peers also may lie in their unwillingness to conform, in the fact they belong to a minority group, or that their father's work is looked down upon by the community. It may be necessary for the leader to effect changes in the attitudes and behaviors of the group rather than in the individual, although, as a general rule, it will be the individual who must change his behavior if he is to be accepted by the group.

Children 4, 6, 2, and 3 form a chain of mutual choices. Why? Does child 6 have to divide his time between 2 and 4? If 2 and 4 do not get along well together is 6 under tension because of his "in-between" position?

A small subgroup, or clique, is formed by children 2, 3, and 8. What do they have in common and what is the effect of this clique on the

[5] Gronlund, op. cit., pp. 221–222.

group? What can the leader do to integrate these three boys more completely with the group? Only one mutual choice exists between the sexes, but the leader need not be concerned over this obvious cleavage between the boys and girls because this is a common occurrence at this stage.

How to Group Children

The immediate responsibility of a leader following the administration of a sociometric test is to keep his promise to the children with respect to their choices. Jennings states the principle involved:[6]

Each individual should be given the highest degree of satisfaction compatible with maximum happiness for everyone else and maximum stimulation for all. In other words, the object is to provide for each child the best possible arrangement from *his* point of view, but since the same consideration must be shown to all . . . , there will have to be some compromise.

Steps in the grouping procedure will follow these rules:

1. Give the unchosen or seldom chosen child his own first choice. For example, Hope S., number 13, received no choices, but her first choice was Grace K. She should be placed in a group with Grace K.
2. Give any child in a pair relation the highest reciprocated choice from *his* point of view. If his first choice is returned he is given this choice. If it isn't, then give him the next highest choice that is returned. Our matrix chart shows that Betty T.'s first choice was Alice B., but Alice did not choose Betty. Her second choice was Ruth W. who also chose her first, so we place Betty with Ruth.
3. If a child is chosen by others, but chooses none of those who choose him, give him his first choice.
4. If the sociometric test provides for children to indicate rejections— those children with whom they do *not* wish to play—do not put any child with those who rejected him.
5. Give each child, regardless of status, at least one of his choices and more if possible.

Leaders should understand that the higher the total number of mutual choices, the better since mutual choices reflect a common desire for association and are actually a measure of a group's social cohesiveness. All other factors being equal, that group is best which has the fewest

---

[6] Helen Hall Jennings, *Sociometry in Group Relations* (Washington, D.C.: American Council on Education, 1948), p. 45.

isolates. Unfortunately, numerous sociometric tests have revealed an almost chronic persistence with which socially neglected and socially isolated children of all ages appear in our society. Gronlund reports that school studies "indicated that between 11 and 22 percent of the pupils were neglected or ignored by their classmates."[7]

The extent and nature of this problem presents a four-fold challenge to recreation leadership:

1. Identify these unwanted and unliked children.
2. Analyze carefully all aspects of the situation in a determined effort to discover the reasons why they are unwanted and unliked. Is it because they are physically unattractive? Perhaps they lack social skills. Or is it possible their low social status could be greatly improved by encouraging athletic participation?[8]
3. Conduct programs which include special efforts to improve the social relationships of children. Guidance in personal grooming may be indicated; or the development of social or athletic skills may be a partial answer; or keeping a list of the unpopular, lonely, and rejected children and giving them some responsibilities which put them in contact with the majority of the group may prove effective. Mixing children from two different racial groups generally will reduce the social cleavage between them.
4. Determine the results of the procedures you have taken to improve these social relationships. For example, if your first sociometric test revealed a racial cleavage in your group which you attempted to overcome by sociometric grouping, a retest some weeks later will indicate the effectiveness of what you have done by revealing the change in the number of choices exchanged by the members of the two groups. You also may be concerned with determining the effects of your procedures on the behavior of a particular child, on the climate within which the group operates, and on the visible interactions of all the children. This, generally, will necessitate some supporting evaluative measures since data provided by any method of evaluation should be supplemented by other evidence whenever possible.

One such valuable technique is the anecdotal record which is simply a record of the leader's observations of a child's behavior in a specific situation. If the leader is desirous of determining a child's relations with his peers, he will record what the child says and does that throws light on this particular problem. Is he accepted by the

---

[7] Gronlund, *op. cit.*, p. 112.

[8] A Study by McGraw and Tolbert indicates that athletic ability is a dominant factor in achieving sociometric status by junior high school boys. L. W. McGraw and J. W. Tolbert, "Sociometric Status and Athletic Ability of Junior High School Boys," *The Research Quarterly*, March 1953, pp. 72–80.

group? Are they friendly to him and he to them? Is he a coöperative team-player or an individualist who thinks only of himself? Is he a good sport? Does he play well with certain children and not with others? The leader who records carefully his observations of the child's behavior will be able to answer these and similar questions—answers which will go far toward explaining why this individual is accepted or rejected by his peers and what remedial action, if any, must be taken to improve his inadequate social relationships.

EVALUATING GROWTH IN DEMOCRATIC HUMAN RELATIONS

We need to keep constantly in mind that one of our most vital responsibilities is that of furthering the ideals of a democratic society primarily by contributing to the development of the kinds of people who believe deeply in democracy, are dedicated to its preservation and refinement, and who possess the qualities basic to its effective functioning. In Chapter 4 we learned that five of the most important of these qualities of the democratic citizen to which recreation should make a major contribution are: (1) respect for human beings and regard for the welfare of others; (2) respect for both the letter and the spirit of the law; (3) ability and desire to coöperate for the common good; (4) a preference for excellence rather than mediocrity; and (5) a high level of moral and ethical behavior.

How shall we evaluate our work in terms of what we contribute to democratic citizenship? Should we not be more concerned with the kind of person the child is becoming than with what he knows, or even with what he can do? As our process of evaluation proceeds we must get to the heart of the matter by raising questions based upon democratic values and seek the answers by whatever evaluative procedures seem to promise the most accurate results. Relevant questions then will include: Is the child becoming a person who believes that a human being is the most important thing in the world? Is he beginning to treat all human beings as he, himself, would like to be treated? Is he sensitive to their needs and to their welfare? Does he obey both the letter and spirit of the rules governing his game world? Does he accept gracefully the decisions of the officials? Is he growing in the ability to discipline himself—to do the right thing without the compulsion of rules and officials? Is this self-disciplined behavior transferring from the recreation situation to other situations? Does he work and play in a coöperative and friendly manner with others? Is he becoming the kind of person who is satisfied with mediocrity or is he developing a taste for excellence? Is he willing to pay the price of excellence? Is he becoming an honest and truthful person? Does he call his own foul if he touches the net in volleyball? Is he "obedient to the unenforceable?"

Unfortunately, evaluation in recreation has not yet progressed to the point where valid and reliable instruments are available for the measurement of child growth in democratic citizenship in the recreation situation. Future research must provide these instruments. Answers to the questions raised above, and to similar questions, must be sought primarily through simple day-to-day observations by the leader, assisted by rating scales of his own construction.

Behavior Rating Scales

The usual rating scale provides the leader with a set of qualities, traits, or types of behavior which are to be evaluated. The rater assesses the individual by checking a point on the scale representing a level or degree of the trait generally indicated in one of the following ways:

1. By numbers—1, 2, 3, 4, 5.
2. By frequency of occurrence—always, usually, seldom, never.
3. By qualitative terms—excellent, superior, good, fair, poor.
4. By relative terms—outstanding, above average, average, below average, inferior.

The effectiveness of any rating device depends largely on the competencies of the leader doing the rating. These competencies involve skill in constructing the rating device as well as administering it. The traits to be evaluated should be selected carefully. They should bear a definite relationship to the goals sought. For example, if the goal sought is improved democratic citizenship, such traits as coöperation, honesty, and truthfulness are relevant, but selfishness is not.

It is well to define the traits so objectively that they will mean the same to all people. The best kind of definition, for rating purposes, is that which describes the trait in terms of observable behavior. *Coöperation* might be clarified by defining it as: The child's ability to work or play harmoniously with others. The definition is important, but it should be supplemented by types of child behavior that indicate growth toward the coöperative citizen.

372

CREATIVE LEADERSHIP IN RECREATION

The leader's rating sheet with respect to just this one trait might look like this:

Behaviors Which Indicate That One Is Growing In The Ability to Coöperate

Leader _____ Child _____

"Average" means that the child exhibits the behavior indicated to about the same degree as the average child of his age group.

	Much below average	Below average	Average	Above average	Much above average
1. Works harmoniously with others for the common good	___	___	___	___	___
2. Accepts decisions of groups and leaders	___	___	___	___	___
3. Is loyal to his group	___	___	___	___	___
4. Is unselfish	___	___	___	___	___
5. Takes turns and shares	___	___	___	___	___
6. Participates actively in group planning and execution of plans	___	___	___	___	___

Rating devices, as a means of securing information to be used in the evaluation of children have been criticized because of their subjective nature and lack of depth. And yet, a leader constantly is rating the children with whom he works, in one way or another. Every time he coaches an athletic team and selects the players for the various positions, he is rating them in terms of their abilities to play these positions. If he is a judge at a diving contest, he must rate the divers before flashing their scores. Some degree of rating is a prerequisite to the selection of every child for the slightest responsibility assigned by the leader. The rating scale is simply a device by which the leader is enabled to be more objective than he otherwise would be. Their limitations can be minimized by (1) careful selection, definition, and description of the traits to be rated; (2) utilizing only a relatively small number of traits; (3) clearly defining each point on the scale; (4) careful selection and preparation of the raters; (5) using more than one rater whenever possible; and (6) resisting the tendency to rate highly in everything those whom you like and the reverse in the case of those whom you dislike.

Behaviors Which Indicate That One Is Growing
In Moral And Ethical Character

Leader _____   Child _____

	Much below average	Below average	Average	Above average	Much above average
1. Calls fouls on himself when touching the net in volleyball	____	__	__	__	____
2. Immediately admits it when tagged	____	__	__	__	____
3. Is honest in his scorekeeping	____	__	__	__	____
4. Refuses to take an unfair advantage of opponents	____	__	__	__	____
5. Obeys the rules even when no official is present	____	__	__	__	____
6. Tells the truth when an official asks him a question	____	__	__	__	____

HOW TO EVALUATE THE LEADER

The leader is the most important single factor influencing the success or failure of any recreation department. Therefore, the effectiveness of a program of evaluation must be judged ultimately in terms of the degree to which it improves the quality of leadership and fosters the professional growth of the leader by practices which harmonize with the values of a democratic society. Since autocratic methods never result in the achievement of democratic values and wrong means never lead us to good ends, we must be as concerned with the techniques and procedures involved in the evaluation of leadership as we are with the information gained through their use. In deciding upon the evaluative procedures to be used we should ask ourselves such questions as these: Is the plan a coöperative enterprise in which evaluation is considered to be the privilege and responsibility of every person affected by the department's program? Or is the leader looked upon as a target for administrative sharpshooters? Do we, in a democracy, want a type of authoritarian evaluation which emphasizes conformity and unquestioning obedience to one's superiors? Does the proposal actually help the leader discover his weaknesses and encourage him to overcome them? Or will the plan result in greater tension, anxiety, insecurity, unhappiness, and thus, less effective leadership? Is there a reward or punishment provision implicit in this plan and, if so, is this an effective way of motivating the professional growth of leaders?

Leaders in a democratic society can make their best contribution toward improving the quality of the recreation experience when basic principles of democracy operate in the department. Two of these principles throw light on the type of evaluative procedures we should adopt:

1. Democracy is based upon a belief in the worth and dignity of the individual.

    All individuals are important, leaders as well as supervisors and administrators. Each is different; each has the capacity for growth; each has something of value to contribute to the group; each should be encouraged to make his contribution and be respected for it. This leads us to the second principle which is an outgrowth of the first.

2. Since the basic tenet of democracy is belief in the worth and dignity of the individual it naturally follows that all individuals who are to be affected by a decision should participate in making the decision. This is the principle of involvement previously discussed in Chapter 4. This principle emphasizes the importance of coöperative social action as a means of mobilizing all the resources inherent in the group and of stimulating all individuals to carry out the purposes of the group which, in essence, are their own purposes arrived at through consensus.

It is in the light of these democratic principles that issues regarding the evaluation of leadership should be considered. Certainly self-evaluation is indicated provided: (1) a self-evaluation form is coöperatively devised by leaders, supervisors, and administrators and used by the leader to help gain a better understanding of what constitutes good leadership; and (2) this form is used in conjunction with an intensive program of in-service education. Furthermore, with slight modifications, this form should be used by the leader's supervisor or director in a joint evaluation procedure. Democracy rests upon belief in the worth and dignity of the individual and upon coöperative social action, but it does not insist that administrators should abdicate their positions and ignore their responsibilities. The success of any joint evaluation plan depends largely upon the degree of mutual respect and confidence that exists between the supervisor and the leader.

A Self-Evaluation Form

Self-evaluation can lead to tangible self-improvement only when professional competence can be defined so objectively that the leader can appraise his own ability in a given area. Furthermore, it is difficult to see how leadership in recreation can become truly professionalized until we can say what it is in fairly precise behavioral terms. A listing of leadership competencies or leader behaviors is basic to evaluation because no matter who the evaluator is he needs certain specific criteria upon which to base his observations. These criteria should revolve about this one basic question: "What are the characteristics of all good leadership?" The self-evaluation form should consist primarily of behaviors, competencies, what the leader does, or the specific techniques used in attaining the goals of recreation. The evaluator is more concerned with evaluating the leader's skill in the specific techniques he must use in order to attain the goals than he is with determining the extent to which the goals are accomplished.

Rose presents this point of view with respect to teaching:[9]

To consider the evaluation of *teaching* is at once to focus on a process, a complex of acts, certain patterns of behavior, rather than on the person performing them or on the consequences of his behavior. The consequences deserve the most careful study, but they should be clearly distinguished from the behavior and circumstances which produced them.

A checklist which may be used by a leader in evaluating his own behavior is given as an illustration.

Basic Areas	Leader Behaviors	I do this	I need to improve
1. Personal Relationships	1.1 I judge everything I do in terms of what it does to human beings	_____	_____
	1.2 I know everyone is different so I find out all I can about each person's needs, abilities, and interests and try to help him meet them	_____	_____
	1.3 I know, like, and am friendly with every person in the group	_____	_____
	1.4 I help each person experience success as early and as frequently as possible	_____	_____
	1.5 I give special assistance to the unskilled, the unable, and the unaccepted, but I do not neglect the talented	_____	_____
	1.6 I involve as many people as possible in the planning and conduct of their own activities	_____	_____

---

[9] Gale Rose, "Toward the Evaluation of Teaching," *Educational Leadership,* January 1958, pp. 231–238.

Basic Areas	Leader Behaviors	I do this	I need to improve
2. Preparation and Planning	2.1 I plan carefully each day's work	____	____
	2.2 In advance of each activity, the group and I agree upon the goals	____	____
	2.3 For some special events, I begin planning weeks in advance	____	____
	2.4 I seek constantly to improve the quality of the recreation experience	____	____
	2.5 I encourage the selection of activities that will help us attain our goals	____	____
	2.6 I plan *with* people rather than *for* people	____	____
3. Motivation	3.1 I attempt to arouse enthusiasm in others by displaying enthusiasm myself	____	____
	3.2 I introduce people to new interests by helping them develop understandings, appreciations, and skills	____	____
	3.3 I present each activity in as interesting a manner as possible	____	____
	3.4 I note carefully when interest begins to decline and take steps to renew it	____	____
	3.5 I motivate participation by showing how one can achieve self-enhancement through an activity	____	____
	3.6 I use praise, peer approval, reward, and success as means of motivation	____	____
4. Professional Growth	4.1 I read widely in an attempt to keep up with new developments in recreation	____	____
	4.2 I am a member of my state and national professional associations	____	____
	4.3 I keep myself informed in the area of the basic sciences underlying the field of recreation	____	____
	4.4 I work and study with professional groups to improve my competencies as a leader	____	____

Basic Areas	Leader Behaviors	I do this	I need to improve
	4.5 I seek excellence in all that I do and am not satisfied with mediocrity		
	4.6 I contribute to our professional body of knowledge through articles and research	———	———
5. Leadership Techniques	5.1 I possess considerable skill in certain activities and use this skill for demonstration purposes	———	———
	5.2 I seek constantly to improve both individual and team skills	———	———
	5.3 I help individuals gain acceptance by their peers	———	———
	5.4 I abide by the laws of learning in my leadership practices	———	———
	5.5 I encourage leadership in others and try to make myself increasingly unnecessary	———	———
	5.6 I seek multiple values because I know that the unified nature of man demands it	———	———
	5.7 I am more democratic with mature groups than with immature	——— ———	——— ———
6. The Environment	6.1 I attempt to create a friendly climate in which everyone will feel secure and wanted	———	———
	6.2 I achieve control of my group through democratic methods	———	———
	6.3 I maintain our facilities in a clean, safe, and attractive condition	———	———
	6.4 I have established an effective organization that is responsible for the issuance and care of equipment and supplies	———	———
	6.5 I utilize volunteer leadership on playground safety patrols	———	———
	6.6 I make available the tools, supplies, and equipment essential to the proper functioning of the program	———	———

MEASURING PUBLIC OPINION

A program of evaluation that makes any claim to completeness must measure the attitudes and opinions of taxpayers, parents, leaders, and both youth and adult participants toward recreation and the operation of the local recreation department. Superintendents and boards of recreation should not be obliged to guess how the public feels toward the department of recreation and an adequate program of research will replace conjecture with facts and darkness with light. When recreation leaders know what the public thinks, feels, and wants the department to do; when they realize the extent to which the public understands the recreation program; when the spotlight of research reveals points·of satisfaction and dissatisfaction, strengths and weaknesses, shifts occurring in public opinion, and support or opposition to policies and practices, the capable administrator and his staff of leaders are able to make constructive changes in the management of the department because they are operating on the basis of facts rather than guesswork.

An Inventory of Parent Opinion

This survey is included here solely for the purpose of giving a few examples of the types of questions that might be asked parents about their summer playgrounds. It is not intended to serve as a "model" poll. Every such study must be tailored to fit the specific situation involved.

Directions To Parents

How do you feel about the playground which your children attend? We are asking you to tell us that so we can further improve the recreation program at this playground. *It is easy to do.* It will take you but a few moments as in most cases you merely check the answer that tells how you feel. *Do Not Put Your Name on This Paper.* We want you to say exactly what you think and we do not want anyone to know who says what.
Please answer every question.
Please mail the completed inventory as soon as possible.
A stamped return envelope is enclosed.

Personal Facts

We need this information in order to make the study more meaningful.
A. Which parent filled out this form? (Check one)
_____1) The father
_____2) The mother

_____3) The male guardian or stepfather

_____4) The female guardian or stepmother

B. How many children do you have attending the summer playgrounds and what are their ages?

Number of Boys	Ages	Number of Girls	Ages
_____	_____	_____	_____

C. How far did you go in school? (Check one)

1 2 3 4 5 6 7 8   9 10 11 12   1 2 3 4
(Elementary school)   (High school)   (College)

D. In what age group do you belong? (Check one)

_____1) I am under 30 years of age.

_____2) I am in my 30's.

_____3) I am in my 40's.

_____4) I am in my 50's.

_____5) I am 60 years of age or older.

E. What is your occupation or that of your husband if you are a housewife?

_____

- -

1. In general, are you satisfied or dissatisfied with the playground which your children are attending? (Check one)

_____1) Very well satisfied

_____2) Satisfied

_____3) About half and half

_____4) Dissatisfied

_____5) No opinion

2. How good a job do you feel the playground leaders are doing in developing: (Check in one column only for each trait)

	Good	Fair	Poor
Honesty	____	____	____
Coöperation	____	____	____
Fair play	____	____	____
Sports skills	____	____	____
Good health	____	____	____
Respect for rules and officials	____	____	____

3. Do you believe that proper emphasis is being placed on the performing arts—music, dance, and drama—on your playground? (Check one)

_____1) Too much emphasis

_____2) Too little emphasis

_____3) Emphasis about right

_____4) Don't know

4. Rank the order of importance to your community of: (1 = most important, 2 = second most important, etc.)

_____laywers

_____clergymen

_____public school teachers

_____playground leaders

_____merchants
_____public officials

5. Is it your impression that the playground leaders in your community generally are underpaid, overpaid, or would you say they get about the amount of pay they should receive? (Check one)
_____1) Underpaid
_____2) Overpaid
_____3) Right amount
_____4) Don't know

6. Are you in favor of highly competitive sports for boys under 12 years of age in which city, state, and national championships are determined? (Check one)
_____1) Yes
_____2) No
_____3) Can't say

7. Are you satisfied or dissatisfied with the quality of the leadership on your playground? (Check one)
_____1) Very well satisfied
_____2) Satisfied
_____3) About half and half
_____4) Dissatisfied
_____5) No opinion

8. Do you think your children feel they are "part of the gang" on their playground? (Check one)
_____1) Yes, I think they feel they "belong," that they are "accepted," and are "wanted."
_____2) I am not sure.
_____3) No, I think they feel they are "outsiders" and are not "wanted."

9. a. In general, are you satisfied or dissatisfied with the way your children are treated by the playground leaders? (Check one)
_____1) Very well satisfied
_____2) Satisfied
_____3) Half and half
_____4) Dissatisfied
_____5) No opinion
  b. If you are dissatisfied with the way your children are treated, tell what things are done that you don't like.

_____

_____

10. a. Are there activities that your children should be taking part in right now that are not being offered on their playground? (Check one)
_____1) No, none
_____2) Yes, a few things
_____3) Yes, many things
_____4) No opinion

  b. If there are activities that you think your children should be taking part in which are not offered on their playground, tell what these activities are._____

_____

11. a. Does your playground have as much equipment (swings, slides, bars, jungle gyms, sandboxes, balls, bats, nets, etc.) as it needs? (Check one)

_____1) It has everything it needs
_____2) It has most of what it needs
_____3) It has very little of what it needs
_____4) No opinion

b. If you think your playground needs more equipment, tell what it needs.

_____
_____

12. Is your playground kept clean? (Check one)

_____1) Yes, always clean
_____2) Yes, usually clean
_____3) No, sometimes dirty
_____4) No, always dirty
_____5) No opinion

13. a. Are you treated as well as you think you ought to be treated when you visit the playground? (Check one)

_____1) Yes
_____2) Sometimes yes, sometimes no
_____3) No
_____4) I have never visited the playground

b. If you don't like the way you are treated when you visit the playground, tell what you don't like._____

_____

14. Do you feel that the recreation department does a good job or a poor job of telling you about the work of your playground? (Check one)

_____1) Very good
_____2) Good
_____3) Fair
_____4) Poor
_____5) Very poor
_____6) No opinion

15. What is the one thing you like most about your children's playground?

_____

16. What is the one thing you most dislike about your children's playground?

_____

17. What do you think should be done to improve your children's playground? We shall deeply appreciate your suggestions._____

_____
_____

EVALUATING AREAS AND FACILITIES

A major factor influencing both the quality and quantity of recreation programs is the physical plant. Any attempt to answer this evaluative question, "What kind of a recreation program does this community have?," must involve careful consideration of the nature, number, size, and quality of its land and water areas and its buildings and indoor facilities.

Criteria, or standards, for the evaluation of healthful, safe, and adequate recreation areas and facilities have been developed by specialists in these areas and are available in published form.* These standards are important and serve a useful purpose, but they must be applied with intelligence and discretion.

Where standards do not exist communities have no common yardstick by which to determine their relative status at any given time. Thus, a city's recreation areas and facilities may be wholly inadequate, but in the absence of standards who is to say they are inadequate? Standards, therefore, can be used to awaken a backward community to the fact that it *is* backward and stimulate it to more progressive action. Furthermore, standards may serve to assure the progressive communities that they *are* progressive and in the most advanced cities standards are looked upon as goals to be exceeded, not just to be attained.

It is well to understand the limitations inherent in national standards and the caution with which they should be utilized. Standards are developed with the average community in mind, but there is no average community. Hence, they can never be applied completely to any specific city without modifications made in light of the particular, or unique, conditions which exist there. Standards provide a point of reference, a norm, a measure of quality or quantity which may serve as a basis for the development of an intelligently conceived local plan. Some communities may look upon standards as maximal rather than minimal goals. When so viewed they can retard progress because these communities have a tendency to say, "We meet the national standards so there is no good reason why we should exert ourselves any further." Standards are not absolutes, inflexible, and unchanging. They should be reviewed and revised from time to time as conditions change and as the ideas, ideals, and attitudes of people toward recreation change.

* See Selected References at end of this chapter: Butler; Gabrielsen; National Commission on Safety Education; The Athletic Institute.

Standards must be applied with intelligence and sound judgment. For example, climate is a vital factor in the determination of facilities and, therefore, of standards; a Florida city will not have toboggan slides or ski jumps. Furthermore, a nine-hole golf course may be relatively unused in an economically backward community of 27,000 population in which the schools fail to include golf in their physical education program, and be completely inadequate in a similarly sized, economically progressive community where the schools emphasize golf as a vital part of their education for leisure.

Also, design, construction, and maintenance are important factors to consider in evaluating areas and facilities. A poorly designed, constructed, and maintained playground or playfield of forty acres may give less maximum recreation use than one half this size that is properly designed, constructed, and maintained.

At the beginning of this chapter we pointed out the importance of evaluation as a factor in the improvement of a recreation program as well as the fact that very few people engaged in recreation were making any serious efforts to evaluate their practices, their programs, their leadership, or their facilities. Some relatively simple evaluative techniques have been presented in this chapter which can be utilized by anyone who is interested in his own professional growth, in improving the quality of the recreation afforded people, and in the refinement of administrative, supervisory, and leadership practices. As professional people we are obligated to evaluate our work to the very best of our abilities.

Selected References

Anderson, Jackson M., "Evaluating Community Recreation," *Journal of Health, Physical Education, and Recreation,* 24, No. 5, 1953, 25.

Baron, Denis and Bernard, Harold W., *Evaluation Techniques for Classroom Teachers* (New York: McGraw-Hill Book Company, Inc., 1958).

Boykin, Leander L., "Let's Eliminate the Confusion: What Is Evaluation?," *Educational Administration and Supervision,* 43, No. 2, 1957, 115.

Butler, George D., *Standards for Municipal Recreation Areas* (rev. ed.) (New York: National Recreation and Park Association, 1962).

Edgren, Harry D., "Yardsticks for Evaluating Your Recreation Program," *American Recreation Annual,* 1, 1960, 66.

Gabrielsen, M. Alexander and Miles, M. Caswell, eds., *Sports and Recreation Facilities for School and Community* (Englewood Cliffs, N.J.: Prentice-Hall, Inc., 1958).

Gronlund, Norman E., *Sociometry in the Classroom* (New York: Harper and Brothers, 1959).

Hughes, Marie M., "Whither Evaluation?," *Educational Leadership*, XV, No. 4, 1958, 208.

Jennings, Helen Hall, *Sociometry in Group Relations* (Washington, D.C.: American Council on Education, 1948).

Kindred, Leslie W., *School Public Relations* (Englewood Cliffs, N.J.: Prentice-Hall, Inc., 1957).

Kinney, Lucien B., "Self-Evaluation: The Mark of a Profession," *Educational Leadership*, XV, No. 4, 1958, 228.

Latchaw, Marjorie and Brown, Camille, *The Evaluation Process in Health Education, Physical Education, and Recreation* (Englewood Cliffs, N.J.: Prentice-Hall, Inc., 1962).

National Commission on Safety Education, *Checklist of Safety and Safety Education in Your School* (Washington, D.C.: National Education Association, 1953).

Orcutt, Dorothy J., "Evaluative Criteria for Administrative Measurement of Recreation Programs for Senior Citizens." Unpublished Doctoral dissertation, Colorado State College, 1968.

Peterson, Carl H., "Seven Keys to Evaluating Teacher Competence," *The American School Board Journal*, 136, No. 5, 1958, 34.

Planning Facilities for Health, Physical Education, and Recreation (rev. ed.) (Chicago: The Athletic Institute, Inc., 1956).

Chapter XIV

The Challenge of Tomorrow

WITHIN THE PAST half century we have witnessed advances in science and technology so astounding and so revolutionary as to challenge the imagination. Today's jet from Denver to Washington, D. C., covers approximately 1,600 miles in about three hours. Our first astronauts circled the globe twice in the same period of time. Compare the fantastic changes in travel during this half century with those of previous centuries. Nothing faster than a horse was available to George Washington or to Julius Caesar. We live in a world of space ships, man-made satellites, jet propelled transportation, atomic submarines, automation, and computers.

Miraculous as these changes have been, there is every indication that our children will live in a world that will not even remotely resemble our own. As Commager predicts: "Now we seem to be moving across another great watershed into a new country and a new environment, an environment as different from that which we have known and explored in the past two generations as that was from the environment of the nineteenth century."[1] To many people, this new world, lying under a constant threat of nuclear warfare, seems like a double image of hope and doom.

The hazards of prediction are sufficiently great to deter most people even in a relatively static world; to undertake the role of a prophet today appears to be the height of folly, particularly when many of us cannot

---

[1] Henry Steele Commager, "Brave World of the Year 2000," *The New York Times Magazine*, November 1, 1959, p. 24.

predict even our own behavior in basic matters. And, yet, there are sound reasons why we should make every effort to pierce the veil between the present and the future. In the conduct of public recreation over the remaining years of the present century, we must have in the back of our minds some picture of the problems that lie ahead—problems that are new or likely to become vastly more serious—for the degree to which we are successful in solving these problems depends largely upon our ability to foresee them in time to do advance planning in relation to their preven-tion, solution, or alleviation. "Where there is no vision the people perish," applies to recreation as to all other aspects of life.

Whenever we make plans of any nature, these plans are based upon our view of what we think the future course of events may be. Business-men shape their policies and practices in the light of future probabilities as they see them and a board of education purchases land for a new elementary school in terms of anticipated future enrollments and resi-dential building trends. The leader of recreation, therefore, must be able to see the present, not as something complete in itself, but as a step between the past and the future.

Some people are inclined to predict on the basis of their own inter-ests, desires, and prejudices. If they believe strongly that something ought to exist which at present does not, they are quite likely to foresee it as a future probability, especially if their own welfare, pride, or ethical stand-ards are involved. The authors are not immune to the temptations and the pitfalls that lie along the path of the amateur oracle, but will do all in their power to prevent his imagination from transcending the evidence.

LEISURE WILL INCREASE
IN AMOUNT AND SIGNIFICANCE

No nation in all history has experienced the amazing acceleration of scientific and technological advances which now characterize life in this country and appear to be limitless both in scope and consequences. We stand at the threshold of a new world—a world powered by atomic energy, guided by electronics, and geared to automated systems that perform with a precision and a rapidity unmatched in humans. As Michael points out, "cybernation," an invented term which refers to both automation and computers, "presages changes in the social system so vast and so different from those with which we have traditionally wrestled that it will challenge to their roots our current perceptions about the viability of our way of life."[2]

All available evidence leads to the inevitable conclusion that leisure will continue to increase although this gift of free time probably, at least for many years to come, will not be distributed evenly among our people. Many managerial and technical workers, as well as members of the professions, may have to work longer hours in the immediate future, rather than fewer, while this increase in leisure will fall upon less capable workers. Eventually, following a period of transition to a way of life based on the widespread use of atomic energy and other technological developments, it may reasonably be expected that everybody will have more leisure and the security to enjoy it.

We can be fairly sure that work in the future will be increasingly intellectual in nature, more highly specialized, more automated, require more education, and probably be even less satisfying than in the past. The more highly specialized a job becomes, the less does it challenge the whole man. This decreases the satisfactions to be found in work and spurs man on to find in his leisure compensatory gratifications. But as we turn from labor to leisure we find ourselves trapped between two guilt complexes. As Kerr points out, "In a contrary and perhaps rather cruel way the twentieth century has relieved us of labor without at the same time relieving us of the conviction that only labor is meaningful."[3] The philosophy of our work-oriented society drives us on to work harder while new discoveries in medical science warn us that we may kill ourselves if we don't give recreation an important place in our lives. Thus, we feel guilty whether we work or whether we play. We have become schizophrenics—split between our traditional obsession that only work is significant and a growing understanding that our health, in fact our very lives, depend upon relief from work. Until this conflict is resolved we can be happy neither in our work nor in our play.

The authors believe that the conflict will be resolved, but it will necessitate a transformation of values, of philosophy, and of ethics as deep as any that has ever taken place in America—and it is not likely to come about in our time. The deep-seated convictions of people, well founded or not, are not changed overnight. Our nation came into being under the influence of both religious and secular codes which emphasized the vital significance of work in a man's life. This Puritan emphasis has been

---

[2] Donald N. Michael, *Cybernation: The Silent Conquest* (Santa Barbara, California: Center for the Study of Democratic Institutions, 1962), pp. 13–14.

[3] Walker Kerr, *The Decline of Pleasure* (New York: Simon and Schuster, 1962), p. 40.

re-enforced by the "utilitarian ethic" which measures the value of all things by their usefulness and which can find nothing useful beyond the confines of work. But, as Lincoln said, "A house divided against itself cannot stand," and we cannot continue indefinitely to pursue a course that produces leisure in ever greater quantity while our national conscience condemns this leisure as meaningless.

Slowly, over many years, the people of America will come to recognize leisure as a positive aspect of modern culture and recreation as a vital part of the good life. They may never agree with Aristotle that leisure, rightly used, is the end and purpose of life, but they will cease to regard it merely as time for foolish diversions and ephemeral amusements, or even for hobbies. Part of this change in attitude will result simply from the quantity of leisure in relation to the amount of time devoted to work. Broudy describes this probable reorientation:[4]

With few hours of leisure, recreation, hobbies, and harmless amusements were needed for relaxation. When, however, the work week is reduced to thirty hours, where in the world is one to find enough amusements and hobbies to fill the leisure hours? Karl Marx made much of the principle that if quantity is increased beyond a certain point, one gets a change of quality. . . . Courage, for example, is a state of mind appropriate to the total danger situation, so that if you increase fearlessness beyond a certain point, it will in many situations become foolhardiness instead of courage. Similarly, a little leisure is appropriately regarded as time left over from work. But given enough leisure, work is more aptly regarded as time left over from leisure. An even more serious weakness in the hobby-recreation prescription for leisure, is, therefore, that it does not take into account the prospect that under the new dispensation life will have to become leisure-centered instead of work-centered.

Both Broudy and the American people need to understand that recreation in the deeper meaning of the term, goes far beyond the hobby-amusement concept to include those activities of highest creative, cultural, and civic value which enrich the lives of human beings and elevate the tone of a democratic society. To develop, accept, and widely interpret a basic philosophy of recreation is one of the most needed, most sensitive, and most controversial issues of modern recreation. This is a priority of the highest rank and is a professional obligation that will be met in the near future; it should have been met years ago. No one believes that all members of any professional group need think alike on all matters, but there should be general agreement on certain basic concepts and values.

---

[4] Harry S. Broudy, *Paradox and Promise* (Englewood Cliffs, N.J.: Prentice-Hall, Inc., 1961) p. 37.

With the recognition, acceptance, and attainment of these higher values, recreation and recreation leaders will attain a status and prestige they do not at present possess. Education and recreation will discover that they have a great deal more in common than either presently recognizes. This discovery of common values, interests, activities, and methods will bring about a closer relationship between these two great professions than they have experienced in the past.

The new and broadened concept of leisure and of recreation will embody the point of view that the primary responsibility of leadership is to help every individual develop to his highest potential within a framework of social, moral, and ethical purpose.

Sorenson suggests that the leisure of the future will be more leisurely, less high pressured, and that there will be time in which to enjoy activities of a more simple, voluntary, and spontaneous nature; time to seek a more healthy balance between work and recreation; to enrich family recreation, achieve social competence and end social isolation; stimulate youth participation in community affairs; encourage the individual to be himself; achieve a balance between "activity and passivity, action and reflection, gregariousness and solitude"; cultivate creativity and the cultural arts; achieve a higher level of physical and mental health; and time for self-education as we widen our knowledge and comprehension in those areas of human endeavor that command our interest.[5]

GOVERNMENTAL AGENCIES WILL EXPAND THEIR RECREATION SERVICES

Ample evidence exists that government on the Federal, state, and local levels increasingly is recognizing its basic responsibility for the provision of recreation facilities, programs, and services. There are valid reasons to believe they will intensify their efforts in the future.

On the Federal level, nine cabinet-level departments and fifty-seven agencies, bureaus, services, and administrations contribute to the recreational life of the American people. The National Park Service, for example, increased its land acreage by 4,659,421 acres during the period 1960 through 1968. Attendance at all areas in 1968 exceeded 150 million visitors, as compared with approximately 80 million in 1960. Other Federal agencies also are improving and expanding their services.

---

[5] Roy Sorenson, "Directions for the Future," *Recreation*, November 1960, pp. 412–413, 441–442.

The recent establishment of the Bureau of Outdoor Recreation in the Department of the Interior should accelerate the rapid expansion and development of this phase of recreation by the Federal government. Especially should it advance the public interest, which clearly requires that America's dwindling heritage of wilderness grandeur be preserved to inspire and enrich future generations. Eventually, the term "Outdoor" probably will be deleted from the title and the Bureau will enlarge its scope of responsibility to include the entire field of recreation.

The National Recreation and Park Association reports that in 1964 statistical data related to their work in recreation were submitted by 233 state agencies. A total of $247,335,000 was reported spent by 233 agencies in 1964, a 61 percent increase over the figure reported in 1960 by 165 agencies. It seems reasonable to anticipate that the states will continue to expand their recreation services.

Stimulated, in part, by recent developments in outdoor recreation at the national level, it seems quite probable that each state may establish a central agency for the development of long-range plans for outdoor recreation. This may well be accompanied by a Federal program of grants-in-aid to provide matching funds to the states for recreation planning and to assist in acquiring lands and developing facilities for public outdoor recreation.

In 1965, 3,142 local governmental units—cities, counties, towns, villages, and school and park districts—reported their work in recreation. Of this number 358 were county agencies as compared with 290 out of a total of 2,968 in 1960. Full-time year-round leaders totaled 9,216 in 1960 and 19,208 in 1965, more than double in the five-year period. Total acreage in parks and recreation areas, not including school recreation areas, exceeded 1,496,378 acres in 1965, an increase of more than 50 percent over the acreage reported five years previously. In 1965 playgrounds conducted under leadership totaled 24,298 as compared with 20,107 in 1960; during the same period total park and recreation expenditures increased significantly, from $567,000,000 to $905,000,000.

The trend in municipal administration toward enlarging administrative units by combining departments with similar or allied elements and purposes resulted in a marked increase during the decade of the 60's in park and recreation agencies. This trend very probably will continue as will the growth elements reflected in the above statistics. Sixty-eight more county agencies reported in 1965 than in 1960, but the number, 358, is still pathetically small when we realize there are more than 3,000 counties in the fifty conterminous states alone. Nevertheless, the increase provides a basis for predicting that recreation administered by county-wide authorities will continue to grow.[6]

SCHOOLS WILL MAKE A GREATER CONTRIBUTION TO RECREATION

Increasing involvement of the schools in recreation seems inevitable. In the past, education aimed primarily at preparing students for work in a work-oriented society. Are we to continue to place major emphasis on preparation for work when work constitutes a constantly decreasing segment of our lives? If leisure replaces work as the central life-interest of a large proportion of our people will not this necessitate a major revolution in the schools? Broudy poses a vital problem: "If this reorientation does occur, the schools will likewise have to turn their emphasis upside down. This would really entail a revolution because there is little in the public school curriculum that has not tried to justify its tenancy by its usefulness in the economic, civic, and moral enterprise."[7]

An ever greater degree of involvement of the schools in recreation most likely will take the following forms:

1. A higher proportion of the people will be educated. In 1900 only one person in 50 stayed in school beyond the age of 15; now 30 out of 50 finish high school. At the end of the 1947-48 school year, 272,311 students were graduated with bachelor's or first-level professional degrees from the colleges and universities of this country. In 1958-59, this number had increased to 385,151, an increase of more than 41 percent.[8] In 1959, the total number of college graduates in the United States was 8,323,000 about two and one half million more than in 1950. Education is a powerful force influencing both the nature and extent of one's participation in recreation.

2. The schools will place greater emphasis on education for leisure. As leisure increases in quantity and as school people see more clearly the relationship between education and the quality of the leisure experi-

---

[6] All the above data relating to growth of Federal, state, and local government agencies in the area of recreation derived from: Donald E. Hawkins, ed., *Recreation and Park Yearbook 1966* (Washington, D.C.: National Recreation and Park Association, 1966), pp. 1–28.

[7] Broudy, *op. cit.*, p. 38.

[8] Wayne E. Tolliver, *Earned Degrees Conferred-1958-1959* (Washington, D.C.: U.S. Department of Health, Education, and Welfare, 1961), p. 2.

ence, there is little doubt they will accept as one of their imperative responsibilities the development of skills, appreciations, and understandings basic to the effective and satisfying use of leisure.

3. Some 25 to 30 million Americans are involved at present in adult education of one kind or another; this may well double in the next generation. Our educational leaders should begin to plan now for this tremendous development in a program that because of its magnitude and significance must be considered a central rather than a subordinate function of the schools. Its relationship to leisure and recreation should be apparent to everyone.

4. The schools will expand opportunities to students wherein the various recreation activities taught can be practiced, interests deepened, and skills perfected. Just as libraries are made available to students who have learned to read, so will gymnasiums be made increasingly available to those who have developed skills in and a love for such games as basketball, volleyball, badminton and other sports of a similar nature. Intramural programs will be enriched and emphasized perhaps even above the program of interscholastic athletics. Athletics for all will become a reality in the progressive school of the future. Numerous clubs, each organized around a common leisure interest, will be recognized as a fundamental part of the curriculum of the future. Nor will this phase of the program be demeaned by labeling it "extracurricular"; it will constitute a vital aspect of the central core of an educational program designed to prepare youth for a life in which leisure is of paramount significance.

5. School facilities will be used more extensively for community recreation. Recent years have witnessed a remarkable growth in the number of school buildings used for community recreation purposes during the late afternoon, evening, and Saturday hours when the day school is not in session. In 1950, the National Recreation and Park Association reported the use of 5,575 school buildings as centers for community recreation; in 1960, this figure had risen to 12,208, an increase of 119 percent during the decade. Almost 72 percent of all buildings used for recreation purposes in 1960 were school buildings.

The use of school buildings as community centers is one aspect of the expanding community school concept which is being increasingly accepted throughout the nation. In the progressive community the approach to development of a comprehensive program of recreation will be one of joint planning and mutual coöperation. Where the total resources of a community are mobilized for the welfare of all the people, the use of public school buildings as centers of community life is simply an expression of sound educational and public policy.

Although the provision of community centers is one of the most pressing needs in every community, far too few have recognized it as an obligation. The school people, who should be particularly sensitive to this need and especially alert to the desirability of utilizing school buildings for this purpose, traditionally have been somewhat less than enthusiastic about doing so. There are today many thousands of communities totally devoid of community centers while more than 100,000 school buildings throughout the nation lie completely, or largely, unused during non-school hours when people are free to use them. Less than 11 percent of the public school buildings of this nation are being used for community recreation purposes.[9] There are indications, however, that the blindness, indifference, and lethargy of the past is gradually being supplanted by an awakening consciousness of the enlarged role of the school as a social institution concerned with the total improvement of community life.

6. The school as a public agency, concerned with the well-being of the public, will become more active in helping to provide a widely diversified program of community recreation.

The schools, increasingly recognize the vital significance of leisure in the modern society; understand and accept their responsibility to educate for this leisure; provide expanded opportunities for students to participate in leisure interests while under jurisdiction of the school; make their facilities available for community recreation purposes; and appreciate the degree to which unsound programs of recreation operated by non-school agencies may vitiate the work of the schools. It is unrealistic to assume that the schools, in light of these developments, will remain aloof from active participation in the conduct of community recreation. This does not necessarily mean that the schools will assume direct administrative responsibilities for community recreation. The National Recreation and Park Association reports that in 1960 a total of 2,968 local and county agencies administered recreation and park areas or programs in the United States; of this total only 274 were school authorities, a decrease of 13 during the decade. If we assume that all school authorities operating community recreation programs reported this fact to the National Recreation and Park Association, we must recognize the absence of any trend toward greater school participation in the management of community recreation. However, as the schools become more and more active in discharging those leisure responsibilities universally recognized as belonging to the schools, they may very well, in increasing numbers, assume the additional managerial responsibility, especially where their failure to do so would result in no community recreation program whatsoever.

Regardless of what agency administers the recreation program, the school people of the future will provide effective leadership to work with other community leaders in mobilizing the total resources of the community to the end that the best possible program may be provided.

---

[9] The United States Department of Health, Education, and Welfare reports that for the year 1959-1960 there were 92,111 public-elementary and 25,744 public-secondary school buildings in the United States.

CERTAIN RELEVANT SOCIAL AND
ECONOMIC TRENDS WILL CONTINUE

By the year 2000, our population will approximate 350 million; about 73 percent of these people will reside in metropolitan areas; the proportion of those in the 15–24 year age bracket, the most active of all, will rise from the current 13 percent of the total to about 17 percent by 1976; incomes will soar to new heights—"disposable consumer income is expected to rise from $354 billion in 1960 to $706 billion by 1976 and to $1,437 billion by 2000"; mobility will continue to increase with the number of passenger cars projected at 100 million by 1976 and 200 million by 2000.[10]

Both the total number and proportion of aged persons will continue to increase. By the year 2000, the present trend indicates between 30 and 40 million persons over sixty-five, a total in excess of 10 percent of the population. Projections indicate that in 1975 there will be about 138 older women for every 100 older men. An increasingly higher proportion of the aged will be kept off the labor market. Young people also will be excluded from work for longer periods of time. Broudy points to one of the most acute and potentially explosive problems of the future: "Unless medical science develops tranquilizers that one can administer to these young people systematically, e.g. with their orange juice or milk, their leisure may constitute the greatest problem of all."[11]

Thus, the working population which supports the whole will become relatively smaller as the number of children and the number of the aged continue to grow. A highly significant and potentially disturbing aspect of this problem with respect to the aged of the future is outlined by Lang:

For more than 80 percent of today's Americans who are now 40 to 44 years old (the other 20 percent will not survive beyond the age of 60), there will be not only the problems of preparation and provision for their *own* retirement years, but also the challenge of responsibility for older relatives.[12]

Farm employment over the next decade will decline; opportunities for unskilled workers will not increase; only a slow growth will occur in

---

[10] Outdoor Recreation Resources Review Commission, *Outdoor Recreation for America* (Washington, D.C.: U.S. Government Printing Office, 1962), pp. 30–31.

[11] Broudy, *op. cit.,* p. 26.

[12] Gladys Engel Lang, *Old Age in America* (New York: The H. W. Wilson Company, 1961), p. 14.

skilled and semi-skilled jobs; growth rate in the professional and technical occupations will be twice that of the labor force as a whole; job opportunities in the service fields will increase greatly. Many workers may have to acquire both occupational and geographical mobility if they are to remain employed.

PROGRAMS WILL BE EXPANDED AND ENRICHED

As leaders become better prepared for their work; as they acquire a more thorough understanding of the nature and needs of human beings in a democratic society; as they are guided by their efforts to achieve higher values through the recreation experience and appreciate more fully the relationship between ends and means, we may reasonably anticipate that the program of the future will be characterized by:

1. A great expansion in the range of activities with considerably more emphasis upon arts, crafts, music, drama, dance, hobbies, social activities, outdoor recreation, and individual and dual sports which appeal to both sexes and a wide age span. The performing arts in particular are experiencing an almost explosive growth.
2. Significant developments in adult recreation particularly for the aged.
3. An emphasis upon the more active types of recreation as people become better educated, engage in larger numbers in professional, technical, and white collar occupations, and understand more clearly the relationship of exercise to health. Greater participation by women and girls in sports. Less emphasis upon the highly competitive team sports limited to skilled players and more upon programs of a friendly, coöperative nature for all the people.
4. A tremendous increase in the more expensive activities, such as golf, water and snow skiing, horseback riding, boating, skin and scuba diving, and travel. As income rises so will participation in these and similar activities. As the demand exceeds the budgets of recreation departments, we may expect an increase in the number of activities for which a fee is charged, as well as an increase in the amount of many fees.
5. A greater demand for activities invested with more intellectual content, such as drama, nature recreation, art, opera, and activities in the category of the language arts.
6. Expanded use of state and national forests and parks as mobility

increases and income rises. Camping in these areas will increase greatly.

7. An increase in opportunities for the handicapped, convalescent, and institutionalized.

8. More activities involving travel—bus trips to points of interest, hosteling, bike rides, horseback trips, even plane trips to foreign countries.

9. Heightened participation in all kinds of activities involving water—boating, canoeing, sailing, swimming, fishing, skiing, skin and scuba diving. Numerous studies disclose that the key factor in outdoor recreation is water.

10. A vast increase in facilities for walking and bicycling. The Outdoor Recreation Resources Review Commission recommends, "Along the broad rights-of-way of our new highways—particularly those in suburban areas—simple trails could be laid out for walkers and cyclists. Existing rights-of-way for high tension lines, now so often left to weeds and rubble, could at very little cost be made into a 'connector' network of attractive walkways."[13]

11. The provision of enriched opportunities for family recreation.

12. The inclusion of more activities that are characterized by an element of danger, daring, and adventure. Deep within the nature of every human being is the desire for adventure; in some this drive is more powerful than in others. The popularity of many recreation activities is due in large part to their hazardous nature, for man loves the thrill and excitement of danger. The appeal of skin diving, skiing, motorcycling, motorboating, football, and ice hockey is compounded of a number of elements not the least of which is the danger involved. To mountain climbers, danger in itself is "an honorable destination." Remove entirely the dangers inherent in these activities and you drain them of much of their appeal and value. Especially is this true in the case of adolescent boys to whom in the words of Pindar, "deeds of no risk are honourless."

13. Elimination of all boxing and of highly organized competitive sports for boys below the age of 12, especially those involving state, regional, and national tournaments.

14. An increase in activities of a community service nature.

15. An emphasis upon the integrated program in which relationships among activities is stressed.

16. An improvement in the quality of activities as leaders influence people to prefer the beautiful and the excellent and reject the crude and vulgar.

17. Efforts to evaluate the program in terms of its effect on human beings; to judge it in terms of the degree to which leaders are successful in attaining the values deemed important.

---

[13] Outdoor Recreation Resources Review Commission, *op. cit.*, p. 83.

RECREATION WILL PROGRESS TOWARD FULL PROFESSIONAL STATUS

The history of all professions, such as medicine, law, engineering, and education proves conclusively that professional status does not come about accidentally, but is achieved only by what Churchill would have called "blood, sweat, toil, and tears." No occupation becomes a profession simply because those who engage in it call it a profession. An area of work achieves professional status only when it possesses certain specific characteristics, just as a building becomes a house rather than a barn or a gymnasium only when it possesses certain unique qualities. Any attempt, therefore, to determine recent progress made toward professional status and to estimate future probabilities must begin with an identification of the specific characteristics of a profession.

Fortunately, these are not difficult to determine as a number of studies have identified them for us, chief among which is the study by A. M. Carr-Saunders and P. A. Wilson published under the title, *The Professions*.[14] In general, these are the tests or unique characteristics of a profession:

1. A profession serves a distinctive and permanent social function in the community.
2. A profession has a highly specialized body of knowledge complex enough to require a prolonged special education and a technique.
3. The members of a profession form professional associations or societies to improve its standards and extend its public acceptance.
4. The professional work must be of sufficient social importance to warrant the exercise of some form of control over its practice by society, the practitioners themselves, or by both operating together.
5. A profession develops and follows a code of ethics.
6. A profession is characterized by professional behavior, attitudes, and workmanship of those who comprise it.

Within the past decade recreation has advanced along a wide front toward professional status. Progress has been uneven, rapid in some areas, slow in others. But the trend is encouraging and the future, in general,

---

[14] A. M. Carr-Saunders and P. A. Wilson, *The Professions* (New York: Oxford University Press, 1933).

promising. By the turn of the century, there is every reason to believe that standards will be raised immeasurably, recreation services vastly improved, the public benefited greatly, and recreation will have become a profession.

THREATS FROM WITHIN

Most of the predictions ventured in the earlier pages of this chapter present a future highly favorable to public recreation. But probabilities are not inevitabilities and recreation is not an island in American society immune to the impact of forces originating outside itself. The future of recreation will be determined by what happens to the nation in every facet of its existence. A healthy program of recreation cannot exist in an otherwise sick society; its welfare is inextricably interwoven with the welfare of the nation at large. It is imperative, therefore, that occasionally we forget for a while our immediate, day-to-day problems, climb the highest peak and from this vantage point attempt to catch a vision of recreation in its broadest possible perspective—to see it in its entirety throughout all human history; to understand what it has meant in the lives of men and of nations; to appreciate its relationship to the society of which it was a part and the reactions and interactions of each upon the other; and to gain a deeper insight into its potentialities for enriching the lives of people and for improving our democratic society.

When we attempt this broad appraisal we immediately are struck by one of the bitter lessons taught by history—that as civilizations rise they create the conditions that lead to their fall. A nation's decline slowly and insidiously begins when it is at the peak of its strength and prosperity; when the life of action has been displaced by the life of ease; when overemphasis upon the intellect has eaten away at the virility of the nation; when its citizens, in their complacency, no longer possess the qualities of their forefathers who led the nation to greatness; when the termites of corruption have gnawed away at the moral foundations of society; and when leisure, increasing in quantity, becomes synonymous with boredom, emptiness, unrest, apathy, and a desperate search for relief through entertainment designed to stimulate the emotions and excite the senses.

Civilizations decay from within. Some of the destructive forces which led to the downfall of other democracies, other cultures, in the past are now at work in our own society. If we are aware of what these disintegrating forces are we can be more effective in our efforts to overcome or to limit their destructiveness. As educated people we possess the ability to shape our own destinies, at least to some degree, for as Socrates observed "Whom, then, do I call educated? First, those who control circumstances instead of being mastered by them, those who meet all occasions manfully and act in accordance with intelligent thinking . . . ."

The Threat of the Easy Life

As our leisure continues to increase in quantity, can we resist the temptation of the soft and easy life? More and more is our economy involved in the production of those things that make life easier and more comfortable—electric carts to make our golf easier, all kinds of gadgets to eliminate muscular effort from our work, and numerous contraptions to make our drinks cooler, our domestic duties lighter, and our chairs and beds softer. Historically, men have proved they cannot be trusted with easy alternatives. Pericles, speaking of conditions in Athens in 431 B.C., described one of the few occasions in history when they could be trusted:

When our work is over we are in a position to enjoy all kinds of recreation for our spirits. . . . Our love of the beautiful does not lead to extravagance; our love of the things of the mind does not make us soft.

In Athens, the national ideal was the man of wisdom *and* the man of action, and "What is honored in a country is cultivated there." But even Athens was unable to maintain indefinitely a society which believed in the wholeness of man and which created a place where men lived well together. Eventually, this nation of athletes succumbed to the temptation of the easy option and became a nation of spectators. Gardiner might have been describing modern America when he tells us what happened to the Athenians:[15]

The result of specialization is professionalism. There is a point in any sport or game where it becomes over-developed and competition too severe for it to serve its true purpose of providing exercise or recreation for the many. It becomes the monopoly of the few who can afford the time or money to acquire excellence, while the rest, despairing of any measure of success, prefer the role of spectators. When the rewards of success are sufficient there arises a professional class, and when professionalism is once established the amateur can no longer compete with the professional.

We are witnessing the same growth of professional athletics that sounded the death knell of amateur athletics in ancient Greece. New pro-

---

[15] E. Norman Gardiner, *Greek Athletic Sports and Festivals* (London: Macmillan and Co., Limited, 1910), p. 130.

fessional leagues are being organized and old leagues expanded. As our population becomes more highly concentrated in metropolitan areas, opportunities for the amateur athlete are likely to decrease and the number of spectators increase. Where professional athletics flourish, amateur athletics die out.

The Threat of the City

Can we solve the complex and urgent problem of renewing, redeveloping, and revitalizing our decaying urban centers? Carrying within themselves the seeds of social and biological degeneration, they constitute a challenge to all agencies and individuals concerned with the improvement of living. The recreation department can play a vital role in helping to put together again our disintegrated communities by providing common neighborhood meeting places or community' centers, which will serve as social instruments to help strengthen the bonds of friendship and mutual understanding so essential to the maintenance of a healthy community life.

The Threat of Corruption

A breakdown in the moral standards of at nation invariably threatens its stability and vitiates its strength. Considerable evidence exists which indicates that in the moral and ethical spheres we have no justification for viewing either the present or the future with optimism. The extent of crime and delinquency, alcoholism, drug addiction, gambling, bribery, graft, and other forms of corruption and dishonesty in America do not promise well for the future of democracy; and anything that weakens democracy is a threat to the future of recreation.

The late Robert F. Kennedy painted a sorry picture of gambling in this country: [16]

No one knows exactly how much money is involved in gambling in the United States. What we do know is that the American people are spending more on gambling than on medical care or education; that in so doing, they are putting up the money for the corruption of public officials and the vicious activities of the dope peddlers, loan sharks, bootleggers, white-slave traders, and slick confidence men.

---

[16] Robert F. Kennedy, "The Baleful Influence of Gambling," *Atlantic,* April 1962, p. 76.

Investigation this past year by the FBI, Internal Revenue Service, the Narcotics Bureau, and all other federal investigative units disclosed without any shadow of a doubt that corruption and racketeering, financed largely by gambling, are weakening the vitality and strength of this nation.

In those states where gambling has been legalized this question must be raised: How can a society survive that finances itself by exploiting the weaknesses of its citizens?

The growth of crime in the United States has reached staggering proportions. The FBI reports:

During the calendar year 1968 there were an estimated 4,467,000 crimes of murder, forcible rape, robbery, aggravated assault, burglary, larceny $50 and over, and auto theft in the United States . . . . The 1968 total was seventeen percent rise above the peak reached in 1967 or 665,000 more serious crimes than the previous year. . . . [17]

The alarming increase in juvenile crime is reflected in police statistics revealing that during the period 1960–1968 arrests of young people, ages ten to seventeen, for specific criminal code offenses increased 78 percent while this segment of the population increased but 25 percent.

As the leader of the free nations of the world, we have both the opportunity and the obligation of becoming the showcase of democracy. But first we must determine the well-springs of our greatness and in what shall we lead the world. Whether there is to be a great growth of democracy or a vast shrinkage of liberty in the world of the future will depend very largely upon the power of our example. If we can demonstrate that nowhere else in the world is the ordinary citizen so much the center and purpose of all social, economic, and political institutions; that under no other form of government does he have as much freedom to develop his own innate capacities and to follow the dictates of his own conscience; and that democracy offers the best way of life known to man, the victory over communism will be assured.

As recreation leaders, we can make a vital contribution to this victory through our efforts to help people add dimensions of enjoyment and grace to life, uplift the human spirit, and strengthen democratic human relations.

Selected Reference

Statistical Abstract of the U.S. 1969, 90th Annual Edition (Washington, D.C.: U.S. Department of Commerce, 1969).

[17] J. Edgar Hoover, *Crime in the United States* (Washington, D.C.: U.S. Department of Justice, 1968), p. 1–15.

Index